If Is the Only Peacemaker

If Is the Only Peacemaker

The Catholic Humanist Rhetoric of *As You Like It*

GREG MAILLET

☙PICKWICK *Publications* · Eugene, Oregon

IF IS THE ONLY PEACEMAKER
The Catholic Humanist Rhetoric of As You Like It

Copyright © 2022 Greg Maillet. All rights reserved. Except for brief quotations in critical publications or reviews, no part of this book may be reproduced in any manner without prior written permission from the publisher. Write: Permissions, Wipf and Stock Publishers, 199 W. 8th Ave., Suite 3, Eugene, OR 97401.

Pickwick Publications
An Imprint of Wipf and Stock Publishers
199 W. 8th Ave., Suite 3
Eugene, OR 97401

www.wipfandstock.com

PAPERBACK ISBN: 978-1-6667-0520-1
HARDCOVER ISBN: 978-1-6667-0521-8
EBOOK ISBN: 978-1-6667-0522-5

Cataloguing-in-Publication data:

Names: Maillet, Greg, 1965–, author.

Title: If is the only peacemaker : the Catholic humanist rhetoric of as you like it / Greg Maillet.

Description: Eugene, OR : Pickwick Publications, 2022 | Includes bibliographical references.

Identifiers: ISBN 978-1-6667-0520-1 (paperback) | ISBN 978-1-6667-0521-8 (hardcover) | ISBN 978-1-6667-0522-5 (ebook)

Subjects: LCSH: Shakespeare, William, 1564–1616—Religion. | Shakespeare, William, 1564–1616—Criticism and interpretation. | Christian humanism. | Christianity and literature. | Christianity in literature. | Criticism and interpretation. | English drama. | History and criticism. | Humanism, Religious, in literature.

Classification: PR3011 .M35 2022 (paperback) | PR3011 .M35 (ebook)

06/09/22

For Jennifer, whose wit and beauty have brought
so much comic joy to my life

Contents

Preface		ix

PART I | UNDERSTANDING CATHOLIC HUMANISM

1	Catholic Humanism in Judeo-Christian Scripture and Tradition	3
2	Historiography and Catholic Humanism	16
3	Italian Catholic Humanism	23
4	English Catholic Humanism	33
5	Erasmus and the Play of Sapiential Rhetoric	49
6	More and the Humor of Holy Rhetoric	65
7	The Marriage of Wit and Wisdom: The Book of Sir Thomas More	80
8	"When Words Do Well": Reviving Renaissance Rhetoric	88
9	Totus Mundus Agit Histrionem: *As You Like It* in 1599	104

PART II | *AS YOU LIKE IT* AND THE RHETORIC OF CATHOLIC HUMANISM

1	"The Old News": Brotherly Conflict and Masculine Rhetoric	117
2	"Never Two Ladies Loved as They Do": The Feminine Rhetoric of Celia and Rosalind	128

3	"Sermons in Stones":	142
	"Translating" Eden in the Forest of Arden	
4	"Ambitious for a Motley Coat":	155
	The "Matter" of "Melancholy" Jaques	
5	"Learn of the Wise":	170
	Touchstone and the Foolish Wisdom of Catholic Humanism	
6	"Not True in Love?":	188
	Comical Confusion of Male and Female Identity	
7	"A Woman's Wit":	202
	Debating Jaques and Educating Orlando	
8	"If You Be a True Lover":	217
	Rounding Up Imaginative Realists in the Forest of Arden	
9	"Sweet Lovers Love the Spring":	229
	Finding the Time for Love	
10	"To Make All This Matter Even":	247
	Hymen and the Catholic Humanist Marriage Song of *As You Like It*	

Conclusion: "If Is for Children":   267
Rhetoric and the Value of *As You Like It*

Glossary   277
Bibliography   283

Preface

Your "if" is the only peacemaker; much virtue in "if."

(Touchstone, 5.4.100)[1]

What care I for words? Yet words do well

When he that speaks them pleases those that hear.

(Phoebe, 3.5.112–13)

I like this place, and willingly would waste my time in it.

(Celia, 2.4.93–94)

What is "Catholic Humanism", and how can it be seen in Shakespeare's *As You Like It*? The epigraphs chosen from this play suggest an almost indecorous, even oxymoronic juxtaposition of the serious and comic. Peace and the war between nations or, even more commonly in human history, the war between the sexes, men and women, suggest as serious themes as literature is capable of considering. Yet how can a single word, "if," help create peace, especially when it is spoken by the designated fool of the play, Touchstone? The second line here, which sounds so serious and hopeful, is actually spoken by a hilarious and ludicrous character, Phoebe, as she pursues the seemingly unattainable love of the shepherd Silvius. The entire play

---

1. All Shakespeare references, unless otherwise noted, are to *William Shakespeare: The Complete Works*, edited by Stanley Wells and Gary Taylor. This pioneering edition revolutionized Shakespeare Studies by printing and distinguishing Quarto and Folio texts for each play. Because *As You Like It* was not published until the First Folio, there are less textually debatable elements than in some other Shakespeare plays.

can seem silly, yet as the girl Celia discovers upon arriving in the forest of Arden, and speaking the third epigraph here, *As You Like It* is a place whose virtues redeem any loss of human time. Amidst its abundant laughter, there is the eternal spirit of joy that enlivens the rhetorical language of the play's characters, especially its heroine, Rosalind, surely one of Shakespeare's most exceptional creations.

What others have called the "serio-comic"[2] art of men like Erasmus and More has many connections to the nature of this play, giving my own book three primary purposes. First, to see the drama of Shakespeare through a cultural lens that can be shown to be central to the formation of this theatrical art, fourteenth- to sixteenth-century Catholic Humanism. Second, thus aware of this formative literary culture, to read Shakespearean drama through the union of *eloquentia* and *sapientia*, of wit and wisdom, found in the rhetorical ideals of Erasmus and More, who most directly convey Catholic Humanism to Shakespeare's England. Finally, and most importantly, given the complexity and literary value of one of Shakespeare's most under-estimated plays, to closely read *As You Like It* through this ideal, finding in this play an outstanding example of the Catholic Humanist rhetoric central to his art. Each purpose has its own significance and rationale.

Because it is clear that Shakespeare is a pioneer of dramatic literature in English, it is natural for us today to view his work as a founding jewel rather than the culmination of anything previous to him. Yet Shakespeare was not divine, and his art does not appear *ex nihilo*. Scholars aware of the historical roots of his work have found numerous elements of literary and cultural tradition in Shakespeare's writing. Because it is these elements of the past that would most clearly have been present to Shakespeare's historical audience, it is essential that scholars also see these elements in his work. Pre-Reformation Catholicism is an obvious example of this kind of historical culture. It is unsurprising, further, that recent scholars have often noted this culture's persistence in post-Reformation England, even in popular literary art like Shakespearean drama.

Of course, to describe this era as "pre" or "post" Reformation is a clearly Protestant means to describe the historical period, and begs the question that, from a Catholic point of view, is the very heart of the dispute: is it necessary or even possible for humans to re-form the Church once created by Christ, or should we hope only to "reform" it in every age, in the sense of improving rather than radically remaking the Church? Protestant and Catholic ecclesiology can respond to this central issue in various ways not central here, for there are Protestants who assert one continuous Church

2. See, for example, Gordon, *Humanist Play and Belief*.

from the time of Christ, and there are Catholics willing to admit that the Church needs constant reforming, or the constant cleansing of problems caused by human sin. Perhaps the more essential question to directly address here, though, is the obvious question raised by my title: why is it necessary to speak of "Catholic Humanism" rather than the more common "Christian Humanism"?

Answering this question is part of the purpose of the first half of this book, but the point here is not partisan politics or ecclesiastical argument. Rather, it is the ability to see and discuss the elements of theology most central to human identity as they are expressed by great artists. My claim is not mainly that Shakespeare or Chaucer or Dante were Catholic, though they may well have been (arguments for Shakespeare's Catholicism in particular have been a common part of much recent biographical work, as I discuss in chapter 9 of part 1). Rather, elements of what may broadly be termed "theological anthropology," or the Catholic understanding of what it means to be human, are essential to understanding and correctly evaluating Shakespeare's *As You Like It*.

Cultures (and countries) have an obvious bias towards claiming genius as their own, so it is unsurprising that non-Catholic critics, whether secular or Protestant, have often described the work of Shakespeare and his forerunners without reference to the Catholic faith. Of course, to try and describe such artists solely through reference to their religious faith, or any biographical element, is inevitably reductive of their imaginative achievement. Yet it is also true that to assume a secular or atheistic understanding of a human being can easily distort religious conceptions of the human relationship to the Divine. A balance that attempts to correct bias must be part of any serious literary hermeneutic. Neither religious nor non-religious interpreters can entirely escape their own biases, but one can hope to contribute in a broad sense to critical understanding and appreciation of these artists.

The broad value of doing so, however, is surely more possible because the Catholic Humanism of the fourteenth to sixteenth century, like Catholic humanism in any era, is founded on a view of the human person that aims to transcend its cultural origins. Even if these origins can be traced to particular thinkers or places that exert key influence on adjacent cultures, it is of the essence of Catholic Humanism that its key tenets should appear "naturally" in another culture. Paradoxically, this "natural," ahistorical claim makes it especially essential to articulate clearly the central ideas of what many scholars today now call "early modern" Catholic Humanism, in order to distinguish it sharply from the secular, atheistic form of humanism common today, and even from the "Christian Humanism" that scholars have often studied as part, albeit a moderating, creative force, within the Protestant "reformation" that affects European culture in the subsequent decades of the fifteenth and sixteenth century.

Erasmus and Thomas More are both Roman Catholic Humanists especially learned in this prior tradition, yet again often classified, and misread, as founding fathers of the humanism that follows them. Many of the most distinctive and influential actions of Erasmus and More were in the service of Catholic orthodoxy, though today this is better known of the latter than the former. But the more important point for us here is the theological anthropology that both affirm, which must consider the Catholic understanding of Mary, and many other doctrines that divide Catholicism from the Protestant Reformation that follows the time of Erasmus and More (the early 1500s), even as these doctrines tend to unite Catholics with the Eastern Orthodox who first formally divide the Church in 1054. Politically, no unity is possible in the sixteenth century, but Erasmus and More help to create what one Catholic historian, Brad Gregory, has called a "Republic of Letters."[3] In this country, the goal is not conquest or power but rather peace, to be achieved through a rhetoric that unites, to use their Latin terms, *eloquentia* and *sapientia*, wit and wisdom. Given the wars of religion common throughout sixteenth-century Europe, this republic could be deemed a failure, but many of its ideals live on and continue to influence both the Catholic and broader human culture.

Rhetoric, whether speech or writing, was not understood by Erasmus and More as the amoral acquisition of literary skills, but rather a spiritual gift that God both gives and grows within the human soul. So far from the dry as dust lists of figures of speech into which rhetorical pedantry can descend, for Erasmus and More rhetoric was a means to respond with human words to the divine Word that has established the eternal, a-temporal Kingdom of God that both transcends and subsumes human culture.

This ideal, though often eloquently expressed in the early fifteen-hundreds by Erasmus and More, had deteriorated in many ways by the time its echoes are heard in the grammar schools that educate Shakespeare, born in 1564. Later the playwright will mock the rhetorical excess of Holofernes, the babbling, un-eloquent, and certainly unwise teacher who cannot give the young good advice in *Love's Labour's Lost*. In 1598, Frances Meres listed amongst Shakespeare's plays one called, *Love's Labour's Won*, but sadly it is lost;[4] we do not know if it redeems a rhetorical ideal.

---

3. Gregory, *Unintended*, 114.

4. Meres, *Palladis*. For quotation on *Love's Labour's Won* and discussion of Meres, see Schoenbaum, *Lives*, 26–22.

We do know that 1599 was one of the most extraordinary years of Shakespeare's career, as James Shapiro has recently reminded us,[5] a year that saw the production of *Henry V*, *Julius Caesar*, *As You Like It*, and *Hamlet*. Of these, of course, the latter is usually seen as the great breakthrough. *Hamlet* certainly marks a level of stylistic skill and philosophical seriousness, likely related to the death of Shakespeare's only son, Hamnet, in 1596, that still astounds today. Yet each play in the extraordinary year of 1599 has its own breakthroughs, and *As You Like It* is especially important to understanding the Catholic Humanist rhetoric that is significant throughout Shakespeare's career.

As men like Erasmus and More recommended, the rhetoric of *As You Like It* is a union of *sapientia* and *eloquentia*, conveyed both through its main themes and the witty expression of its wisdom. This play's language is exceptional, its slender plot constructed on a series of artful rhetorical debates. Often these debates become meta-linguistic, allowing glimpses of Shakespearean reflection on basic human questions: what is the purpose of words? Of rhetoric? Of poetry? A comical tone pervades the work, as is often found in Erasmus and More, but it is a mistake not to take seriously the play's major themes.

The play's heroine, Rosalind, is as eloquent as the hero of *Hamlet*, and no less than him gives her own answer to the fundamental *raison d'etre*, the "to be or not to be" question that must be answered in every human life. Her character is an oft-noted theatrical conceit—a male actor playing a female who in the play disguises herself as a boy in order to teach the play's obtuse hero, Orlando, of how to properly woo and truly love the feminine heroine she truly portrays—but her clever wit should draw us towards important, imaginative reflection upon gender roles. Perhaps most significantly, towards gender roles within married love, though the play also includes a political battleground, a tale of strife and exile between two brothers, Duke Signor and Duke Frederick, to which the timeless "battle of the sexes" between Rosalind and Orlando could be figuratively compared, especially within the conflicted, often violent political contexts of Reformation era Europe.

All of the major themes of *As You Like It* are important to Catholic Humanism, but it is the witty, comical tone of the play that most reminds us of Erasmus and More. Unfortunately this tone has led some scholars to regard the play as trivial, and there is definitely a bias, even within Shakespeare Studies, against book-length studies of Shakespeare's major comedies. It can be difficult to avoid pedanticism when attempting to describe

---

5. Shapiro, *A Year*.

both the linguistic detail and comical but philosophical themes of the play, its marriage of wit and wisdom, but criticism must attempt to understand Shakespeare's immense achievement. As Jonathan Bate says in the excellent PBS documentary, *Shakespeare Uncovered*:

> Historically, people have paid more attention to Shakespeare's tragedies and history plays than his comedies, but that's a huge mistake. In terms of thinking about what it is to be human, what it is to live in society and, above all, what it's like to live in personal relationships—men and women, together, families—the comedies are the place where Shakespeare really works that out in a profound way.[6]

Learning to understand the rhetoric of *As You Like It* is not only a way to avoid this "huge mistake"; more positively, it should allow us both to revel in the play's wit and at least partially, God helping, to reveal its wisdom.

---

6. Sutherland, *Shakespeare Uncovered*.

PART I

Understanding Catholic Humanism

DEATH CAN LEAVE THOSE left behind appreciating the meaning of experience rather than taking life for granted, but is tragedy essential to such realization? Could not the meaning of laughter, friendship, joy, even perhaps marriage itself allow one to catch the meaning of such experiences as they are intended by God in human life? This entire book is written according to the bias of an affirmative answer to this question, but part 1 is necessary to changing our "horizon of understanding" and thus make possible an accurate evaluation, in part 2, of Shakespeare's *As You Like It*.

Whether gaining such understanding would actually change the world or even one single human life has always been a matter of controversy and debate. The religious humanists focused on in the first half of this book were often criticized for believing that book learning could be a primary element of social change. The Shakespearean drama focused on in the second half of this book is often dismissed as "high culture" irrelevant to present or future human concerns. This is perhaps especially true of comedy, often regarded as trivial entertainment alongside the high seriousness of tragedy. People often have a pleasant, "fun" experience watching a play like *As You Like It*, but miss its meaning, its marriages enlivening the human heart less than the multiple deaths of a play like *Lear* create permanent catharsis.

To have the experience but miss the meaning seems to be a common but extremely significant element of human life. Most can give examples from youth, such as attending school but not retaining its lessons, or of going to church but not focusing upon the meaning of the service or scripture. We forgive ourselves easily of such lapses, but missed meaning can affect one's entire life. One may be unable to learn something crucial to budget management (as I have failed to learn to maintain vehicles) or, of far greater import, one or both of the key persons involved may have missed the meaning of their marriage ceremony, with sad consequences for their future life together. Complex human meaning often involves others, for better or worse, and we can learn to expand our understanding of what it means to be a husband, wife, father, mother, brother, sister, son, or daughter. Whatever our role, we are learning part of what it means to be human. According to Christianity, we ultimately learn what it means to be part of a family with God as our Father. According, further, to the complexity of Catholic Christian revelation, we learn what it means also for Jesus to be our brother in this family, and Mary to be our Mother.

The failure to comprehend meaning happens often in life, and clearly it is also a common part of our experience of reading literature. How often does one begin to read a book, only to find that it is beyond one's horizons, and its author's language and concerns so foreign to us that we cannot grasp the meaning of many words, sentences, or paragraphs, let alone any unified understanding of an author's vision. Trained guides or teachers can help introduce the basic concepts needed to minimally comprehend a book's vision, but interpretative dialectic seems essential to any even temporarily valid evaluation of literature. Whether hearing a poem read aloud, reading a novel silently, or watching a play or film in performance, it remains possible even for highly trained readers to experience a literary work without understanding its meaning or, to use the term more common in evaluative literary criticism, its significance to human life. Skeptics will doubt whether such knowledge is ever possible, but the following chapters are intended to create a horizon from which truth can be enjoyed.

1

Catholic Humanism in Judeo-Christian Scripture and Tradition

So God created man in His own image, in the image of God He created he him; male and female created He them (Gen 1:27).[1]

What can this mysterious verse possibly mean? Given the horrors of human history, not necessary to name here but clearly obvious, in what sense is it true that human beings reflect the divine image? If we are skeptical about this claim, should we not also be skeptical about the "scripture" in which we find this idea, the Bible? Should we not especially be skeptical of the God whom the Judeo-Christian scriptures portray? In its very next chapter, in Genesis, scripture turns to the story of the "Fall," and begins answering these questions. Yet every traditional Christian account of the meaning of the Fall implies at least one more troubling question: what power is strong enough to turn the "good" of God's creation, so often affirmed in the first chapter of *Genesis*, into the evil so common in our world today? Henri

---

1. The biblical quotations in this book are from the 1611 King James Bible (KJV). I am aware of the hermeneutical issues surrounding biblical translation, and of the fact that *As You Like It* was first performed before this Bible was published, though the play was first printed afterward in the First Folio of 1623. However, for the purposes of intensive study of Shakespeare's plays, such issues seem less important than the value gained through language similar to Shakespeare's own style.

de Lubac wrote, of Genesis 1:27, that "Christian tradition has not ceased to annotate this verse, recognizing in it our first title of nobility and the foundation of our greatness."[2] Yet given the puzzling questions raised in the opening chapters of Genesis, can one believe in either God or Humanity, let alone Christianity? Who is the God in whom Christians believe, and what difference should this make to humanity?

Such questions may seem beyond the scope of this present book. Yet anyone seeking to understand Catholic Humanism, or its role in a play such as *As You Like It*, must begin with the scriptures that Catholicism believes reveal the most important truths about God and Humanity. Yet to begin explaining the meaning of Catholic Humanism through "scripture" and "tradition" is already, according to some theologians, evidence of bias. For it is true that pitting Catholic "tradition" vs. Protestant "sola scriptura" is one of the enduring conflicts popularized by the sixteenth century division of Western Christendom. Yet anyone in the West who is afflicted by this division, i.e. everyone, cannot help but be affected by the bias of their own deepest beliefs and motivations. Many scriptures allow multiple interpretations, though some seem to contradict each other and interpretative authority requires spiritual authority such as can only come from the Spirit whom Jesus promises will lead us into "all truth" (John 16:13). Catholicism and Protestantism agree on this significant point, though historically they have often differed on how humanity is most likely to hear the voice of the Spirit.

Long before this principle affected Catholic and Protestant relations, its relevance to the relationship of Judaism and Christianity was crucial. In just the second verse of the Bible, for example, we read "the Spirit of God moved upon the face of the waters" (Gen 1:2). Is this the spiritual movement of the one, purely monotheistic God of Judaism, or the "triune" monotheism that the New Testament requires Christians to believe exists before the beginning of time, when the Word who was God was with God, before becoming "flesh" in the historical person of Jesus of Nazareth (to cite the famous prologue of John's Gospel, one of many New Testament passages that make the Trinity one of the most widely accepted of all Christian doctrines). The distinction is crucial to both religions, of course, because on it depends the metaphysical status of Jesus, yet there can also be no question that these two religions share many scriptures and even, in an important sense, believe in the same God. Both Christians and Jews, for example, think that it really is the one, living God of the universe who appears to Moses in the burning bush (Exod 3:14) before revealing foundational aspects of human ethics in the Ten Commandments. Both share scriptures, or writings, that must be

---

2. Lubac, *Atheist Humanism*, 19.

regarded as sacred, yet the meaning of key passages are determined by the meaning of key parts of scripture as revealed elsewhere than in the initial passage itself.

This often overlooked point affects many aspects of biblical interpretation, even within Judaism itself. There are key questions, such as, just who is the snake seen in the garden of Eden in Genesis 2 and 3? It is not there named as the fallen angel Satan but usually interpreted as such, by both Jews and Christians, with reference to the Lucifer later described in Isaiah 12. One should not, then, hope to understand biblical revelation on the relationship of the Divine and human in a chronological way, or expect that authentic, universal doctrine is warranted by our linguistic interpretation of key scriptural verses. Rather, truth is warranted by the living God; for Catholic biblical interpreters, as in every other area of life, there is no way to our Father except through the Way, Truth, and Life who is Jesus. For those seeking to know what public revelation should be universally shared with humanity, as compared to the private interpretation that might occur in one's own silent reading, one can interpret scripture well only through the Wisdom of Christ, Who in history has revealed the realities that the church can accept as Revelation.

That many of these truths are revealed in history, to living human beings, should not diminish the value of the ancient text. We must start where we are, as twenty-first century interpreters somewhat aware of our biases in the many controversies that have affected tradition, and yet open to hearing how scripture still speaks of the most significant truths we can ever know, at least in this life. We should not avoid, then, reading scripture and summarizing those aspects of revelation most relevant to our topic, but nor can we avoid relying on Catholic tradition for the lenses by which to see this significance. To aid our ability to explain this revelation, diverse elements of Christian literary, philosophical, and theological tradition have always been invaluable. Usually my focus is on writers prior to the time of Shakespeare, but of course there are Catholic Humanist writers who chronologically follow Shakespeare and are of the same tradition, despite apparent differences. One of the defining characteristics of Catholic Humanism is its capacity to transcend any historical culture. We here test this hypothesis through the delightful play that is *As You Like It*, but understanding its Catholic Humanism first requires significant review of both scripture and theological as well as literary Catholic tradition.

Revelation of the first chapter of Genesis should fill us with wonder, and questions. The creation of humanity is clearly part of an original blessing in which God speaks into being all that exists and several times judges His creation as "good" (Gen 1:11, 18, 21, 25), indeed "very good" (Gen

1:31). Well aware of the evident problems in human life, we first have to ask how things became "not so good"? Yet given God's evident power to make so much that we cannot make, what power do we imagine strong enough to make God's creation go from "good" to "bad"? The force of this question as it applies to human rather than general nature is further elevated when we learn, at 1:27, that humans are made "in the image of God." What might this possibly mean, given the good world we have just heard God create, and the evident evils of the subsequent human world? The same verse further tells us, "male and female created He them," ensuring that we must take seriously two halves of the human race, and the importance of gender difference, real from the beginning of creation. Yet we are pointed also towards another mystery: for all their apparent differences, men and women are similar, as human beings, in both sharing within themselves an image of the divine. How can men and women learn to see this in each other?

Chapters 2 and 3 of Genesis further give some of the most crucial elements of theological anthropology in the entire Bible. They offer a second creation account, Eve from the rib of Adam, which could again suggest the common nature of male and female. Perhaps the most obvious question these chapters evoke, though, is who is the snake, "more subtil than any beast of the field" (Gen 3:1), and how did it (or is it "he," since this snake talks and seems to have personality) get in the garden? No direct answer in Genesis is given, but Christian tradition will point ahead to Isaiah's account of the "son of the morning" fallen from heaven (Isa 14:12)—often translated as Lucifer himself, and Jesus' meeting and rebuke of Satan (the enemy of God) in the desert (Luke 4:1–12)—to interpret the tempter of Genesis as a fallen demon who had already rebelled against God and led a war in heaven. Milton's *Paradise Lost* becomes the most famous account of this interpretation, but Milton himself based it upon a traditional, widely held view crucial to Judeo-Christian anthropology: before the creation of humanity, God made another sort of creature, angels, whose form and relationship to time and eternity is fundamentally different than humanity, but share a rational capacity to obey or disobey God.

The Bible's opening chapters include many other crucial elements of theological anthropology. Why does God forbid the "tree of the knowledge of good and evil" (Gen 2:17)? Has God created Adam and Eve in an infantile state, utterly dependent on him and unable to acquire further knowledge? Is God, in fact, a tyrant? This is exactly what Milton's Satan tells Eve, reflecting the rebel angel's original temptation in Genesis: "Ye shall not surely die: for God doth know that in the day ye eat thereof, then your eyes shall be opened, and ye shall be as gods, knowing good and evil" (Gen 3:4–5). Humanity's destiny, according to Satan, is to become more than human, to be as gods comparable in nature to their Creator. Is this what the "divine image" means?

That it does not, that the snake here lies, is revealed not only by subsequent human history, but by the obvious consequence of the fall as Adam and Eve eat of the forbidden tree and then are expelled from Eden by God. Scripture records many other negative consequences, such as the pain of work and childbearing, general alienation from God, and perhaps most painfully of all the evil murder of Abel by his elder brother Cain, Adam and Eve's two oldest sons. Yet these facts do not settle the primary point of dispute about the fall that later divided Catholic and Protestant tradition: the extent to which the Fall eliminates the possibility of good human will, of the human capacity to choose good, God helping, rather than the evil inevitably also part of human nature, both traditions agree, after the Fall.

The negative answer to this question is well known in Luther and Calvin, whose stress on complete human depravity leads logically to their conception of salvation by God's grace alone, God alone choosing who to damn and who to save, as Calvin explicitly argues, mainly through his interpretation of Paul's letter to the Romans, especially chapter 9. Many other issues were at stake in the Reformation controversies, but the relationship between the human will and divine grace cannot be taken as "academic" or unimportant. Not only is God's nature at issue, but moreover the question of the relevance and role of the human will, of human choice itself. Catholic thought both affirms the necessity of the human will to accept divine grace if salvation is to occur, and, as a logical corollary, that it is possible for humanity to reject God. From the Apostle John to Augustine to Aquinas to Erasmus to Newman to Tolkien to John Paul II, despite the obvious differences between such figures, Catholic Humanism consistently affirms both the necessity of human choice and the reality of Divine Providence. Both are real elements of human life, and further teach us the need for the central virtue most clearly violated in the Fall, the virtue seemingly necessary to allow humanity to remain close to God: obedience.

The importance of obedience is perhaps most memorably, and shockingly, portrayed in the story of Abraham. God promises him that he will be patriarch to millions but then keeps him childless for so long, then asks Abraham to sacrifice his only son, Isaac (Gen 22). Many find this command sadistic, but Catholicism sees in the story "typology" that helps us to understand how great a sacrifice it is when God the Father later will actually allow the sacrifice of His only Son, whose obedience even to the Cross will reestablish the communion between God and Humanity caused by the Fall. Many other examples of Old Testament typology help us to understand the Christ, or Messiah, such as the stories of Noah, Joseph, Moses, Job, David, or many others. Jesus himself will read the Old Testament in this way by affirming, "as Jonas was three days and three nights in the whale's belly; so shall the Son of Man be three days and three nights in the heart of the earth" (Matt 12:40).

All of these Old Testament figures shed light on the meaning of theological anthropology as understood by Catholic Humanism. While we must be clear that "old" here is not pejorative but a synonym for venerable or ancient, clearly none can be as important as the shocking turn of the New Testament, which occurs when the eternal, infinite, immaterial God, the divinity generally believed in by Judaism, enters time to take form as one human man in the person of Jesus Christ. It is impossible to even suggest the Incarnation's full implications, or its impact upon human culture, but perhaps four key elements of scripture and tradition can be clarified to suggest the importance of Christ to Catholic Humanism. Each of the four stems, as we shall see, from Jesus' utterly unique status; in the church's paradoxical, incomprehensible, yet absolutely dogmatic words, Jesus is both "fully divine" and "fully human." In their own way, each of the four elements is crucial to how Jesus fulfills the meaning of his Jewish name, "Yahweh saves."

It is, of course, reductive to classify Jesus' impact on humanity in four categories. But perhaps each of the four helps us remember truths that our fallible, finite minds might otherwise forget. The first, obvious area is as ethical example and moral teacher. This is the way the world tends first to categorize Christianity, especially in its obvious contrast to the ethic of this world. It is certainly possible to summarize Christian ethics in relation to the two great commandments that Jesus gives: to love God, and to love our neighbor as ourselves (Mark 12:28–31). This ethic is central to how the world tends first to categorize Christianity, especially in its obvious contrast to the ethic of this world.

However, so long as such ethics remain abstract and impersonal, there can seem little difference between Christianity and the Jewish ethic that formed Jesus (cf. Deut 5–6, Moses teaching the Israelites both the ten commandments and the love of the Lord essential to Judaism). In the Gospel of John, however, Jesus' teaching to his disciples seems more personal, and requiring both faith and works. "*If* ye continue in my word, then are ye my disciples, indeed; and ye shall know the truth, and the truth shall make you free" (John 8:31–32). The contingent relationship of freedom and truth also seems part of Jesus' promise to send the Apostles the Holy Spirit; later in the Gospel of John, Christ tells his Apostles:

> If ye love me, keep my commandments. And I will pray the Father, and he shall give you another Comforter, that he may

> abide with you for ever; even the Spirit of truth; whom the world cannot receive, because it seeth him not, neither knoweth him: but ye know him, for he dwelleth with you, and shall be in you. (John 14:15–17)

My italicizing of "if" in both passages reminds us that Catholic Humanism regards "if" as necessary to peace between God and Humanity, and the scriptural foundation for peace of any kind.

These passages also remind us that when Jesus does stress the unique nature of his Gospel, in context this often becomes a call for inner spiritual transformation rather than simply adherence to an outward rule. Jesus' "Sermon on the Mount," for example, does not rescind God's commandment against adultery (Exod 20:14), but extends it to call us not even to think adulterous thoughts (Matt 5:28). Clearly this is a much harder task, but consistent with Jesus' broad effort to change not only human behavior, but the human heart itself. Sometimes this effort seems so hopeless as to be absurd—few of even the best Christians have truly succeeded in loving their enemies—but perhaps Jesus himself is aware of irony in his later words in the Sermon on the Mount: "Be ye therefore perfect, as your Father which is in heaven is perfect" (Matt 5:48).

Though these words have helped some to become ethically earnest, Catholic Humanism has typically interpreted them as ironic. Being well aware of what is "in man" (John 2:25), Jesus knows well that most human beings are unlikely to approach perfection in this world. But our conclusion should not, therefore, be despair; rather, there is humor in the gap between what humanity is and what we should be, and an awareness that we *must* be dependent on God in the way that small children sometimes realize they are dependent upon their parents. Even that analogy can break down, of course, but Jesus' insistence that we must become as little children to enter the kingdom of heaven (Matt 18:3), which can seem so puzzling as part of a rational Christian ethic, is for Catholic Humanism confirmation of a greater truth: God surely laughs at us while loving us, and even after all our efforts to love God, at some point we must laugh at ourselves and run into God's arms in the way that the Prodigal Son does in returning home to his Father.

Our need to refer to Jesus' parables gives another key element that Catholic Humanism typically sees in Jesus as ethical teacher: an apparent preference for teaching through parables, stories, figures of speech, rather than through rational or logical propositions. We cannot know Jesus' entire rationale for this choice, nor can one deny the clear ethic often drawn from his teaching, but Catholic Humanism has usually posited that Jesus chose figurative language as a more likely mode by which to reach, and save, the sinful human heart. The most commonly recurring image of Jesus' parables is a call for those with "eyes to see" and "ears to hear" (Matt 13:16). Literal minded response might think this includes at least most human beings; but in reality, as most teachers know, humans are quite capable of "ever learning" but never coming "to the knowledge of the truth" (2 Tim 3:7). The New Testament often refers back to the Jews' treatment of their prophets; when God to Isaiah, for example, lamented how the people badly need, though are obstinately unaware, of being "healed" (Isa 6:10). Similarly, Jesus often seems aware that his parables are likely to fall "on stony ground," as the parable of the sower puts it (Mark 4:1–20), the parable that gives the clearest hermeneutic guide to understanding Jesus' parables. Yet Jesus continues teaching via parable throughout his ministry, perhaps suggesting that there is no more effective way to reach the human heart. Accordingly, Catholic Humanists have typically stressed the value of figurative speech as a preferred means to express truth.[3]

Any awareness of the range and power of Jesus as ethical teacher leads to an obvious question: why did God the Father further deem it necessary that Jesus also die on the cross, in a most painful death usually reserved for criminals? What could humanity possibly gain through this piteous spectacle, so painful that Christ himself, in the garden of Gethsemane, prays that "this cup pass" (Matt 26:39) if possible. Again, no one can presume to know God's full answer to this pressing question, but Catholic Humanists are likely to point to the cross' power to move the human heart. Of the three enemies that Christianity typically sees vanquished on the cross—Satan, death, and sin—it is the third enemy that Catholic Humanists tend to stress. To the childish question, "who killed Jesus?," a mature Christian knows to reply, "I did." Hymns like "Amazing Grace" and "When I Survey the Wondrous Cross" essentially express this; that both hymns emerge from the sin and grace of the Protestant tradition does not make them less relevant to Catholic Humanism. On the contrary, such hymns are artistic expressions capable of moving the human heart.

The further, more obvious consequence of the cross, after just three days, is the resurrection of Christ that follows from it. What are the consequences of Christ's Resurrection, if it is true? As Holly Ordway's teacher put it in the moving account of her conversion, "that is the big question."[4] It is, again, impossible to even suggest the value of the resurrected Jesus to humanity. All of the hymns of joy composed by all of humanity's great artists cannot convey the joy of this sudden turn, which Tolkien terms a

---

3. A point that David Lyle Jeffrey and I make repeatedly in *Christianity and Literature*.
4. Ordway, *Not God's Type*, 126.

CATHOLIC HUMANISM IN JUDEO-CHRISTIAN SCRIPTURE AND TRADITION

"eucatastrophe"[5] and which Catholics have always followed St. Paul in seeing as absolutely crucial to their faith (1 Cor 15:14). For me, no work of art better conveys the human importance of Christ's Resurrection than G. M. Hopkins' poem, "That Nature is a Heraclitean Fire, and of the Comfort of the Resurrection." This poem acknowledges the tendency of human nature to mimic and even become part of the sinful world around us, but the last two lines reach an astonishing conclusion:

> I am all at once what Christ is, / since he was what I am, and
> This Jack, joke, poor potsherd, / patch, matchwood, immortal diamond
> Is Immortal Diamond.[6]

To begin with this claim, of course, would be astonishing arrogance, yet as a conclusion of what Christ's resurrection does for humanity, Hopkins here claims the promise that impels Catholic artists to attempt being "sub-creators" with God. Tolkien coins this word in his "Mythopoeia,"[7] a poetic defense of art that complements the prose of "On Fairy Stories." Just after the latter text's prose epilogue speaks of the Incarnation and Resurrection as an "eucatastrophe," a sudden turn from catastrophe to joy, Tolkien further claims that God's "primary story, which begins and ends in joy," has "hallowed all other stories, especially the "happy ending."[8] Because of Christ's cross and resurrection, in other words, happy human conclusions are no longer vain hopes; they are, rather, divine offers, awaiting only the time and setting within which both God and individual creatures endowed with free will shall write the human story.

Even a dim awareness of the nature of Jesus' ethical teaching and the meaning of his passion is certainly enough to enliven the artistic tradition of Catholic Humanism. Yet there are two other key areas of the Gospel that further stem from taking seriously the dogma that Jesus is both fully divine and fully human.

First is the paradoxical promise that humanity will receive both ultimate justice and eternal mercy. Both promises might seem irrelevant to Catholic Humanist art in this world, unless we see both the act of writing and the actions of human life itself as part of a script whose ultimate Author is God. Both historians and literary writers often know of stories that might cause one to despair of justice, whether due to human error, the power of

---

5. Tolkien, "On Fairy Stories," 66.
6. Hopkins, "Nature is a Heraclitean Fire," 105.
7. Tolkien, "Mythopoeia," 98.
8. Tolkien, "On Fairy Stories," 66.

criminals, or the corruption of a legal system. However, a legitimate hope for divine justice allows victims to retain some hope, and it is exactly this hope that Christ offers, especially in the Book of Revelation. At the end of time, Christ will be a just Judge, and allow the peace and beauty of a city of God called the New Jerusalem (Rev 21). The belief that human history is ultimately hopeful, not nihilistic, fuels the pens and lives of Catholic Humanist writers, who are free to speak of evil precisely because God ensures the partial, limited, temporal nature of evil.

While the evils of human history fuel our need for divine justice, how much more do human beings need the promise of divine mercy. In the New Testament, one of the most striking ways that the divinity of Jesus is claimed is by granting him "the power on earth to forgive sins" (Mark 2:10; Luke 5:24). Logically, such authority could be held by God alone; after the Resurrection, this same point seems to be made when, just before commanding the "great commission" and giving the full name of God, Jesus says, "All power is given unto me in heaven and in earth" (Matt 28:18). For humans aware of their own sin, this is especially good news. From the perspective of one whose sin would lead to death—i.e., the perspective of any self-aware human being—forgiveness is a key part of the power and promise of Christ's resurrection, and even so great an artist as Shakespeare concludes what is probably his last play by praying to "Mercy Itself" (*The Tempest*, Epilogue: 18). Mercy here is another name for the divine grace that allows Catholic Humanist artists to continue their quest for truth and beauty.

All three elements of the Gospel discussed thus far might be imagined as Jesus communing with an individual human heart. Indeed this is possible, and a key part of His ministry. However, Catholic Humanism also asserts the divine creation of a church that offers a community of grace. The nature of Christ's church is far too complex to detail here, but New Testament metaphors consistently make the point most stressed by Catholicism: it is not possible to separate Christ and His church. The Catholic sacraments and commitment to Christ's "real presence" often make the Catholic "Word" more concrete but less articulate than Protestant ministry of the Word in preaching and Bible study, but this point also leads to many other emphases.[9] One is Christ as the Bridegroom, His Church the Bride, an image presented several times in the New Testament (e.g., Rev 19:8). This theological reality is the model for human marriage (rather than the reverse, as anthropomorphism assumes) as St. Paul implies when he quotes Genesis on the meaning of marriage (Gen 2:24), then adds, "this is a great mystery, and I am applying it to Christ and the church" (Eph 5:23). Or, as

---

9. See my *Word Awake*.

St. Paul also puts it, Christ himself is the head of the body that is the church, a highly complex organism that furthers infinitely God's communion with humanity.

Usually Catholicism distinguishes "the Church Triumphant," or those alive in heaven, and the "Church Militant," those suffering here on earth, with all its human sin. Such distinctions are crucial to Catholicism, though space here does not allow room to adequately review controversial doctrines such as the papacy or the meaning of infallibility in Catholicism, but suffice it here to say that the "hands and feet" of Christ's body have frequently been the material means within which work those artists granted the "eyes and ears" of Catholic Humanism. In other words, concrete matter, through what some term the "sacramental imagination" is part, typically, of Catholic Humanist art.

This is true not only of "sacred art," but also of the oft misnamed "secular art" by which Catholic artists have often explored the mysteries of human and divine nature. Again, this point is especially obvious in the work of a great Catholic artist such as Tolkien, who acknowledges in a letter to a friend and priest that *The Lord of the Rings* is "of course a fundamentally religious and Catholic work"; paradoxically, this meant, for Tolkien, that he "cut out . . . practically all references to anything like 'religion.'"[10] Why this cut? It is hard to answer this complex question, but in sum I would point to Tolkien's humble respect for the priority of Divine Revelation over any human art. "The Incarnation," he says in another letter, is "something much greater than I could ever imagine."[11] Yet, as already noted, rather than rejecting human art, Tolkien's view is that the great "eucatastrophes" of Christian revelation, such as the Incarnation, Crucifixion, and Resurrection, have not negated but rather have "hallowed all other stories especially the 'happy ending.'"[12]

It is the Catholic sense of revelation, usually called the "deposit of faith," which grounds the nature of Catholic Humanism. The importance of this seemingly obvious point cannot be overstated, existentially. Supernatural revelation, in other words, cannot be prevented from suffusing "natural" reality with divine grace. Within this revelation, each of the seven Catholic sacraments, and Mary herself, offer endless means of aesthetic grace. There are many further topics that could be considered relevant to Catholic Ecclesiology, but perhaps of broadest importance is "the problem of evil." St. Augustine famously defines evil as an "absence of being," and other theologians

---

10. Tolkien, "Letter 142," 171–73.
11. Tolkien, "Letter 181," 235.
12. Tolkien, "On Fairy Stories," 66.

offer compelling explanations like "free will" or the "original sin" of the Fall. However, for those suffering personally through evil, such as in a period of corruption in the visible church, all purely abstract or intellectual answers can seem empty. This is a key reason for the Incarnate suffering of Christ, of why Jesus could not simply be a wise teacher, for Jesus' personal involvement with human suffering is perhaps the most compelling theodicy.

Catholic Ecclesiology thus points, paradoxically, to Judas, to the mystery of why Christ chose Judas to be one of his first disciples. Even acknowledging that it was Satan who "entered into" Judas at the time of Christ's passion (Luke 22:3), Judas himself clearly makes some of his own choices. The story of Judas is necessary for humanity to really believe and understand that no evil can ultimately stop the good intended by God. This conclusion does not diminish the tragedy of Judas, which reminds us that humans can choose the temporal separation from God that is hell, but it also reminds us that the church Jesus creates will survive into eternity for the same reasons as Christ's other promises.

The masculine focus of Catholic Humanism is typically balanced, especially in ecclesiology, by the role of Mary. Mary's unique role, as the human creature who first receives the special graces of the New Testament, accounts for why two texts so far apart in time and genre—Dante's *Divine Comedy* and the first encyclical of John Paul II, *Redemptor Hominis*—both conclude with a lengthy praise of Mary. John Paul does go out of his way to acknowledge the truth of Protestant "proof-texts" such as 1 Timothy 2:5, which remind us that all humans need Jesus to be saved, by clarifying that Mary too is saved through Christ. Yet Mary's influence upon Catholic Humanism must be understood both theologically and culturally, impacting on many levels our understanding of what redeemed men and women should be.

Mary's "Immaculate Conception," for example, which refers not to the Virgin Birth of Christ but rather to the claim that Mary was conceived without sin, is a doctrine partially derived from the Catholic understanding of the Fall. As the "second Eve," the New Testament's "mother of all [spiritually] living," it is Mary's son, Jesus, who fulfills the Genesis promise that Eve's offspring will defeat Satan (a promise whose literal meaning seems lost in the crimes of Cain). Catholicism thus posits that Mary must have a pre-fallen nature, like the pre-fallen Eve, in order to freely accept or reject the Angel Gabriel's "annunciation" of God's plan for the Incarnation; otherwise, Mary's obedience, reversing the disobedience of Eve, can have no meaning. One could see Mary's immaculate nature as unnecessary, as one could imagine the Incarnation without human figures at all. But clearly this is not the record of biblical revelation. In addition to many further scriptural verses, Catholic scholars are likely to cite Revelation 12, where Mary seems the mother of the Messiah, or the wedding at Cana, where Mary tells the servants of Jesus: "Whatsoever he saith unto you, do it" (John 2:5).

To note the other Marian doctrine that most divides Catholics and Protestants, perhaps because it too was "infallibly" defined by modern Popes, Mary's "Assumption" into heaven after death (soul and body), is also a long held belief that Catholic Humanism, following the Apostle's Creed, foresees for all redeemed human beings. Thus understood, it is surely unsurprising that Mary is such an important subject in Catholic Humanist art, both in herself and as a spiritual example for all men and women who seek to follow her to life in Christ. In Mary is the eternal evidence that both men and women are made to be obedient to the image of God in them. In contemporary Catholicism, the Marian revelations at Fatima and Akita are also important to transcendent human faith in divine providence.

The transcendent reality of the church sometimes is used to diminish its relevance to this world, but Catholic Humanism is entirely faithful to Catholic tradition in rejecting any abstract alienation opposed to the fullness of grace intended and ultimately certain to be achieved by God. There is no human means to separate Christ from His Bride the Church, no means to prevent the Word from speaking through the word that is Scripture. Yet God's book is also history, both physical and spiritual, and both books give glimpses of the glory of God's grace to humanity. Thus there is also no means to keep Christ in the grave, or to prevent Logos from Rising.[13] Catholic Humanism can never be an abstract idea, or bloodless myth. Yet apology and humility, exemplified by the papacy of St. John Paul II, are essential starting points for any comprehension of Catholic Humanism. To see the way forward, it is also valuable to look back to other key thinkers and artists whose human lives show us the presence of God. As Tolkien's Baggins rightly sings, "the road goes ever on,"[14] but to enter the road sometimes it is necessary to retrace our steps.

---

13. See Jones, *Logos Rising*. My gratitude to Patrick Coffin for this reference.
14. Tolkien, *The Lord of the Rings*, 42.

2

Historiography and Catholic Humanism

In 1998, Harold Bloom brought rare public attention to literary criticism by claiming that Shakespeare "invented human nature," at least "human nature as we know it."[1] In many ways, Bloom's claim was simply the latest in a long critical line of praise for the "infinite variety" of characters in Shakespearean drama; but, in his radical, bardolatrous edge, Bloom also appealed to late twentieth-century atheism or, as it is also known, secular humanism. Though carefully substituting the rhetorical term "invention" for the traditional term "creation," Bloom subtly compared Shakespeare to deity while granting the bard far more contemporary influence than any traditional god. Christians, however, could not join a secular chorus of praise, if only because of the centrality to their religion of the Incarnation, the belief that God became human in the historical person of Jesus. What difference should this obvious clash of worldviews make to anyone's interpretation of Shakespearean drama? Apart from the probably unanswerable question of Shakespeare's own religious faith, but aware that the historical age which produced Shakespearean drama was at least in some important respects a Christian society, to what extent does a Christian rather than secular conception of human nature affect our ability to perceive both the aesthetic form and ethical intent of Shakespearean drama?

---

1. Bloom, *Invention*, 717.

To begin exploring this complex question, let us begin with the hard question suggested by the title of this chapter, and of this entire book: Why is it important, to appreciate Shakespeare's art, that we speak of "Catholic Humanism," rather than the more commonplace "Christian Humanism," and view key humanists of the sixteenth century, such as Erasmus and More, not as early pioneers of a movement that follows them, in the sixteenth or seventeenth century, but rather as late representatives whose origins must be traced to at least the Italy of the fourteenth century?

The key figures in this tradition were most likely to have accepted a shorter, simpler term—the Latin term "*umanista*"[2]—though the term itself was controversial even in its own time, and these pioneering figures would probably see themselves, if part of any movement, as part of a literary revival against the philosophical method of medieval scholasticism. Though clearly engaged in the retrieval of classical studies, most *umanista* also seem to have been faithful Catholics, at least in the doctrines that they publicly affirm. Yet this historical fact is not my primary reason for speaking of "Catholic Humanism"; rather, the first part of my rationale can be called, *historiographical*, the second, *cultural*.

Perhaps our most influential contemporary historian of Humanism, Charles D. Nauert, traces the dominant twentieth-century view of Humanism to a nineteenth-century Swedish scholar, Jacob Burckhardt, whose *Civilization of the Renaissance in Italy* told a story that became widely accepted:

> According to this story, after the collapse of ancient civilization in the fifth century AD, a thousand years of darkness ensued, with the Christian church acting simultaneously to preserve some few shreds of ancient civilization and to suppress any intellectual or religious revivals that might weaken the stranglehold that the higher clergy and the warrior aristocracy held over the minds as well as the bodies of ordinary people. Eventually, however, a revival of commerce and urban life . . . laid the foundations for a rediscovery of ancient literature and simultaneously for a secular, even anti-religious, set of values. These values, which constituted a new and distinctly modern philosophy of life, glorified the individual and the attraction of earthly life;[3]

Yet as Nauert pithily comments, in conclusion, this story "has only one major flaw: both in its general thrust and in virtually every detail, it is untrue."[4] The other major problem, though, is that the man most scholars believe

---

2. Crane, "Early Tudor Humanism," 13.
3. Nauert, *Humanism*, 1.
4. Nauert, *Humanism*, 2.

to be the founding father of Humanism, Petrarch, coined the term "dark ages,"[5] using it to cover all the way from his own time in the fourteenth century back to St. Augustine of Hippo, not only a key Church Father but perhaps also the last great Latin classicist. Yet if historians speak of a "dark ages" today, most date this precisely from 410 with the withdrawal of the Romans from England, to 597, when missionaries sent by Pope Gregory the Great began to evangelize the Anglo-Saxon tribes, a process we mainly learn about from a learned scholar who becomes famed as the Venerable Bede.[6] While there are few written records from this "dark age," archaeology has, over the past thirty years, discovered much evidence of the survival of a vibrant Anglo-Saxon culture in the fifth and sixth centuries.[7]

Regardless of how one views the recent English archaeology, a wide variety of historians are certainly aware that seeing any revival or "renaissance" of culture depends on the country under consideration. St. Patrick's work and life in the 400s was certainly epochal, but though Ireland is so close geographically to England its medieval history is almost entirely separate. Most who value literacy speak highly of the reign of King Alfred the Great in England in the late 900s, while those who focus on continental Europe, such as France or Italy, commonly now speak of a twelfth-century Renaissance.[8] The latter term has become accepted in contemporary historiography, and its meaning cannot be strictly linked to a revival of classical learning. If only through the immense learning of St. Augustine, a Classicist before his conversion to Catholicism, many examples of medieval Christian familiarity with classical culture can be given. What then distinguishes the Medieval and Renaissance periods?

It is instructive that both historical and literary scholars today more commonly refer to pre-seventeen-hundred times as an "Early Modern" rather than "Renaissance" period, presumably seeing in this age primarily the genesis of contemporary culture.[9] Yet those wanting a broader view of medieval culture are likely to notice a secular bias in this view. For while it is arguable that the term "renaissance" referred to a revival of literary study in reaction against the logical theology of scholasticism, the fact remains that the major figures of this age retain some form of Christian faith. Rather than rejecting this faith when there was a growth in classical or literary study, the

---

5. Nauert, *Humanism*, 19.

6. Largely because of "Caedmon's Hymn," usually cited as the first published poem in English, Bede remains well known, and is officially canonized by the Roman Catholic Church. Cf. Bede, *Ecclesiastical History of the English People*, 29–32.

7. See Hinton et al., *Anglo-Saxon Archaeology*.

8. See Novikoff, *The Twelfth-Century Renaissance*.

9. Hattaway, Introduction to *A Companion*, 5.

key issue usually becomes how such learning was integrated with Christian doctrine. In Catholicism, a hierarchy of truth is expected, so, for example, it is obvious in any thorough reading of Augustine that Platonic thought is integrated within Judaeo-Christian revelation, while Aquinas includes more references to biblical and Augustinian sources than to the Aristotelian philosophy for which scholasticism becomes famous. In historical context, the same point holds true for most major Humanist figures; the challenge for us is to understand how they integrated classical thought with the Christian beliefs they held, and the Catholic culture within which they worked.

To meet this challenge, then, requires us to look beyond secular bias against Catholicism, while still appreciating those aspects of Humanism that were reactions against the more established culture of Scholasticism. It is not enough, like many modern scholars, to use the simple "humanist" label that many fourteenth- to sixteenth-century scholars use of themselves; the meaning of this term has radically changed because of crucial cultural differences. Further, we cannot focus solely on those aspects of Humanism that become part of modern culture, or even part of the Protestant culture that gained political power in many parts of sixteenth-century Europe, including England. Rather, to appreciate medieval Catholic Humanism, key individuals and their work must be selected, according to our bias to understanding the aesthetic culture within which Shakespeare eventually lived, wrote, and struck audiences with wonder. These individuals are not cited for how they *directly* influence Shakespeare; in many cases, he may not have read their work or seen the direct products of their art. That is not the point.

The point is how these figures change culture, to allow English culture to become the kind of audience that would applaud and appreciate Shakespeare's art. Given that the precise nature of audience reception or influence cannot be tracked with certainty, even in well documented historical periods (which no one would call Medieval Europe), these figures are not chosen because of immediate influence or popularity. Rather, they are key markers of, as historians put it, "what is going forward"; specifically, what leads to the possibility of Shakespeare and his art, especially *As You Like It*. So the historical figures here briefly considered are chosen in part because of their relevance to the themes of this play, but the dangers of narrow obscurity are belied by the near universal relevance of this play's themes: the role of comedy and tragedy, of good and evil, in art; the human desire for peace; human disagreement over fundamental concepts such as gender and the meaning of socially essential concepts such as authority and marriage; and, perhaps more important of all, of the relationship between Divine and human nature. Catholicism shared much in common on these issues with the classical world, and this is part of why it was important to rediscover classical authors, and much in common with the Protestant Reformers. Victors cannot be relied upon to write accurate history, as everyone today knows, so it is essential to understanding the theological roots of Shakespeare's art to review European Catholic culture of the fourteenth–sixteenth century, which not only precedes Shakespeare chronologically, but also provides the intellectual and spiritual soil in which Shakespearean art grows and thrives.

How can the distinctive features of these complex, often dissimilar figures be recognized while also grouping them within a common movement? I was a championship basketball coach for many years, so to answer this key question, please permit me to develop an analogy of how this childish sport might be applicable to scholarly studies. In youth basketball, especially, there are so many players to choose from, yet only five can go on court at once and it is crucial to both individual development and the eventual strength of the team of twelve that a coach figures out how to group the lines in a way that highlights strengths and addresses weakness.

When it comes to the historiography of fourteenth to sixteenth century Europe, something like this method of coaching youth basketball could be applied to Catholic Humanism. This is especially true of Italy, where famous pioneers of this movement leave a lasting cultural impression. One can certainly debate which Italian figures are most important, as one can debate which players to put on any youth team, but most will find the revival of Classical learning important in Italy, and that is the strength that becomes well known to later ages; yet, as my account will particularly show, most Italian figures of the time were also believing Roman Catholics, and so the way in which they integrate these apparently incompatible elements create the unique culture and art that is almost as surprising and unpredictable as how young basketball players play on any particular day. In England, the situation is often reversed, in which clearly Roman Catholic figures integrate seemingly foreign learning to create their own unique art and lives.

As with Italy, many possible figures could be chosen. For England, I similarly choose five central to the immediate goal, which is to understand how Catholic Humanism created the culture of Shakespeare and his audience. While these chapters must necessarily give very condensed and specific aspects of the influence of both Italian and English Catholic Humanism, the subsequent two chapters attempt something again familiar to any basketball coach: how the insertion of a key sixth player can radically change the course of a game. In Catholic Humanist historiography, Erasmus plays this role in Europe, while Thomas More does the same for England. Because Erasmus and More were close friends, contemporaries whose joint influence can and often has been directly traced to Shakespeare, they help reunify my study, as good sixth men reunify a basketball team. Yet unlike a game, there can be no final score on the immediate success or failure of this admittedly unorthodox historiography. For better or worse, my hopes and methods have been strongly influenced by two very different historians: Thomas Cahill and Brad Gregory.

Cahill is best known for his "Hinges of History" series, which has included volumes on the Irish,[10] ancient Greeks, Jews, Christians, and key figures from Medieval and Renaissance Europe. The inevitable subjectivity of Cahill's survey is accentuated by frequent admission of personal bias; Cahill is often directly or indirectly telling us that he is of the nineteen-sixties generation of liberal American Catholics for whom Vatican II was the next best thing to the Second Coming, and John XXIII a hero sadly followed by the "conservatism" of John Paul II and Benedict XVI.[11] Yet though my own biases are often antagonistic to Cahill's, his account of how the "hinges of history" have unfolded is often compelling for me. This somewhat surprising fact is a reminder both of the objective reality of history, and of the inevitable bias of any historiography, including my own, towards the age that formed it. Though it is important to distinguish history as what is written and remembered from history as the reality that actually occurred, it is wise to remember that real elements of the past are present in the future, whether or not an individual historian's books are also present.

This point is brilliantly made by a much more rigorous and academic historian, Brad Gregory, in his great book *The Unintended Reformation*. As subjective and polemical, in some ways, as Cahill, Gregory uses extensive detail and philosophical argument to demonstrate that our contemporary "secular age" (as philosopher Charles Taylor calls it[12]) has ironic roots in the religious actions and ideals of sixteenth-century Protestant reform. For Gregory, the great US modernist writer William Faulkner had it right: "The past is never dead. It's not even past."[13] In a simpler and more aesthetically focused way, my historical approach follows Gregory's in being "a genealogical approach that emphasizes the continuing influence of the distant past in the present."[14] Though both Cahill and Gregory have influenced my approach to history, as a literary scholar perhaps even more important to me is the work of a contemporary author of historical fiction, Edward

---

10. Cahill's best-known book is probably *How the Irish Saved Civilization*.

11. Cahill, for example, describes John Paul II's theology of the body as, "painfully abstract" and "nearly interminable," in *Heretics and Heroes*, 281. Of course, I disagree.

12. Taylor, *A Secular Age*.

13. Quoted in Gregory, *The Unintended Reformation*, 1.

14. Gregory, *The Unintended Reformation*, 6.

Rutherfurd,[15] and an extraordinary, recently published book of poetry: Michael O'Siadhail's *Five Quintets*.

Neither is widely known, and Rutherfurd especially might be denigrated as an imitator of the sprawling, James Michener style novel that, arguably, reduces historical complexity to fictional entertainment. What redeems Rutherfurd's work for me, though, is not just his careful collaboration with scholars and museums to improve the likelihood of historical accuracy. Moreover, it is the use of a literary trope whereby members of the same fictional family, but living in vastly different historical eras, share both a physical genetic trait and a tendency to think and act in similar ways. Sometimes this link is contradictory, preventing any charge of historical determinism, but in general Rutherfurd's "genealogical" fiction makes the same point as Gregory's historiography: the past, even the distant past, continues to affect us in ways we cannot even articulate.

Rutherfurd's fiction gives an even more vital reminder. So often history is the record of tragedy, of who died when and in which war. Yet even when Rutherfurd depicts clearly tragic historical events, such as 9/11 in his novel *New York*,[16] there are survivors as well as victims. The point here is not simply optimism vs. pessimism, but rather realism vs. despair. Though thousands did die in the 9/11 tragedy, thousands more survived to go on making history in the twenty-first century.

The poetry of Michael O'Siadhail gives another model of historiographical hope and clarity in the twenty-first century. Again his aesthetics are crucial. Modelling his long poem after both Eliot's *Four Quartets* and Dante's *Divine Comedy*, O'Siadhail similarly lets speak, in their own subjective voice, dozens of the historical figures from the past 400 years whose work has been key to creating our contemporary culture. Though God is given the unorthodox title of "Madame Jazz," O'Siadhail's work can be seen as an authentic expression of Catholic Humanism. God is an important actor in O'Siadhail's poem, as God must be in any Catholic historiography. We cannot see humanity the way God does, but we can write with the aim of forming a human face that can at least resemble, and in some sense be "in the image of," the Divine face that we will one day know (1 Cor 13:12).

---

15. Rutherfurd's many long novels include *London*, and my personal favorites, *The Princes of Ireland* and *The Rebels of Ireland*.

16. Rutherfurd, *New York*, 994–1017.

3

Italian Catholic Humanism

To introduce his discussion of Italian Renaissance Humanism, Cahill writes:

> Men like Petrarch came to be called humanists, that is, people interested in human subjects rather than in the divine or theological subjects that had so enticed the previous age. This did not mean that they were irreligious or antireligious (Petrarch himself was a Catholic priest, though openly in love with a married woman, Laura, about whom he wrote obsessively).[1]

This is what might be termed the "soft secular" version of Burckhardt's argument; there is some historical fact here, and some accurate emphases, but it still ignores the importance of Christian theology to most Humanists. It is more defensible with the Italian figures with whom Cahill begins, Petrarch and Boccaccio, though even with them a secular claim must be heavily qualified. It is much less defensible for the first major figure of Catholic Humanism, Dante, whom despite the jealousy and "anxiety of influence" exhibited by the major intellectual closest to him in time, Petrarch, has in subsequent ages come to be seen as one of the most revolutionary and radically successful artists of all time. For Dante, the human relationship with God is of fundamental importance.

1. Cahill, *Heretics and Heroes*, 70.

DANTE (1265–1321)

Despite the claims of Petrarch, to whom we shall turn shortly, it should be obvious to lovers of literature that the towering, unique, and therefore indispensable figure of the Italian Renaissance is Dante Alighieri. Exiled by political strife from his native and beloved Florence in 1300, Dante spent the next twenty years or so wandering Italy, eventually completing and leaving the world the long poem, *The Divine Comedy*. It is primarily this work that will cause T. S. Eliot, much later, to claim that "Dante and Shakespeare divide the modern world between them; there is no third."[2] However hyperbolic the claim, there has been the inaccurate perception that the latter is secular, concerned mainly with this world, while the former focused on eternity. The controlling motif of *The Divine Comedy* is Dante's journey through hell (*Inferno*), purgatory (*Purgatorio*), and heaven (*Paradiso*), but along the way he meets and converses with a staggering variety of figures who made their name in the human world: figures from Italian Politics, but also church history, including Scripture. There are also a remarkable variety of characters from classical literature and mythology, whose imaginative origins are usually not distinguished in the poem from the characters of clearly historical inspiration. Obviously the entire work is a fiction—for Dante had not really died, of course—but one that millions of subsequent readers have found relevant to the reality of human spiritual life.[3]

Dante's religious themes cause some to arbitrarily assign him to the medieval period, but clearly *The Divine Comedy* does combine Classical and Christian motifs in the manner most associate with Renaissance art. Yet while both sources are essential to the poem, they certainly are not equal or equivalent. Compare and contrast, for example, the role played first by Virgil, author of the Roman epic *The Aeneid*, and Beatrice, an Italian woman whom Dante had known in his youth. The former acts as Dante's guide through *Inferno* and about two thirds of *Purgatorio*, while the latter guides Dante further up into the highest realms of *Paradiso*. A clear hierarchy between the two guides is thus established, though both are essential to Dante's journey. Virgil gives Dante the calm and clear eye of reason to look at the painful reality of what humanity does to itself; there are times when this is so frightening that Dante the pilgrim literally faints. What modern readers unfamiliar with *The Aeneid* fail to understand, however, is the Roman epic poet's profound belief in the reality of divine providence.[4] Though

---

2. Eliot, "Dante," 227.

3. One contemporary American cultural critic, Rod Dreher, even wrote a book entitled *How Dante Can Save Your Life*.

4. See Markos, *From Achilles to Christ*.

Virgil lives before the Incarnation of Christ, it is probably his faith in the providential destiny of Rome that draws Dante to him, and it is a mistake to be certain that he cannot further ascend Mt. Purgatory after his sudden separation from Dante in canto 30 of *Purgatorio*. Though virtuous classical philosophers such as Aristotle and Plato are met by Dante in early, less painful regions of *Inferno*, the subsequent journey does contain many surprises, such as the Roman Emperor Trajan's redemption through the prayers of Gregory the Great, or the appearance of unbaptized infants in *Paradiso*, there because in eternity, after human life, they have exercised the free will of human reason to choose to be with God, just as those more infamously found in the initial chambers of Dante's *Inferno* have similarly chosen to be there.

Whereas Virgil allows Dante to look upon human nature, Beatrice directs his eyes towards the reality of the living God. Whatever the oft debated historical facts, or even the question of what inspires Dante's *La Vita Nova*, his *Commedia* strongly moves away from any suggestion of romantic love. Beatrice is, after all, guiding him where people "neither marry, nor are given in marriage" (Matt 22:30), and when she does look at Dante it is usually to frown, and then help him to direct his eyes towards God. A characteristic passage, near the top of Mt. Purgatory, is:

> Regally, in her gesture still severe,
> She went on, like a speaker who keeps back
> The sharpest things he has to say till last:
> "Look at me well! I am indeed Beatrice.
> How were you able to climb the mountain?
> Did you not know that men are happy here?" (30.70–75)[5]

In *The Divine Comedy*, then, human nature is raised up by divine love, and this Catholic Humanism is especially relevant to feminine human nature. Not only Beatrice but also Mary, St. Lucy, and other good women of heaven begin Dante on the journey to God when he is "lost" in middle age,[6] and it is by the hard gaze and tough love of Beatrice, always directing Dante's eye up, to the mystic rose of Mary, symbolic of the eternal beauty of redeemed human souls, that he sees the highest realms of heaven. As this study will show, Dante's portrayal of the relationship of human to Divine nature, and its expression in male and female gender, is entirely characteristic of Catholic Humanism.

---

5. Dante, *The Divine Comedy*, 331.
6. Dante, *The Divine Comedy*, 51–55.

PETRARCH (1304-74)

As already suggested, of all the players on my Catholic Humanist "team," Petrarch is the one most easily singled out to represent the secular humanism sought by historians following in the footsteps of Burckhardt. Petrarch does seem to be responsible for coining the term "dark ages," to signify the time between Augustine and his own.[7] To further this potent myth, Petrarch had an almost heroic devotion to the recovery of old classical manuscripts, and to the return of Rome to its ancient glory. Petrarch also made the curious claim of never having read Dante's *Divine Comedy*, even though his own father was exiled with Dante from Florence in 1301, and though Dante's great poem was available in numerous manuscripts in fourteenth-century Italy. Petrarch clearly sought to publicly establish his own leadership of a "re-naissance" of classical texts and even, infamously, orchestrated his own coronation as Rome's poet laureate in 1347.[8]

Yet Petrarch was ordained a Catholic Priest (at a time when clerical celibacy was neither well understood nor often practiced, leading him to father two children), and he maintained a life-long devotion to St. Augustine. One of Petrarch's earliest recorded manuscript purchases, in 1325, was *The City of God*, and Petrarch frequently referred to *The Confessions*. Augustine appears as the prime interlocutor in Petrarch's own autobiographical dialogue, *The Secret*. The editor of a recent English edition of this text, however, follows many modern scholars in misunderstanding Augustine's role in this text. Justly noting that Petrarch directly quotes from several classical authors, but not from Augustine's texts themselves, this editor concludes that Petrarch's Augustine is a fictional construct whose main function was to help Petrarch imagine how classical literature "could be made to serve in a (Christian) quest for happiness, spiritual health, and salvation."[9] In *The Secret*, however, especially in the Third Dialogue, "Augustinus" serves as a serious, existential rebuke of the known foundations of Petrarch's poetic career, especially the fame he has gained by writing of Laura. We cannot know today if Laura herself was a historical woman or fictional construct, but *The Secret* very directly rebukes how "Franciscus" (as Petrarch is here called, by his first name) has throughout his life sought "love and glory." Justification for the love of Laura is given, and purely spiritual affection is claimed, but "Augustinus" steadfastly rejects such claims (whether or not they are true), because of a more fundamental Christian principle:

---

7. See Hattaway, Introduction to *A Companion*, 3–12.
8. Nauert, *Humanism*, 19–24.
9. Quillen, Introduction to *The Secret*, 34.

> She has kept your soul aloof from the love of heavenly things, and she has turned your desire from the Creator towards a mere creature. And this is the one sure way leading down to death.[10]

Petrarch may not be directly quoting Augustine here, but surely he is referring to one of the best known teachings of the historical Augustine: the crucial distinction between *caritas*, the love of things that leads to God, and *cupiditas*, the love of things for their own sake, leading ultimately to death.[11]

It is surely a mistake to claim Petrarch as an "Augustinian" in a serious, fully Catholic way, but *The Secret* leaves little doubt that a Catholic metaphysic remains the atmosphere of Petrarch's inner soul. Outwardly he "self-fashions" an image and livelihood as a radical, revolutionary classicist, but Catholic spirituality remains important for the meaning and influence of his work. When the Petrarchan Sonnet tradition is passed on to Wyatt and others in sixteenth-century England, the tradition there retains many physical and spiritual ironies, such as sonnets about Henry VIII's lust like "Whoso List to Hunt."[12] Even in conventional Petrarchan sonnet sequences such as Sidney's *Astrophel and Stella*,[13] the human heart (common English synonym for the "soul") becomes the primary means for admitting truth. Even when Shakespeare rejects the by then clichéd Petrarchan love tradition in poems like Sonnet 130 or, as we shall see, plays like *As You Like It*, the errors of Petrarch retain their humor, and Catholic Humanism, by being recognized as spiritual folly.

BOCCACCIO (1313-75)

If Petrarch is not signaled out as the leader of secular Italian Humanism, the honor is usually given to his contemporary and friend, Boccaccio. The bawdy humor of Boccaccio's masterpiece, *The Decameron*, is well known, so to claim its author as "humanistic" in a modern, atheist sense is unsurprising. Historians such as Cahill can easily quote from the *Decameron* to justify sexual sin, but proof-texts are not evidence of an entire story's effect, as every literary critic knows. Though the two men were friends, by all accounts, the vast difference between Boccaccio and Petrarch is clearly seen by their completely different attitude to Dante; the latter, as noted, tries to ignore his great predecessor, but Boccaccio is arguably the first serious

---

10. Petrarch, *The Secret*, 112.
11. See Jeffrey, "Charity and Cupidity," 55–74.
12. Wyatt, "Whoso List to Hunt," 350.
13. Sidney, "Astrophel and Stella," 53–211.

Dante scholar. In 1360 he publishes a short treatise in praise of Dante, and he dies in 1375 amidst a series of public lectures and commentaries on *The Divine Comedy*.[14]

These facts do not imply a rejection of classical learning. Boccaccio published *The Genealogy of the Pagan Gods* in 1360, and he recopied, by hand, the entire text of *The Decameron* in 1370, after first finishing writing it in 1352.[15] Crucial to the former, though, is the allegorical reading of classical literature typical of medieval Christian hermeneutics, and the integration of classical and Catholic Humanism is also clearly seen at the beginning of *The Decameron*. Its first narrator begins by telling us:

> It is fitting that everything man does should take as its origin the wonderful and holy name of Him who was the maker of all things. Thus, since I am the first and must begin our storytelling, I intend to start off with one of His marvelous works so that, once you have heard it, our hope in Him, as in that which is immutable, will be strengthened, and we will forever praise his name.[16]

The collection's first story does not easily achieve this aim for modern readers, concerning as it does the erroneous elevation of a sinner to pseudo-saint status. The point of the story, though, is clearly given in the tale's conclusion:

> We may recognize how very great God's loving kindness is toward us, in that He does not consider our sinfulness, but the purity of our faith, and even though he make our intercessor of His enemies, thinking him His friend, God still grants our prayers as if we were asking a true saint to obtain his grace for us.[17]

It is God's holiness that makes sense of the Catholic practice of prayer to the saints. An even more controversial issue, papal primacy, is similarly understood in the second tale of *The Decameron*, in which a Catholic named Giannoto attempts to convert a Jew named Abraham. When Abraham travels to Rome, Giannotto fears that corruption there will prevent conversion, but on return home Abraham says:

> I saw no holiness there, no devotion, no good works or models of life—or of anything else—in any member of the clergy. . . . Still, since I see that what they're trying to do hasn't happened,

---

14. Rebhorn, Introduction to *The Decameron*, xv–xlvii.
15. Rebhorn, Introduction to *The Decameron*, xv–xlvii.
16. Boccaccio, *The Decameron*, 18.
17. Boccaccio, *The Decameron*, 27.

and the fact is that your religion is constantly growing and becoming more resplendent and illustrious, I think I'm right to conclude that the Holy Spirit must indeed be its foundation and support, for it is truer and holier than any other.[18]

As Vatican I will clearly explain and confirm, it is the holiness of God, despite human corruption, that allows the infallibility of the Church. Through Boccaccio, we are reminded that this is not a development of the nineteenth century, nor the thirteenth century, but a timeless, true insight about the nature of the human and divine relationship in Catholic Humanism.

While an important reminder of the divine source and meaning of infallibility, especially in times of papal corruption, perhaps the broader importance of Abraham's insight, at least for literature, is the value of honestly portraying evil. This Boccaccio will go on to do in many further stories in *The Decameron*, but its early examples help explain why. Boccaccio's purpose is not to celebrate sin, but rather to understand it and even to laugh at it. This intention is obvious in the writer on my English Catholic Humanist "team" most directly influenced by Boccaccio, Chaucer. The Clerk, a pilgrim-narrator in *The Canterbury Tales*, borrows from *The Decameron* its final, infamous story of patient Griselda, a long-suffering wife who endures ludicrous levels of abuse from an evil husband. For neither the Italian nor English author is the story a model for marriage, but rather about how self-sacrifice—so often the lot of the powerless in human life, among whom have often been women—allows us to follow Christ in not only taking up our cross but also ultimately to triumph over sin. The feminine emphasis of the *Decameron*, which has seven female narrators and three male, is no accident but rather typical of Catholic Humanism. The sword in Mary's heart continues to bleed throughout history, and comic literature is one place to feel both its pain and its power. This is an important reality that helps to develop Shakespearean comedy into plays such as *As You Like It*.

ST. FRANCIS OF ASSISI (1182–1226)

Boccaccio memorably portrays the presence of the sacred within the sinful world of humanity. The reverse might be seen through St. Francis of Assisi, for certainly the personal holiness of this man is almost universally acknowledged. Francis works within the world of human sin, answering God's call to rebuild His church through self-denial and a humble commitment to the traditional monastic ideals of poverty, chastity, and obedience.

---

18. Boccaccio, *The Decameron*, 30.

This commitment never becomes dour or joyless, and it is part of the lesser-known story of Francis' saintly vocation that he inspires not only individual and church moral reform, but also the reinvention of a major form of literature, commonly known as the "medieval lyric."

The pioneering book on this topic, *The Early English Lyric and Franciscan Spirituality*, was written (as a young man) by my teacher, friend, and subsequent coauthor, David Lyle Jeffrey. I cannot help but be biased towards it, but any reader can study it and gain an objective sense of how Franciscan Catholicism helped to give the medieval lyric what Jeffrey, in a later book, resurrecting a traditional term, called "the beauty of holiness."[19] St. Francis was known for his concrete expressions of faith, whether with the poor, animals, or even in the later, partially hidden sign of sharing in the Cross of Christ, the stigmata. Perhaps his most influential contribution, though, is the artistic expression of the *crèche*, or nativity scene, to help us remember the original, concrete setting of Christmas. God came, in the Incarnation, into the simple world of the stable, with all its dirt, sin, and yet transcendent human love shared by Mary and Joseph. This extraordinary setting inspires the song of the angels, and the journey of the Magi, and the desperate, bloodthirsty attempt by Herod to cling to power.

Jeffrey shows how medieval lyric poets were inspired by Franciscan spirituality to write concretely of things in this world, but never for their own sake; rather, creation points to the Creator. Traces of the Trinity can be found in the most commonplace forms of nature, as in "I Sing of a Maiden," the famous lyric that explains the Virgin Birth of Christ through the three successive images of the morning dew; it concludes:

> As dew in Aprille
> That falleth on the spray,
> Moder and maiden
> Was never non but sche;
> Well may swich a lady
> Godes moder be.[20]

As in so many early English lyrics, the Catholic Humanism of this poem especially celebrates Mary, the model for human holiness.

---

19. Jeffrey, *In the Beauty of Holiness*.
20. "I Sing of a Maiden," 661.

MICHELANGELO (1475–1564)

While the aesthetic models of St. Francis have clearly been overshadowed by his religious reputation, the opposite has even more clearly happened to Michelangelo. One way to see this is his poetry, particularly if one accepts "Love" as a synonym for God's name; the scriptural letter 1 John biblically authorizes this (1 John 4:7–21), so its prevalence is unsurprising. The sonnet sequence is interrupted, though, by this even clearer four-line poem:

> He Who made all there is, made every part
> At first, then put those loveliest of all
> Together, to show what beauty's at His call,
> As here, in this triumph of celestial art.[21]

The much more common experience of Michelangelo's celestial art, of course, comes when visitors to the Vatican see the ceiling of the Sistine Chapel. This work of art, whose cost helped fuel the Protestant Reformation because it was largely funded through the immoral sale of indulgences,[22] has probably been seen by more people than all the other examples of art cited in this book. Has it produced comparable spiritual fruit? Why would the Vatican, in good times and bad, want tourists to see this extraordinary example of Catholic Humanist art?

Cynical responses aside, Michelangelo's representation of God the Father is also often rebuked, intellectually, as a prime example of anthropomorphic error, of "god" as an old man in the sky. Also contrary to my argument, Michelangelo's Adam is often extolled as Renaissance Man drawn large. Both objections are understandable, but both miss key theological points. As with so many Catholic dogmas, paradox is key. For few things are clearer in Catholicism than that God the Father is not a man, but rather the sublime Spirit taught by Christ in John 4:24, the eternal reality of Being from which all creatures come and to which all must return. At the same time, the church understands very well that such doctrines are difficult to grasp, and may not move even believers to pious action. It was therefore also part of Jesus' teaching, and of subsequent scripture and doctrine, that God is our spiritual father, and believing in God makes us one of the "children of God" (John 1:12). But never has physical, material, or sexual regeneration of any kind been part of the Catholic doctrine of God the Father. It is thus, of course, an error to view Michelangelo's God as a literal representation, or his Adam as an exaltation of the human being. The crucial theological element

---

21. Michelangelo, *Complete Poems*, 12.

22. See a recent book on this well-known fact: King, *Michelangelo & the Pope's Ceiling*.

of the Sistine Chapel is not Adam's size, or beauty, but first of all the famous finger that shows him touched by God. Within a painting that further shows Adam surrounded by the figures of sacred history, Adam's unique, personal relationship to God is not an exaggeration of human status, however mistakenly the proud wish to interpret it, but rather a vivid reminder of the reality of God's providence within human life, a way of showing that God has his hand upon every human being, as Psalm 139 so memorably teaches.

It is therefore true that the Sistine Chapel exalts the dignity of every human being, but does so in a way characteristic of Catholic Humanism. Michelangelo's masterpiece affirms—right from the start of human history—that God personally cares for each human person. Understood in this way, the Sistine Chapel inspires even the profound theological poetry of a much later champion of Catholic Humanism, John Paul II. In *Roman Tryptich*, a long poem published near the end of his life at the Vatican, John Paul II reflects on a central paradox of Catholic Humanism; given the history of human error, what can it possibly mean that humanity is made in the image of God? John Paul writes:

> Why was it said about that one day alone:
> "God saw all that he had made and found it very good"?
> Is this not denied by history?
> Even our twentieth century!
>   And not only the twentieth!
> Yet no century can obscure this truth
> Of the image and likeness.[23]

---

23. John Paul II, *Roman Triptych*, 18.

4

English Catholic Humanism

ANYONE LOOKING FOR MEDIEVAL forerunners of Shakespeare is tempted to start in fourteenth-century Italy, when so many great artists first develop new literary forms that uniquely express Catholic Humanism. While the sonnets of Petrarch become mediated to Shakespeare's England by poets such as Wyatt, as is well known, the influence of *The Divine Comedy* or *The Decameron* can less precisely be traced, but may be even more profound. Shakespeare may have read these texts himself, but their aesthetic was certainly mediated to him by the greatest poet of fourteenth-century England, Geoffrey Chaucer.

Chaucer visited Florence in 1372, and surely learned something of the aesthetic of Dante, Petrarch, and Boccaccio.[1] All three are personally mentioned in *The Canterbury Tales*, written in the final decade of Chaucer's life, the 1390s. The telling of stories in a "game" format certainly reflects the influence of Boccaccio, and the first-person discourses of Chaucer's pilgrims clearly recalls the dramatic voices given souls at each level of Dante's epic. In the social context that develops in Europe as the fourteenth century progresses, however, perhaps an even more influential element of the Italian influence in England concerns a key element of Catholic understanding: the

---

1. Crane and Leland, "Chaucer's Life," xix.

Petrine ministry, or the primary spiritual authority of the Pope, the Bishop of Rome, in the Roman Catholic Church.

A full discussion of this complex question leads beyond the scope of my historical approach to Catholic Humanism,[2] but suffice to say that the Italian artists discussed in chapter 3 clearly cause one to consider the issue. Roman corruption, as noted, paradoxically leads Boccaccio to rediscover the infallible holiness at the center of the church in God himself, known through the Holy Spirit, but the insights of Dante are more complex. On one hand Dante places specific popes, such as Nicholas III, in hell (cf. Canto 19 of *Inferno*), which probably accounts for the *Divine Comedy* (possibly the greatest Catholic poem ever written) being on the pre-Vatican II list of prohibited books until the nineteenth century; on the other hand, Peter himself appears in Dante's *Paradiso* (Canto 24) to clarify and define the Petrine ministry. Fourteenth-century Europe was far from paradisal, however, and the Avignon papacy that began in 1307 developed into the Western Schism between Avignon and Rome, 1378–1478, which surely tested Christian faith in a Roman Papacy.

In this context, it is not unreasonable to find in John Wyclif an intellectual articulation of questions that must have occurred in any Christian conscience. In the summary of David Jeffrey, it is probable that many fourteenth-century Catholics followed Wyclif in asking,

> What is the relationship between spiritual purity and spiritual authority? . . . Are Peter's apostolic successors necessarily bishops of Rome? What is the precedent in Scripture for election by a college of cardinals, most of whom are not even priests? Who is then Christ's true vicar?[3]

Aside from the contrast between Wyclif's answers to these questions and those eventually authorized in Roman Catholicism, a scholar of English Catholic Humanism must look for faith beyond the intellectual achievement of Scholasticism. In England, this distinction did not often involve alienation from local churches. As Jeffrey eloquently explains:

> The actual experience of churchgoing in medieval England was mercifully removed from the worst elements of the papal controversy. Even in large communities, the ordinary Christian would focus spiritual life in the tranquil and beautiful sung worship of the abbey church or cathedral. Here a mass was offered in the splendor of fractured light and articulate images;

---

2. A good guide to this question is Ray, *The Papacy*.
3. Jeffrey, *The Law of Love*, 8.

the altar centered at once a moment of prayer and a pageant of history, and the beauty of holiness was figured amply in the beauty of art.[4]

The very useful, traditional phrase here, "the beauty of holiness," can remind scholars to look for religious faith, even Catholic theology, in diverse, even popular forms of art. If one rejects the extreme bias whereby one notes only the secular aspects of medieval art, and is rather open to the complexity of its religious vision, one easily finds Catholic Humanism expressed in many forms. The following "bus tour" of English artists is surely incomplete, but it does help us to see the "serio-comic" Catholic Humanism that eventually creates an English audience, and in that sense makes possible, the theological aesthetic of Shakespeare's *As You Like It*.

GEOFFREY CHAUCER (1343–1400)

The aesthetic diversity of English Catholic Humanism in the fourteenth century is most easily seen in the work of the major poet already mentioned, Geoffrey Chaucer. It is perhaps an inevitable effect of the dramatic aesthetic of Chaucer's most famous poem, *The Canterbury Tales*, that people tend to remember the almost comically diabolical evil clerics on this pilgrimage. The Friar, Summoner, and Pardoner, as many critics have noted, all abuse (in both the old and newer sense of this term) believers through means familiar to any fourteenth-century Catholic. The latter, the Pardoner, is perhaps most wicked of all; because his financial fraud depends on the selling of indulgences, the same kind of spiritual fraud that later spurs the rebellion of Martin Luther and other Protestant Reformers, it is natural and just to view Chaucer as critical of the Catholicism of his age.

So vicious are the clerical villains of *The Canterbury Tales* that many casual readers never realize how Chaucer balances the text to make it also exemplify Catholicism. Although the Pardoner may well be the most wicked pilgrim, the best might be the Parson, seemingly a very good man who concludes the pilgrimage with a sermon on repentance and a prologue that, despite all the evil that has been alongside him, dares to compare their pilgrimage to Canterbury to the human journey to the New Jerusalem, the Holy City of God promised in the Book of Revelation. The Parson says:

> I wol yow telle a myrie tale in prose
> To knytte up al this feeste and make an ende.
> And Jhesu, for his grace, wit me send

---

4. Jeffrey, *The Law of Love*, 9.

> To shew yow the way, in this viage,
> Of thilke parfit glorious pilgrimage
> That highte Jerusalem celestial.[5]

Chaucer taught solely via the *Norton Anthology* is more likely to focus on the medieval technological trivia such as the astrolab or the grim humor of human flatulence and sexuality, which famously collide in *The Miller's Tale*. Important though such *fabliaux* are to entertaining Chaucer's audience, and certainly in the tradition of Boccacio's *Decameron*, one also understands the angst of modern Christian apologist Holly Ordway, who laments never hearing of Chaucer's religious faith during her university English courses. In the moving account of her journey out of atheism and into faith, *Not God's Type*, Ordway recalls:

> I remember an upper-division English literature class on Chaucer's Canterbury Tales. We discussed his criticism of corruption and hypocrisy in the medieval church, without considering the faith that would move people to go on pilgrimage in the first place; I was left with the impression that Chaucer was a forward-thinking humanist, not a believing Christian. I never noticed that Chaucer asks readers to give thanks for anything valuable in the poem to "Our Lord Jesus Christ . . . from whom proceeds all understanding and goodness."[6]

The critique of medieval culture and especially the medieval church is an element of Chaucer's work that is essential to learn, but Ordway's point is that perhaps an even more essential thing to learn is what motivated Chaucer to make this critique, and whether it resulted in the loss of his faith.

Beside the Parson, there is much further to say about Chaucer's Catholicism. The best-known contemporary portrait of him, the 1411 painting by Thomas Hoccleve, depicts Chaucer with pen in right hand, rosary in the left, the latter clearly visible in his pocket as a sign of his devout Catholic faith. One could also cite the large number of more directly spiritual writings that Chaucer produced, but even within *The Canterbury Tales* itself there are clear reasons for a Catholic hermeneutic. One can't know if Chaucer completed the text, to his own satisfaction, before dying in 1400. Certainly the text, as we have it, does not fulfill the ambition stated in "The General Prologue" that each pilgrim will tell two tales on the way to Canterbury, two on the way back. Nor do we learn which tale earns the free supper offered by the pilgrimage's host, Harry Bailey. Bailey's criteria for judgment,

---

5. Chaucer, *Canterbury Tales*, 287.
6. Ordway, *Not God's Type*, 29.

though, are given: tales will be judged according to their "sentence" and "solas" (General Prologue, line 798),[7] Middle English words that probably intend not only "meaning" and "consolation," as they are often translated in Modern English, but also "wisdom" ("sententia" are "wise sayings" in Latin) and "spiritual joy," the ultimate consolation found only in God (Chaucer had, we note, translated Boethius's *Consolation of Philosophy*, which teaches this theology). Many of Chaucer's *Tales* are as full of bawdy entertainment as Boccaccio's, for both use realistic first-person narration; in Chaucer, moreover, normally, a prologue spoken via the character's own persona precedes each tale. Chaucer is himself a pilgrim and story-teller within the narrative, giving the text an exceptional level of rhetorical complexity that recalls Dante's own role within the *Divine Comedy*.

A highly complex level of aesthetic meaning is thus found in *The Canterbury Tales*, and one must consider such meaning before simplistic acceptance of the "retraction" that Chaucer writes near the end of his life, which regrets any *Tale* that "tends" to lead others to sin. Any realistic presentation of evil could potentially do that, but Chaucer's own "entente," to use the Middle English word that regularly appears as we consider the intention of all the pilgrims on the way to Canterbury, is perhaps defined most clearly by the Nun's Priest. His epilogue cites the Second Letter of Paul to Timothy on scripture, "al that written is / To our doctrine it is ywrite,"[8] and advises us to sift the chaff from the wheat in all of our interpretations. The principle is intended first for scripture, reminding us that even what seems obscure or unclear in scripture remains intended by God, in ways we may not understand, of teaching us some important truth at some point in our lives. Yet this same teaching also appears in the closing note to *The Canterbury Tales*, commonly called Chaucer's "Retraction"; modern connotations of this term, however, can distract readers from what Chaucer then writes in his "retraction": "Al that is writen is writen for oure doctrine," stressing "that is myn entente."[9]

Could this same principle hold in the book of history, the book of humanity, in which God must also be counted as at least the primary author? Diverse aspects of human nature instruct us in the nature of the God who created us, ultimately intending to help us live in harmony with God amidst the entire communion of saints in heaven. Evil example is a warning, perhaps, and how one interprets it largely depends on the conscience of

---

7. Chaucer, *Canterbury Tales*, 36.

8. The Nun's Priest is citing 2 Tim 3:16, translated in the KJV as: "All scripture is given by inspiration of God, and is profitable for doctrine, for reproof, for correction, for instruction in righteousness." Chaucer, *Canterbury Tales*, 261.

9. Chaucer, *Canterbury Tales*, 328.

each reader. This hermeneutic is clearly indebted to Christ's Parable of the Sower, so that we see how Catholic Humanism again returns to its roots in Christ's ministry.

Particularly relevant to Chaucer's key role in creating an audience that can appreciate a play such as *As You Like It* is the conversation about the nature and purpose of marriage that takes place in several *Canterbury Tales*. Most critics today cite *The Franklin's Tale* as the most likely representation of Chaucer's own view, finding in this tale the "mutual submission" ideal of marriage that John Paul II taught in our time.[10] Yet another famous, key figure in Chaucer's conversation is the Wife of Bath. One might initially take her as representative of a class or group in medieval society, like pilgrims such as the Knight or Cook, but she emerges as one of the most unique characters in all of literature. The Wife of Bath's *Prologue* opens with two lines that foreground a crucial question in human philosophy: "Experience, though noon auctoritee / Were in the world, is right ynogh for me."[11] What should be the ultimate foundation of our knowledge, experience or divine authority? Reason or Revelation? Can either be trusted? But the Wife's *Prologue* opening lines do not conclude with a period; rather, for her, experience is enough "to speke of wo that is in mariage."[12] From a modern perspective, her married life cannot be called happy; from a medieval perspective, much of it is expected. For both, it is crucial to decide whether it is best to be guided by the harsh reality of experience or by whom one accepts as an authoritative teacher of what marriage truly is.

The Wife of Bath has been married five times, but not because of divorce; as would be expected, given the short medieval male life span, all of the husbands have died. Still, the facts of her life do raise another very pertinent question for medieval Catholics: whom should one trust on the nature of marriage, someone who has been married several times or the Incarnate Christian God who never married? Moreover, what authoritative knowledge can be given by men like St. Paul, who also never married, or by a church led by so many evidently corrupt men? Perhaps the Wife must interpret scripture via her own experience and authority. When she does so, she makes some obvious errors, such as forgetting the New Testament's teaching on monogamy (Matt 19), claiming that the gospels never speak of "nombre," in marriage, never distinguish "bigamye" from "ocotogamye" (lines 32–33).[13]

---

10. John Paul II, *On the Dignity and Vocation of Women*, 101.
11. Chaucer, *Canterbury Tales*, 105.
12. Chaucer, *Canterbury Tales*, 105.
13. Chaucer, *Canterbury Tales*, 105.

One might guess that the "deafness" attributed to her in the General Prologue[14] is at least in part a spiritual deafness, or that through her Chaucer is reinforcing the importance of clerical authority. But during her prologue, the wife is interrupted three times by the most wicked clerics on the Canterbury Pilgrimage—the Pardoner, Friar, and Summoner—and like the Host Harry Bailey most readers are happy to let the Wife continue to speak. If we listen to the end of the Wife's Prologue, we learn that she is physically deaf after being hit on the ear by her fifth husband, who had been reading commonplace medieval misogynistic literature when the Wife ripped pages from the book. The ensuing fight turns comical, however, when the Wife pretends to be mortally wounded, allowing her to wring from the repentant husband a promise to give her "maistery" and "soveraynetee" (line 817) in their marriage. After this, she reports, the couple "hadden never debaat"[15] (line 821).

Women gaining authority in their marriages also seems to be the main point of "The Wife of Bath's Tale."[16] Set in the days of King Arthur, the Wife's Tale tells of a knight convicted of rape who, to avoid execution, must answer the age-old riddle: what do women want? He gets the true answer from an old hag who mysteriously appears; her answer, "maistery" and "soveraynetee" (line 1037–40) is of course the same as the Wife of Bath's "remedies of love"(*General Prologue* line 475)[17] in marriage, and it satisfies all the women in her Tale. As compensation, though, the old Hag demands that the Knight marry her; this he is initially reluctant to do, so eventually she gives him a choice: have her old and faithful, or young and he takes his chances against other suitors. Having learned his lesson fairly well, the Knight lets her decide, and when she pulls back her veil she is both beautiful and true to him always (l.1241). Before this fantasy, though, the Old Hag has given a long talk, almost half the tale, praising the Christian value of poverty and not judging others according to their appearance (lines 1109–215). To the plot of the tale, this material is unnecessary, but it probably is intended by Chaucer to suggest some of the virtues that make life-long monogamy both possible and enjoyable.

The Wife's "entente" seems clear, but so too does Chaucer's "entente" in extending further our vision for what constitutes happy marriage. One might yet reject the Wife of Bath's "sentence" or "solas," but there is no question that she reminds us of marital issues that males tend to forget. In

---

14. Chaucer, *Canterbury Tales*, 30.
15. Chaucer, *Canterbury Tales*, 116.
16. Chaucer, *Canterbury Tales*, 116–22.
17. Chaucer, *Canterbury Tales*, 30.

this way, her narrative is also "written for our doctrine," and thus confirms Chaucer's rationale for studying both good and evil characters: one learns something from both, provided one stays on the road where one can continue learning. To do so, the essential virtue is humility; this allows repentance, the main topic of the Parson's concluding sermon, which he prefaces with a short principle that sums up both his own morality and Chaucer's Catholic Humanist aesthetic:

> I take but the sentence, trusteth weel.
> Therefore I make protestacioun
> That I wol stond to correccion.[18]

WILLIAM LANGLAND (1332–86)

The influence of Chaucer's Catholic poetic is extensive, and this is part of why so much more is known about him than of most Medieval and Renaissance authors. Obscure voices can leave a key mark as well, though, and one example of this is William Langland, a near contemporary of Chaucer's who is widely thought to be the author of the visionary poem *Piers Plowman*. This authorial attribution is solely due to an obscure fifteenth-century text, and to obscure traces of the author's name found in the poem. For most of this poem we have solely what exists for most medieval texts: anonymous manuscripts that preserve the poem, but little to nothing of the text's immediate historical contexts.[19] We do know that there are three versions of *Piers Plowman*, known as the A, B, and C text,[20] which appear at different points in the second half of the fourteenth century, all of which are written in the alliterative form typical of Northern British English poetry of this time. However, the poem's clear reliance on allegorical characters and obscure mystic vision have made it less popular with modern audiences then, for example, *Sir Gawain and the Green Knight*. Yet the length, epic scope, and serious subject matter of the poem give it, in many critics' estimation, a claim to be considered the greatest single poem of the English Middle Ages. In the Peasants' Revolt of 1581, the priest John Ball (one of the revolt's leaders) cites the inspiration of *Piers Plowman*, so we know the text had some

---

18. Chaucer, *Canterbury Tales*, 287.
19. Schmidt, Introduction to *The Vision*, xi–xliii.
20. It was the B text that Shakespeare or other sixteenth-century authors might have read, which Robert Crowley printed in 1550. My quotations are from this modern publication of the B text: Langland, *The Vision of Piers Plowman*.

social audience, but its significance for Catholic Humanism is a mystery wrapped within a most complex literary rhetoric.

Clearly a mix of theological allegory and social satire, *Piers Plowman* is usually classified by medieval literary historians as "dream vision literature." A dreamer sees clearly, paradoxically through allegorical distortion, many aspects of his own time and culture. Yet as in *The Dream of the Rood*, the Anglo-Saxon prototype of this genre, history soon melts into eternal vision as the dreamer eventually sees Christ, who appears in Langland's poem as an allegorical rural figure named Piers Plowman. A very early suggestion of the plowman whom Erasmus will hope can "sing some portion" of scripture while working "at the plow,"[21] in Langland this plowman has all the ultimate authority of Christ the Pantokrater in Eastern art. The historical suffering of the peasantry will one day be replaced by the City of God, and in the climax of the poem the dreamer has a vision of Christ's passion, like the dreamer of *The Dream of the Rood*; whereas Christ in that poem is an Anglo-Saxon warrior who would "hasten with stout heart" to the cross,[22] here Christ is a medieval knight but one who takes the symbolic form of Piers Plowman. This medieval Christ defeats Satan and sin on the cross by redeeming the good fruit of the peasant-farmer's harvest. Even in Northern Middle English, this vision is perceivable for a modern reader:

> "Jesus," he seide,
> "And fecche that the fend claymeth—Piers fruyt the Plowman."
> "Is Piers in this place?" quod I, and he preynte on me.
> "This Jesus of his gentries wol juste in Piers armes,
> In his helm and in his haubergon—humana natura.
> That Christ he noght biknowe here for consummatus Deus
> In Piers paltock the Plowman this prikiere shal ryde." (VIII.19–25)[23]

In modern language, in Langland's vision it is in the form of Piers Plowman that Christ again becomes incarnate in human nature. The *Dream of the Rood* clarifies the relevance of Christ to the Anglo-Saxon in order to convert them to a true faith in Jesus, so Langland offers a devout vision of Jesus Incarnate to allow true faith even amidst the agricultural trials and ecclesiastical conflicts inescapable in fourteenth-century England.

The literary rhetoric[24] of such a passage seems unrelated to Shakespeare and even far from Langland's contemporary, Chaucer, but *Piers Plowman* is

---

21. Erasmus, *The Paraclesis*, 97.
22. *The Dream of the Rood*, 25.
23. Langland, *The Vision of Piers Plowman*, 220.
24. For a recent and fascinating account, see Gruenler, *Piers Plowman and the Poetics of Enigma*.

a key marker of Catholic Humanism because it reveals the Divine reality of Eternal life within which English history discovers its identity. Not a distant, obscure, island of uncultured peasants with funny accents scraping out a hard agricultural living, but a blessed realm personally cared for by a loving Shepherd who seeks out even very lost sheep. There is a radical difference in these identities, and that is the point of a visionary poem such as *Piers Plowman*.

The poet, whoever he was, clearly takes his motivation and authority from outside the public realm, and hence might be regarded as one whose faith is not dependent on the established authority of either this world's monarchs or princes of the church. In literal terms, Langland's hope is a peasant farmer who is Christ. However simplistic, the implied respect for the peasantry and common man is important to the kind of pastoral vision that Shakespeare will develop in *As You Like It*. Again, however, Langland cannot be classified as a "proto-protestant" or even spokesman for either Ball or Wyclif. The poem's dreamer does mock indulgences as "*ingratus*," (or "unkind"), the purchase of which "The Holy Ghost hereth thee nought" (Passus XVII.256–57). However, his vision normally builds faith in Christ's Church, which is "salt for Christene souls," if "they holy were" that is, if holy (XV.427–28). In Passus XVII.l.120, the Dreamer is "hostele" ("lodged") and "heele" ("healed") "thorugh Holy Church bileve" ("through the faith of the Holy Church"). *Piers Plowman*, then, reflects a radical faith in both God and Man, and the hope that poetic vision can inspire ecclesiastical wisdom.

JULIAN OF NORWICH (1343–1416)

Another way to see the diversity of fourteenth-century Catholic Humanism is in the artistic visions of its many mystical writers. Best known in the century itself were Richard Rolle, Walter Hilton, and the anonymous author of *The Cloud of Unknowing*, but very little is known for sure about Julian of Norwich; the often unreliable Margery Kempe reports being counseled by her, though there is also manuscript evidence, chiefly wills, which suggest that she was a historical person. But little more is known for sure. Why, then, do I propose focusing upon this obscure author, whose text of mystical revelations, or what she called "Shewings," was not published until the seventeenth century? Is it because of the widespread twentieth-century popularity of Dame Julian; she is often praised, for example, by modern feminist theologians for teaching that Christ is both our father and mother.[25] But how can Julian of Norwich possibly be relevant to Shakespeare in 1599?

---

25. See Glasscoe, *English Medieval Mystics*, 215–67.

The key point, paradoxically, is that Julian, whoever she was, chose to live as an "anchoress," i.e., not just as a "hermit" who lived in isolation from the rest of a nunnery, but one who, on a specific date complete with farewell ceremony, chose to live in an "enclosure" that would be permanently walled off from the outside world, but for delivery of the food and water necessary to survive and avoid the sin of suicide. Again, this life-choice seems the antithesis of any form of humanism, so what can justify her presence on my English Catholic Humanist team? While "enclosure" is a problematic practice that one cannot lament passing, it is a radical witness to one's absolute faith in the reality of the eternal world and the possibility for the human soul to prepare to live there through contemplation.

Julian's witness to these key truths of Catholic Humanism is enhanced, of course, through her visions of Christ. These have often struck many as authentic because of the powerful way in which she conveys the goodness or holiness of Christ. In context of the vision, Julian's theology of "father" and "mother" has no literal meaning, but is obviously a means to attempt the inherently impossible description of an infinite, triune Being. Many other analogies are used, as is common for writers on the Trinity, but it is certainly the doctrinally orthodox vision of the Incarnate Christ by which Julian understands the nature of humanity:

> I saw that our nature is complete in God, in which He makes a diversity of things flowing out of Himself to do His will, and whose nature preserves and mercy and grace restore and fulfill. And none of these shall perish, for our nature in its higher part is knit to God in its creation, but God is knit to our nature, in its lower part, when He takes on our flesh.[26]

It is this same "shewing" which includes Julian's praise of God as "our mother," but just prior to this she has also written the far more commonplace Catholic belief that "our Lady is our mother."[27] What is unusual, however, is for a female writer to be literate enough to articulate Catholic Humanist truths in writing. Even though this writing was not printed in her lifetime, Julian becomes well enough known to make clear that the female soul was as capable of divine transcendence as the male, as Genesis 1:27 promises. It is this "feminist" truth that is important for Shakespeare's *As You Like It*, which certainly shews, in all its infinite incomprehensibility, the interior life or "soul" of a woman, Rosalind.

---

26. Julian of Norwich's Middle English cannot be read by modern readers, so translation must be given. This translation is from Jeffrey, *The Law of Love*, 218.

27. Jeffrey, *The Law of Love*, 218.

Julian's status in English Culture might be compared to Hildegard of Bingen, though the German abbess made a far larger historical mark on her social culture and has now been proclaimed as an official "doctor" of the Catholic Church. Potential for a similar status for Julian has long been rumored, though she has never been officially canonized. Benedict XVI did devote an entire general audience, however, to praising her, particularly recalling

> with admiration and gratitude the women and men's cloistered monasteries. Today more than ever they are oases of peace and hope, a precious treasure for the Church, especially since they recall the primacy of God and the importance, for the journey of faith, of constant and intense prayer.[28]

In *As You Like It*, Rosalind will make fun of those who "forswear the thick stream of the world and live in a nook merely monastic" (3.2.405); paradoxically, her very ability to express this humor was surely pioneered by those, like Julian, who proved the reality of the female soul.

THE WAKEFIELD MASTER (EARLY 1400s?)

The individual spiritual vision achieved by a poet like Langland or mystics such as Julian is in many ways extended and developed by English communities in medieval drama, especially the mystery plays. Not at all related to modern detective cases, the medieval mystery plays were dramatizations of biblical scenes performed by members of a "mysterium," medieval Latin for a working guild; the shipbuilders of a town, for example, might perform the story of Noah's ark. In the extensive surviving records of towns like York, mystery play cycles encompass the entire Bible, from Creation to the Last Judgement, simultaneously giving both a theological education and a civic festival.[29]

Such plays were banned in England in 1567, when "Reformation" leaders expressed worry that their depiction of God could be blasphemous. Most mystery play texts seem theologically harmless, however, at worst simplistic but certainly entertaining versions of well-known Biblical stories. Modern productions of the mystery plays have been successful not only in York, but in public performances in places like the University of Toronto. At their best, the mystery plays can be theologically profound, with the

---

28. Benedict XVI, "General Audience."
29. See Beadle, *Cambridge Companion to Medieval Literature*.

best example probably the *Second Shepherd's Pageant*.[30] By an anonymous author whom modern critics have named the "Wakefield Master," this play is clearly connected to the Christmas season but artistically develops its dramatic representation.

The play opens with three shepherds, but they are not the famous ones of Bethlehem. It is cold outside, and their status as medieval English shepherds is confirmed by the arrival of Mak, supposedly a "yeoman of the king," but actually a poor thief about to steal one of the sheep. He returns with it to his oft-pregnant wife Gill; when the three shepherds come looking for their sheep, Gill comically disguises the sheep as a baby. Mak's plot is soon uncovered, but rather than exacting some harsh penalty the three shepherds engage in more medieval fun: they "toss him in a blanket," but never actually hurt Mak. Then an angel appears, singing *Gloria in Excelsis Deo*, and leads them to see Jesus born to Mary at Bethlehem. As in the dream visions, historical and eternal time has suddenly intersected. This may have been related to the English popularity of the crèche, or nativity scene invented in Italy by Saint Francis, but the three shepherds remain medieval Englishman, bringing gifts such as a tennis ball and bob of cherries. A broader, typological interpretation of the Christmas story is also given to an imaginative audience: the good Shepherd disguised as a human baby will become the lamb who saves all the world.

Mak's vice has not only not participated in this providential action, but actually helped both those onstage and off to grasp its immense importance. Though always festive and never solitary, a mystery play such as *The Second Shepherd's Pageant* points, just as surely as individual poetic or mystic vision, to the graceful presence of Christ in the world. The Catholic Humanism of such plays' imaginative vision may have been underappreciated by Protestant political leaders, but Shakespeare himself may have seen such plays performed when he was a youth in Stratford, and he seems to fondly remember them through Bottom and the workingmen of A *Midsummer Night's Dream*.

Bottom and the "rude mechanicals" (3.2.9) work valiantly for the imaginative vision to put on a play for their Duke, but the play perhaps suggests that his vision is finally given to them. In one of the most creative Biblical allusions in Renaissance drama, Shakespeare confounds physic and logic yet makes clear that spiritual vision has been acquired by Bottom through his time in the fairy kingdom, after he was "translated" into a donkey. Though he cannot recall it clearly (4.1.199–240), in awakening from

---

30. Probably the most anthologized medieval play, as in vol. 1 of *The Norton Anthology of English Literature: The Major Authors*.

this dream Bottom describes a vision that the "eye of man hath not heard," that "the ear of man hath not seen" (4.1.208–9) of the kingdom that God has prepared for those who love him. St. Paul in 1 Cor 2:9 is clearly evoked, but in a Catholic Humanist tone that owes much to the traditions of medieval drama that preceded Shakespeare.

JOHN COLET (1467–1519)

The fifth and final member of my English Catholic Humanist team cannot be credited with any similarly extraordinary works of art, but John Colet's contribution to this movement is absolutely critical. As the Dean of St. Paul's and a respected member of first Henry VII's and later Henry VIII's court in late fifteenth, early sixteenth-century England, Colet plays the crucial role of opening up central English institutions to the influence of Catholic Humanism. Colet welcomes Erasmus to Oxford on the Dutch scholar's first visit to England in 1499, and fosters the friendship between Erasmus and Thomas More that will be so important to English Catholic Humanism. In 1504, he becomes spiritual director to More, though the two may have been friends even before that.[31] In 1505, Colet, More, and Erasmus open the grammar school at St. Paul's, for which the basic curriculum of *humanisti litterae*, of the classical trivium applied to both classical and Christian texts, will be the primary means of educating the great writers of England for almost two hundred years. The friendship of More and Erasmus is central to the Humanism that became available to Shakespeare, as the next two chapters show, but Colet's friendship with both men is the open gate by which Catholic Humanism enters England and directly shapes its major institutions.

We must also note the influence of Colet's biblical scholarship. As Michael Massing explains, Colet was educated in Scholasticism, which tended to refer to scripture "as an assemblage of proof-texts for use in theological dispute,"[32] but Colet's lectures at Oxford "treated Paul as a real human being wrestling with urgent moral, social, and spiritual problems."[33] Colet's approach can be seen in his commentary on 1 Corinthians, in passages that one expects especially influenced Erasmus; on St. Paul teaching, for example, that "the weakness of God" is "wiser and stronger than men," Colet says:

> His meaning is, that those who were accounted foolish and weak in the world, provided they have now been drawn to God

---

31. Monti, *The King's Good Servant*, 26.
32. Massing, *Fatal Discord*, 72.
33. Massing, *Fatal Discord*, 72.

and abide in God, and have all their wisdom and actions from God, are, in God, both wiser and more powerful than men."[34]

It would be difficult to give a clearer, more concise account of the theological meaning of Erasmus' *Praise of Folly*, one of the key texts of Catholic Humanism. Colet is perhaps best known for his famous praise of Erasmus, when in 1516, upon first receiving a copy of Erasmus' New Testament, he said that, "the name of Erasmus will never perish."[35] Yet Colet had his own substantive cultural influence upon Catholic Humanism, one that affects England and our Lord's kingdom beyond even our present time.

CONCLUSION

By the time of Erasmus' arrival in England at the start of the sixteenth century to meet Colet and More, England was, in many respects, a deeply Catholic country.[36] This is not to say that the ecclesial abuses noted by Chaucer and others were not real, only that there is also a story of piety that needs to be told. Partially because of the disruption that was to follow, the contrast between Henry VIII's early life—marriage to a Spanish princess, and the ardent defense of the seven sacraments of the Catholic Church against Luther in 1521[37]—and his later folly, schism, and mortal sin, Henry VIII's madness is usually focused on and offered as one of the many obvious evidences of the corruption of state and church as this point in history. Undeniable though such arguments are, my "teams" of Italian and English Catholic Humanists are a reminder of the ongoing light, the one life in the Spirit, that also continued to animate elements of English culture in the fourteenth and fifteenth century.

There are many other worthy figures to note, some of whom will be mentioned in the following chapters on Erasmus and More. But there may be some value in listing the number of luminaries that can be counted by one's own hand. "Figures of Five," we recall, aid Sir Gawain as he prepares to again meet the Green Knight, especially the pentagram, that "token of Solomon" whose five points are interdependent but in a grace-filled way, so that if one point fails then the others prop it up, but even if all four fail one may yet prop it up.[38] There is a statue today in Worms, Germany, erected

---

34. Colet, *Corinthians*, 17.
35. Quoted in Olin, *Christian Humanism and the Reformation*, 1.
36. See Duffy, *The Stripping of the Altars*; Saward et al., *Firmly I Believe and Truly*.
37. Massing, *Fatal Discord*, 482–84.
38. *Sir Gawain and the Green Knight*, 127–28.

in 1868, which depicts Luther supported by four pillars or forerunners of his reformation (Waldus, Wycliffe, Hus, and Savanarola). Again, five figures are needed to convey the roots and thrust of the movement. Whereas the foundations of Luther's movement are so self-evident that moderns may be provoked to irony or even parody, the roots of Catholic Humanism are as green as the hue of the Green Knight's horse, and as strong as his axe.

5

Erasmus and the Play of Sapiential Rhetoric

DESIDERIUS ERASMUS (1466–1536)

Paradoxically, it is difficult both to overestimate and to appreciate the influence of Desiderius Erasmus upon the history of Catholic Humanism. Long recognized as a crucial figure in any historical conception of the "Renaissance," Erasmus' career practically defines that value laden term via the extraordinary productivity of his scholarly life. Replacing the sometimes dry logic and obscure argument of the Scholastics with virtuoso rhetoric in diverse imaginative genres, Erasmus almost literally brings Italian Humanism north, not so much to his home country of Holland but to adopted homes in Switzerland, Belgium, France, and especially England, where he develops a number of crucial friendships. One of these, already discussed, is the partnership with John Colet that results in the Humanist curriculum at St. Paul's Grammar School, which goes on to educate most of the major English writers of the seventeenth century. But for my purposes here, perhaps even more important is Erasmus' friendship with Thomas More, which particularly influences the kind of comedy eventually written by William Shakespeare.

How can we today appreciate the influence of Erasmus? Where, in my account of Catholic Humanism, does Erasmus fit in? The key to understanding Erasmus' influence, in my opinion, is to closely read his work within the historical contexts of his life and career. This commonplace is hard to apply for centuries after his death, however, due both to the mixed reception of Erasmus' work, and to his work's role within the infancy of a publishing industry that (with Luther) he practically invented. Multiple editions of most of his works and innumerable references to his activity (from the writings of scholars, popes, and his fellow humanists) testify to his influence, though today historians are largely restricted to apparently a-temporal texts that do not explain their own contexts. The dates and interplay of letters are an obvious antidote to this problem, and Erasmus did leave no less than 1,314 letters; like most of Erasmus' work, most of these letters are written in Latin, and though many were published in his lifetime, as a group they were not collected until the early twentieth century;[1] later in the twentieth century, though, there were a number of English translations of selected letters as well. The University of Toronto's massive, ongoing attempt to publish all of Erasmus' works in English translation have further aided scholarly approaches that are biographical and historical.[2]

There is also an excellent recent book, *Fatal Discord*, in which a modern journalist, Michael Massing, year by year reconstructs the conflict of Erasmus and Martin Luther. Massing helps us to understand that Erasmus, the illegitimate son of a priest born about the year of 1469, is until the rise of Luther mainly himself a Humanist advocating the reform of the Catholic Church. Economic desperation caused him to experience the corruption of late medieval monastic life, and he escapes from this only to enter the dry scholasticism of the University of Paris. As Humanism grows to oppose Scholasticism, the former movement's intellectual energy and elegance attracts good young scholars such as Erasmus. But does he become a Ciceronian, a Christian, or both?

Due to his immense influence and productivity, much of it inspired by classical models, Erasmus is often paired with Petrarch as a key figure in the "rebirth" of classical study. Yet far more than with a text such as *My Secret*, even a cursory glance at Erasmus' texts usually makes clear his commitment to the priority of Christian truth. Even Erasmus' oft-quoted invocation of "St. Socrates," for example, occurs in a dramatic text, or "colloquy," "The

---

1. Under the editorial lead of P. S. Allen, *Opus Epistolarum Des. Erasmi Roterodami*.

2. Now at eighty-nine volumes, under the editorial lead of Craig Thompson et al., *Collected Works of Erasmus*.

Poetic Feast,"[3] in which Erasmus is not speaking in his own voice, but rather through a variety of characters whose conversation is almost entirely concerned with Christian topics and biblical exegesis. Erasmus did edit new editions of major classical authors, such as Lucian and Cicero (for whom he has a strong affection that also becomes typical of the age), but he is even more productive with editions of the Church Fathers, most notably publishing editions of St. Jerome (1516) and St. Augustine (1529).

Yet surely the most influential text of Erasmus is his Greek New Testament of 1516, translated back into Latin for the first new translation since St. Jerome in the fourth century AD. This work clearly inspires the vernacular Bibles that became common in the coming century, something Erasmus explicitly speaks of in the "Paracelsus," calling on the Holy Spirit to allow "the farmer" to "sing some portion of them at the plow."[4] Whether or not recalling Lollards or the Peasants Revolt of England of the fourteenth century, Erasmus' scholarly work on the Bible was independent of the Catholic hierarchy, and the controversy over this independence accounts in large part for the general condemnation of Erasmus' writings at the Council of Trent. With the slogan of *ad fontes*, or back to the sources, Erasmus in the first two decades of the sixteenth century is clearly part of a movement to reform the Catholic Church, and it is during this time that there begins to circulate the adage that the Reformation was "the egg which Erasmus laid and Luther hatched." Yet both Erasmus and Luther would come to vehemently deny this claim, and it is important for us today to understand why.

In the case of Erasmus, it is not simply because he remains loyal to the early sixteenth-century popes, though that is significant. As Lutheranism grows, Erasmus is prodded by several Catholic leaders to intervene, but he does not do so until the early fifteen-twenties, waiting to write on a theological issue that will prove especially important to the Catholic Counter-Reformation: the freedom of the will. For however right Luther was to castigate the Catholic Church for the abuse of political power and financial stewardship inherent in practices like indulgences, both Luther and later Calvin are clearly wrong about the notion that salvation is purely the work of God's grace alone, involving no element of the human will, for such a doctrine logically requires the corollary that God chooses to "damn" or at least not save (practically, the same thing) those not predestined to be saved. Such a notion cannot be reconciled with Christian revelation of God's goodness, holiness, and love for all humanity.

3. Erasmus, "The Poetic Feast," 158–76.
4. Erasmus, *The Paraclesis*, 97.

The concrete, significant contrast between Luther and Erasmus' theology is perhaps most memorably shown in the contrast of their imagery for the human will, and its corresponding understanding of the nature of God. Michael Massing explains Erasmus' position well to a modern audience in "The Freedom of the Will" (*De Libero Arbitrio*):

> Erasmus took up the biblical image most favored by opponents of free will—that of the potter and his clay, from Jeremiah 18. Just as clay in the potter's hand is to be shaped as he wills, so is man in God's hand. In its place, Erasmus proposed another image—that of a young child learning to walk.... Though the child is completely in his father's debt and so has no reason to glory in his own powers, he has still done something on his own. So it is with God the Father and his children. If he works in us simply as the potter shapes the clay, what blame can be imputed to us if we err?[5]

By contrast, Luther's *On the Bondage of the Will* (*De Servo Arbitrio*) acknowledges that human beings can choose in some matters, but "pertaining to salvation and damnation," as Massing again explains well, Luther argues that a human being

> has no choice, but is a captive, subject and slave either of the will of God or the will of Satan. The human will is placed between these two "like a beast of burden." If ridden by God, it goes where God wills; if ridden by Satan, it goes where Satan wills. The beast itself is incapable of choosing its rider.[6]

The contrast between Erasmus and Luther is not simply linguistic or "rhetorical" in any decorative sense. Rather, it stems from a very different understanding of the *sapientia* of God that must be united to *eloquentia*.

Erasmus does share with the Reformers, however, a strong concern to save Catholicism from "dead ritual," superstition, or external action that becomes disconnected from the normally interior movement of the Holy Spirit. Erasmus could be aligned with Protestant movements in this respect, though violent revolution was always something he resolutely rejected as incompatible with his understanding of the Christian God. Set aside each other, as Erasmus and Luther dueled in tracts even as many later Catholic and Protestants would fight on the battlefield, it is not hard today to see which view of the human will is more likely to inspire human art, and which image of God is closer to the Father to whom Jesus asks us to pray. Even

---

5. Massing, *Fatal Discord*, 603.
6. Massing, *Fatal Discord*, 673.

before the German Peasant Revolt of the later 1520s exposes the deep divisions within Lutheranism, or how unlikely it was that all might accept the Lutheran notion of the Bible as a self-interpreting text, Erasmus wins a rhetorical battle that preserves human creativity and rejects the false notion of a God for whom human choice is irrelevant.

It remains for other scholars to discuss the complex connection of Paul, Augustine, and Aquinas to the issue of free will at the heart of the intellectual conflict between Erasmus and Luther, or to the opposition later to develop between Catholicism and Calvinism. It is happily true that Erasmus' basic theology, his *philosophia Christi*, is a practical Christian ethic that can be profitably read and learned by most Christians of any age (much like *The Imitation of Christ*, which directly influenced Erasmus). Yet what is most important in Erasmus's career for the dramatic art that so brilliantly develops later in the sixteenth century, in the work of William Shakespeare? In my opinion, five texts are especially important.

Copia: Foundations of the Abundant Style

The first, *Copia: Foundations of the Abundant Style* (*De duplici copia verborum ac rerum commentarii duo*)[7] or simply *Copia*, as it became known even in its own day, might seem a historical curiosity, appropriate only as preparation for future courtiers, hence its widespread use in Humanist Grammar Schools throughout Europe in the 1500s. Erasmus first wrote it as curriculum for Colet's St. Paul's, and today the text is perhaps best known for teaching writers the opposite of the "clarity-brevity-sincerity" mantra so common in today's compositional manuals. Erasmus hopes that writers will learn an "abundant" style and then offers a "practical demonstration" of almost 200 different ways of varying a simple Latin sentence: "*tuae litterae me magnopere delectarunt*" ("your letter pleased me mightily").[8] But what is the point of all this verbal variety? Is it the kind of courtly politeness that Shakespeare will later satirize in characters such as Polonius or Osric in *Hamlet*?

That the purpose of *Copia* is more sublime has been apparent to readers because of two commonplace associations and assumptions so familiar to Erasmus' audience that his text does not need to spell them out. The first is the union of *eloquentia* and *sapientia*, eloquence and wisdom, which was fundamental to Cicero and Quintilian, the two classical writers whom Erasmus most often references. Against pejorative views of "mere rhetoric," or

---

7. Erasmus, *Copia*, 284–659.
8. Erasmus, *Copia*, 348–54.

rhetoric designed to manipulate political gain, the ideal of sapiential rhetoric asserts that only eloquence rooted in wisdom has any lasting power to move human hearts. For Judeo-Christian rhetoricians such as Erasmus, the notion of wisdom as a foundation of creativity can be traced to Proverbs 8; to quote just the final two verses, here Wisdom tells us that while God was creating the world:

> then I was by him, as one brought up with him:
> and I was daily his delight, rejoicing always before him;
> rejoicing in the habitable part of his earth; and my delights
> were with the sons of men. (Prov 8:30–31)

While many later theologians and Church Fathers comment on this passage, perhaps the most influential for rhetoric is St. Augustine's *On Christian Doctrine*, whose entire third book is devoted to the role of rhetoric to interpret scripture. For Augustine, it is the wisdom of God that must remain united to human thought if eloquence is to retain value. The interdependence of eloquence and wisdom is perhaps most easily seen in Erasmus' early work, such as in this passage from *The Antibarbarians*:

> Those seeds of fair arts that God our Father places in us—understanding, intellectual power, memory and the other gifts of the mind—are talents entrusted to us to lend out; if we, as it were, double them by practice and effort, the Lord will praise us on his return as hard-working servants, and will allow us to keep what we have earned; but if we bury the talent we have been given, how will we feel, confronted with our Lord's eyes and face and voice at his return, when others count out the profit from the share they received but we through our idleness merely hand back the useless talent?[9]

As most Renaissance Christian readers would recognize, Erasmus' argument here is not a proud appeal to humanistic gifts or a call to value-free capitalism, but rather a humble exegesis of Christ's "Parable of the Talents," and a Christo-centric, biblical faith that we will face a Last Judgment when we come face to face with the Lord himself.

Erasmus' Catholic Humanism is suggested further by the reference to "words" ("verborum") and "things" (or "res") in the full Latin title of Erasmus' *Copia*. As is suggested in more detail in the book that acts as almost a companion or guide to *Copia*, the *De Ratione Studii* ("On the Rationale of Study") written by Erasmus in 1511, to speak of "words" and "things" is to reference a long tradition of education that both attempts to take seriously

---

9. Erasmus, *The Antibarbarians*, 160.

the complexity and beauty of elegant communication through language and the attempt to use language in a wise way that eventually brings us to a realistic knowledge of the things of the world. As Brian McGregor puts it in the University of Toronto translation of *De Ratione Studii*, commenting on the text's opening sentence claim that "knowledge as a whole seems to be of two kinds, of things and words":

> To sophisticated readers this phrase would have recalled a more complex subject than pedagogy or curricula. "Things and words" suggests or describes a topic that had been debated by philosophers for centuries: the question of universals, the reality of genera and species.[10]

Within the Christian tradition, the foundation of all universals, of all reality, is God. Hence Augustine's *On Christian Doctrine* is not an abstract theory of signs, distinguishing two kinds of signs, words and things, but a means to interpret the signs that God has authored in scripture, nature, and history. If Erasmus' Catholic Humanism has a "secular" bent, as many claim, it is simply that copious eloquence united to divine sapience can develop human nature to positively build human society and culture in this world. Of course, Erasmus would add, such a hope is not new . . . it could be traced to the *philosophia Christi* in the simile of the Lord's Prayer: "as it is in heaven" (Matt 6:9).

As the sixteenth-century wars of religion tragically demonstrate, however, the human sword often severs any lasting human attempt to unite *eloquentia* and *sapientia*. Hence the importance of the other assumption within Erasmus' *Copia* and entire educational program: the hope that the linguistic facility gained through real eloquence can inspire art of lasting wisdom. Humanist grammar schools did not teach rhetoric simply as a means to interpret great writing of the past, but also as a way to practically enable the linguistic skills of writers of the future.[11] In our time, the effect of Erasmus' *De Copia* on Shakespeare's art has been well written about by Marion Trousdale. She begins by quoting the venerable classicist R. R. Bolgar:

> If we want to trace how the Humanist practice of imitation affected creative writing, if we want to go behind the scenes and cast an eye on the mechanics of the process . . . our best guide is Erasmus.[12]

---

10. McGregor, *On the Method of Study*, 666n1.
11. Baldwin, *Shakespeare's Small Latine & Lesse Greek*.
12. Trousdale, *Shakespeare and the Rhetoricians*, 45.

Trousdale goes on to show how Erasmus' many methods of developing *copia* ultimately aim at an experience of language especially related to dramatic writing. For Erasmus, she argues, "the description of a thing, placed before the reader and painted with all the colors of rhetoric, draws the hearer or reader outside himself, 'as in the theatre.'"[13] By "varying something copiously," Erasmus teaches, "one is able to see it in as many ways and from as many points of view as it can possibly be seen."[14] The value of such a perspective is obvious to civic rule, and also to the dramatist; but perhaps it is "the poet who is best able to do this through his rich and varied use of specific example."[15] Trousdale goes on to demonstrate the applicability of Erasmus' rhetoric to a number of Shakespeare's play, and I shall return both to her work and Shakespeare's attitude to rhetoric in chapters 8 and 9 of this prelude to *As You Like It*, but here we simply see the connection between Erasmus' seemingly dry linguistic distinctions and the artistic creativity apparent in so many of the pupils of Catholic Humanist schools.

As T. W. Baldwin shows in the most detailed study ever published of the curriculum of these schools,[16] the linguistic eloquence of Erasmus' literary program was never for its own sake, nor isolated from the study of ethics, scripture, or Christian *sapientia* in general. Apart from reading Baldwin's entire book or applying the entire curriculum in a school ourselves, as many have in the classical Christian educational movement that has blossomed in the twenty-first century, perhaps our best means to glimpse the meaning of this experience is through the Renaissance iconography of rhetoric. For their volume of *De Copia* and other educational writings by Erasmus, the University of Toronto translators selected as a frontispiece a 1628 icon of "Rhetorica" in which from her mouth "stream three golden chains," speech that "has power even to hold beasts," pictured in the bottom right of the icon. Perhaps the most striking part of the icon, though, is what also appeared on the cover of the final edition of Erasmus' *Copia*, in 1534.[17] Entwined serpents are wrapped around a wand, perhaps the "caduceus" associated with Mercury, herald of the gods, whose eloquence has reconciled opposing arguments. Divine desire to bring peace, an end to bickering and violent division, is the sapiential ideal of eloquence, not the endless expression of self by which some might abuse verbal skill.

---

13. Trousdale, *Shakespeare and the Rhetoricians*, 48.
14. Trousdale, *Shakespeare and the Rhetoricians*, 49.
15. Trousdale, *Shakespeare and the Rhetoricians*, 49.
16. Baldwin, *Shakespeare's Small Latin & Lesse Greek*.
17. Shown in Erasmus, *Copia*, 656.

The Praise of Folly (Morae Encomium)

As the sixteenth century is engulfed by religious warfare, it is easy in retrospect to see Erasmus' hopes as foolish rather than wise. Yet Erasmus' most popular text throughout that century, and perhaps even in our own, is the seemingly more foolish exercise of *The Praise of Folly*. Ostensibly written on horseback on the way back to Europe after a visit to England, the Latin title is a joking jab towards Thomas More: *Morae Encomium*. In it, the goddess Folly comically mocks the plethora of foolishness in human life and, in language that later critics will often use to seriously attack Erasmus, mocks especially the outward ceremony and lack of inward piety of monks and other corrupt clerics in the early sixteenth-century Catholic church. Towards the end of her discourse, Folly also praises the wisdom of foolishness in texts like the first chapter of 1 Corinthians, which reflects on the "foolishness" of the "cross" of Christ (1 Cor 1:18) and of how God chose "the foolish things of the world to confound" the powerful (1 Cor 1:27). Here Erasmus' foolish text surely turns serious, becoming a praise of the unique combination of humor and holiness in More. As Thomas Chaloner puts in the preface to his 1549 edition, one of many editions that circulate widely in the sixteenth century, Erasmus "never showed more art, nor wit, in any of the gravest book he wrote, then in this his praise of Folly."[18]

In addition to the historical and religious relevance of the text, though, *The Praise of Folly* is crucial to the development of Shakespearean comedy, especially *As You Like It*, because of one key concept: to "counterfeit." The concept here has little to do with money, as in our day, but rather trades in another currency especially dear to humanists like Erasmus, the human imagination. Erasmus' concept here could be described in logical terms, as a hypothetical syllogism, or as the most familiar of figures of speech, metaphor or simile, in which different things are likened to each other directly, or through the use of "like" or "as." In an important sense, the very title of the play focused on in this study, *As You Like It*, is a complex *simile* for what makes humanity happy, a *hypothetical syllogism* inviting us to imagine human relationships, especially the romantic love of man and woman, in new ways.

The Praise of Folly, though, further explains "to counterfeit" through a single word that Shakespeare will also use to construct many of *As You Like It*'s key lines: "if." Erasmus' conception of this key concept can be understood through a long passage so important to my topic that it is worth reading in full in Erasmus' Latin or the first English translation of this text,

---

18. Quoted in Trousdale, *Shakespeare and the Rhetoricians*, 113.

by Thomas Chaloner in 1549. However, Chaloner is unintelligible to most modern English speakers, so here is the key passage in the 1668 prose of John Wilson:

> If anyone seeing a player acting his part on a stage should go about to strip him of his disguise and show him to the people in his true native form, would he not, think you, not only spoil the whole design of the play, but deserve himself to be pelted off with stones as a phantastical fool and one out of his wits? But nothing is more common with them than such changes; the same person one while impersonating a woman, and another while a man; now a youngster, and by and by a grim seignior; now a king, and presently a peasant; now a god, and in a trice again an ordinary fellow. But to discover this were to spoil all, it being the only thing that entertains the eyes of the spectators. And what is all this life but a kind of comedy, wherein men walk up and down in one another's disguises and act their respective parts, till the property-man brings them back to the attiring house. And yet he often orders a different dress, and makes him that came but just now off in the robes of a king put on the rags of a beggar. Thus are all things represented by counterfeit, and yet without this there was no living.[19]

For Erasmus, this passage suggests, the need for imagination caused by disguise or "counterfeit" is not to be lamented, nor accepted simply as a practical necessity for the theatre, but rather seen as an essential element of human life. As Erasmus further implies, the human imagination is an especially important element of comic drama.

One can quickly think of how "counterfeit" later becomes essential, for example, to the comic drama of Feste in *Twelfth Night* (4.1), but why, in his own time, was imaginative theatre important to Erasmus' Catholic Humanism? Why, in other words, is "if" an important religious word? John D. Cox has shown the relevance of Lucianic satire to Shakespearean comedy,[20] and there is no doubt that both Erasmus and More loved the humorous satire of Lucian, and used "barbed wit" of this kind to poke fun at decadent yet still arrogant elements of the late medieval church. Yet both also saw humor as a means to laugh at oneself, and by the end of *The Praise of Folly* we are reminded that God uses the foolishness of the cross, the foolish things of the world, to build in humanity a real humility that allows us to laugh at

---

19. Erasmus, *The Praise of Folly*, translated by John Wilson.
20. Cox, *Seeming Knowledge*.

ourselves. If Erasmian satire can cause us to laugh at ourselves, then it might also allow us to imagine a better world.

A Complaint of Peace (Querela Pacis)

The association between "if" and peacemaking can perhaps most easily be seen in this text, which Erika Rummel calls "Erasmus' most celebrated plea for peace."[21] Another text that, like *Praise of Folly*, uses *prosopopoeia* to personify the text's main topic, here Peace develops *copia*, and the union of *eloquentia* and *sapientia*, through obvious rhetorical repetition of "if":

> If then I am Peace, praised aloud by gods and men, the fount and source, the sustainer, amplifier, and preserver of all good things of heaven or earth; if without me there can be no prosperity, no security, nothing sacred or undefiled, nothing pleasurable for men or acceptable to the gods; if on the other hand war is a kind of encircling ocean of all the evils in the world, if through its inherent wickedness prosperity immediately declines, increase dwindles, towers are undermined, sound foundations are destroyed, and sweetness is embittered . . . in the name of the immortal God I must say this: who would believe those beings to be human or possessed of any spark of sanity when they devote so much expenditure and application, such great effort and artifice, so many anxieties and dangers, to rid themselves of me—such as I am—while they are willing to pay the heavy price they do for such a burden of evils?[22]

Even in this shortened form—which omits two other fairly long "if" clauses—this passage makes clear the connection Erasmus sees between the rhetoric of "if" and the wisdom of religious peace that he believes essential to faith in both the Christian God and humanity itself.

Colloquies (Colloquia familiaria)

As influential as *The Praise of Folly* certainly is, there may be no more commonly read demonstration of Erasmus' comic wit than his *Colloquies*. Modeled after the classical genre of the "dialogue" that is central, most famously, to the philosophical texts of Plato, Erasmus' *Colloquies* deal with a very wide variety of both intellectual ideas and concrete, everyday elements of life in

---

21. Rummel, *Erasmus Reader*, 288.
22. Erasmus, *A Complaint of Peace*, 289.

sixteenth-century Europe. Sometimes the speakers are entirely fictional, other times thinly disguised figures known to Erasmus, other times historical persons likely to be known by most readers. The criterion for inclusion is neither historical accuracy nor entertainment value, but rather usefulness to the education of the young. One of the most oft-quoted lines on this work comes from Erasmus' prologue to an edition of the *Colloquies*: "I'm not sure anything is learned better than what is learned as a game."[23] Here, the "game" is dialogue, but the broader goal is *sapientia*, the wisdom attainable through education.

The *Colloquies* were popular, published in many editions in the sixteenth century,[24] and Erasmus took their development seriously, adding many new colloquies throughout his life. Their influence on Renaissance literature is incalculable, since we simply can't know how many creative writers read them. But certainly one can agree with Craig R. Thompson, who translated the *Colloquies* before moving to the University of Toronto Erasmus project, that the literary style of Erasmus' work makes it "deserve the more dignified name of literature," for Erasmus "had the dramatist's eye; he saw everything and could recreate scenes with his pen."[25]

While even a casual reading of the *Colloquies* reveals their literary style, what of substance in these "dialogues" or series of "one act plays" is most influential upon Shakespeare's comic art? As noted already in "The Poetic Feast," most *Colloquies* suggest Erasmus to be more a Catholic Humanist than a Classicist, but there are several that reveal the range of his theological and ethical imagination. Recalling Chaucer, for example, there are eight colloquies that might be called a "marriage" group.

The first of these, "Courtship," features a heroine named Maria whom Thompson calls, "a delightful creature, comparable in poise, intelligence and wit to the women of Shakespeare's romantic comedies."[26] Maria's wit, like Shakespeare's heroines', is practical, almost pragmatic; when faced with the exchange of vows or "*de praesenti*" commitment often thought to be binding by canon law, Maria shows the patience and imaginative wit we will later see in Rosalind. But both heroines rarely talk on the level of abstract legalese. Rather, Maria is always ready to sharply rebuke her suitor's romantic idealism and stupidity (which often amount to the same thing, as we shall see with Orlando, suitor to Rosalind), as in the colloquies' opening lines:

> Pamphilius: Hello—you cruel, hardheated, unrelenting creature!

23. Erasmus, "The Usefulness of the Colloquies," 625.
24. Thompson, Introduction to *The Colloquies of Erasmus*, xxi–xxix.
25. Thompson, Introduction to *The Colloquies of Erasmus*, xxvi.
26. Thompson, Introduction to *The Colloquies of Erasmus*, 87.

> Maria: Hello yourself, Pamphilus, as often and as much as you like, and by whatever name you please. But sometimes I think you've forgotten my name. It's Maria.[27]

Maria also outwits the love-lorn Pamphilius with logic and rhetoric, playing the "sophist" with him, as Rosalind will with Orlando, but the main reason for her sharp wit seems to be avoiding a loveless marriage to a man who "wouldn't return love for love."[28] There is a point later in the dialogue where she affirms that "I do return" the love Pamphilius offers, but long-term commitment must withstand several more disputes. Maria closes the colloquy by poking further fun at Pamphilius' abstract notions of the soul in love while also proposing future dialogue and even, romantically, rewarding a continuation of the courtship:

> You say your soul has passed almost entirely into my body and that there's only the slightest particle left in yours. Consequently, I'm afraid this particle in you would skip over to me in a kiss, and you'd then become quite lifeless. So shake hands, a symbol of our mutual love; and farewell. Persevere in your efforts. Meanwhile I'll pray Christ to bless and prosper us both in what we do.[29]

Not exactly what Pamphilius wants to hear, of course, but very close to the union of *eloquentia* and *sapientia* that Shakespeare will later dramatize in Rosalind.

The meaning of Maria for Erasmus' Catholic Humanism is highlighted at the colloquies' opening, when Pamphilius responds to Maria's initial rebuke by saying her name derives from Mars, the god of war. This seems a deliberately obtuse classicism, for every Catholic reader in Erasmus' audience would know that Maria derives from "Mary." For such readers, Mary is the exemplar of brave virginity, who in accepting patiently the hardship of the Virgin Birth of Christ gives the eloquent song later termed the "magnificat" (Luke 1:46–55). It is not inaccurate to see Erasmus' Maria as a type of Mary, boldly affirming her virgin identity against false male notions of love. The miracle, both in the colloquy and in Shakespeare's later comedies, is that such women sometimes also assent to share their soul's love with a human male.

---

27. Thompson, Introduction to *The Colloquies of Erasmus*, 88.
28. Thompson, Introduction to *The Colloquies of Erasmus*, 88.
29. Thompson, Introduction to *The Colloquies of Erasmus*, 98.

On Mending the Peace of the Church (De Sarcienda Ecclesiae Concordia)

It is fair to say that no issue more deeply divides sixteenth-century Protestants and Catholics than Marian questions. Yet by the time, 1533, that Erasmus writes the final text considered here, *On Mending the Peace of the Church* (*De Sarcienda Ecclesiae Concordia*),[30] it is certainly true that division has multiplied over so many doctrines, within also the Protestant movement itself, that it is hard by then, as now, to imagine a way to regain unity. By 1533, as John P. Dolan puts it, "all of Europe seemed in travail," and "More's fate had been sealed," but *De Sarcienda* can be taken as Erasmus' "last will and testament."[31] The text's goal now becomes not so much doctrinal unity, nor the broad cultural revitalization once hoped for by Catholic Humanism, but rather peace. Religious warfare has brought an end to political peace, but beyond that Erasmus still prays for spiritual peace, peace in one's heart where one might hear the still, small voice of the living God. It this kind of peace, which Erasmus has long known can be given only by Christ, that he finally prescribes as the only way to mend the church.

Jumping ahead in time, to this text, should not allow us to think Erasmus idle during this period. He brought out numerous editions of Church Fathers' writings, including Jerome, Cyprian, Hilary, Irenaeus, Ambrose, Augustine, and Origin. This output must be considered alongside the editions of classical authors that he also published, yet contexts usually suggest the hierarchy of Catholic over Classical thought which is central to his work. Like Newman in the nineteenth century, Erasmus' humanism was profoundly shaped by the Church Fathers, and by his engagement with the philology and biblical exegesis of Jerome and Augustine that is necessitated by Erasmus' edition of the New Testament, which went through numerous editions in the final nineteen years of his life. The influence of the Church Fathers is especially relevant to Erasmus' view of language, as we shall see in chapter 8, but it could also be argued from even a casual reading of *De Sarcienda*, for Erasmus' main remedy for heresy is the rational, communal consensus of the historical Catholic Church. Very directly he says, "if we seek true peace of soul, let us remain in the tabernacle of the Lord of Hosts, let us remain in union with the Catholic Church."[32] But the "if" here always depends, Erasmus throughout insists, on the mercy that can be given to humanity by God alone. So he affirms that "outside the Church there is

---

30. Erasmus, *On Mending the Peace of the Church*, 331–88.
31. Erasmus, *On Mending the Peace of the Church*, 327.
32. Erasmus, *On Mending the Peace of the Church*, 357.

not real hope of blessedness," but "this blessedness will be had only in the resurrection of the dead."[33]

If *On Mending* shows Erasmus in continuity with Catholic tradition, it also contains the emphases of his contemporary program of Catholic Humanism. Erasmus claims to follow Jerome by arguing that "the word 'man' does not exclude women," and he follows this by quoting St. Paul to the Galatians: In Christ "there is neither Jew nor Greek, there is neither bond nor free, there is neither male nor female . . ." (Gal 3:28). Erasmus has many different names for God, turning at one point to the familiar Humanist emphasis on play to argue: "Our Gamemaster calls His followers to the contest."[34] Yet he also seems to respond to one of the major objections that the Reformation, rightly or wrongly, makes to Catholicism, the relationship of faith to works. Erasmus writes:

> Whatever God has given to you He has given through His Son and because of His Son, not because of the works of justice that we perform. "For all of us have offended in many things." He alone is the lamb without spot. Therefore O God our Protector, if our face or our conscience offend You, then look upon the face of Christ Thy Son, whom You love without exception and through whose merits you have granted us what we do not deserve.[35]

This obvious attempt at peacemaking is followed by an argument to "hold fast to what the Catholic Church has handed down to us from Holy Scripture," but by essay's end it is clear that Erasmus is attempting to rise above ecclesial politics and remind all Christians that there is one God above them all. "The power of neither the angels nor the prophets nor the saints confers true beatitude," he argues, for "this is only accomplished by the God of Gods."[36] By this point in his life, humanistic study has made Erasmus deeply aware of the complexity of the human soul, and of why God alone can bring real peace: "So immense and so capacious a thing is the human soul that only God can fill it, even if you add to it, besides God, six hundred worlds."[37]

Erasmus' God is the "God of Angels," and the "God of powers," but also the "God of men," he sees an apt model for humanity in Jacob, the Old Testament patriarch who "when wrestling with the angel, merited

---

33. Erasmus, *On Mending the Peace of the Church*, 355.
34. Erasmus, *On Mending the Peace of the Church*, 366.
35. Erasmus, *On Mending the Peace of the Church*, 370.
36. Erasmus, *On Mending the Peace of the Church*, 375.
37. Erasmus, *On Mending the Peace of the Church*, 355.

a benediction and said, "I have seen the Lord face to face and my soul is saved."[38] Though always conscious of the Triune God and accepting the Old Testament as revelation, there is also definitely a Christ-centric quality to Erasmus' Catholic Humanism. He writes:

> To look upon God is true beatitude, but we are unable to behold Him until He has first looked upon us. Since we were blind and living in darkness rather than mist, He has deigned to look upon us and has opened our eyes. And since we became His enemies by loving ourselves, He has enabled us to love Him once again. Look upon the face of your Christ.[39]

This Christo-centric mixture of ethical insight and theological metaphor is typical of *On Mending*, especially in its concluding pages. But for literature lovers perhaps the most moving passages of this text come earlier and are figurative, as when Erasmus follows Christ in comparing men to sparrows, both utterly humble before the providence of God. Erasmus teaches:

> The Holy Spirit does not love souls that are swollen with pride, burdened with love for corporeal goods and therefore walking on the ground; He loves souls that are birds and rejoices in dealing with the heavens; He loves those who are little in their own eyes and disregarded by the world; He loves all who depend upon the providence of God.[40]

Erasmus did far too much in his career to ever be disregarded by the world. Yet in passages like these, one senses the entire Erasmian program of Catholic Humanism. Seemingly consumed in the flames of sixteenth-century religious strife, it tends to rise again, phoenix-like, wherever the souls of human beings seek the peace that only God can give. We can turn now to Erasmus' close friend, Thomas More, whose fate in this world was politically sealed, but the divine influence of his soul—forged partly through friendship with Erasmus—continues to bring peace to many.

---

38. Erasmus, *On Mending the Peace of the Church*, 369.
39. Erasmus, *On Mending the Peace of the Church*, 369.
40. Erasmus, *On Mending the Peace of the Church*, 351–52.

6

More and the Humor of Holy Rhetoric

ST. THOMAS MORE (1478-1535)

We can begin thinking about the importance of More through the always provocative comments of G. K. Chesterton:

> Blessed Thomas More is more important at this moment than at any moment since his death, even perhaps the great moment of his dying; but he is not quite so important as he will be in about a hundred years time. He may come to be counted the greatest Englishman, or at least the greatest historical character in English history. For he was above all things historic; he represented at once a type, a turning point and an ultimate destiny. If there had not appeared that particular man at that particular moment, the whole of history would have been different.[1]

In what sense, if any, is Chesterton right? Especially today, about 100 years after Chesterton's words? Are Chesterton's claims about More, as critics might contend, nothing more than the biased historical revisionism of one who wishes to advance his own claims as a Catholic convert? How could

---

1. Chesterton, "A Turning Point in History," 63, quoted in Monti, *The King's Good Servant*, 15.

More be seen as such an essential type of human being, either in his own time or ours? More is now not merely "blessed" but a fully canonized saint in the Catholic Church, but what of his life in early sixteenth-century England is so exemplary? Further, to ask a question especially relevant to my study here, to what extent was More still influential within England when Shakespeare wrote *As You Like It* at the end of the sixteenth century?

Many today are familiar, from the excellent film, with More as "a man for all seasons," who was famously martyred in opposition to the clearly evil desire of Henry VIII to divorce his wife and establish himself as head of an English "church." Yet few are aware of the complex life that More lived before this, and fewer still understand how More's Catholic Humanism impacts both his own age and future generations, in England and the universal church. Unlike Erasmus, More published texts in both English and Latin but, apart from the Latin text *Utopia*, the 1516 work that proved to be even more popular a fiction than Erasmus' *Praise of Folly*, most of More's vast writings were largely unread by modern scholars before Yale University Press, in 1963, began publishing More's complete works in English.[2] Scholars today can contextualize this writing, and are fortunate to have a literary biography comparable to *Fatal Discord*, Massing's work on Erasmus and Luther. James Monti's *The King's Good Servant but God's First: The Life and Writings of St. Thomas More* considers More's writing in the chronological order and context of More's life. Monti allows us to understand More not only through his famously holy martyrdom, but also in the humor, and human sin, that makes him such an important man in the history of English Catholic Humanism.

More as Humanist

More was born in 1478, and thus was already twenty-one when he met Erasmus in 1499. By then, he was already committed to both Catholicism and the cultural movement of Humanism, even translating the biography of one of the most influential, if at times controversial, thinkers in Italian Humanism, Pico Della Miranda. Pico, much like Petrarch, is often critiqued as heterodox, and in some ways he was, but More's translation[3] (into English from the Italian) reminds us of the Catholic Faith that runs throughout Pico's life. More was perhaps drawn to Pico because of the many parallels between their lives, as laymen, scholars, who turn their minds ultimately to

---

2. More, *Complete Works of St. Thomas More.*
3. More, *Life of John Picus.*

the service of Christ's church. The Bible was central to this Catholic Humanism, as is shown by a passage from More's Pico biography:

> Thou mayest do nothing more pleasant to God, nothing more profitable to thyself, than if thine hand cease not day nor night to turn and read the volumes of Holy Scripture. There lieth privily in them a certain heavenly strength, quick and effectual, which with a marvelous power transformeth and changeth the reader's mind into the love of God.[4]

Though educated in a monastic school and living the drudgery of professional life as a lawyer, as well as the duties inherent in becoming father to a large family and husband to two women, after the first died when More was only twenty-seven, More nevertheless shows great literary creativity in his translation of Pico's biography. As Monti notes, the last third of the *Life of John Picus* "is taken up by poems"[5] inspired by the Italian Humanist. This poetry is not only theological, and deeply Catholic, it often shows the interest in Christ's Passion characteristic of More's entire life:

> When thou in flame of temptation friest,
> Think on the very lamentable pain,
> Think on the piteous cross of woeful Christ,
> Think on his blood beat out at every vein,
> Think on his precious heart carved in twain,
> Think how far thy redemption all was wrought,
> Let him not lose that he so dear hath bought.[6]

The unity between More's piety and Catholic Humanism could be shown in a variety of other ways. As already noted, in 1504 Colet became More's spiritual director. In 1505, More married, confirming the difficult decision to live as a lay person rather than cleric, but in the same year he worked with two clerics, Colet and Erasmus, to found the grammar school at St. Paul's. In 1505, More also worked with Erasmus to translate works by the Roman satirist Lucian, but their mutual love of satire has an ultimate Christian purpose, as we saw in *The Praise of Folly*, for it ultimately reminds us to trust revelation more than strictly intellectual reason. More also wrote a *History of Richard III*, whose major theme—the claim that the hand of God was upon the rise of England's Tudor House—is one of many aspects of his Humanist work that seems a difficult, even ironic way to prepare for More's later trials under the tyranny of Henry VIII.

4. More, *Life of John Picus*, 13, quoted in Monti, *The King's Good Servant*, 38.
5. Monti, *The King's Good Servant*, 40.
6. More, *Life of John Picus*, 27, quoted in Monti, *The King's Good Servant*, 42.

In all, More's complete works, translated into English in the last half of the twentieth century, come to no less than fifteen volumes—not quite as prolific as Erasmus, but certainly a noble amount of writing for any major literary figure. More's professional life did keep him busy, but in domestic life he made clear the importance of humanist education in his own home by using the curriculum that a Spanish Catholic Humanist, Juan De Vives, had used to educate Queen Catherine of Aragorn, in order to teach his own oldest daughter Margaret. Such might not seem radical today, but Vives' and More's advocacy of female education became one of the most famous aspects of Humanism in More's time. Many aspects of this program distinguish it from modern feminism, of course, but Margaret does become a prolific author and wife to William Roper, the son-in-law who, in 1535, gives us our first biography of More.[7]

Utopia

None of More's humanist efforts have proven as influential, however, as the fictional text whose brevity and profundity might be compared to Erasmus's early gift of *Morae Encomium*. More's *Utopia*,[8] published in 1516, is similar to *The Praise of Folly* in being relatively brief, and also in being by far the most commonly read text, today, of its respective author. Both authors would probably have found this highly ironic, for both texts are comical, playful texts over which their authors shed much less toil and sweat than over many longer works. Both texts do have serious intentions, but neither More nor Erasmus would likely view either as comparatively important to their longer theological works. For both texts, as already discussed for *The Praise of Folly*, it is essential to have some understanding of their rhetorical form in order to interpret them well. Even more so than with Erasmus, the lack of understanding of the rhetoric of More's text, and of More himself, has often led to misinterpretation.

Perhaps the best place to start with this notoriously complex issue is with the obvious ways that one must *not* interpret *Utopia*. Despite the misguided enthusiasm of the many who hope to find in the book a pioneering effort to imagine a perfect society, a utopia, More's *Utopia* cannot be taken as a simple, "ideal" model for how to reform either the European society of More's day or as a literal model for later political reform. Nor, though, is it a cynical critique of a failed political system initially claimed to be utopian.

7. Roper, *The Lyfe of Sir Thomas More*.
8. More, *Utopia*, translated by Turner. Unless otherwise noted, all references to *Utopia* are to this edition.

More's *Utopia*, in other words, is not a dystopian novel like that which has become common in reaction to the numerous political utopias that have been attempted in the centuries since this text's publication. The issue of communism, the conception of which is certainly part of More's *Utopia*, is usually part of either misreading, whether praise or ridicule. Regardless of one's attitude to this issue, or to many other social or political notions presented in the text, it is certainly a misreading to claim More's *Utopia* as a simple proposal arguing for the advancement of a social agenda.

Readers can ascertain, first, from the text's title and opening pages, other rhetorical purposes. A deliberately silly opening poem immediately uses Latin puns to suggest the text's fictionality, and clarifies the meaning of its title. As any student of Latin would know, *u-topos* means "no place," suggesting that the book is about a purely fictional place, though the text's introductory poem also refers to "eutopia," a good place. The suggestion is to not take the book too seriously, because it is about no-place, nowhere, but also that we might yet learn some valuable things from this place. Students of *As You Like It* cannot help but here think of Celia's wonderful comment on the Forest of Arden: "I like this place, and willingly would waste my time in it" (2.4.93–94).

Further confirmations of *Utopia's* status as fiction follow in a letter presented as written by More himself, with the author creating a "persona," putting himself in the text in a way commonplace amongst Medieval and Renaissance authors, while the second later purports to be written by Peter Giles, another historical person whom the historical More actually knew and did write letters to. These letters are part of an easily seen through "realistic" introduction which also refers to the travels of Amerigo Vespucci, the historical adventurer who did actually discover the American continent (after Columbus' 1492 voyage ended in the Caribbean). The ironic effect of these "realistic" touches is surely skepticism, since it is all so unlikely, but the first obvious indication that the text is an imaginative fiction, in the tradition of speculative satire that Erasmus and More translated from Lucian, is the sea traveler that Giles soon introduces to More: Raphael Hythlodaeus.

The fictional nature of this traveler could be guessed from the unlikely story of his voyages, but readers who know Latin, the language in which More wrote the original text, can quickly guess this from Hythlodaeus' last name, which suggests that he is the "peddlar of nonsense." Those interested in Humanism in 1516, however, might have kept reading not only because this sea-traveller has the first name of a great Italian painter, but also because the Latin spelling of his last name, "hytholodaeus," suggests a pun on "deus," the Latin word for God. Quite possibly, the joke or pun here, achieved with the addition of a simple "a," is a response to the title *Morae*

Encomium (which makes More a fool to be praised along with the goddess of the text), for was not Erasmus an oft-travelling pedlar of nonsense about God? But the pun is an intellectual joke, not satire against Erasmus himself. Even without any reference to Latin, finally More suggests the imaginative nature of his subject because both he and Giles have "forgotten" the location of the wonderful island about which More will speak.

However, just as it would be a ludicrous misinterpretation to then argue that Erasmus intends worship of the goddess Folly, so it is clearly incorrect to see this as some sort of "pre-conversion" text in which More is presenting one who speaks for God as speaking nonsense. Nor would any intelligent person take literally More's praise of himself, in the opening letter, as "one of the glories of the age," nor take seriously Giles' repetition of this phrase in the second letter. Even apart from what we know of the historical More in 1516 or from his later writings, we can recognize that this mock serious "pride" actually conveys a deep humility. Similarly, much more likely than religious apostasy is the hint that comes from *Praise of Folly*, where Erasmus starts out satirizing human folly, but leads us toward the foolish wisdom of the gospel in 1 Corinthians 1.

Can a similar pattern be found in *Utopia*? More is far too witty to be pinned down by any simplistic schematic, but attending to the rhetorical form of the text can suggest insight. After the opening two letters, we have a discussion in Book One between More, Giles, and Raphael which focuses on political issues in sixteenth-century Europe. Then, for most of Book Two, Raphael alone speaks of what he saw in the country of Utopia. Finally, More gives a very short response to Raphael, inviting further discussion after dinner. By attending to this rhetorical structure or, to put it more directly, actually reading the book, one avoids the simplistic tendency to equate Raphael's enthusiasm for this country he has "visited," to the notion that More himself is proposing it as a blueprint for European society. Rather, one can far more plausibly view the book as the witty "conversation starter" that Humanist writers generally took dialogues and satires to be. *Utopia* is not a novel, an unknown literary genre at the time, and still less a political manifesto of the kind that Marx will popularize over three centuries later.

One does not have to be any kind of historian to see this, for in the opening letter, More's literary *persona* tells us almost exactly the same thing. In the colloquially-conscious modern English translated by Paul Turner in the twentieth century, near the end of the opening letter More laments:

> Most readers know nothing about literature—many regard it with contempt. Lowbrows find everything heavy going that isn't completely lowbrow. Highbrows reject everything as vulgar that

isn't a mass of archaisms. Some only like the classics, others only their own works. Some are so grimly serious that they disapprove of all humor, others so half-witted that they can't stand wit. Some are so literal minded that the slightest hint of irony affects them as water affects a sufferer from hydrophobia.[9]

Utopia is a form of serio-comic literature designed to amuse men like Erasmus, and we have to be wary of taking any comment within it in too literal minded a manner. Because Hythlodaeus effusively praises the absence of private property in Utopia, and there are comical elements of anti-wealth humor in the book, such as the Utopians' use of gold for urinals, perhaps the most common form of literal misreading has been to see *Utopia* as an early Communist tract. Turner himself seems to fall into this trap by attaching an appendix, to his twentieth-century Penguin Classic edition of the book, which attempts to analyze other writings by More to conclude, with non-mock seriousness, "I have yet to see any evidence that More did not mean what he said about communism in Utopia."[10]

By which even this learned translator means, of course, that, in his opinion, the historical Thomas More would not clearly reject the praise of communism offered by Raphael Hythlodaeus. At the conclusion of *Utopia* itself the literary *persona* of More seems to do exactly this, however, saying:

> While Raphael was telling us all this, I kept thinking of various objections. The laws and customs of that country seemed to me in many cases perfectly ridiculous. Quite apart from such things as their military tactics, religions, and forms of worship, there was the grand absurdity on which their whole society was based, communism minus money. Now this in itself would mean the end of aristocracy, and consequently of all dignity, splendour, and majesty, which are generally supposed to be the real glories of any nation.[11]

One does not have to interpret these words via reference either to the historical More's wealth or friendship with the aristocracy, nor to his working-class origins and ascendancy through effort to professional life as a lawyer. It is enough to be aware of the absurdity, as can also be shown in any post-Marxian political example, of any nation attempting to administer money through purely public means. Advocacy of the passage just quoted might appeal in a literal-minded way to opponents of class structure in Britain,

---

9. More, *Utopia*, 32.
10. Turner, "More's Attitude to Communism," 151.
11. More, *Utopia*, 132.

where class distinctions have been central for so long, but in More's day aristocracy was an immovable fact of life essential to the cultural and economic well being of all.

If there is added irony in the literary More's comments here, it is via reference to the Latin that the historical More would regularly have seen on the door of St. Paul's Cathedral: "Sic transit Gloria Mundi." All glories of this world pass, a final self-deprecating joke in response to the mock-pride of the opening letters, and finally we must only hope to enter into the glory of God. The origins of communism are in the shared property of Christ's first apostles (Acts 4:32–37), as the historical More well knew, but the complex structures and sad reality of human sin cannot allow communism to be the political system of a Christian nation. Perhaps some of Hythlodaeus's proposals could be applied to European society, but the historical, clearly Roman Catholic More speaks most clearly through comical understatement when he says, "things will never be perfect, until human beings are perfect—which I don't expect them to be for quite a number of years."[12]

The critique of Hythlodaeus given by the persona of More does not develop into any kind of bitterness. Rather, the text closes with an invitation to supper and further discussion. There are many further fascinating aspects of *Utopia* that one can discuss, such as Hythlodaeus's simultaneous praise of the Utopians' openness to divorce and capital punishment for adultery, but perhaps the topic most relevant to my study here is religion. Far from being atheists, like modern communists, the Utopians practice a religion that stresses tolerance. The Utopian people show both the good possible and the evil inevitable in human nature unenlightened by divine revelation, but given the tolerance advocated by Erasmian humanism, especially before the violence prompted through Lutheranism, it may be that in 1516 More himself thought it important to season claims of divine revelation with doses of human humility. Though this interpretation might reveal my own bias as a post-Vatican II, ecumenical Catholic, one could acquire this idea through the prayer Utopians say each day:

> O God, I acknowledge Thee to be my creator, my governor, and the source of all good things. I thank Thee for all Thy blessing, but especially for letting me live in the happiest possible society, and practice what I hope is the truest religion. If I am wrong, and if some other religion or social system would be better and more acceptable to Thee, I pray Thee in Thy goodness to let me know it, for I am ready to follow wherever Thou shalt lead me.[13]

---

12. More, *Utopia*, 64.
13. More, *Utopia*, 128.

Even for the historical More, this seems a worthy prayer of reverence and respect for divinity, even if it reminds us that the Utopians themselves have not yet heard the revelation of God in Jesus Christ. It may be an obvious admittance of bias to see in the Utopia prayer the "if" that allows peace both in Erasmian ecumenism and in *As You Like It*, but it is a hypothesis that any Catholic might hope to discuss further with More in a better world than ours.

More as Catholic Apologist

For once, there can be no doubt about the Catholicism of someone who is a key figure in the development of Catholic Humanism. Even more than Erasmus' response to Luther on the will, More gives clear, reasoned opposition to the Protestant Reformation, first through his own lengthy response to Luther and then an even longer dialogue with William Tyndale, the Englishman so often later praised for the first vernacular translation into English of the Bible. More's "Response to Luther" comes in 1523 while "A Dialogue concerning Heresies," in 1529, specifically responds to Tyndale, whose written response causes More to write another polemic against him called, "The Confutation of Tyndale's Answer" in 1532.[14] By this time, More is "Lord Chancellor," an important political post in the pre-Protestant court of Henry VIII, and naturally concerned, as any government official would be, with the potential for Lutheranism to cause strife and division within England. There were numerous incidents of mass violence even in the 1520s, such as the German Peasants' War; from the very early days of the Reformation, Luther often found himself involved in conflict with those who wanted a more radical or immediate application of Protestant ideas. One could imagine More's opposition to Tyndale in these terms. Yet More's apologetic writings are the opposite of the political bureaucracy and legalese that one might expect.

The scholarly detail of More's apologetic writings is extraordinary, especially given that he worked full-time as a lawyer or in government, writing normally late into the night. Modern Catholics used to post-Vatican II ecumenical dialogue will likely find these writings by More a bit contentious, but we should also be impressed by their logic and rhetoric. More's apologetic writings are exceptionally clear and intelligent, giving modern readers a thorough overview of all the theological issues at stake in the Reformation. Real ecumenism, which seeks truth rather than compromise, requires the kind of specific knowledge that More provides. Perhaps even more important is the faith and spiritual depth that More brings to his

---

14. Monti, *The King's Good Servant*, 140–45.

argument. More's response to Luther is not impersonal, or purely intellectual, but full of the faith, spirituality, and conscience that one might expect from a future saint. More defends many theological truths of Catholicism with very detailed logic and biblical knowledge, but one passage may here suffice; whereas God, More argues,

> Wrote the old law first on stone, later on wood, yet always externally, He will write the new law inwardly by the finger of God on the book of the heart. Thus what lasted a very short time on harder material, He will cause to last forever on the most pliant material.... The tablets made of rock were broken immediately; those of wood lasted a long time; but what He has written on the heart will last indelibly.... On the heart, therefore, in the Church of Christ, there remains inscribed the true gospel of Christ which was written there before the books of all the evangelists.[15]

More here responds to Luther not only with the doctrinal point essential to counter Reformers' claims of *sola scriptura*—that the Church clearly exists, historically, before the Bible is compiled or even written down—but is also spiritual enough to understand that God's revelation is a gracious gift and holy reality known in our own souls (as Moses explained in Deut 30). It is this combination of doctrinal clarity and spiritual call that makes More's apologetic writing so compelling.

Also characteristic of the More we know from his other writings is the humor occasionally found even in his apologetic writings. Given the political and personal stakes involved in the Protestant Reformation for a man like More, even a bit of such humor is surprising, and indicative of how important such humor was to More's spirit. When Tyndale, for example, responded to the scripture vs. oral tradition issue by rhetorically asking, "Who taught the eagles to spy out their prey?," More appeals both to St. Augustine and Luther on the priority of the living apostolic church, but also to the humor and common sense of humble readers:

> But now ye see well good readers by this reason, that Saint Augustine in respect of these noble eagles that spy this prey without the means of the Church, was but a silly poor chicken. For he confessed plainly against such high eagle heretics, that himself had not known nor believed the gospel but by the Catholic Church. Howbeit it is no great marvel, since God is not so familiar with such simple chickens, as with his glorious eagles. But one thing is there that I cannot cease to marvel of, since God

---

15. More, *Response to Luther*, quoted in Monti, *The King's Good Servant*, 157.

inspireth Tyndale and such other eagles, and thereby maketh them spy this prey themselves, how could it hap that the goodly golden old eagle Martin Luther himself, in whose goodly golden nest this young eagle was hatched, lacked that inspiration?[16]

More refers, of course, to Luther himself admitting that the historical apostolic church historically preceded the proclamation of Christian scripture, but more important than this point here is More's tone. As Monti comments, a humorous "mock seriousness"[17] frequently appears in More's writing, showing his ability to laugh amidst situations of dire seriousness. Such laughter is only possible when accompanied by extreme confidence in God.

Perhaps the most moving apologetic work of More comes late in his life, largely written from imprisonment in the Tower of London during the dark time of Henry VIII's break with Rome. Pope Clement VII had proclaimed Henry VIII "defender of the faith" after the 1522 publication of *Assertio Septem Sacramentorum*, which defended the validity of the seven Roman Catholic sacraments against the claims of Luther. By the late 1520s, however, Henry's quite possibly demonic lust for power involved not merely the assertion of independence but also the gruesome execution and theft of land and property of any churchman who opposed him. This opposition and subsequent martyrdom is the most famous part of More's life, made still more known by films such as *A Man For All Seasons*,[18] but the apologetic writings that More composed in the Tower give us special insight into the soul capable of such courage.

The first, *A Dialogue of Comfort against Tribulation*, employs the familiar humanist literary form of a dialogue, in this case between an elderly man named Anthony and his nephew, Vincent, who is facing persecution from Turkish invaders. Probably an allegory intended first for his family as they helplessly watched More himself persecuted by his enemies, Monti describes this dialogue as "the most widely disseminated of More's Tower writings" and "a rich treasury of spiritual wisdom."[19] Two other works from this time, *A Treatise Upon the Passion* and *A Treatise to Receive the Blessed Body of our Lord*, return to the example of Christ and the nourishment of His eucharist to inspire the extraordinary spiritual will that sustains More during this time.

---

16. More, *Confutation of Tyndale's Answer*, 723, quoted in Monti, *The King's Good Servant*, 167.
17. Monti, *The King's Good Servant*, 167.
18. Zinnemann, *A Man for All Seasons*.
19. Monti, *The King's Good Servant*, 329.

Perhaps the most moving apologetic work of More, however, is his last, *On the Sadness of Christ* (*De Tristitia Christi*). In this extraordinary work, seemingly completed just a month before More's execution and known only through imperfect copies until the original Latin text was rediscovered in 1963,[20] More "takes us into the Garden of Gethsemane" and demonstrates, in Monti's words, "a serenity of spirit and controlled dramatic intensity"[21] that combines rhetorical eloquence with spiritual sapience of Christ's human and divine nature. In addition to its inspiring circumstances, though, what makes *De Tristitia Christi* a spiritual masterpiece is its rhetoric, which shows both the influence of the humanist influences upon More, and medieval approaches to biblical interpretation that were still common in More's time.

As a Catholic Humanist, it is unsurprising that More often uses dramatic writing to "takes us deep into the Garden of Gesthemane."[22] The rhetoric of More's narrative combines concrete physical detail with spiritual insight to seek some comprehension of Christ's suffering. Imprisoned and about to face execution, More perhaps sees his own human situation in the final trials of Christ:

> He knew that His ordeal was now imminent and just about to overtake Him: the treacherous betrayer, the bitter enemies, binding ropes, false accusations, slanders, blows, thorns, nails, the cross, and horrible tortures stretched out over many hours.[23]

Moving though this passage is, More's meditation on Gethsemane further considers doctrinal questions such as why the Lord allowed himself to endure tribulation. Arguing that this was a way to demonstrate his true humanity, More imagines Christ speaking to future followers:

> See, I am walking ahead of you along this fearful road. Take hold of the border of my garment and you will feel going out from it a power which will stay your heart's blood from issuing in vain.[24]

In these dramatic, moving passages, More is often employing, whether readers realize it or not, the common medieval form of biblical interpretation known as the "four-fold method." The kind of figurative language common in this method—which distinguishes literal, allegorical, moral, and anagogical

20. Monti, *The King's Good Servant*, 382–83, tells the story of Bullough's discovery.
21. Monti, *The King's Good Servant*, 383.
22. Monti, *The King's Good Servant*, 385.
23. More, *De Tristitia Christi*, quoted in Monti, *The King's Good Servant*, 385.
24. More, *De Tristitia Christi*, quoted in Monti, *The King's Good Servant*, 388.

(or eternal) meaning in any biblical passage—is often contrasted with classical rhetoric. However, as our next chapter shows, this approach is also found in the rhetoric of Erasmus, and the medieval method often seems to inspire the imagination of many sixteenth-century writers, including More.

In reflecting on the Garden of Gethsemane from his own dire circumstances in the Tower, for example, More clearly sees allegory when Christ's enemies arrive to arrest him, as "they carry smoking torches and dim lanterns," avoiding being "enlightened by the light of Him who enlightens every man that comes into this world."[25] Monti likens this "powerful passage" to the "poetic imagery of the Church Fathers," who often use allegory, but similar readings are often given today of Judas' kiss identifying Jesus.[26] More comments: "in just this way is He kissed by those priests who consecrate the most holy body of Christ."[27] Within this allegory, it is unsurprising that Peter is enraged and cuts off the ear of a Roman soldier, but More gives mainly a moral interpretation of Christ's response to this act. Commenting on Christ's words here to Peter, "Shall I not drink the cup which the Father has given Me?" More sees Christ teaching Peter the meaning of obedience.[28] Yet Christ not only uses this moment to teach morality, but also to show His ultimate, eternal power over the body, pain, and all of life and death. More writes:

> But now behold the most gentle heart of Christ, who did not think it enough to check Peter's strokes but also touches the severed ear of His persecutor and made it sound again, in order to give us an example of rendering good for evil.[29]

More never uses the terms allegorical, moral, or anagogical, and he might have called all his words a "spiritual" sense, as did many medieval theologians who sought to simplify the four-fold sense. Yet More uses close fidelity to the literal details of the biblical text to develop a figurative understanding of Gethsemane that is not fanciful, but rather of great spiritual relevance to any (i.e., every) human soul facing death.

The literary achievement of *On the Sadness of Christ* should not cause us to divide the man who wrote it, under such dire circumstances, from the humble, happy soul of the man whom More showed himself to be in most of his life. As late as 1532, just after resigning as Lord Chancellor once

---

25. More, *De Tristitia Christi*, quoted in Monti, *The King's Good Servant*, 396.
26. Monti, *The King's Good Servant*, 397.
27. More, *De Tristitia Christi*, quoted in Monti, *The King's Good Servant*, 397.
28. Monti, *The King's Good Servant*, 398.
29. More, *De Tristitia Christi*, quoted in Monti, *The King's Good Servant*, 398.

Henry VIII's evil course was set, More wrote to Erasmus hoping for the life of humane scholarship which the great Dutch Catholic Humanist had largely pursued:

> It has been my constant wish almost since boyhood, dearest Desiderius, that some day I might enjoy the opportunity which, to my happiness, you have always had, namely, of being relieved of all public duties and eventually being able to devote some time to God alone and myself; at long last this wish has come true, Erasmus, thanks to the goodness of the Supreme and Almighty God.[30]

More goes on, ironically, to thank his sovereign King for this opportunity, and to lament that the physical trials of old age are already upon him, but the more important point of the letter here is the late reminder that More had always envied the life of a scholar but chose to serve others. Especially, as the title of Monti's book reminds us, the Ultimate Other who is God.

More and Shakespeare

More's apologetic writings teach many other theological truths. To conclude, though, by returning to the questions raised by Chesterton at the start of this chapter, what is it that makes More such a uniquely important figure in our world? Too direct an answer to this question from a twenty-first century perspective would distract from my topic here, but somewhat surprisingly there are some significant sixteenth-century texts to also consider. The extraordinary 1590s play on which Shakespeare seems to have collaborated, *The Book of Sir Thomas More*, will be considered in detail in my next chapter, but here let us cite in full the sonnet that many scholars have thought to be a direct reference to More. In Sonnet 23, in the otherwise needless repetition of the line bolded, Shakespeare seems to clearly but subtly allude to More. Because the line comes at the end of a well unified poem, it is necessary to quote the sonnet in full:

> As an unperfect actor on the stage,
> Who with his fear is put besides his part,
> Or some fierce thing replete with too much rage,
> Whose strength's abundance weakens his own heart;
> So I for fear of trust forget to say
> The perfect ceremony of love's right,
> And in mine own love's strength seem to decay,

---

30. Quoted in Monti, *The King's Good Servant*, 308–9.

> O'ercharged with burden of mine own love's might:
> O let my books be then the eloquence,
> And dumb presagers of my speaking breast,
> Who plead for love, and look for recompense,
> More than that love which more hath more expressed.
> O learn to read what silent love hath writ,
> To hear with eyes belongs to love's fine wit.

Sonnet 23 may or may not signal Shakespeare's support for Roman Catholicism, as twenty-first century scholars regularly debate. What seems indisputable, though, if one accepts as allusion the sonnet's twelfth line, is reverence and respect for More. Read as a means to interpret this sonnet as a whole, Shakespeare seems to associate More with the Catholic Humanism of Erasmus, the vision of an imaginative literature that uses eloquent language to search for sustainable wisdom about both the world and human nature. The superb final couplet, especially, reminds us of the imaginative, transcendent wit gained by Bottom when he was in the spiritual world (*MSND*, 4.1.198–215), with its famously irreverent allusion to the biblical text lectured on by Colet and animated by Erasmus' Folly and St. Paul's letters to the Corinthians. We may remember More best for losing his head to Henry VIII, but it is surely the holy, often humorous wit inside More's head, a sapiential eloquence both wise and humble, that lives on to exert a vast and indispensable influence upon the Catholic Humanist literary tradition.

7

The Marriage of Wit and Wisdom

The Book of Sir Thomas More

M‍ore and Erasmus are separated, historically, by the lustful, power-crazed, and quite possibly demonic violence that sadly turns the initially noble idea of reforming the Church into an ongoing war whose borders re-form around ever shifting borders of politics, ego, and greed. One must still debate what the term "Reformation" really signifies. Does it mean correcting the practices of the church to make them more Christ-like, or is it a vain human attempt to re-form the church itself, created once for all eternity by Christ himself, a re-formation whose inevitable fruit is bloodshed and misery? This latter use of this term, whether naively liberal and Protestant or pejorative in the manner of pre-Vatican II Roman Catholicism, typically rejects any positive, lasting legacy to the work of Erasmus and More, seeing the former's books, especially, as merely more fuel for the bonfires that tragically engulf much of sixteenth-century European culture. Yet in addition to their vast literary and cultural legacy, Erasmus and More appear together again in "history," though in a very unlikely time and place: late Elizabethan English Drama. One can't quite say the two meet onstage, in the theatre, because of the apparent fact that the play-script in which both appear, *The Book of Sir Thomas More*, was apparently prevented by censors from ever being acted onstage.

    The play's text is now in the British Museum, preserved as a document of extraordinary historical interest. As one of the few original manuscripts that survives today from the Elizabethan era, the text is important for multiple reasons, but is perhaps best known because it includes one of the few surviving examples of what most scholars today accept to be Shakespeare's handwriting, in the speeches attributed to "Hand D." Authorship of the play is usually attributed to Anthony Munday, a public official and prolific playwright of the day whose fascinating character is, as I shall explain, hard to pin down, but the text is clearly an example of the collaboration between playwrights that scholars increasingly believe to be commonplace in the English theatre of the time. In addition to Munday and Shakespeare, the manuscript of *The Book of Sir Thomas More* also suggests the work of Henry Chettle, Thomas Dekker, and Thomas Heywood. Despite the clearly collaborative nature of the play, it has seemingly entered our contemporary Shakespearean canon. The first edition of Stanley Wells' and Gary Taylor's *Oxford Shakespeare* printed the parts of the play ascribed to "Hand D,"[1] while the second edition prints the entire play.[2] Modern theatre companies such as the RSC have had successful runs producing the play.[3] But apart from the play's current cultural status, perhaps the more essential intellectual question is historical: what possibly could have motivated all of these writers to pen a play that, as can be readily shown, is extremely sympathetic to More, the man who, in living memory, had so publicly opposed the authority of Elizabeth I's father, Henry VIII?

One obvious and recently popular answer to this key question is Catholicism, with Shakespeare's involvement in the project typically cited as further evidence of his connection to the "old Faith." As just noted, Shakespeare's Sonnet 23 had long been similarly cited for seeming to inscribe More's own name in the text. The great difficulty with this interpretation of *The Book of Sir Thomas More*, however, relates to the ambiguity of what is known historically of Munday's character. As noted even as late as Evelyn Waugh's twentieth-century biography of Edmund Campion,[4] the Jesuit missionary burned at the stake in England in 1581, Munday himself claimed to have taken a personal role in betraying Campion's disguise to the English authorities. Moreover, Munday published several tracts, such as *The Roman Lyfe* of 1582, in which he claimed to have spied on the English Jesuit college in Rome. Could Munday really be the author of *The Book of Thomas More*, and would Shakespeare really have collaborated with this infamous Protestant?

1. Munday and Chettle, "Sir Thomas More," 785–88.
2. Munday and Chettle, *The Book of Sir Thomas More* (2005), 873–908.
3. See John Jowett, Introduction to Munday and Chettle, *Sir Thomas More*.
4. Waugh, *Edmund Campion*.

Radically challenging the assumptions of these rhetorical questions is the work of Donna B. Hamilton, whose *Anthony Munday and the Catholics, 1560–1633* is one of the most detailed and scholarly works ever written on an early modern playwright.[5] Covering the whole of Munday's life and career, Hamilton rejects both popular and scholarly opinion to make the case that Munday was a kind of Roman Catholic that became more common in England after the 1589 failure of the Spanish Armada, as the long reign of Elizabeth I solidified the status and power of the English State church. Munday, Hamilton argues, was a "loyalist Catholic," one who continued to hold Catholic religious views, but made political loyalty to England and the monarch a professed part of his identity.[6] Such a Catholic might have opposed the Jesuit missions into England, and Hamilton concedes that it is "possible to conclude that, at this point," Munday "did turn fully against the Catholic community."[7]

Yet Hamilton also argues that, even in his outwardly anti-Catholic polemics, Munday gives a "ventriloquized Catholic polemic" while also keeping "his loyalist face intact."[8] In *The Roman Lyfe*, for example, Munday mocks Catholic relics, but also offers "what amounts to a guidebook for travelers"[9] interested in seeing these same relics; an example is the baptismal font where Constantine was christened, "a tradition that Protestants denied" because it helps to "locate the roots of Christianity in Rome."[10] Hamilton thus sees "rhetorical complexity" in the text, and a double meaning, applicable to Munday's past in Rome and his present identity "as a conformed and loyal Englishman, when the text further explains, "he that is in Rome . . . must live as he may, not as he will," for "favour comes by conformity, and death by obstinacy."[11] These words could be taken, Hamilton suggests, as a motto for English Loyalist Catholics.

Stronger support for Hamilton's claims of Munday's Catholicism comes from his fictional writing, which also falls into specific periods and focuses on particular genres. For the longest of such periods, from 1581–1619, Munday translated a large number of "Iberian Romances," old tales extant in Spanish or French. Though elements of Catholic culture were excised in

---

5. Hamilton, *Anthony Munday and the Catholics*.
6. Hamilton, *Anthony Munday and the Catholics*, xvi–xvii.
7. Hamilton, *Anthony Munday and the Catholics*, 41.
8. Hamilton, *Anthony Munday and the Catholics*, 42.
9. Hamilton, *Anthony Munday and the Catholics*, 49.
10. Hamilton, *Anthony Munday and the Catholics*, 49.
11. Hamilton, *Anthony Munday and the Catholics*, 49.

Munday's translation, Hamilton argues that the ideological purpose of such texts remained fairly clear:

> In reviving the romances of Spain and Portugal, Munday transferred into the English language narratives in which the Constantine of Catholic ideology provided one of the organizing principles. Whatever the neutralizing effect of Munday's excision of details of Catholic religious practice, those changes did not eliminate the plot elements that represent the normative as a world unified politically and religiously by way of Catholicism.[12]

In addition to his literary work translating romances, Munday becomes from 1590–1602 a prolific writer for the theatre, working with a number of companies and playwrights to author or coauthor a wide variety of plays. Again, a number of these plays suggest sympathy for Catholicism. For Hamilton, especially *The Book of Sir Thomas More* is a landmark for "contested issues" that "impinge on virtually all of the assumptions that underlie and guide study of early modern drama, including issues of authorship, date, censorship, sources, revision, and referentiality."[13] To focus primarily on the last of these, Hamilton supports David Bevington's view that the stance of Munday's More "appeals" beyond public Roman Catholics, of which there must remain very few alive late in Elizabeth's reign, "to all those who are troubled in their religious allegiances."[14] For Hamilton, Bevington's interpretation suggests the "social ecumenism" that historian Brad Gregory often finds in the early modern period,[15] but still "does not satisfy all the questions we have about how a work so sympathetic to Thomas More could have been attempted for the public stage."[16]

Closer study of *The Book of Sir Thomas More* itself confirms Hamilton's interpretation of this extraordinary play. A principle source of the most controversial scenes of the play, those showing More's later life, is *The life and death of Sir Thomas More* by Nicholas Harpsfield, whom Hamilton describes as "a major figure in Marian and Elizabethan Catholicism."[17] Not merely "biographical in nature," Harpsfield's *Life* is "a devotional work that tells the story of More as a martyr"[18]; for Munday to draw on it as a source "should leave no doubt about" his "attempt to put confrontational

---

12. Hamilton, *Anthony Munday and the Catholics*, 78.
13. Hamilton, *Anthony Munday and the Catholics*, 119.
14. Hamilton, *Anthony Munday and the Catholics*, 120.
15. Gregory, *The Unintended Reformation*, 129–79.
16. Hamilton, *Anthony Munday and the Catholics*, 120.
17. Hamilton, *Anthony Munday and the Catholics*, 122.
18. Hamilton, *Anthony Munday and the Catholics*, 122.

material on the stage."[19] The initial plot of the play, based upon Holinshed's *Chronicles*, recounts More's role, as Sheriff of London, in quelling the London riots against foreigners on the "Ill May Day" of 1517, which led to More's promotion to "Lord Chancellor" of England under Henry VIII.

In the play, More's rhetoric is praised after we see it in action, as we are told that "Not steel but eloquence hath wrought this good" (6.201–2). More begins, "Let me set up before your thoughts, good friends / One supposition," the notion that "'twere not error if I told you all / You were in arms against God" (6.101–2). More proceeds to argue that the rebels "rise 'gainst God" by "Rising 'gainst him that God himself installs," but More's further appeal is based upon the *ethos* of Christ's second great commandment, like unto the first, which asks us "to love our neighbour as ourselves" (Matt 22:39). In the most-quoted speech from this scene, the play's More concludes by arguing:

> Would you be pleased
> To find a nation of such barbarous temper,
> That, breaking out in hideous violence,
> Would not afford you an abode on earth,
> Whet their detested knives against your throats,
> Spurn you like dogs, and like as if that God
> Owed not nor made not you, nor that the claimants
> Were not all appropriate to your comforts,
> But chartered unto them, what would you think
> To be thus used? This is the strangers' case. (6.145–55)

Using techniques familiar from Renaissance rhetoric, this theatrical More is asking the mob to imagine how they might wish to be treated if they were refugees. As controversy over immigration has grown throughout the post 9/11 world, this speech has become one of the most quoted examples of the golden rule.

The speech also employs key elements of the Catholic Humanist rhetoric that we have traced. The key line is a clumsy, repetitive string of "conditional" similes central to that rhetoric; the play's More asks the mob to imagine the plight of immigrants "like as if that God / Owed made not you." The easy part in this line to understand is the familiar Catholic Humanist doctrine that the strangers too are "made" in the image of God, and thus deserve good treatment. Moderns are likely to misread "owed," here, however; the commonplace sense in Shakespeare's time is not "financial obligation" but rather commitment of relationship such as "own, possess, have."[20] In

---

19. Hamilton, *Anthony Munday and the Catholics*, 123.
20. Crystal and Crystal, *Shakespeare's Words*, 312.

other words, the strange immigrants are God's people as much as any citizen of London. Thus understood, the Catholic Humanism of the play's More is radical both metaphysically and politically.

Even apart from this main story, other elements of the play help us to understand More's Elizabethan and Jacobean cultural *persona*, such as his famous sense of humor. When we first meet More in the play, he is creating a "merry jest" (2.750) by employing a common thief, the aptly named "Lifter," to pick-pocket the self-righteous "Justice Suresby." After the joke, designed to teach Suresby some commonsensical awareness, the play's More returns the purse and concludes the scene by saying: "Fear nothing of More / Wisdom still [?] the door." The corrupt text's missing word would likely be "bars" or "guards" in a modern, edited text, for the entire play shows the unity between More's "wit and wisdom."

When players arrive to put on a play, More will have "none but" (9.65) one entitled, "The Marriage of Wit and Wisdom," a play in which More inserts himself in the role of "Good Counsel." A fictional Erasmus also makes a visit, prompting More to use humor based upon the Catholic Humanist love of disguise, or "counterfeit." More presents his servant, "Randall," as himself, in order to "see if great Erasmus can distinguish / Merit and Outward Ceremony" (8.40–41). Once Erasmus hears Randall's poor Latin, however, the truth is revealed. Erasmus praises More's humor as "best physic" against "melancholy," and More returns the praise, proclaiming that "Erasmus preacheth gospel against physic," deeming him, "My noble poet" (8.195–96). A humorous temperament, and love of comical wordplay, are certainly among the most oft-cited elements of More's historical *persona*.

The Catholic Humanist roots of More's rhetoric are further suggested by another scene that many scholars ascribe to Shakespeare, though its handwriting makes it less certain. At the start of scene eight, about the middle of the play, in soliloquy More begins by reflecting on the eternal reality of the human soul, before distinguishing fortune and providence through the theological distinction familiar to any educated person in Shakespeare's day:

> It is in heaven that I am thus and thus,
> And that which we profanely term our fortunes
> Is the provision of the power above,
> Fitted and shaped just to that strength of nature,
> Which we are born withal. Good God, good God,
> That I from such an humble bench of birth
> Should step as 'twere up to my country's head
> And give the law out there. (3.1–8)

In part this soliloquy might be attributed to Shakespeare because of Sonnet 23, which, as noted in the previous chapter, seems to allude directly to More. Given More's controversial status in Shakespeare's age, the likely allusion is probably not simply verbal wit. Midway through the soliloquy from *Sir Thomas More* just cited, its author has the actor pun on his own name: "More, the more thou hast / Either of honour, office, wealth, and calling" (3.1.14–15). Several other examples of the same pun also occur in the play, suggesting its historical commonplace. The scene 8 soliloquy thus reminds us that even as More's political fortunes unwound in historical time, his spiritual influence became "more," and lived on to guide future generations.

The most significant element of this influence, More's martyrdom, is portrayed in the last part of the play. More is shown imprisoned in the Tower of London, along with fellow martyr John Fisher, bidding farewell to his wife and daughters with faithful prayer, "God send us all his everlasting light" (16.126), but also maintaining his humour even upon the scaffold, saying he has come there for "a headless errand" (17.51). The play's More also suggests the Catholic Humanist mingling of art and life, noting how his "offense" makes him both "a state pleader" and a "stage player," one who must "act this last scene of my tragedy" (17.74–76). His final words in the play speak to many future audiences:

> Here More forsakes all mirth; good reason why:
> The fool of flesh must with her frail life die.
> No eye salute my trunk with a sad tear.
> Our birth to heaven should be thus: void of fear.
> (17.121–24)

The final scene of *the Book of Sir Thomas More* presents a noble, religious figure, and perhaps suggests the way towards the many eloquent and often wise spiritual aspects of the great plays of the second half of Shakespeare's career, especially the last plays.

Does the clearly Catholic content of *The Book of Sir Thomas More* confirm Hamilton's account of Munday's religious identity? I doubt very much if it is possible, at least for many Early Modern playwrights, to define authorial identity in anything close to as clear a form as that used to establish rhetorical relationships for clearly Anglican poets such as Spenser or Puritan poets such as Milton. If Hamilton is correct to see Munday as a Loyalist Catholic, then he clearly evaded detection in his own time; how can we then be sure, over four hundred years later, that we are able, to employ the fine phrase of Hamlet, another play much concerned with spying and surveillance, to "pluck out the heart of" Munday's "mystery" (*Ham.*, 3.2.369)? Perhaps the virtue in this "If," however, lies in the Catholic Humanism that the *Book of*

Sir Thomas More foregrounds. To further understand this play's "wit" and "wisdom," we must continue to look for the legacy of both More and Erasmus in the rhetorical theory and practice of Shakespeare's own day.

8

"When Words Do Well"

Reviving Renaissance Rhetoric

NOTHING SEPARATES US MORE from the sixteenth century, and its literature, than language itself. Bridging this distance surely requires revival of the noble discipline of philology, but the challenge is more than simply the historical change of linguistic meaning. As important as the annotations are of any critical edition of this literature, we cannot be satisfied with mere translation or paraphrase. However much we feel distant from and need to learn of the period's politics, philosophy, theology, or material conditions, literature is made from the reality of language. Thus fundamental, the language of any literature can be difficult to describe in its formal features, but how much more when the Catholic Humanism of the age insists that linguistics is closely tied to ethics, or *eloquentia* to *sapientia*? As is shown by the lives and language of Erasmus and More, Catholic Humanist rhetoric was never simply a formal method for developing linguistic skill, but rather a pedagogical program in which the form of words and its content, often ethical and theological, were understood to be connected.

Style is the "man," according to the proverb often suggested by the literature of Catholic Humanism, but in *As You Like It* style is also the woman, personified in the witty wisdom of Rosalind. On a more basic level even than gender, the play also asks us to consider, through foolish Phoebe, a still more fundamental question: how can words do well? Deceptively simple, this question suggests many of the most complex questions of any communication theory that attempts to demonstrate how language functions. To what extent is the meaning of words controlled by the intentions of the words' speaker, or author? To what extent is the effect of words determined by the interests or "interpretative horizons" of the audience? Or, rather, do words do well because of their intrinsic ability, apart from authorial intention or an audience's intention, to refer to the extra-textual world? What difference does it make if the words in question are spoken within an aesthetic text, such as the script of a play being performed in a theatre? Beyond the theatre, how can words contribute to the building of a healthy human society? Beyond human society, what role can words play in contributing to the reign of peace that shall accompany the city of God?

Historically, such questions have primarily been considered not by literary theory, but by the discipline of rhetoric, a highly developed theory of communication from Classical Greece to Renaissance Europe. Some contemporary literary theorists consign rhetoric, along with many traditional elements of philosophy, to a historical dustbin. At the same time, reaction against the extreme subjectivity of literary theory has caused others to focus upon "objective features" of language that can provide an objective basis for interpretation.[1] In part this was the impetus behind the structuralism of the mid-twentieth century, but Sausserian linguistics were largely co-opted by Derrida's post-structuralism, which clearly adopts a Nietzschean approach to the linguistic sign.[2] Other linguists, however, established the literary theory known as "stylistics."[3] Focusing upon grammar as it is studied by contemporary linguistics, stylistics stands in the tradition of "objective interpretation" outlined by E. D. Hirsch, whose distinction between "interpretation" and "evaluation" seems to me fundamental to literary criticism.[4] Stylistics can seem narrow, however, in comparison to the philology of the nineteenth century, and even more so compared to the theory of communication developed in earlier centuries as the discipline of rhetoric, which also included grammar and logic to comprise what medieval or Renaissance educators called the *trivium*.

Specialized linguistic study seems narrow, perhaps, because communication theory must be concerned not with language alone, but rather with language in its social environment. Thus the whole of social reality, indeed all of human reality, becomes an element of literary debate, as many of my opening questions suggest. Renaissance rhetoric itself is a theory of

---

1. See Barry, "Stylistics," in his *Beginning Theory*, 196–213.
2. Derrida, "Structure, Sign, and Play," 915–25.
3. Barry, "Stylistics," 196–213.
4. Hirsch, *The Aims of Interpretation*.

communication that did not spring out of thin air, nor did it exist only in the learned books that have survived into our age. Rather, it was primarily the product of the social, cultural, and religious movement that has been here described as Catholic Humanism. This movement, though gathering cultural force in the fourteenth to sixteenth centuries, goes back at least to Book Three of St. Augustine's *On Christian Doctrine*, which teaches that learning rhetorical techniques helps one to interpret and compose words that contribute to the *caritas* of the Kingdom of God.[5] Though Augustine intended his work primarily to teach biblical interpretation, its ideas influence secular medieval literature in many ways. Though Catholic Humanist education focuses upon classical and biblical rather than medieval texts, as a writing curriculum for Renaissance writers it similarly stresses the unity of eloquent wisdom.

It is necessary to clarify the nature of classical rhetoric in Shakespeare's age, and to explain how we can explore, today, Shakespeare's use of the art of rhetoric in his plays. It is important to appreciate, first, that classical rhetoric offered Renaissance educators, playwrights, and critics alike a very comprehensive approach to the art of communication, and that this approach influences both the internal world of plays themselves and the external interaction between a playwright and a play's audience. Thus, classical rhetoric offered a remarkably detailed system both for stylistic analysis and artistic expression. Finally, however, it is also essential to recognize that this system intended far more than what we generally mean today by "style." Rather, for Catholic Humanists, rhetoric was not merely a method to build intellectual knowledge, but a mode of language designed to inspire the human heart to virtuous action, or at least the "non-action" expressed in spiritual life by prayers for peace. For Catholic Humanists, there is an essential unity between eloquence and wisdom, as expressed in the commonplace Latin phrase, *sapientia et eloquentia*. For Catholic scholars such as Erasmus and More, the full meaning of words can only be found in the Word who is the Wisdom of God (John 1:1).

Despite, or rather *because* of the ethic of Catholic Humanism, the entire classical *trivium*—logic, rhetoric, and grammar—was foundational to the aesthetic forms created by countless Renaissance poets. Such poets built upon rather than rebelled against Medieval foundations, for as early as the twelfth-century rhetoric is one of seven liberal arts—the trivium along with the "quadrivium" of arithmetic, geometry, music, and astronomy. Moreover, rhetoric developed a strong presence in medieval culture through homiletic

---

5. Jeffrey, "Charity and Cupidity in Biblical Tradition," 55–74. This article also appears in Jeffrey's magisterial *Dictionary of Biblical Tradition in English Literature*.

theory, or the method and rationale for sermons. As in any age, practice often did not follow ideals, but medieval sermon theory does display the surviving influence of classical rhetorical theory in Catholic culture.[6] Some even claim connections between the rhetoric of homiletic theory and the popular biblical drama discussed in chapter 4 above,[7] though such connections are difficult to prove directly.

While rhetoric creates many historical connections to Christian culture, *how* to analyze rhetoric in Shakespearean drama remains a very complex matter. In my opinion, it is most essential to relate the rhetorical words of a play, which could be included under the broad category of what the *Poetics* means by "diction," to the broader categories that Aristotle finds common to most poetic compositions: plot, character, and thought (we would say, "theme"). Aristotle also stresses that drama typically conveys meaning through "spectacle" or performance, and this element of meaning also has important implications for dramatic art.[8] Appreciating the influence of classical rhetoric upon Renaissance dramatic art thus requires knowledge of both ancient authors and modern critics who have restored our understanding of this complex system of communication.

CATHOLIC HUMANIST RHETORIC AND THE FOUR MEDIEVAL SENSES OF SCRIPTURE

Through Erasmus and More, in their union of wit and wisdom, one can clearly see the direct connection between Catholic Humanism and the art of William Shakespeare. Yet a serious problem remains: how to apply the Renaissance union of *eloquentia* and *sapientia*, or all that this historical period means by "rhetoric," to the interpretation or performance of Shakespeare's plays today? Though it is easy to hear echoes of the Catholic Humanist education that Shakespeare likely received in the Elizabethan Grammar School, it remains unclear as to how one might apply this knowledge to further our understanding of any work of Shakespearean drama.

There is a real danger here of pedantry, which Shakespeare reminds us of through his mocking portrait in *Love's Labour's Lost* of the schoolmaster Holofernes, who demands "What is the figure? What is the figure?" (5.1.6); perhaps the page Moth speaks for Shakespeare when, in aside, he says that these rhetorically learned men "have been at a great feast of languages and stolen the scraps" (5.1.36–37). Classical rhetoric did offer a plethora of

---

6. See Caplan, "Classical Rhetoric and the Medieval Theory of Preaching."
7. See Owst, *Literature and Pulpit in Medieval England*.
8. On these categories, see chapter 6 of Aristotle's *Poetics*, 684–85.

terms to describe both *schemes*, or arrangements of words, and *tropes*, when figurative rather than literal meaning was suggested, but how can these terms be integrated within Shakespearean literary criticism? To put it in a way that faces the technological challenges of our day, how can we avoid mindless citation of linguistic form, such as can easily now be done with computers? How can stylistics become humane?

This is an especially significant problem for my study, as there has perhaps been no area of sixteenth-century history more affected by the bias against Catholicism than rhetoric, no area in which modern scholars have been as unaware of the historiographical error explained in chapter 2 above. This is perhaps unsurprising, for it is true that Erasmus and other Renaissance Humanists extolled the virtues of classical writers such as Cicero and Quintilian to an extent unknown amongst the medievals. Yet as shown in chapter 5 with Erasmus and Socrates, in large measure the classical rhetorician is "baptized" by the sixteenth-century thinker, and those aspects of rhetoric that can be utilized by Christian theology are stressed. The medieval hierarchy in which theology is the "queen of the sciences," therefore, is rarely forgotten, and often implicitly understood by the terms used to express rhetorical commonplaces. Rhetoric, very clearly, is an important aspect of the Catholic Humanist curriculum developed by Colet, Erasmus, and More.

The easiest way to see this is Erasmus' engagement with the Church Fathers. Throughout his writing career, Erasmus also published as an editor; of the editions he published, there are almost three times as many editions of the Church Fathers as Classical authors. This work began with Erasmus' completion of a nine volume edition of St. Jerome's writings, brought out in 1516 by Froben, Erasmus' primary publisher, to which Erasmus also contributed a *Life of Jerome*. Erasmus thus became very familiar with the infamous nightmare in which Jerome was rebuked by God for being more "Ciceronian" than "Christian," awaking with black-and-blue bruising and a renewed focus upon sacred scripture. Erasmus seems to have loved Jerome the most of any Church Father, and his biography stresses Jerome's love of languages, literature, and the need to translate scripture so that the "philosophy of Christ" (as Erasmus termed the theology to which he subscribed) could be shared with the average person. In all of these ways, Erasmus was anticipating objections to his own Greek New Testament and newly corrected editions of Jerome's Vulgate, but he was also showing that his classical learning could, as Jerome argued, be "made captive," subordinate to Christian theology.

Jerome's explanation of this concept, based upon an exegesis of chapter 11 of Deuteronomy, also found famous expression in St. Augustine, who thought that Christians should accept Egyptian "gold" and think that wherever a Christian finds truth, truth belongs to the Lord.[9] Augustine was often claimed and cited by Erasmus' Reformation opponents, Luther and Calvin, but Erasmus rejected their interpretation of Augustine's views on the will, and many other matters. St. Augustine was especially influential upon rhetoric, and medieval literature in general, because of the extended discussion of rhetoric in book three of his *On Christian Doctrine*, where rhetoric is an important tool of scriptural interpretation. In the preface to the edition of Augustine, published in 1529, Erasmus makes clear that he values the fundamental principle of Augustine's biblical hermeneutic, which argues that interpretation must serve the "reign of charity" or Kingdom of God. Not opposing love to truth, St. Augustine sees both as working together, as those who truly love God desire to know the true meaning of every word that comes from the mouth of God.

In addition to Jerome and Augustine, Erasmus goes on to edit many other Church Fathers, including Cyprian, Chrysostom, and Origen; especially affectionate towards the latter, Erasmus also writes a *Life of Origen*. His comments on Origen make especially clear his attitude to the "four senses of scripture" hermeneutic that one finds so often in medieval biblical theology.[10] Rather than distinguishing a literal from an allegorical, moral, or anagogic sense, Erasmus follows later medieval theologians like Aquinas in simplifying the medieval hermeneutic into a two-fold literal and spiritual sense. Lubac, the French Catholic scholar most responsible for the twentieth-century revival of both the study of the Church Fathers and medieval biblical exegesis, approvingly quotes Erasmus on Origen:

> This is the order that he [Origen] follows: He begins by explaining the history clearly and briefly, each time that the subject demands it. Then he stimulates his audience to discover the deepest meanings of the allegory. And immediately after that he deals with the moral aspects.[11]

This comment reflects Erasmus' respect for allegorical interpretation, and our own modern bias against simplistic allegory should not eliminate allegorical interpretation from biblical exegesis. Erasmus' comments show the emphasis on moral interpretation that is the most obvious element of Catholic Humanist rhetoric. Amongst most sixteenth-century rhetoricians and poets, whether Catholic or Protestant, a stress upon the ethical value

---

9. Augustine, *On Christian Doctrine*, 655.

10. See Lubac, *The Four Senses of Scripture*.

11. Quoted in Lubac, *The Four Senses of Scripture*, 145. Lubac is quoting from the preface of Erasmus' edition of Origen.

of literature retained the standards of what Erasmus calls "the philosophy of Christ," but this could be expressed in more general terms. Sidney, for example, interprets Aristotelian *mimesis* as meaning that literature shows "what should or should not be the case."[12] Because Christian morality is thought to be universally true, it could be expressed by either Classical or Christian sources. When Cicero appears in Shakespeare's *Julius Caesar*, he supports neither the republican rebellion of Brutus and Cassius nor the triumvirate of power formed by Antony, Lepidus, and Octavius. Shakespeare's Cicero, like the historical one, has higher, more objective moral standards, but in the play this could be precisely what costs him his life when he becomes one of the many senators whom the triumvirate "pricked" (4.1.1) or had executed.

The interior role of human conscience could explain why morality might have been included in the medieval "spiritual" sense, but medieval biblical hermeneutics also included *anagogy*, which typically concerned the "ultimate end" or eternal reality of any particular thing. That allegory, morality, and anagogy could be condensed into a single "spiritual sense," though, is apparent whenever the subject being described centrally involves the human soul. Interpretation, in this hermeneutic, converts meaning from the physical to the spiritual, where the soul must make ethical choices, and these choices in turn affect eternal states.

Thus the "spiritual" sense allowed multiple interpretive approaches, and diverse levels of meaning to be intended by any figurative expression. This freedom could be applied to any literary writing, but was especially applicable to Christian writers who taught according to something like the parabolic technique used by Christ himself. The range of parabolic meaning can seem limited in something like the Parable of the Sower, where the seed must be the Word of God and the various grounds seem to clearly correspond to the state of the human soul. However, the range of figurative meaning possible through parable can be suggested by famous stories like the Prodigal Son. Its father seems an obvious image for God, but what brings the son home, and why is his elder brother less than excited about the homecoming? Many other elements of the parables could be explored, of course, and the range of figurative expression possible in even this simple story helps to inspire a similarly broad "spiritual" sense in much Catholic and Christian literature. Writers of Shakespeare's day were giving such stories to a religious audience, regardless of whether one considers the theatre of the day part of a "secular" culture distinct from sacred ecclesiastical structures.

---

12. Sidney, *Defence*, 235.

This is not to claim that all "secular" literature has religious meaning, but only that rhetoric in Shakespeare's theatre participated in a complex discourse that typically mingled political, religious, and spiritual elements, within a culture typically far more interested in theology than our own. Within this culture, Catholic Humanist rhetoric typically employs all the complexity made possible by the linguistics of Classical rhetoric, but unites this to a Catholic Humanist conception of spiritual wisdom. It is usually some element of the "spiritual sense" that becomes the *sapientia* that must be mingled with *eloquentia* in Erasmian rhetoric, and it is this "marriage of wit and wisdom" that critics must witness to glimpse the range of rhetorical meaning expressed by great Renaissance drama such as *As You Like It*. The problem remains *how*, but for examples of those who have worked towards this ideal, we can turn to some of the major rhetorical critics of the past century.

A SHORT HISTORY OF RHETORICAL SHAKESPEAREAN CRITICISM

To even be able to read rhetorical criticism requires some education in the history of rhetorical literary criticism. A good author to begin with here is Cicero, called by Chaucer's Franklin the "lerned Marcus Tullius Schithero,"[13] known to every Renaissance Humanist as "Tully," and perhaps respected above all classical authors for his emphasis on the ethical purposes of eloquence. Cicero can introduce us to the five major parts of classical rhetoric; their Latin names, and English counterparts, are *inventio*, or invention, *dispositio*, or arrangement, *elocution*, or style, *memoria*, or memory, and *pronuntiatio*, and *actio*, the two aspects of delivery. Cicero explains further:

> All the activity and ability of an orator falls into five divisions.... He must first hit upon what to say; then manage and marshal his discoveries, not merely in ordinary fashion, but with a discriminating eye for the exact weight as it were of each argument; next go on to array them in the adornments of style; after that keep them guarded in his memory; and in the end deliver them with effect and charm.[14]

Both classical rhetorical manuals and new rhetorics by English writers became widely available in Tudor England, and a theory of composition based upon classical logic and rhetoric became central to the standard

---

13. Chaucer, "The Franklin's Prologue," in *The Canterbury Tales*, 178.
14. Cicero, *De Oratore*, 142–43.

grammar school education of the day. T. W. Baldwin outlines this curriculum, in great detail, in *Shakespeare's Small Latine & Lesse Greek*.[15] As Rosemond Tuve showed in *Elizabethan and Metaphysical Imagery*, poets made extensive use of rhetoric, and Renaissance critics "accepted without cavil" a clear parallel between the powers of the orator and those of the poet.[16] Yet such critics "are little preoccupied with [the poet's] feelings, greatly preoccupied with those he will evoke."[17] The most important critical question was not "did the poet feel it?" but, "will the reader feel it?"[18] As a possible "type" of the primary heroine of *As You Like It*, we should note that one of the ladies wooed in *Love's Labour's Lost*, Rosaline, expresses this idea clearly and especially applies it to comedy:

> A jest's prosperity lies in the ear
> Of him that hears it, never in the tongue
> Of him that makes it. (*LLL*, 5.2.845–49)

In our age it is essential to add that an important part of the enduring appeal of Shakespeare's art is that its portrayal of humanity, though often referenced through masculine pronouns like that used here by Rosaline, includes an enormous diversity of human beings, including major female as much as male characters. Shakespeare's "prima facia" feminism has been a major topic of debate among critics in our time,[19] but no one disputes the complexity and appeal of his many female characters, despite the obvious problems that afflict women of his time, not least, especially for Shakespeare's dramatic art, their general exclusion from onstage acting of these characters.

Tuve is herself a contemporary female scholar whose work teaches how to integrate rhetorical criticism with great Renaissance authors. Another very influential contemporary female scholar in this area is Sister Miriam Joseph, whose *Shakespeare's Use of the Arts of Language* demonstrates that Shakespeare excelled in applying the grammar school curriculum onstage, regularly using more than two hundred figures outlined by Renaissance rhetoricians.[20] Renaissance rhetorics like George Puttenham's *The Art of English Poesie* or Henry Peacham's *The Garden of Eloquence* divide all figures

---

15. Baldwin, *Shakespeare's Small Latine & Lesse Greek*.
16. Tuve, *Elizabethan and Metaphysical Imagery*, 182.
17. Tuve, *Elizabethan and Metaphysical Imagery*, 183.
18. Tuve, *Elizabethan and Metaphysical Imagery*, 183.
19. See Dusinberre, *Shakespeare and the Nature of Women*; Jardine, *Still Harping on Daughters*; Callaghan, *A Feminist Companion to Shakespeare*.
20. Is it a coincidence that the most thorough modern study of rhetoric is by a Catholic nun, or that Sr. Joseph dedicated her work to another nun, Sr. M. Madeleva?

of speech into *tropes*, in which language changes meaning, and *schemes*, in which the physical arrangement of words is altered. Yet their "concept of figures is so inclusive" that their work does include "an analysis of practically every aspect of grammar, logic, and rhetoric."[21]

The variety of the figures demonstrates the limitations of a rhetorical criticism based upon viewing them as stylistic ornaments. As Puttenham wrote, "a figure is ever used to a purpose, either of beautie or of efficacie."[22] To reflect this, Joseph reorganized the figures of Renaissance rhetoric into four categories, based on function. First, grammar, in its "aesthetic aspects" and then the three means of audience persuasion proposed by Aristotle's *Rhetoric*: *logos*, the appeal to reason, *pathos*, the appeal to the emotions, and *ethos*, the appeal based upon the ethical values of the speaker. Under grammar, Joseph showed that Tudor figures gave "beauty, emphasis, and strength to the thought and feeling" of Shakespeare's characters,[23] while even vices of grammar, which also had specific names, aided in the portrayal of comical fools such as Constable Dogberry. Very often, Shakespeare's characters do heed the advice of Tranio in *The Taming of the Shrew*, who tells his master Lucentio to "practice rhetoric in your common talk" (1.1.35).

Perhaps the most forceful statement of this claim in rhetorical criticism also comes from the mid-twentieth century when Brian Vickers, first in *Classical Rhetoric in English Poetry*, argued that, rather than regarding schemes as ornamental patterns "with no imaginative function, as a modern might, rhetoricians of ancient Greece, Rome, and Renaissance England all argued that figures have definite emotional and intellectual effects."[24] For Vickers, perhaps the supreme classical example of this kind of rhetorical literary criticism is Longimus' *On the Sublime*, which sees a connection between figures of speech, even schemes, and human emotional states. In the classical historian Xenophon, for example, "The words issue forth without connecting links and are poured out"; "Locking their shields," says Xenophon, "they thrust fought slew fell," and this is the origin, Vickers believes, of a scheme such as *asyndeton*, which omits all conjunctions. "In real life," Vickers argues, the "genesis of a rhetorical figure" occurs when one sees the "syntactical root," of an emotional state, and gives it "a name," thus allowing another writer to "re-create the emotional state" by using the same figure.[25]

---

21. Joseph, *Arts of Language*, 17–18.
22. Puttenham, *Art*, 202.
23. Joseph, *Arts of Language*, 89.
24. Vickers, "Shakespeare's Use of Rhetoric," 90.
25. Vickers, *Classical Rhetoric in English Poetry*, 103.

Vickers' theory often proves useful in Shakespearean literary criticism, as he himself went on to show in learned volumes on Shakespeare's prose.[26] A more recent approach to rhetoric in Shakespearean drama is Lynn Enterline's *Shakespeare's Schoolroom: Rhetoric, Discipline, Emotions*. Throughout her book, Enterline relies "on the axiom that rhetoric has two branches that continually interact: tropological (requiring formal, literary analysis) and transactional (requiring social and historical analysis)."[27] This approach allows rhetorical criticism to incorporate insights of New Historicist criticism, as I do with James Shapiro's book in the next chapter. However, perhaps the area of contemporary literary criticism most closely connected to the history of rhetorical criticism is performance criticism.

Performance criticism studies Shakespeare's plays as they are performed live, in front of theatre audiences or in front of cameras, as for tv or film. Performance criticism tempers the potential pedanticism of close linguistic analysis by another of rhetoric's traditional categories: delivery. In 1664, Richard Flecknoe, an English Catholic dramatist, tells us in his *Short Discourse of the English Stage* that Richard Burbage, a leading actor in Shakespeare's company, had "all the parts of an excellent Orator (animating his words with speaking, and Speech with Action."[28] Perhaps Flecknoe was recalling Burbage as Hamlet, advising the players visiting Elsinore to "Suit the Action to the Word, the Word to the Action" (*Ham.*, 3.2.17–18). Voice (known in Latin as *pronuntiatio*) and gesture (Latin, *actio*) were the two major aspects of delivery distinguished by both Classical and Renaissance rhetoricians. "All delivery," wrote Quintilian, is concerned with "voice and gesture, of which the one appeals to the eye and the other to the ear, the two senses by which all emotion reaches the soul."[29] References like this to the soul are an important part of why Catholic Humanists "baptized" classical philosophers such as Socrates and Quintilian.

Both *pronuntiatio* and *actio* are central to the just cited lines from Hamlet's famous advice to the players, and both concepts were also referenced when he initially warns them: "Speak the speech, I pray you, as I pronounc'd it to you—trippingly on the tongue;" and "Nor do not saw the air too much your hand thus, but use all gently" (3.2.1–5). Again, Shakespeare warns us of the dangers of applying to art a rigidly defined external system, and critics must base comment upon potential delivery of a particular dramatic line,

---

26. Vickers, *The Artistry of Shakespeare's Prose*.

27. Enterline, *Shakespeare's Schoolroom*, 157, notes that she borrows this formulation from Berger.

28. Flecknoe, *Discourse*, 2.

29. Quintilian, *Institutio Oratoria*, XI.iii.4.

understood through the context and conventions of a specific actor in a particular play. In this effort, the contemporary practice of "performance criticism" can be an important ally of rhetorical criticism, and remind us to test critical theory, ancient or modern, against performance practice within the theatre or, as contemporary technology often allows, within film or television versions of Shakespeare's plays.[30]

RHETORICAL CRITICISM IN THIS STUDY

My approach will thus trace Catholic Humanism in *As You Like It* through rhetorical literary criticism. Specifically, my study here names specific figures of English rhetoricians, then connects these figures both to the dramatic meeting of characters within the context of a particular scene, and to the traditions of Catholic Humanism that form the cultural background of the play. There are times when my study refers to Puttenham's *The Art of English Poesie*, and to modern rhetoricians like Sr. Miriam Joseph or Richard Lanham, but my preferred source is the 1593 edition of Henry Peacham's *The Garden of Eloquence*. Peacham's second edition, substantially revised from the first in 1577, is the most complete English rhetoric, and one that reflects late sixteenth-century linguistic changes and literary fashions. As William G. Crane argues in his Introduction to this text, by 1593 "the style of Lyly's *Euphues* had risen to immense popularity and had then begun to suffer a reaction," so that those interested in rhetoric were conscious both of its use and potential abuse.[31] There is also a link between Erasmus' work on rhetoric and Peacham's, though filtered through several intermediary English rhetoricians,[32] and Peacham can himself be considered a Christian Humanist. Ordained at the age of 28 in the Anglican church,[33] many of Peacham's examples in *The Garden of Eloquence* are biblical, though he also includes the classical sources characteristic of Catholic Humanism. Peacham's 1593 *Garden* is also the "only one" of the rhetorical manuals in which Sr. Joseph

---

30. The following study is informed by six performances of *As You Like It*: the 1936 film, directed by Paul Czinner; the 1978 BBC version, directed by Basil Coleman; a 1983 Stratford, Ontario theatre production, directed by John Hirsch; the 2006 film, directed by Kenneth Branagh, which reset the play in nineteenth-century Japan; 2009 film performance at London's new Globe theatre, directed by Thea Sharrock; finally, a 2016 performance at Stratford, Ontario, which reset the play in a contemporary East Coast Canadian setting, directed by Jillian Keiley.
31. Crane, Introduction to *The Garden of Eloquence*, 23.
32. Crane, Introduction to *The Garden of Eloquence*, 5–23.
33. Crane, Introduction to *The Garden of Eloquence*, 5.

found compelling verbal parallels that strongly suggest inter-textual awareness of Shakespeare's plays.[34]

As well, Peacham's rhetoric is the primary source of Willard Espy's *Garden of Eloquence*, to my mind the modern book that best captures the spirit and humor of Renaissance rhetoric.[35] My approach does not aim at anything close to a complete listing of all the figures of rhetoric employed by Shakespeare in *As You Like It*, but rather the serio-comic delight intended in the Catholic Humanist union of *eloquentia* and *sapientia*. To achieve this, I largely follow the reclassification of the figures made by Sr. Joseph, who distinguished figures of thought and grammatical schemes, but then listed the other figures according to their appeal to the central Aristotelian categories: *logos, ethos*, or *pathos*. One could translate these three terms as logic, ethics, and emotions, but such a translation barely begins to suggest the broader aims of each category: truth, character, and the beauty made possible by the most sublime feelings. Drama often considers the obverse of each aim, of course, and both literature and philosophy often illustrate the overlap of each aim as "transcendental,"[36] or different ways of knowing the reality of the one living God.

Joseph's reclassification is justified first not through philosophical theology but rather because her close study of primary Renaissance texts showed that "logic was clearly regarded as the most important factor in composition"; of the more than two hundred figures of speech defined by men like Peacham, a majority are "derived from the topics and forms of logic."[37] This emphasis is consistent with Catholic Humanism which, prompted by the preeminent meaning of *logos* at the start of John's Gospel, could see all appeal to reason as a road to the reality of truth. As we saw, however, in our study of texts such as Erasmus' *Praise of Folly* or More's *Utopia*, the Catholic Humanists eschewed formal logic in favor of humorous, often paradoxical appeals to truth, and it is this emphasis that dominates Shakespearean comedy. As seen most easily in Shakespeare's fools, often it is irrational foolishness that points towards the wisdom of truth, so dramatic context becomes essential to note.

Similarly, figures of *ethos*, which Joseph classifies as means of showing "courtesy, gratitude, commendation, forgiveness of injury,"[38] often point not

---

34. Joseph, *Arts of Language*, 44.

35. Espy was the subject of my first academic article; Maillet, "Theoretical Foundations," 41–52.

36. In short, the notion that the true, good, and beautiful are interdependent manifestations of the one living God.

37. Joseph, *Arts of Language*, 398.

38. Joseph, *Arts of Language*, 36.

to good character, but rather to foolishness. Figures of *pathos*, which Joseph classifies as showing "vehemence and affection,"[39] often reveal the foolishness of human emotions. In drama generally, appeals to *ethos* and *pathos* often indicate both the character and emotions of a speaker at the same time. In *As You Like It*, specifically, appeals to *ethos* or *pathos* are often ironic signs of foolishness rather than direct forms of wisdom. Practical criticism, such as part 2 of my study here, unlike linguistic theory, must proceed according to how speech is actually used in a literary text, rather than how speech might be used by an inspired orator. Joseph also notes the limits of her own categories, that her "reclassification makes no claim to apodictic exactitude," for "one figure may fit into any one number of classes, and some figures may not fit precisely into any one."[40]

My glossary thus does not attempt the complexity of Peacham's *Garden* with its many distinctions between kinds of "schemes," the physical arrangement of words, and tropes, figures of speech whose meaning extends beyond the literal. In the more practical kind of approach of my study here, necessitated by focus on a particular text by a specific writer, in this case Shakespeare's *As You Like It*, my glossary lists only those figures actually used to discuss this play. My glossary normally gives Peacham's definitions in his own words, with modernized spelling and occasional help from modern rhetoricians like Joseph, Lanham, or Espy, because sometimes there are important connections between Peacham's diction and the nature of the figures, such as the term "translation" in his definition of *metaphora*.

However, following Joseph, my glossary reclassifies the categories of Peacham's *Garden* to reflect my aim to understand this particular text, *As You Like It*. For example, my glossary begins with major "tropes of thought," which for the most part are terms that remain commonplace in literary criticism today, but this part of my glossary also includes the three different kinds of pun distinguished by Peacham. Insignificant though literary critics might find the pun, it is central to the thought and rhetoric of *As You Like It*. Even more important, though, is the *conditional* or *hypothetical syllogism*, which modern rhetorician Richard Lanham defines as a "hypothetical clause" composed of an "if" clause, "called the antecedent," and a "then" clause, called the consequent."[41] Sr. Joseph understandably treats this as a figure of *logos*, of logical argument, and Shakespeare's characters, especially the fool Touchstone, both use and abuse the intellectual purpose intended by this figure. However, as we shall see, the *conditional* or *hypothetical*

---

39. Joseph, *Arts of Language*, 36.
40. Joseph, *Arts of Language*, 39.
41. Lanham, *Handlist*, 58.

syllogism occurs in so many different dramatic moments within *As You Like It*, and is used for so many diverse purposes, that it becomes a central "figure of thought" for the entire play.

After the complex "figures of thought" familiar to modern critics, which often appeal to truth, ethics, and beauty at the same time, my glossary continues with figures that appeal to *logos*, *ethos* and *pathos* in *As You Like It*. Here I am considering the function of the figure; rhetorical questions, for example, are a means to *logos*, of pointing to a truth that everyone recognizes. Even the detailed description of style made possible by the schemes usually becomes relevant, in drama, through an emphasis of *ethos* or *pathos*, as my commentary usually notes. Such schemes are thus categorized in my glossary to prompt reflection on how their stylistic expression relates to character relations in drama. My glossary is thus not intended as any sort of guide to the complexity of a work such as Peacham's *Garden of Eloquence*, but rather a means to describe the rhetoric of one Shakespearean play, *As You Like It*.

Rhetorical criticism should not be dry or pedantic. Certainly it should never recall Holofernes shouting, "What's the figure? What's the figure?" (*LLL*, 5.1.180) whilst seemingly unaware of the romantic reality all around him, nor should it ever be "as dry as the remainder biscuit after a voyage" which Jaques will see in Touchstone's wit (2.7.38–39). Yet it is certainly true that the technical precision and Latinate construction of the figures often makes them sound archaic and outdated. Joseph is surely right that Renaissance rhetoricians such as Peacham appeal to all three of the major Aristotelian categories, and thus engage with the union of truth, action, and feeling which must cohere within any traditional conception of wisdom. Post-Enlightenment readers like ourselves, however, must remember that each of these three categories have relevance to the soul that, as my study has highlighted, is especially developed in Catholic Humanism.

Tuve also saw this clearly and similarly argued that rhetoric and poetry were so interlocked in the Renaissance mind because both had "the final aim of the communication of truth from one mind to another."[42] Perhaps the best guide to Shakespeare's aesthetics, as usual, are his own words. For the unity of beauty, virtue, and truth inherent in rhetoric, and the paradoxical power of this unity to allow incredible complexity, seems to be the main theme of Sonnet 55, a text where Shakespeare seems to be directly reflecting on his writing process; this sonnet concludes:

> "Fair, kind and true" is all my argument,
> "Fair, kind, and true" varying to other words;

---

42. Tuve, *Elizabethan and Metaphysical Imagery*, 282–83.

> And in this change is my invention spent,
> Three themes in one, which wondrous scope affords.
> "Fair, kind, and true," have often lived alone,
> Which three till now never kept seat in one.

Rhetorical figures cannot be "ornaments of style" because they were never created as such, but as means to communicate the most serious matters of the human mind. Shakespeare's echo here of the medieval transcendentals is not as well known, for example, as Keats' conclusion to "Ode on Grecian Urn," but it is arguably more coherent. Paradoxically, Shakespeare suggests this most directly through his comical fools, who—as we shall see through Touchstone—combine appeals to *logos*, *ethos*, and *pathos* all while making us laugh at the human condition. Thus the fool in *As You Like It* is first addressed by his central rhetorical function in the play when Celia sees Touchstone in the Forest of Arden and greets him, "How now, Wit; wither wander you?" (1.2.53). "Wit" might be the best summary word for wisdom in Shakespeare, though typically in Shakespearean comedy the wit of fools needs completion through the wisdom of comic heroines.

On some occasions, unsurprisingly, the "intra-textual" rhetoric of Shakespeare's plays also becomes "extra-textual" and appeals to the cultural contexts particular to Shakespeare's historical audience, contexts created in no small part by the long development of Catholic Humanist culture. A last historical glance at Shakespeare's relationship to this culture is given in the final chapter of part 1, which situates *As You Like It* in 1599, the year it was first performed.

9

Totus Mundus Agit Histrionem

As You Like It in 1599

Part I of this book has explored the meaning of Catholic Humanism since biblical times, but to what extent is this tradition relevant to *As You Like It* in 1599, in London? James Shapiro reminds us that *As You Like It* first appeared onstage as part of an extraordinary group of four plays that introduced the newly built Globe Theatre to the paying public.[1] In their order of performance in that extraordinary year: *Henry V, Julius Caesar, As You Like It* and *Hamlet*. While the latter is almost universally acknowledged as one of Shakespeare's most important plays, and a major creative breakthrough in the writer's career, Shapiro also strives to show the significance of the other three plays. For Shapiro, this significance is primarily topical, how these plays speak to the cultural concerns of London theatregoers at that moment in history, in London 1599.

Many of Shapiro's arguments, however, can be put in aesthetic terms to suggest how the plays of the Globe's initial year not only broke new creative ground, but also drew on Catholic Humanism. These plays, though unique in many ways, are in a tradition which, as part 1 of this book has shown, was crucial to the formation of English culture to this point in its history. *Hamlet* is the obvious breakthrough, but if *As You Like It* is not to be dismissed as silly summer fun, via the common bias against comedy, then

---

1. Shapiro, *A Year*.

the significance of its aesthetic should also be seen in relation to the other three plays of 1599. Rhetorical criticism like that suggested in my previous chapter can help us, provided that, as Catholic Humanist Rhetoric, we are able to see how the aesthetic form of the play and its language is united to *sapientia*, to wisdom, which speaks to more universal human concerns. Though *As You Like It* is not an overtly religious play that one might easily associate with Catholicism, its matter does reflect the traditions of Catholic Humanism in profound ways.

The dramatic art that Shakespeare develops in 1599 is often connected to the theological concerns of Catholic Humanism. To see this, it is helpful to begin with aesthetic and historical elements of English culture, circa 1599. Like most critics, Shapiro sees, in Hamlet's famous soliloquys and dramatic conversations with the play's Ghost, new creative forms by which Shakespeare depicts a character's inner life. The human mind and heart is also a major theme in *Henry V*. He is not only a great public king, one whose charisma leads to military and political victory, Henry V is also a nervous man who wanders his campsite the night before battle, arguing military ethics with his soldiers before concluding with his own long soliloquy (4.1.230–82). As already suggested, much of the interest of *Julius Caesar* lies in the complexity of its characters' inner lives. Though Brutus recommends to the conspirators a pleasant public face, inwardly Brutus is haunted by the ethics of the rebellion. The extraordinary 2.1 opens with Brutus wandering in the garden, and then shows him most unwilling, perhaps unable, to share his inner life either with his "honourable wife" (2.1.287) Portia, or with fellow conspirators such as Lucius or Ligarius. For her part, in *As You Like It* Rosalind seems at first to be a typical young woman falling in love with a handsome young man after seeing him in a wrestling match; her subsequent dialogues with Orlando, however, reveal a wise soul who has thought deeply and yet still smiles at the idea, and ideal, of marriage.

Each main character from the extraordinary plays of 1599 answers a question asked succinctly by Dympna Callaghan: "Do characters have souls?"[2] Hamlet reflects on his eternal soul even before first seeing the Ghost, trying to judge whether its call is from heaven or hell (1.4.21). Henry V angrily tells his men, after over-hearing them claim that the justice of any war falls only on a leader's head, "every subject's soul is his own" (4.1.177). Brutus speaks more of Rome than of his own soul right after the assassination, but in his subsequent arguments with Cassius perhaps we see the doubts that he has kept beneath his breast, particularly when Caesar appears to him in dreams (4.2.325; 5.5.18–19). Rosalind is too cheery to often

---

2. Callaghan, "Do Characters Have Souls?," 41–46.

speak directly of her own soul, but her eloquent language reveals a deep, compassionate heart.

In all of these examples, internal rhetoric is crucial, but each play also develops "external rhetoric" that defy conventions and redefine expectations for their audience. *Henry V* is not simply about a heroic English leader, but also a reflection upon how difficult it is to unify the diverse peoples of the British isles, of how the rag-tag army created by enforced "muster" requires spiritual unity and leadership if it is to have any chance of survival. *Julius Caesar* is clearly not simply a tragedy, given that Caesar dies midway through the play and is at most its third most important character; rather, instead *Caesar* might be seen as a history play whose main subject, like Shakespeare's other history plays, is England itself. The mixing of genre in *Hamlet* gives us Polonius' famous speech on the subject of "tragical-comical-historical-pastoral . . . scene individable or poem unlimited" (2.2.400–401); the play's radical experiment, however, might be within the genre of revenge tragedy. *As You Like It* is easily defined as a pastoral play, due to its rural sheep and shepherds, but it also includes many elements that stretch the conventions of comedy. As comedy, many of its elements advance past the plays of the 1590s, and look forward to the complex generic experiment that is *Twelfth Night*.

External rhetoric thus inspires aesthetic innovation in each play. *Henry V* opens with a Chorus who asks us to reflect specifically on what the new Globe, the "wooden O" (1.0.13), will allow its audience to see. *Julius Caesar* shows the power of external rhetoric to sway public crowds, as Antony overcomes the speech of Brutus, and a rhetorical contest is played out in the Globe's public crowd. *Hamlet* turns on the private rhetorical appeal of the Ghost, and the power of an aesthetic form, the play, to "catch the conscience of the king" (2.2.607). *As You Like It* is constructed around a series of rhetorical debates, within which is not only the romantic story of Rosalind and Orlando but also a political and religious story of battling brothers. In each play, Shakespeare's audience is reminded that the microcosm of the human soul is often mirrored by the public macrocosm of social and political conflict. Rhetoric is an important part of both worlds, as foreseen by Humanist educational curriculum, which explicitly hopes to produce civic leaders who could speak and act publicly while retaining inward virtue and sensitivity.

Other aspects of *As You Like It* also suggest its unique aesthetic creativity, and link to Catholic Humanism. Shapiro details how 1599 saw the departure from Shakespeare's acting company, the Lord Chamberlain's Men, of perhaps its most famous actor: the clown, Will Kempe. Popular especially for the extended "jigs" that audiences had come to expect would conclude both comic and tragic plays, Kempe was leaving for a cross-country tour that he recorded in print, after playing characters such as Bottom and Dogberry. These fools normally employed an "unconscious comedy" in which they were more humorous than the character intended or realized; the "malapropism," or misspoken word, was a primary tool of such comedy, along with antics that cause Dogberry, for example, of making clear to everyone, "I am an ass!" (*MA*, 4.2.74). With Kempe's departure, however, later fools in Shakespeare, such as Feste or Lear's Fool, are more intellectual creatures who often use logic and argument to make a comical point, as when Feste will "catechize" his Lady Olivia to expose false melancholy for her long dead brother (*TN*, 1.5.36–49)

Both kinds of fool could convey the Erasmian praise of foolish wisdom, for even Dogberry had the wisdom to catch villains while Bottom spent time in the fairy's spiritual world, but clearly the second kind of fool allowed Shakespeare to present a more developed figure of wisdom. One of the many fascinating things about *As You Like It* is that its clown, Touchstone, seems midway between the two conceptions. Probably played by the new fool, Robert Armin, Touchstone certainly has moments of the unconscious, roguish, sometimes bawdy humour of Kempe, however he also offers the wisdom that gives my book its title. From the viewpoint of Catholic Humanism, which both celebrates the importance of Armin-style foolish wisdom and acknowledges the possibility of foolish wisdom even in the Kemp-style fool, Touchstone is a "best of both worlds" blend who simultaneously entertains and instructs audiences throughout *As You Like It*.

Shapiro points out many other topical ways in which the comedy of *As You Like It* was relevant to 1599. He notes, for example, the 1599 publication of a book called *The Pilgrim's Progress*, a collection of love poems published under Shakespeare's name (even though only a few of the poems were his) by an unscrupulous publisher before the advent of copyright. What made it commercially attractive for the publisher to do this was Shakespeare's reputation as a poet of romantic love, established largely through the popularity of his early 1590s narrative poems "Venus and Adonis" and "The Rape of Lucrece." *The Pilgrim's Progress* also included the dueling love shepherd repartee of Christopher Marlowe and Sir Walter Raleigh, highly rhetorical pastoral love poetry that *As You Like It* at times mimics or even mocks. This play also seems to include a direct allusion to Marlowe's tragic death in a pub, "a great reckoning in a little room," (3.3.11–12), and surely it is Marlowe that is referenced when Phoebe, in an aside, speaks of "A dead shepherd" who taught her a line from Marlowe's "Hero and Leander" that she calls a "mighty saw": "Who ever loved that loved not at first sight?" (3.5.81–82).

To what extent does *As You Like It*, in the England of 1599, convey topical reference to Catholicism, as we learned was possible through the literary networks related to *The Book of Thomas More*? Very different but equally interesting answers to this question can be gleaned by contrasting the ideas of Shapiro with those of one of the most historically learned, albeit still highly controversial, studies of the relationship of Shakespeare to English Catholicism, Claire Asquith's *Shadowplay*. It is especially instructive to compare how these two writers treat two key aspects of the play's meaning: first, the play's relationship to its primary source, *Rosalynde*, a popular prose romance published by Thomas Lodge in 1590. Second, the topical significance of Rosalind herself, whose alleged extra-textual significance almost seems as important, for these two critics, as the extraordinary intra-textual role given this complex heroine in *As You Like It* itself.

For Shapiro, Lodge's *Rosalynde* is a dusty old text whose primary interest, for us today, lies in what it teaches about Shakespeare's artistic creativity in adapting a source for the stage. Shakespeare regularly does this in his career, but what Shapiro especially admires about Shakespeare's treatment of Lodge is the ability of *As You Like It* to convey the main points of Lodge's quite conventional romance, but to update it in a manner that allows compelling theatre. Shapiro admires, for example, how the Rosalind and Orlando relationship takes over center stage from the "old tale" of Sir Rowland and his three sons, allowing us to see a "natural" love affair in the midst of what is presented by Lodge, heavily under the influence of the euphuistic style of John Lyly, as the "most artificial" of tales.[3]

Asquith, by contrast, sees in Lodge's *Rosalynde* an example of the artistic resistance that Catholic writers could give to the ruling Anglican regime of Elizabethan England. Asquith reminds us that the "Ardennes," the French mountainous region where Thomas Lodge set *Rosalynde*, was the home of Catholic communities, such as Douai, Rheims, and Louvain, where Catholic exiles from England often took shelter. Asquith further reminds us that Lodge was himself a Catholic exile, who while abroad published a poem entitled, "Truth's Complaint over England," which seems to summarize the situation of, in Asquith's words, "all those who believed that Truth had been driven from England by the Reformation."[4] For Asquith, Lodge was "the embodiment of Catholic loyalty," a man who returned to his native country to treat victims of the plague after studying medicine at Avignon.[5] Asquith goes on to argue that "beneath the idyllic, jeweled pastoral" of Lodge's *Rosalynde* is "a story simply adapted to the situation of English dissidents," and

---

3. Shapiro, *A Year*, 207–11.
4. Asquith, *Shadowplay*, 138.
5. Asquith, *Shadowplay*, 138.

that "Shakespeare follows Lodge's plot so closely that in many ways *As You Like It* can be seen as a tribute to the exiled writer."[6]

Both Shapiro and Asquith stress the topical significance of the play being set in the English Forest of Arden, in Shakespeare's native Warwickshire region. For Shapiro, this setting reminds us of many of the struggles that Shakespeare likely endured by maintaining a home in Stratford-upon-Avon, where he eventually retired and died, while working most of his life in the city of London. Shapiro also stresses how *As You Like It* avoids becoming an idealistic pastoral fantasy by reminding us of difficult economic issues relevant in 1599, such as the "enclosure" of forests, the limiting of forest resources for the average rural person.[7] Asquith, however, reminds us that the family of Shakespeare's mother, Mary Arden, was a long established Catholic family in the Warwickshire region (Shapiro himself notes that the Ardens were a Catholic family implicated in at least one failed assassination attempt against Elizabeth I).[8] The tyrannical actions of Duke Frederick in the play, where he makes an "extent" upon the "house and lands" of anyone who opposes him (3.1.17), could have reminded English Catholics of Henry VIII's seizure of the monasteries after his break with Rome.

The incompatible topical perspectives of Shapiro and Asquith are even more striking in relation to Rosalind herself, the central heroine of the play. For Shapiro, Rosalind is an advance in dramatic representation comparable to the creation of Hamlet. Noting that she speaks about one-quarter of the plays' lines, Shapiro sees Rosalind as the full representation of the character of the same name whom Romeo loved, in Petrarchan style, before meeting Juliet.[9] Rosalind is also an underdeveloped heroine in perhaps the most rhetorical of Shakespeare's plays, *Love's Labour's Lost*, where her role is tragically stunted due to the stupidity of Berowne and the play's other male suitors. For Shapiro, the Rosalind of *As You Like It* is the fulfillment of these disappointed hopes, allowing us to see a real woman in the full glory of wit and wisdom that not only allows but actually creates the play's comic conclusion.[10]

It is central to the thesis of Asquith's *Shadowplay* that Shakespeare writes in "coded" language that allows him to distinguish between the historical country of England, which has fallen into the heresy of Anglicanism, and the land of all the faithful who would return to Roman Catholicism. Within this code, "Rosalynde" is the proper name of the latter, making *As*

6. Asquith, *Shadowplay*, 139.
7. Shapiro, *A Year*, 230–49.
8. Shapiro, *A Year*, 142.
9. Shapiro, *A Year*, 210, 214.
10. Shapiro, *A Year*, 214–16.

You Like It a successful attempt—begun earlier in *Romeo and Juliet* and *Love's Labour's Lost*—of a hero successfully learning to love the true faith.[11] Though seemingly not as compelling as Asquith's argument on Lodge, her view of Rosalind is part of the Catholic allegory that she sees in all of Shakespeare's work. In *As You Like It*, another key invented character is Jaques, whom Asquith sees as a representation of Shakespeare's friend and fellow playwright, Ben Jonson.[12] Jonson had converted to Catholicism, in the late 1590s, while serving time in prison for killing a man in a duel (it is an unsurprising fact of the times that one of Jonson's closest friends in prison was a Catholic priest). In *As You Like It*, however, Jaques is defeated in rhetorical duel by the art of Rosalind.

Shapiro also links Jaques to Ben Jonson, and to the kind of satirical comedy often contrasted to Shakespearean comedy.[13] As Benedick puts it at the end of *Much Ado about Nothing*, "man," as a species, without exception, "is a giddy thing" (5.4.106–7), something to laugh at even, perhaps especially, at the moment of triumph in marrying one's true love. Here Shapiro's topical argument tends towards the universal, and begins to suggest my own reasons for generally preferring a universal, Catholic interpretation of literary texts to any topical argument. Topical arguments are often difficult to disprove, or prove, because they are dependent upon very selective evidence. However, as I argued against Asquith in my earlier book on *King Lear*,[14] even if one acknowledges the probability of Shakespeare's Catholicism and the relevance of Catholic literary networks to literary interpretation in his day, it is not clear to me why the topical meaning of Shakespeare's art is more relevant than the universal meaning applicable to any time or place. Cannot Shakespeare's Catholic art, in other words, become catholic or, as Jonson puts it in his 1623 poetic tribute published in the First Folio, "not of an age" but "for all time"?[15]

There is no doubt that the historical work of critics such as Asquith, and Shapiro, have helped us today to consider a more accurate range of topical meaning in *As You Like It*, but I am also interested in the broader aesthetic and philosophical meaning that has allowed Shakespearean drama to speak to so many people of diverse cultures. Hence the appeal of rhetoric for exploring the grand literary exercise that is *As You Like It*. As part 2 of this book strives to show, the play combines *eloquentia* and *sapientia* in a

---

11. Asquith, *Shadowplay*, 139–41.
12. Asquith, *Shadowplay*, 142.
13. Shapiro, *A Year*, 216–20.
14. Maillet, *Learning to See*, xx.
15. Jonson, "To the Memory of my Beloved," 648–50.

witty plot that goes far beyond the "old tale" of Lodge. "Old tales" become increasingly important for Shakespeare, culminating in the most theological of his plays, the late romances, but even by 1599 he was perhaps turning towards traditional religious questions. *Hamlet* is the most well-known example of this, with much of the meaning of that complex play turning on whether its Ghost really is from purgatory (as the Ghost clearly claims in 1.5 of the play) or is a devil impersonating Hamlet Sr. in order to damn his son (as Hamlet himself explicitly asks at the end of 2.2 in that play). Though the imaginative situation was surely prompted by many source texts of Hamlet, few today doubt that the 1596 death of Shakespeare's only son, Hamnet, also affected his interest in the afterlife. Given that the topic of "purgatory" was one of the most divisive elements of the Reformation that throughout the sixteenth century divided the English nation, it is not controversial to see Shakespeare turning towards serious theological questions in 1599. But was *As You Like It* just a bit of silly summer fun to bring crowds into the Globe before the serious matter of *Hamlet*?

One's answer to this question reveals much about how one views comedy vs. tragedy. But perhaps also gender; in what sense, to wit, could the very eloquent Rosalind be compared to the now much more famous Prince Hamlet? To begin suggesting an answer, we can recall that Hamlet's most famous speech, the "To be nor not to be" soliloquy, may not so much be a speech about suicide, as it's often taken, but rather about whether he should "take arms" against Claudius, knowing it will almost certainly lead to his death. Why, then, should he live? Is death the end?

It is this more existential question that Rosalind can be seen as answering when she becomes the chief rhetorical opponent, in *As You Like It*, to Jaques. For his most famous speech, and the play's, uses the motto of the Globe itself, to begin: "All the world's a stage" (Latin, *Totus mundus agit histrionem*). A very traditional structure follows, distinguishing "seven ages" of man, but today we are perhaps struck by how each stage, from the "school-boy" to the "soldier," "justice," and "lean pantaloon," seems very specifically male. Though not definitely excluding women, as "man" is so often in English a general term for all humanity, the speech does not seem to fulfill the promise of its second line: "*All* the men *and* women merely players." This apparently universal claim could be applied to Shakespeare's acting company, which begs the question of whether it illegally might have included some female members in 1599, but Jaques' speech does not clearly become universal until the final, chilling lines:

> Last scene of all,
> that ends this strange, eventful history,

> Is second childishness, and mere oblivion
> Sans teeth, sans taste, sans eyes, sans everything. (2.7.163–66)

Death does seem the universal end of all humanity, and Jaques' French here gives no solace. We, and everyone else, will one day be without "creature comforts," and have to face death.

Will death be nothingness, "mere oblivion"? Why then *is* it worth living, especially through times of adversity? These are the unstated but very existential questions that Rosalind must face in the Forest of Arden, and her ability to do so, and Shakespeare's ability to simultaneously suppress and express their importance, is at the heart of the comedy of *As You Like It*. Perhaps even more important, though, is the closely related question: if we are going to live, how then shall we live? If we are to marry, how shall we court? If nations are to live in peace, how can they do so? As the "if" questions of the play grow in significance, the traditions of Catholic Humanism become monuments of universal wisdom which this play, *As You Like It*, not only refers to, but rather smiles towards, even laughs at, in rhetorical language that is both humorous and holy. Shapiro's final comment on the play is New York, American wit: "we are all players."[16] Perhaps, but as the rhetoric of Catholic Humanism further reminds us, "we are all persons."

---

16. Shapiro, *A Year*, 229.

PART II

As You Like It and the Rhetoric of Catholic Humanism

On first glance, *As You Like It* might seem to lack the "serious" qualities that would allow it to convey the timeless themes of Catholic Humanism. Yet in the very limitations of its primary genre, pastoral, and in its expert use of rhetorical language to explore dramatic conflicts, the peace of this play also endures. Perhaps no more accurate comment upon its value has been made than that from Mark Van Doren:

> As You Like It is so charming a comedy that in order to enjoy it we need not think about it at all. But if we do think about it we become aware of intellectual operations noiselessly and expertly performed. We see an idea anatomized until there is nothing left of it save its original mystery. We watch an attitude as it is taken completely apart and put completely together again. . . . For once in the world a proposition is approached from all of its sides, and from top to bottom.[1]

The "proposition" of *As You Like It* could be taken as the beauty of the pastoral, or some variant of the theme of court vs. country, or urban vs. rural, that is central to Renaissance pastoral literature. More fundamentally, however, one of the play's many "propositions"—for there are many important themes within it—is the far broader, less culturally conditioned claim that it is possible for men and women to overcome their profound differences, and to choose to live together in the state of matrimony.

---

1. Van Doren, *Shakespeare*, 127–28.

The contrast between masculine and feminine rhetoric is thus central in the play, yet the tone of this potential conflict is always confined within the play's comic, pastoral genre. Many critics find a quality of relaxation in it,[2] for this play is so gay, joyful, and given to theatrical artifice and illusion that reason hardly seems to matter in it, and one might rationally believe that the pedantic, comprehensive systems of logic, rhetoric, and grammar outlined by Renaissance Humanists would only weigh down our understanding of this light-hearted work. Yet *As You Like It* does possess qualities that make it extraordinarily amenable to rhetorical analysis. These qualities stem first from the play's genre; as the *Poetics libri septum* of Catholic Humanist author J. C. Scaliger argues in 1561, literature of the "pastoralia" genre contains:

> Arguments, rejoicings, amorous entreaty, love songs, monodies, vows, recitals of deeds, rustic celebrations, praises, oaristiae, wooings or disputes in praise of different girls.[3]

It can make a difference, as Scaliger himself implies, whether it is males or females engaged in these various rhetorical practices, and Shakespeare's play both makes comic capital of this difference and explores the timeless problem of conflict between the genders.

Like most of Shakespeare's plays, in addition to the "intra-textual" rhetoric within its self-contained literary universe, *As You Like It* also draws upon elements of "external" rhetoric, interacting with discourse known both to the playwright and his theatre audience. Initially, one must note that the plot of this play, like most comedies, is biblical: a fall from happiness, a subsequent struggle to overcome problems, and then a subsequent rise in which past conflicts are overcome. Act 1 thus initially stresses old conflicts, "old news" (1.1.94–95), and does so by offering archetypal examples of male conflict; a younger brother, Orlando, seeks a fair amount of the family inheritance from his older brother, Oliver. Meanwhile, another younger brother, Duke Frederick, has usurped the rule of his older brother, Duke Senior, banishing the elder to claim political power. If such machinations are not enough to evoke the age-old problem of egotistical male lust for power, Oliver completes the "old news" by arranging a wrestling match for Orlando in which he hopes that Charles the Wrestler will as likely "break his neck as his finger" (1.1.138).

Yet such physical conflicts are extremely rare in the play. Rather, the primary structural device of *As You Like It* involves pairs of characters coming

---

2. See Frye, *A Natural Perspective*; Barber, *Shakespeare's Festive Comedy*.
3. Scaliger, *Poetics libri septum*, 231.

together to engage in persuasive argument (whether amorous or political), witty dialogue, humorous scenes of railing, or set speeches of considerable linguistic complexity. In this "intra-textual" rhetoric, the characters of *As You Like It* "practice rhetoric" in their "common talk" (*TS*, 1.1.334), often using familiar concepts such as "invention" (2.5.44; 4.3.30, 35), "places" (2.7.40), even a "figure of rhetoric" (5.1.40)—all of the "matter" (2.1.68) required by "very good orators" (4.1.71). When Touchstone says, "we quarrel in print, by the book" (5.4.88), he refers not only to himself, who like most of Shakespeare's fools often uses "good set terms" (2.7.17) while "jesting in and at the sacred terms of rhetoric,"[4] but also to the play's pastoral lovers, shepherds, and even to so unlikely a verbal virtuoso as Charles the Wrestler.

Most, but not all, of these characters are derived from the primary literary source of the play, *Rosalynde*, a popular prose fiction that had been published in four editions by 1598. In its preface, Lodge tells the "Gentleman Readers" of his play, "If you like it, so; and yet I will be yours in duty, if you be mine in favor."[5] Shakespeare clearly adapts this line to title his play, and expands the audience to please a broader audience that could include females—regardless of how many women would actually see the play live in the theatre—and perhaps even to so broad an audience as that envisioned by Catholic Humanists. Because the theatre of Shakespeare's time is popular entertainment but also sometimes regulated by public officials, the documented history of this art is not clear enough for us to be sure of just how broad this audience is; it is possible, though perhaps unlikely, given how prominently female characters figure onstage, that women were entirely excluded from both the cast and audience of Renaissance playhouses. There is a strong possibility that *As You Like It* was the first play performed in the newly built Globe Theatre, in 1599, and the Globe's Latin sign, *Totus mundus agit histrionem*, is certainly alluded to directly within the play, in Jaques' famous "All the World's a Stage" speech.[6]

The play also seems to comment upon an element of external rhetoric that is created by a Renaissance gender reality, the practice of males playing female parts. *As You Like It* portrays a boy playing a girl disguised as a boy pretending to be a girl, an elaborate theatrical conceit in which internal rhetoric both seems to mock and transcend the external rhetoric required by the theatre's social circumstances. For while certainly indirect and unexpected, in that Shakespeare's theatre seems to advocate more for imaginative capacity than gender ambiguity, there is a connection here to

---

4. Baldwin, *Shakespeare's Small Latine & Lesse Greek*, 209.
5. Lodge, *Rosalynde*, xxvii.
6. Latham, *As You Like It*, lxxvi.

Catholic Humanist texts like Vives' *The Education of Christian Women*.[7] In its historical context, gender rhetoric in *As You Like It* is only partly critiquing the clearly flawed practices of Shakespeare's own culture; it is also, more radically, imitating the culture of the City of God, particularly the Catholic sacrament of matrimony, by portraying how it is possible for men and women to gain imaginative empathy for each other's gender reality.

Sociology and theology always seem external to the play, however, for as Van Doren says the "intellectual operations" of the play are "noiselessly performed."[8] We are hardly aware, for example, that Touchstone is a learned logician because we become distracted when he also reveals himself to be a lecherous man rhyming a young shepherdess, Audrey, with "bawdry" (3.3.86–87). Similarly, the play's central heroine, Rosalind, is not only a brilliant orator who can outwit any challenger, but also a young woman whose unfathomably deep (cf. 4.1.196) love for her beloved, Orlando, can leave her with "not a word" to say (1.3.2). Her cousin Celia's later line, "It is as easy to count atomies as to resolve the propositions of a lover" (3.2.227–28) can be taken as a warning to the critic. As Hymen the classical god of marriage says at play's end, "reason wonder may diminish" (5.4.137), but both the broader purposes of language and its technical operation must be noticed if we are to enjoy the wondrous experience that *As You Like It* provides.

---

7. The earliest English edition of this Catholic Humanist text was translated by a member of More's household, Richard Hyrde: Vives, *A Very Fruitful and Pleasant Book*.

8. Van Doren, *Shakespeare*, 128.

1

"The Old News"

Brotherly Conflict and Masculine Rhetoric

THE PLAY'S OPENING WORDS, "As I remember, Adam" (1.1.1) come as close to overtly alluding to the biblical fall as is possible within secular drama. Orlando, the play's lead male actor, opens the play with an impassioned but awkward, prosaic, rhetorically unskilled account of his condition to an old servant of his now dead father. Orlando begins:

> As I remember, Adam, it was upon this fashion bequeathed me by will but poor a thousand crowns, and, as thou sayest, charged my brother on his blessing to breed me well—and there begins my sadness. (1.1.1–4)

As a formal piece of external rhetoric, one could describe Orlando's opening speech as a "prologue." In her closing speech, Rosalind, whom Orlando will learn to love, does begin her final "epilogue," clearly spoken directly to the audience, by telling us that "It is not the fashion to see the lady the epilogue; but it is no more unhandsome than to see the lord the prologue" (5.4.197–99). It is often Shakespeare's "fashion" to open plays with an apparently casual conversation, often between less important characters than the play's "lord," conversations that yet become significant because they often function as a *synecdoche*,[1] or part suggesting the whole, to introduce central themes of the play. Yet Orlando's speech is a more formal prologue

---

1. Peacham, *Garden*, 17.

in the sense given by Aristotle's *Rhetoric*, which tells us that "the prologues of drama" give the audience "a foretaste of the theme," thereby keeping an audience's "mind in suspense" and giving them "a grasp of the beginning" so that they can "hold fast to it and follow the argument."[2] Orlando is clearly angry, believes himself cheated of his inheritance by his older brother Oliver, and is ready to take action to regain what is rightfully his. As external rhetoric, the speech also allows Shakespeare to tell his audience of a general intention to follow the plot of Lodge's *Rosalynde*, a text with which they are likely familiar.

Yet as internal rhetoric, the first thing one notices about Orlando's opening speech is how linguistically unskilled it is. We could ascribe the awkwardness here to Orlando's emotion, and there are critics who commend this opening speech's "convincingly natural manner," for its "curious syntax" may be meant "to reinforce the impression of a conversation of which the audience only overhears the end."[3] Thus the opening speech perhaps omits direct reference to Orlando's father—though some modern editors supply the implied subject "father" for the verbs "bequeathed" and "charged" in the opening line—because to do so would be too painful emotionally. One could argue that the entire opening speech is *anamnesis*, which Peacham calls a figure of emotion and defines as a "calling to remembrance matters past . . . sometimes matters of sorrow."[4] The speech does include some skillful *antithesis*,[5] comparing his brother's upbringing to his own, and closes with *erotema*[6]: "call you that keeping for a gentleman of my birth, that differs not from the stalling of an ox?" (1.1.11–13). As Peacham reminds us, *erotema*, commonly today called a "rhetorical question," is not really a question but rather is a figure of argument, "by which the Orator doth affirme or deny something strongly."[7] As a whole, Orlando's opening speech can be read as the first salvo of the opening scene's masculine rhetoric. I am wronged, Orlando screams, and justice must be done, now!

The rest of the play also suggests another interpretation, the common masculine problem of egotistical self-centeredness. For Orlando's opening speech rambles on for no less than twenty-three lines. Unlike most of the subsequent "pairs" whose debates will define the rhetoric of the play, here Adam is not allowed a single word. There is no debate, reflection, advice

---

2. Aristotle, *Rhetoric*, translated by Roberts, 201–2.
3. Latham, *As You Like It*, 3.
4. Peacham, *Garden*, 35.
5. Peacham, *Garden*, 160.
6. Peacham, *Garden*, 106.
7. Peacham, *Garden*, 106.

shared between the two; instead, the entire speech is the outpouring of Orlando's emotion. Although "naturalistic speech," and "overheard conversation" is a common way for Shakespeare to begin plays, Orlando's opening lines cannot be taken as a sign of psychological or spiritual health. Although wronged, Orlando stands as one in need of education, which will be provided, in the primary action of the play, by Rosalind, the feminine hero of the play.

From the point of view of Catholic Humanism, Orlando's opening lines, "As I remember, Adam," can also be understand as the trope, *ironia*.[8] For clearly Orlando does not remember the doctrine of the human fall, nor wish to be advised in any way by this old man, Adam, who might have some wisdom to offer to understand this condition. In further *allegoria*[9] on these lines, one could also say that Orlando is dominated by the "old Adam" within him, St. Paul's term for the fallen human nature within all men (1 Cor 15:22). Shapiro notes the old legend that Shakespeare might have played Adam, commonly taking "old man" roles in his own plays, and certainly this could add another layer of extra-textual *ironia*.[10] Yet the "Adam" character introduced in this scene will have no substantive role in the play. After ceding the stage to Orlando's brother, Oliver, and briefly trying to reconcile them through the spiritual virtues most essential to Shakespearean comedy—"Sweet masters, be patient," he advises them, "For your father's remembrance, be at accord," (1.1.59–60)—Adam's final words in the scene are bitter, and, again, suggest biblical allegory. "Is 'old dog' my reward?" (1.1.78) he asks, in his own bitter *erotema*[11] after Oliver demeans him by this dehumanizing term. Catholic Humanist readers will recall St. Paul's bitter promise, "the wages of sin is death" (Rom 6:23), and remember Adam as a good man who did good service to the father of Orlando and Oliver.

Such a reading might seem too dark to open a comedy, but in fact Oliver does shortly seek Orlando's death, so the opening *allegoria* remembering Adam does seem to progress to the next story in Genesis, the account of sin's tragic consequence in the world as Cain murders his brother Abel. Yet the play also directly alludes to another biblical story in which there is conflict between a rich older brother and a destitute younger brother, Jesus' parable of the Prodigal Son. In another *erotema*,[12] Orlando asks Oliver: "Shall I keep your hogs, and eat husks with them? what prodigal portion have

---

8. Peacham, *Garden*, 35.
9. Peacham, *Garden*, 25.
10. Shapiro, *A Year*, 220–21.
11. Peacham, *Garden*, 10.
12. Peacham, *Garden*, 106.

I spent, that I should come to such penury?" (1.1.35–37). Both Orlando and the Prodigal Son of the parable are younger sons who have received an inheritance from their fathers, both have a jealous, spiteful older brother, and each of these young men "came to himself" (Luke 15:17) after rhetorical questions that compare their currently impoverished state to the wealth that could be enjoyed if they had received their inheritance. There are many differences, of course, but the similarities are certainly enough, for an audience educated in the literary modes of Catholic Humanism, to wonder if the "spiritual sense" might suggest, as the Prodigal Son is saved by the love of his father, that Orlando could also be saved by love? Although this is the love of a woman he has not yet met, could this love also be a reflection, as in Christ's parable, of the love of God?

Whatever the religious significance of this confrontation, there is also a clearly "naturalistic" element to this opening scene within *As You Like It*, for one brother might in anger murder the other. Yet the potential physical violence is replaced, in the action of the play, by rhetorical conflict in which words become weapons of aggression for use between onstage antagonists. When Oliver appears, we see the first of many examples in the play of an interesting pattern, as Orlando tells Adam: "Go apart Adam, and thou shalt hear how he will shake me up" (1.1.25–26). Orlando is foregrounding the rhetorical nature of the dialogue that follows, designating Adam, and by extension those present within a theatre, as audience of the coming rhetorical exchange. By using the *catechresis*,[13] or implied metaphor,[14] of "shake me up," which can mean both "abuse me violently" and "rouse up an animal to activity,"[15] Orlando is aptly warning this audience of the nature of the dialogue about to take place. Rather than an animal, however, Catholic Humanists would point out that it is the innate, natural eloquence of Orlando, his human capacity for language, that will allow him to repel the aggression of his brother.

Oliver's attack begins with *pysma*,[16] a form of *erotema*,[17] in which an orator uses "many questions in one place" to make his speech become "sharp and vehement," but Peacham notes the aggressive purposes of this figure: to confute, "to provoke," or "to insult."[18] Orlando defends himself,

---

13. Peacham, *Garden*, 16.
14. Peacham, *Garden*, 16.
15. Trautvetter suggests these meanings in her *As You Like It*, 11.
16. Peacham, *Garden*, 106–7.
17. Peacham, *Garden*, 106.
18. Peacham *Garden*, 106–7.

however, through *asteismus*,[19] a figure in which an orator turns "to another sense"[20] the intended meaning of the initial speaker:

> Oli. Now Sir, what make you here?
> Orl. Nothing: I am not taught to make any thing.
> Oli. What mar you then sir?
> Orl. Marry sir, I am helping you to mar that which God made,
> a poor unworthy brother of yours with idlenesse. (1.1.32–37)

Orlando thus begins with the standard Catholic Humanist defense of the dignity of man, the dignity due to any creature created by God. Despite his own lack of formal education, Orlando has no trouble using tropes that do not reflect "rustic simplicity"; rather, Orlando's honesty and eloquence make him appear the more learned of these brothers.

Oliver denigrates Orlando's intellect, however, through more *pysma*, cast in the form of *symploce*,[21] a scheme of repetition in which successive clauses "have the same beginning and ending":[22] "Know you where you are sir? . . . Know you before whom sir?" (1.1.38, 40). The impersonal "sir" here might imply respect, but is more likely *sarcasmus*,[23] as becomes clear when Oliver also soon calls Orlando "boy" and "villain" (1.1.49, 52). Oliver's rhetoric backfires, however, as Orlando clarifies and restates his own identity. Responding directly to Oliver's denigrating language, Orlando affirms: "Ay, better than him I am before knows me: I know you are my elder brother, and in the gentle condition of my blood you should so know me" (1.1.41–42). Orlando then argues against the tyranny of primogeniture (1.1.43–48); when Oliver responds by assaulting him, Orlando reverses Oliver's appeal to the authority of age, saying, "Come, come elder brother you are too young in this" (1.1.50–51). Orlando then clearly asserts his own identity: "I am no villain: I am the youngest son of Sir Rowland de Boys, he was my father, and he is thrice a villain that says such a father begot villains" (1.1.53–54).

There is considerable rhetorical skill in Orlando's reply, though one hesitates to formally enumerate its figures because here Orlando illustrates two of the central pillars of the Catholic Humanist educational program: the innate character of human intelligence, and the "natural" human capacity for eloquence. Orlando clearly has "natural" intelligence, or the good sense given first by God before it can be developed by education, for though

---

19. Peacham, *Garden*, 34.
20. Peacham, *Garden*, 34.
21. Peacham, *Garden*, 43.
22. Peacham, *Garden*, 43.
23. Peacham, *Garden*, 37.

unschooled he accurately perceives the injustice of his circumstances and effectively demands its remedy. Further, the language of Orlando is not only effective argument but, in the general manner outlined by Brian Vickers in *Classical Rhetoric in English Poetry*,[24] utilizes schemes and tropes that allow him to express "natural" emotion or emphasis.

A latent irony within the play, however, results from what may well be a "common sense" opposition to this "natural" Catholic Humanist doctrine that results directly from human experience. The word "natural" in Shakespeare's age commonly denotes mental incapacity, perhaps because a high number of infants born in an age without developed prenatal care are likely to be born "naturally," with mental as well as physical handicaps. Shakespeare perhaps plays on this irony with his "unconscious" fools, characters who employ "malapropisms," or incorrect diction, which often sound humorous.[25] Yet the wit of such Fools also offers uncommon insights, and often such a character can be described by the term the mad Lear applies to himself, a "natural fool of fortune" (*Lr.*, 4.5.187). Nature vs. Fortune is an important, and often consciously articulated argument within *As You Like It*,[26] while the role of "unconscious," perhaps even mentally-incompetent jester is brilliantly played by Touchstone, who often is funnier than he himself appears to realize. Much more seriously, Orlando's "natural" eloquence, although dismissed by Oliver as unlearned foolishness, demands a hearing through its articulate, humane call for justice.

Oliver, by contrast, calls instead for one to appear who can eliminate, through violence, this new threat to his title and position. Charles the Wrestler appears to have the strength to murder any man in hand to hand combat, but his tongue also suggests a man strengthened by rhetorical weapons. The "unnatural" irony here—that a man devoted to physical violence nevertheless possesses verbal wit and skill—reminds us that we are in a play, a pastoral comedy, in which the audience must, in the apt phrase of one of Shakespeare's early comedies, "entertain the offered fallacy" (*Com.*, 2.2.189). Yet there is a naturalistic element here also; for Shakespeare's rhetorically educated audience, a battle with words is almost as welcome as the physical brawling that appeals to human nature in any age.

Charles is "here to speak" (1.1.86), and Oliver immediately greets him with an invitation to political rhetoric: "Good Monsieur Charles—what's the new news at the new court?" (1.1.92). There are schemes here such as

24. Vickers, *Classical Rhetoric in English Poetry*, 103.

25. See Bottom in *A Midsummer Night's Dream* and Dogberry in *Much Ado about Nothing*.

26. See Shaw, "Fortune and Nature in *As You Like It*," 45–50; Hart, *Dramatic Structure in Shakespeare's Romantic Comedies*.

paragmenon, repetition through minimal variance of the same word, but Charles the Wrestler responds with eloquence that belies stereotype: "There's no news at the Court Sir, but the old news: that is, the old Duke is banished by his younger brother the new Duke" (1.1.93–95). Here is *antimetabole*[27] the a-b-b-a structure which is common throughout Shakespeare's work,[28] and which resembles the *chiasmos* in Hebrew poetry,[29] to artfully tell the audience of the key motif within the play: the "old" story of brotherly conflict. Turning Charles' attention upon his own brotherly conflict, Oliver further tells the wrestler that Orlando is a grave threat to his life:

> if thou dost him any slight disgrace, or if he do not mightily grace himself on thee, he will practice against thee by poison, entrap thee by some treacherous device, and never leave thee till he hath ta'en thy life by some indirect means or other (1.1.139–42).

However unlikely the threat of Orlando might seem, however hyperbolic Oliver's claims might sound to the audience, they seem to succeed in persuading the wrestler that his life is in danger. Charles responds with his own hypothetical promise to end Orlando's life: "If he come tomorrow, I'll give him his payment. If ever he go alone again, I'll never wrestle for prize more (1.1.149–51).

Charles' threats are a good example of a common pattern in *As You Like It*: the use of formal techniques of rhetorical argument in casual, colloquial speech. For clearly there is an element of typical bluster in the wrestler's threats, yet they could also be classified, by learned Renaissance rhetoricians, as *hypothetical syllogisms*. The *hypothetical syllogism*, or *conditional*, according to Sr. Miriam Joseph, is an argument preceded by "*if, unless*, or an adverb of time, such as *when*," and "is valid if the minor premise either affirms the antecedent or denies the consequent of the major premise."[30] Charles' *hypothetical syllogism* is entirely valid, in his own mind, because he thinks there is no possibility that Orlando will walk away from their meeting; he thinks, in other words, "either Orlando will be permanently crippled, or die, or I will never fight again." Logicians and rhetoricians often "paraphrase" syllogisms to clarify propositions, but notice also the ambiguities present in Charles' promise: will he not fight again due to his own injuries, or due to dishonor, after losing to so inexperienced a challenger? Such questions may not occur to his own mind, but they could to

---

27. Peacham, *Garden*, 164.
28. Compare Hamlet's "suit the action to the word, the word to the action" (3.2.17–18).
29. Made familiar to English readers today through Robert Alter's *The Art of Biblical Poetry*.
30. Joseph, *Arts of Language*, 361.

the audience; moreover, given the subsequent meeting with Rosalind, could Charles' words be taken as an unwitting prophecy of love, even marriage, which alludes to the familiar biblical idea that "it is not good" for man "to be alone" (Gen 2:18)?

Logical sophistication or biblical allusion might seem odd coming from so unlearned a source, but the *hypothetical syllogism* is central to the themes of *As You Like It*. Arguably even the play's title itself is a compressed *conditional*, if "as" is taken to be an adverb of time, and certainly the figure is used throughout the play, as many critics notice.[31] Renaissance rhetoricians further distinguished many different forms of the *hypothetical syllogism*, and would also describe Charles' repetition of "if" as the first word in successive clauses, *epanaphora*,[32] mirroring the "if" repeated by Oliver's claims of the supposed threat to the wrestler's life. The use of "if" here is clearly contrary to Touchstone's later maxim, central to my study here, that "If is the only peacemaker; much virtue in if" (5.4.100). For Oliver and Charles, "if" is a pledge to be ruthlessly violent, if and when such violence is needed. Their use of "if" does not "disprove" Touchstone's claim that "if" can bring peace, but it does show that the wisdom of this maxim, as with any proverb, depends on the moral character of the speaker for its meaning and purpose. The imaginations of Oliver and Charles are darkened by self-interest, what Shakespeare's age calls "lust," and as in Shakespeare's great Sonnet 129, lust tends towards violence; "till action," this sonnet uncompromisingly affirms, lust is "perjured, murd'rous, bloody, full of blame, / Savage, extreme, rude, cruel, not to trust" (3–4).

Macho violence and masculine rhetoric is not Charles' only contribution to the play. He also tells Oliver that Duke Frederick's elder brother, Duke Senior, is

> already in the Forest of Arden, and a many merry men with him; and there they live like the old Robin Hood of England. They say many young gentleman flock to him every day, and fleet the time carelessly as they did in the golden world (1.1.109–13)

Van Doren argues that this is "the text to be annotated, the idea to be analyzed in the comedy to come."[33] At the very least, one can agree that at least one of the play's major themes is conveyed by setting most of the rest of the play in the Forest of Arden, a pastoral world of imaginative freedom and peace. The play's Forest of Arden has some English roots, and Shakespeare's

---

31. See Young, *The Heart's Forest*; Kuhn, "Much Virtue in 'If,'" 40–50.
32. Peacham, *Garden*, 41.
33. Van Doren, *Shakespeare*, 128.

own wife's family name was Arden, so Shakespeare might well be drawing on his own Warwickshire forest to construct this drama.[34] Yet in Lodge the setting of the play is the French forest of "Ardennes," hence Wells' and Taylor's choice of this spelling.[35] This textual choice is certainly debatable, but what for readers can remain a range of imaginative possibilities, becomes, in performance, an important director's choice.

For it does make a great difference, particularly to the play's pastoral themes, whether the play is performed in a real forest or if the natural world is evoked through symbolic "props." The latter is the normal medium of the media for which the play is written, the theatrical stage, but filmmakers have other options. Walking in the Scottish countryside convinced Cedric Messina not only that he and Director Basil Coleman should film *As You Like It* there, but that the BBC should go on to film each one of Shakespeare's plays.[36] Yet the literary consultant to this initial BBC production later said that "by placing *As You Like It* in a real forest we forced the realism of the location to conflict with the artificial conventions of the play. It became that much harder to believe in."[37] Such incredulity, and the clash of realism and artistic representation, could aid presentation of the play's themes, but the comic potential of many of the play's situations seems best suited to the kind of professional theatre production that John Hirsch directed at Stratford in 1983. For his 2006 film of the play, Kenneth Branagh, in many ways the most accomplished contemporary actor and director of Shakespeare's plays, set *As You Like It* not in medieval France or England but in nineteenth-century Japan. Charles became a fearsome sumo wrestler, and Duke Frederick's men became terrifying Ninja warriors, but the Arden remained a "naturalistic" forest. The realism generally expected by movie audiences is difficult for any director to avoid.

In many ways, the "less" of artistic symbolism is "more" suited to the theatre, for this setting requires active imaginative engagement by both actors and audience. It is also arguable that Shakespeare's Forest of Arden represents not one natural location, but rather the common human longing for the perfect peace of a utopian world, whether imagined as the egalitarian world of Robin Hood, or the "golden world" of the classical age. In *As You Like It*, not only "young gentleman" can "fleet the time carelessly" in the

---

34. Hunt, *Shakespeare's "As You Like It."*

35. A spelling which, to remain with the vast majority of *As You Like It* scholars, I do not use.

36. "Cedric Messina Discusses the Shakespeare Plays," 134.

37. John Wilders, quoted in Wells, "Television Shakespeare," 47.

forest, but young women too, and perhaps more good comes from their time there than one might have predicted.

The playful, aesthetic side of *As You Like It*, the way in which everything in the play—from language to character to plot—can seem artificial, derived from artistic artifice rather than nature, was certainly fore-grounded by Thea Sharrock's 2009 RSC production. Staged at the new Globe Theatre in London, which was rebuilt expressly to allow Shakespearean plays to again be staged in their historical form, Sharrock's production was a triumph filled with laughter and comedy, one that frequently engaged the live audience to achieve its purposes. Something along the same lines, but in a contemporary setting, was attempted by director Jillian Keiley in 2016 at Stratford, Ontario. Keiley set the play in late twentieth-century Newfoundland, on Canada's East Coast, and before the play even began she invited audience participation in "Running the Goat," a traditional Newfoundland dance that both spotlights particular couples and pushes them through circles and swings with a larger group. From the start of the play, the audience is, in Keiley's words,

> part of a kitchen-party culture, a dance-together culture—wherein the art is not to be examined or observed but to be experienced by all of us, together in a circle.[38]

Participation in this "kitchen-party" was further ensured by giving each audience member a "party-bag" which, allowed them, at various times, to portray the forest, a starry night, or even the ocean of the Newfoundland coast. The "party-bag" also included poems written by local grade seven and eight students, which served as the "verse" which Orlando hangs "on every tree" (3.2.9) at the start of act 3. Other audience members were given sticks for roasting marsh-mellows, or carrots to be pulled from imaginary gardens. In one memorable moment, another audience member represented a "dock" which allows the shepherd Silvius to tie up his ocean "dinghy" before going "ashore." Such props not only "re-set" the play on Canada's East Coast, they invited the audience to "re-imagine" the play, though most of the play's lines were unchanged. Comical, poetic, imaginative propositions are at the heart of the *ethos* of any performance of *As You Like It*, but Keiley's production created a particularly playful tone. When a small white whale "swims" down a row in the audience, onstage Rosalind adds to the play's many homonymic puns, or *paranomasia*, beginning 4.3, "Well, well, well . . ."

---

38. These words are found in the program notes for *As You Like It*, performed at Stratford, Ontario, Festival Theatre, directed by Jillian Keiley, August 20th, 2016.

Though not everyone is willing to re-imagine the forest of Arden along Canada's East Coast, the human longing for a utopian world is a very widespread if not universal human desire. This desire, interpreted as a longing for return to Eden or the regaining of communion with God, was an important interest of the Catholic Humanists. More's *Utopia* practically invents this important genre of modern literature, but neither More nor Erasmus ever lose an ironic sense of the contrast between political reality and imaginative hope. The Catholic Humanists' ultimate hope is in Christ, and this hope is at once idealistic and historical, faithful and rational. For Christ not only promises to come again, and to bring the New Jerusalem (Rev 21), but more immediately offers a "peace" that is "not as the world giveth" (John 14:27), a peace that "passeth all understanding" (Phil 4:47). The great question, for them and for us, is whether any place on this earth, even the human heart, mind, and soul, can become a place of true peace. One might hope for such peace in one's family, but the conflict of brothers portrayed early in this play is a reminder that even the first human family, still remembering the perfect peace of the Garden of Eden, soon is doomed to violence and death. Is marriage also a vain, "dystopian" mirage? How can one regain hope in the decision of God in Eden, that a man shall "leave his father and his mother, and shall cleave unto his wife: and they shall be one flesh" (Gen 2:24)? That question, and many others, requires feminine wisdom, particularly the females portrayed by Shakespeare's next scene in the play.

2

"Never Two Ladies Loved as They Do"

The Feminine Rhetoric of Celia and Rosalind

SHAKESPEARE FOLLOWS THE OPENING portrait of quarrelling brothers by portraying its feminine opposite, in affection and language, in two cousins, Celia and Rosalind. The court attendant Le Beau, a relatively minor character, tells us that their "loves" are "dearer than the natural bond of Sisters" (1.2.266); as often happens in Shakespeare's plays, a minor character introduces a major philosophical theme. For Le Beau reminds us of a major claim of the Catholic Humanists: that the Creator of Nature has created natural bonds that can unite humanity even in times of suffering and strife, even beyond what most see as the "natural bond" of family members.[1] Jesus had famously and controversially taught that Christian bonds must supersede any connection to family (Matt 19:29), yet this injunction is not, contra Nietzsche, a justification of "slave" morality.[2] Rather, in the "bond" of Rosalind and Celia, we see and hear an empathetic rhetoric which confirms that the two women seek each other's true good, and real political freedom. The deep bond of this friendship is the true "fortune" of each woman.

The two cousins have perhaps even more reasons for strife than Orlando and Oliver. Celia's father, Duke Frederick, has banished from the court

---

1. As Erasmus rhetorically asks in *Paraclesis*, the introduction to his Greek New Testament, "what else is the philosophy of Christ, which He himself calls a rebirth, than the restoration of human nature originally well formed?" Erasmus, *The Paraclesis*, 100.

2. See Nietzsche, *On the Genealogy of Morals*.

Rosalind's father, Duke Senior. It is important to recognize, though it is part of the play's assumed background rather than realistically described, that in most pre-Industrial Revolution literature, "banishment" is a far harsher, and more dangerous thing than it would be in our modern era. For the banished one is excluded from the necessary protection of civilization, and from the civilized production of the "food chain"; for practical purposes, then, "banishment" could amount to a death sentence. When it did not, however, this is probably thanks to the goodness and free grace of Nature, both human nature and the natural sources needed to sustain the banished person. Eventually, both Celia and Rosalind follow Duke Senior into a place of banishment, the Forest of Arden, in which both forms of essential sustenance are freely offered; but first, Shakespeare portrays both ladies employing the rhetorical language that is foundational to their deep friendship and true peace.

Charles the eloquent wrestler has already introduced the two cousins by telling Oliver of both their personal and political relationship. After Oliver asks him, "Can you tell if Rosalind, the Duke's daughter, be banished with her father" (1.1.100–101), Charles replies not with reference to the main heroine of the play, but rather by focusing upon the role of Celia:

> O, no; for the duke's daughter, her cousin, so loves
> her, being ever from their cradles bred together,
> that she would have followed her exile, or have died
> to stay behind her. She is at the court, and no
> less beloved of her uncle than his own daughter; and
> never two ladies loved as they do. (1.1.102–7)

"Ladies" here likely connotes not only gender, but probably also political class, just as "gentleman" does in the opening scene with Orlando and Oliver. Rosalind and Celia are aristocrats caught in the middle of political struggle, a common and usually not peaceful situation in Renaissance Europe. Yet when we first meet the two "ladies," their political misfortune is not, as one might expect, suppressed to maintain the peace of their personal relationship. Instead, the two begin with an argument, as Celia irrationally begins by exhorting Rosalind to ignore her misfortune: "pray thee Rosalind, sweet my coz, be merry" (1.2.1). Rosalind replies with politeness, but also a rhetorical question that suggests mild irritation: "Dear Celia, I show more mirth than I am mistress of, and would you yet I were merrier?" (1.2.2–3). Yet rather than the *erotemas*[3] of Orlando and Oliver, which progressively become more accusatory until physical violence ensues, Celia and Rosalind

---

3. Peacham, *Garden*, 106.

instead share hypothetical propositions that invite each other to imaginatively alter each other's perception of their apparent suffering.

This rhetorical move allows not only empathy, but also a key goal of Catholic Humanist education: to remember one's true identity.[4] Rosalind tells Celia: "Unless you could teach me how to forget a banished father you must not learn me how to remember any extraordinary pleasure" (1.2.3–6). Yet even without the fulfillment of this hypothetical proposition, great pleasure is available in their immediate relationship. Celia accuses Rosalind of ignoring this reality: "Herein I see thou lovest me not with the full weight that I love thee" (1.2.7–8). This accusation, of course, is playful rather than serious. Celia simply wants her friend to imagine an alternative reality than her obvious political misfortune, and thus offers another *hypothetical syllogism* that clearly continues but has the opposite effect of the *epanaphora*[5] of "if" in the play's opening scene. Here Celia asks Rosalind to consider:

> If my uncle, thy banished father, had been still with me I could have taught my love to take thy father for mine. So wouldst thou, if the truth of thy love to me were so righteously tempered as mine is to thee. (1.2.8–12)

Nor is the imaginative proposition here simply a game, or a means for Rosalind to escape her present, painful reality. For Celia further promises, after her father's death, that "what he hath taken away from thy father perforce," she will "render" Rosalind "again in affection" (1.2.18–19). With this practical promise offered, there is then real force when, in sharp contrast to the denigrating *sarcasmus*[6] which Oliver directed to Orlando, here Celia uses *metaphora*,[7] to translate her friend's name into a traditional metaphor of youthful beauty and, in Dante, of eternal being; Celia concludes: "Therefore, my sweet Rose, my dear Rose, be merry" (1.2.21–22). Willard Espy might also call Celia's words *hypocore*,[8] or the creation of pet names, but Peacham could also use the term *paramythia*,[9] or speech intended to comfort. This term sounds awkward, but reminds us of the connections between rhetoric, poetry, and myth, which work together to enchant and also—for those

---

4. In his initial Catholic Humanist manifesto, Erasmus writes, "the crown of this God-given wisdom is to know yourself." Erasmus, *The Handbook of the Militant Christian*, 42.

5. Peacham, *Garden*, 42.
6. Peacham, *Garden*, 37.
7. Peacham, *Garden*, 3.
8. Espy, *Garden*, 100.
9. Peacham, *Garden*, 100.

such as these young women who are trapped in painful circumstances—to escape.

Celia's comfort is more personal rather than philosophical, however, as usually becomes clear in performance. All of the productions noted here present Celia as a funny, fun-loving friend to Rosalind, someone whose warmth and smile are as important as her words. In Czinner's 1936 film or Thea Sharrock's 2009 production at the new Globe Theatre, though, Elizabethan costuming is used to historicize the play and, in the case of these two cousins, remind us of the many constraining features of Renaissance aristocratic clothing, especially for women. Yet the words of both Rosalind and Celia step forward from the constraints of clothing and exist as their own imaginative reality, and the potential for feminine freedom through rhetoric, paradoxically, is vividly displayed. The power of such historicized productions, even with females playing the role reserved to males in Shakespeare's age, can be further demonstrated by comparison with modern dress productions such as the 2016 Stratford production set on the modern Canadian East Coast. There Celia is shown in pajamas, having her hair done with curlers, and the linguistic play is quite naturalistic. Yet the rhetoric seems casual, nonchalant, rather than the lifeline to freedom which, within the narrative of *As You Like It*, the play of language actually provides.

The friendly feminine rhetoric here soon inspires Rosalind to imagine "falling in love," but Celia cautions to avoid taking this too seriously, but rather "to make sport withal" and to "love no man in good earnest" (1.2.23–24). Like "game" in medieval romances such as *Sir Gawain and the Green Knight*,[10] "sport" in *As You Like It* is an invitation to test and reveal character through trial. Yet Celia's rational reluctance to allow such "sport" to progress towards physical reality also suggests the Catholic Humanist emphasis upon imaginative "play." As Walter M. Gordon's excellent study of Erasmus, *Humanist Play and Belief*, further explains, for Catholic Humanism the concept of play has little to do with leisure, much more to do with the imaginative freedom created for humanity by God's free gifts of grace.[11] With the emphasis on argument, debate, and rhetorical eloquence, Catholic Humanist "play" often prioritizes intellectual before physical activity. When Rosalind asks, "What shall be our sport, then?" Celia replies by proposing a "commonplace" of Renaissance rhetoric: to "mock the good housewife Fortune from her wheel, that her gifts may henceforth be bestowed equally" (1.2.29–32).

10. *Sir Gawain and the Green Knight* has two primary "games," the initial "beheading" game between the heroes and the "felawschip" game between Gawain and the Lord and Lady of the castle.

11. Gordon, *Humanist Play and Belief*, 125–48.

This "sport" plays off one of the most well-known images of Renaissance culture, Fortune personified as a woman sitting by a wheel that doles out good or bad luck randomly, by chance. As a trope, personification is known to Renaissance rhetoricians as *prosopopoeia*,[12] and it also often appears in Renaissance iconography. As an iconic image, or *emblem*,[13] Fortune's wheel can be casually alluded to, or become the foundational "invention" that develops into further argument. Yet though such images are familiar, it would be a serious error to dismiss the arguments connected to them as trivial or simplistic. For Fortune and her wheel are rarely solitary figures of despair, but more commonly in dispute with "Nature," whose iconic images normally refer at some point to the Creator of Nature, or God. This is the debate within one of the most influential literary texts of the period, Boethius' *Consolation of Philosophy*, a sixth-century Latin text translated into English by key figures such as King Alfred, Geoffrey Chaucer, and Elizabeth II.[14] In this text, Dame Fortune vies with Lady Philosophy for the soul of an unjustly imprisoned man; seen as ill fortune, such suffering might lead one to despair, but taken as providential healing, a man of wisdom finds God. Such debates are also developed by medieval scholasticism and Protestant Reformers, who typically contrast the common grace of nature with the providential grace of God, or what C. S. Lewis will later term the "Natural Supernatural" when he explains the concept of "miracle" to modern readers.[15]

In this play, the Fortune vs. Nature debate is not between theological divines, but rather the "sport" of these young ladies, who are all too aware that in the "gifts of the world" that Fortune dispenses "she doth most mistake" in her allotment "to women" (1.2.214). Shakespeare's development of this commonplace, though, is not limited to Celia and Rosalind. As John Shaw argues, in *As You Like It* the conflict between Fortune and Nature "creates an underlying philosophical strife" that forms "an important pattern throughout the play."[16] In addition to the women, Fortune has misplaced her gifts to Duke Senior, unjustly usurped by Frederick, and to Orlando, cheated of his inheritance by Oliver. Shakespeare's invention "especially pointed up the Nature-Fortune conflict by omitting certain motives"[17] that in *Rosalynde* provide rational explanations for the villains' treachery. In

---

12. Peacham, *Garden*, 136.
13. Puttenham, *Art*, 102.
14. See Boethius, *The Consolation of Philosophy*.
15. Lewis, *Miracles*.
16. Shaw, "Fortune and Nature," 45–50.
17. Shaw, "Fortune and Nature," 49.

Lodge it is clear that Torismond dismisses Rosalynde in order to prevent a courtier from marrying her and thus laying claim to the dukedom, but Shakespeare's Duke Frederick never explains this political rationale;[18] similarly, whereas Lodge portrays Saladyne as having been "cheated out of most of his rightful patrimony as eldest son,"[19] Shakespeare has Oliver state that he "know[s] not why" he hates Orlando.

By contrast, Nature is understood to bestow "gifts of the body and mind," such as "wisdom and virtue," that allow one to "flout at Fortune."[20] Despite his hatred of Orlando, the younger brother's natural virtues cause Oliver to admit, "yet he's gentle, never school'd, and yet learned, full of noble device, of all sorts enchantingly beloved" (1.1.156–58). Oliver here uses *antanagoge*, the "balancing of an unfavorable aspect with a favorable one,"[21] an appropriate linguistic form to portray the gifts by which Nature offsets Fortune's cruelty. Puttenham calls this figure the *recompenser*,[22] a term that seems particularly apt when, on his way to the forest of Arden, Adam says that "fortune cannot recompense me better / Then to die well and not my master's debtor" (2.3.76–77). The gifts of nature are further employed in Arden, where the good Duke Senior translates the "stubbornness of fortune" (2.1.19), the fool Touchstone rails "on Lady Fortune" (2.7.16), and all of the forest's courtiers scorn Frederick by living idyllic, carefree lives.

There can be little doubt that Shakespeare's extensive development of the Fortune vs. Nature commonplace would have evoked an intelligent, rational response from a Renaissance audience. Yet the entrance of Touchstone the Fool turns the entire discussion towards the less serious tone of comic humor, as Celia comments that "Fortune" has "sent in this fool to cut off the argument," while Rosalind develops this point to include elements of Nature particular to Touchstone's identity: "Fortune makes Nature's natural the cutter-off of Nature's wit" (1.2.47–48). A "natural" is Elizabethan slang for a mentally handicapped person, which at times a Fool might seem to be, but this type of character often provided Shakespearean drama, and European political courts, with uncommon wisdom. Even the most unlikely or limited gifts of nature, according to Catholic Humanist thinking, contain graces to remind us that the troubles created by bad Fortune are temporal, passing, to be replaced one day by eternal reality.

18. Shaw, "Fortune and Nature," 49.
19. Shaw, "Fortune and Nature," 49.
20. Shaw, "Fortune and Nature," 46.
21. Joseph, *Arts of Language*, 138.
22. Puttenham, *Art*, 216.

Both the tongue and thought of Touchstone offer a more "mixed bag" of folly and wisdom than comparably intellectual Shakespearean Fools such as Feste and Lear's Fool. There are lines that could place Touchstone in the "holy fool" tradition of the "learned" fools, or even of the "unconsciously" or sometimes wise buffoons like Bottom or Dogberry. Yet Touchstone also shares with many of these fools a comical bawdry whose often concrete rhetoric appeals more to the common man in Shakespeare's audience than the philosopher or theologian. The fool's entrance into this play provides an excellent example. Celia tells us that Touchstone is the work of Nature, "who perceiveth our natural works too dull to reason of such goddesses" (1.2.50–51) as Fortune or Nature, and all of the abstractions associated with them in the Elizabethan worldview; instead, Nature "hath sent this natural for our whetstone; for always the dullness of the fool is the whetstone of the wits" (1.2.50–52). The concrete image here, the "whetstone," or stone used to sharpen other things, refers to an object familiar to the Elizabethan audience, but clearly there is *metaphora* implied by Touchstone's name. This fool will sharpen the ladies wit, keep them "in touch" with concrete reality, and even "whet" their appetite further for romance, though Touchstone's interests seem very different than their own.

Whereas the ladies might dream of "falling in love," Touchstone is well aware of the more foolish, fallen elements of human nature, particularly male nature. After Celia introduces him and invites his thought with a question, "How now, wit; wither wander you?" (1.2.53), Touchstone claims that he has learned "oaths" of a source whose concrete images are surely unfamiliar to both Celia and Rosalind:

> Of a certain knight that swore "by his honour" they were good pancakes, and swore "by his honour" the mustard was naught. Now I'll stand to it the pancakes were naught and the mustard was good, and yet was not the knight forsworn. (1.2.60–64)

For the first time in the play, both the theatre audience and onstage listener have to be perplexed as to what the spoken words might mean. Celia and Rosalind dare not ask exactly what Touchstone means, and even learned editors debate the clearly figurative connotations. Behind any "private joke" here surely stands the general Christian commandment against taking oaths (Matt 5:34), but very likely there are other specific sins also implied. Christine Trautvetter, a German critic who edited an "old spelling" and "old meaning" edition of the play,[23] thinks the passage "almost certainly

---

23. Trautvetter, *As You Like It*.

bawdy,"[24] one which uses *metonymy*[25] in which "honour" means the knight's chastity (a claim for which one can find similar usages in Shakespeare) "pancakes" stands for prostitutes, and "mustard" for sexual ardor. Touchstone's dishonest "knight" has surely not been out for breakfast, but far more likely has been to a brothel. Comically, Touchstone portrays the traditional romantic hero, a knight, swearing that he has not brought his sexual heat, or "mustard" to the prostitutes, or "pancakes," whereas Touchstone finds the prostitutes "naught" and essentially brags about his own "mustard," finally affirming the right of any "knight" to make any public claim whatsoever.

Clearly, such humor is a long way from the aristocratic world that Celia and Rosalind have grown up in, and it is likely that some members of Shakespeare's audience would find Touchstone's words not slightly indecorous. Yet as a comic, concrete foil to abstract notions of romantic love common both in the urbane world and eventual pastoral setting of the play, Touchstone's wit does serve as a "whetstone" against which the feminine wisdom of the play must be tested. Yes Celia and Rosalind, Shakespeare seems to say, through Touchstone, men really are this base! Lasting peace or love with such a creature may require more than one might initially guess; men are sinners, and this is surely an important part of why God says, in the Garden of Eden, that "it is not good that the man should be alone" (Gen 2:18). Yet even more surely it has to be a brave woman who seeks out male company, and a very wise woman who can teach men how to fight against their fallen nature.

Celia and Rosalind are not yet ready to take on such a task, but one possible approach to this daunting mission, explored more fully later in the play, is to imagine the condition of men by pretending to be one. That seems to be what Touchstone now proposes to Celia and Rosalind: "Stand you both forth now. Stroke your chins, and swear by your beards that I am a knave" (1.2.68–69). Needing no time to debate entering this sport, Celia replies with another hypothetical or "if" conditional: "By our beards—if we had them—thou art" (1.2.70). Via this "logic," in which an impossible condition voids any positive conclusion, Touchstone wriggles out of possibly being accused of slandering either an actual knight or himself:

> By my knavery—if I had it—then I were; but if you swear by that that is not, you are not forsworn. No more was this knight, swearing by his honour, for he never had any; or if he had, he had sworn it away before ever he saw those pancakes or that mustard. (1.2.71–76)

24. Trautvetter, *As You Like It*, 23.
25. Peacham, *Garden*, 19.

By a negative hypothetical similar to Sidney's famous defense of poets, who "never affirmeth" and therefore "never lieth,"[26] Touchstone's argument logically affirms the impossibility of conclusions without factual evidence, and thus demonstrates the value of imaginative fictions to avoid the direct accusations typical of any male conflict. Though adapted to Touchstone's foolish bawdry, and the folly of the common man, this is the same imaginative impulse that creates Erasmus' *Praise of Folly* or More's *Utopia*. In *As You Like It*, neither Celia nor Rosalind can directly imitate Touchstone's rhetorical argument, but his comical self-critique does suggest the possibility of humbling male pride. There is thus much direct wisdom when Touchstone, as in similar lines from Feste or Lear's Fool, summarizes the fool's vocation: "The more pity that fools may not speak wisely, what wise men do foolishly" (1.2.82–83).

To this claim, Celia—being Duke Frederick's daughter—can readily agree, in the most serious terms: "By my troth, thou sayest true, for since the little wit that fools have was silenced, the little foolery that wise men have makes a great show" (1.2.84–86). It is quite possible that this line is also external political rhetoric, spoken as much by Shakespeare as by Celia, for it is a possible allusion to the "recent restraint imposed upon the theatrical companies by the Puritan authorities, or to the burning of satirical books on the First of June, 1599."[27] This allusion helps explain Touchstone's bawdry, for rhetorically his speech could be termed *cacemphaton*, the figure of foul speech that Puttenham considers "tolerable" when used "to the intent to move laughter, and to make sport" as a "railing companion" for others.[28] Touchstone clearly becomes such a companion for Celia and Rosalind, as is first illustrated when "Monsieur Lebeau" arrives to invite all to see another foolish male sport, the "great show" of Charles, the Duke's wrestler.

Before viewing this "sport," the ladies and their fool mock the messenger's clearly affected habits of speech; much like Osric in *Hamlet*, Lebeau affects the prestige and power of the court of Duke Frederick, despite his own lowly status as a common messenger. Rosalind tells us first that he arrives, "mouth full of news" (1.2.88), which in our age of email or even "slower" mass transport mail might be a dead metaphor, if we forget the practice of messenger pigeons to deliver mail. Celia makes the image more explicit, saying that Lebeau will put the news "on us, as Pigeons feed their young" (1.289-90), an appopriate *simile*[29] if Lebeau has "mincing speech" and his

---

26. Sidney, *Defence*, 235.
27. Trautvetter, *As You Like It*, 25.
28. Puttenham, *Art*, 254.
29. Peacham, *Garden*, 158.

"lips pursed, as if they held grains of corn."³⁰ Rosalind then puns on the image, replying, "Then shall we be news-crammed," a "mew" being "a cage in which fowls were confined for fattening" and "cram" being the technical term for "fattening poultry for the table."³¹ Few modern audiences grasp the pastoral comedy here, but Celia clearly understands, concluding, then "we shall be the more marketable" (1.2.92).

After further banter, Touchstone comments upon the general incongruity of Lebeau's invitation, satirically remarking, "Thus men may grow wiser every day. It is the first time that ever I heard breaking of ribs was sport for ladies" (1.2.127–29). Yet Rosalind appears to be a romantic woman still interested in "falling in love"; she "longs to see this broken music" of wrestling for she "dotes upon rib-breaking" (1.2.131–33). Is the latter *synecdoche*³² an indirect allusion to the biblical account of the creation of Eve (Gen 2:21–22) that parallels the indirect allusions to Adam in scene 1 of the play? In a comedy of manners or a strictly romantic drama we would think not, but in Catholic Humanist rhetoric, we expect such "second meanings." One could argue that Rosalind's role as the biblical "woman" of the play makes her open to the sport of "falling in love," and leads her and Celia towards the wrestling match of Charles and Orlando.

Duke Frederick and his court then come onstage, which can be played as a moment of pomp and spectacle. Yet an audience's attention is quickly refocused upon the rhetoric of romance when the Duke tells Rosalind and Celia, gesturing towards Orlando, "Speak to him, ladies, see if you can move him" (1.2.150–51). Duke Frederick means, of course, "move him from the madness of fighting so fearsome a wrestler as Charles," but Orlando's reply shows both a physical desperation and an imaginative mind:

> If I be foiled, there is but one shamed that was never gracious, if killed, but one dead that is willing to be so. I shall do my friends no wrong, for I have none to lament me; the world no injury, for in it I have nothing. Only in the world I fill up a place which may be better supplied when I have made it empty. (1.2.176–81)

Perhaps because of his depressing conclusion here, Orlando's hypothetical "if" clauses seem more despairing than combative, even though he is pledging to fight rather than open to peace. Yet in this Renaissance version of a modernist commonplace, apparent nihilistic desperation leaves Orlando open to the romantic love about to replace it.

    30. As Trautvetter, *As You Like It*, 25, suggests, following a suggestion from John Dover Wilson.

    31. Trautvetter, *As You Like It*, 25.

    32. Peacham, *Garden*, 17.

The wrestling match itself seems almost more rhetorical than physical. Charles begins with another rhetorical question that could also be called *misterismus*, which Puttenham calls "the fleering frumpe":[33] "Come, where is this young gallant, that is so desirous to lie with his mother earth?" (1.2.188–89). Orlando hears this "question" for what it is, mockery, stressing this point through *paragmenon*: "You mean to mock me after: you should not have mocked me before" (1.2.196–97). In the actual wrestling, Orlando handles Charles so easily that, even as the Duke is crying, "no more, no more," Orlando uses *metaphora* to indicate he would enjoy both more exercise and more speech: "I am not yet well breath'd" (1.2.200–206). Charles, by contrast "cannot speak" (1.2.208); the eloquent wrestler silenced, Duke Frederick briskly commands: "Bear him away" (1.2.208). In this play, rhetorical defeat is equivalent to the loss of any reason for being onstage.

Far more significant than the wrestling, within the scene and play as a whole, are the first words between Orlando and Rosalind. The brevity of this conversation can surprise modern audiences, but is based upon a commonplace of the time: intense emotion can render speech impossible. One could see this commonplace as an obverse, paradoxical corollary of the standard Catholic Humanist emphasis on *copia* in speech and words. In *A Midsummer Night's Dream*, Duke Theseus recalls visiting towns that intended "premeditated welcomes," yet upon his arrival could not speak; "Out of this silence yet I picked a welcome," he continues, describing a situation often experienced also by Elizabeth I, before concluding with this maxim: "Love, therefore, and tongue-tied simplicity / In least speak most" (5.1.94, 100, 104–5).

In *As You Like It*, Duke Frederick speaks the most lines following the wrestling match, establishing simply that Orlando is the son of a friend of his rival, Duke Senior, and therefore shall not be a friend of Frederick. Orlando affirms his patrimony anyway, a dignified pride overheard by the ladies, causing Rosalind to recall that, "My father loved Sir Rowland as his soul" (1.2.224), but none of this potentially important information is spoken between them. Celia urges words to Orlando, saying, "Let us go thank him, and encourage him," but at this point Rosalind is moved, we are told by a rare stage direction, to give Orlando "a chain from her neck," and says only, "Gentleman, / Wear this for me—one out of suits with fortune, / That could give more but that her hands lack means" (1.2.234–36). The term of address here could be *paradoxon*,[34] for what truly constitutes a "gentleman" was an oft debated topic throughout the English Middle Ages and Renaissance.

---

33. Puttenham, *Art*, 201.
34. Peacham, *Garden*, 112.

Rosalind's words could reflect the polite assumption of a young woman first meeting an eligible young man, but could also alienate Orlando, who certainly does not possess a "gentleman's" wealth, though Rosalind's own admittance of ill fortune might modify any such embarrassment.

We cannot be sure exactly how Orlando takes this because he does not respond directly to Rosalind, instead saying in an aside:

> Can I not say "I thank you"? My better parts
> Are all thrown down, and that which here stands up
> Is but a quintain, a mere lifeless block. (1.2.238–40)

The implied *metaphora*[35] here, the image of a wrestler throwing down elements of human nature that cause us to be "lifeless blocks," becomes central both to Orlando's eventual relationship with Rosalind and to the themes of the play as a whole, but momentarily both potential lovers are silenced. A second, even rarer stage direction explicitly tells us, "Rosalind and Celia turn to go," and only when Orlando calls them back does Rosalind speak any lines that might be called "romantic"; she tells Orlando, "Sir, you have wrestled well, and overthrown more than your enemies" (1.2.243–44). Certainly he has no reason to believe that Rosalind overheard his aside, so the use of the same metaphor here indicates imaginative combatibility, but Orlando still cannot reply. After Celia and Rosalind leave, Orlando exclaims: "What passion hangs these weight upon my tongue? / I cannot speak to her, yet she urged conference" (1.2.247–48). He must learn to communicate with Rosalind to share the stage, and a life, with her.

Ironically, and sadly, Orlando's primary speech partner in the rest of the scene becomes, rather, the loquacious court messenger. As LeBeau reenters, Orlando sees the irony but has a rare moment of insight into his own emotions: "O poor Orlando! Thou art overthrown. / Or Charles or[36] something weaker masters thee" (1.2.249–50). Here, as often in the rest of the play, the "weaker sex" exercises strange power over the young man's heart, though he cannot yet describe the attraction. LeBeau has by far the longest remaining speech in this scene, taking no less than sixteen lines to inform Orlando which of the two young women that Orlando has spoken to is "daughter to the banished Duke" (1.2.261–75). Lebeau concludes with what can here only be taken as religious cliché, telling Orlando, whom he hardly knows, "Hereafter, in a better world than this / I shall desire more love and knowledge of you" (1.2.263, 274–75). Orlando gives a one-line response, then concludes the scene with final exclamatory works that express

---

35. Peacham, *Garden*, 3.

36. The correlative conjunction "or ... or" is common in Shakespeare, and equivalent to the modern use of "either ... or."

the incarnate vision on his mind, and in his heart: "heavenly Rosalind!" (1.2.276, 279).

Act 1, scene 3 is the final scene of the first act, and begins with a brief conversation between Rosalind and Celia. Like her romantic counterpart, Rosalind at first has "not a word," not even one "to throw at a dog" (1.3.1–3) but it is one of the benefits of female friendship to dig below the surface of emotions and uncover the heart at the source of language. "But is all this for your father?" inquires Celia, to which Rosalind replies, in the blunt eroticism that occasionally gives concrete contrast to her romantic rhetoric, "No, some of it is for my child's father" (1.3.10–11). Honesty expressed, Celia and Rosalind continue to chat until Duke Frederick enters and formally banishes Rosalind at least "twenty miles" from "our public court" (1.3.43). Rosalind protests, like many historical counterparts in Shakespeare's own time, that the edict of a single political authority cannot prove her a "traitor," but to no avail. Celia similarly pleads on her cousin's behalf, and is twice called "a fool" by her father (1.3.78, 86). As becomes even more clear in later plays such as *King Lear*, to suffer as "a fool" in this play is far wiser than to remain in the "security" of political power represented here by Duke Frederick.

It is thus an ironic but socially realistic part of the play that Celia and Rosalind then decide, in order to survive the "assailants" (1.3.113) whom they are sure to meet in banishment, to disguise themselves as males. Rosalind chooses the name of "Ganymede," after "Jove's own page," while Celia takes the name "Aliena," "something that hath a reference to my state" (1.3.124–27). Celia's name thus seems directly allegorical, in the manner familiar to the Elizabethan audience from medieval morality plays, but Rosalind's name might express a "second meaning" also expected by a Catholic Humanist audience. For when a text such as Chaucer's *Knight's Tale* concludes its allegory of the conflict between classical gods such as Mercury and Venus by appealing to the "high god of love" whose providence can decide events, so here Rosalind will become servant to Jove, the high classical god, whom often represents the "highest" God who "is Love" according to Christian scripture (1 John 4:8). Such a "second meaning" might seem arbitrary to a secular modern audience, but it would be expected by those familiar with the Catholic Humanist "baptism" of classical culture, and it certainly fits with Rosalind's subsequent role in the play, as she will teach Orlando not only how to love, but further what love is.

There is another element of "social realism" here more often commented upon by modern critics, the well-known fact that male actors generally played female roles in Shakespeare's theatre. Hard to imagine today, this historical fact of the theatre has today led many modern critics to see suppressed homosexuality within Shakespeare's theatre, and to claim Rosalind as an exemplar of bisexual androgyny.[37] Since the Elizabethan theatre has very little, if any, explicit sexual action, it is difficult to prove, or to disprove, such claims, but in the case of *As You Like It* it is impossible not to notice a rather elaborate "play" on the gender question. For Rosalind is a male actor playing a female role who takes on disguise only to, in the Forest of Arden, "pretend" to be a female (Rosalind herself) in order to teach a man how to love her. Various forms of gender and / or sexual commentary could thus be posited, but what seems most essential to the play's Catholic Humanist rhetoric is both an actor and audience's ability to construct and imagine diverse identities which conspire together to teach Orlando one central thing: how to love Rosalind as she loves him, and therefore be prepared to marry according to the conception of married love taught by the Son of the High God of Love while He was on earth. An inability to imagine constructed identities or disguises would not only make theatre in Shakespeare's time impossible, but moreover make it impossible to learn how to love any "disguised other," perhaps most importantly, for Catholic Humanists, the Ultimate Other who, as both human and divine, leaves eternity to take on a human identity and teach us how to love.

Such a claim is not an esoteric, gnostic, "religious interpretation" of *As You Like It*, but rather a teaching so central to Catholic Humanism that it can be relied upon, by artists such as Shakespeare, to inform a theatre audience as it informs many other elements of Medieval and Renaissance culture. The "heavenly Rosalind!" (1.2.278) becomes not an object of male fantasy, as in Orlando's initial exclamation, but rather a divinely-directed teacher who can both shatter the egotistic illusions of such a fantasy and rebuild the male to allow a relationship in which God "joins together" even two creatures as different as the male and female, which is Christ's teaching on the meaning, and miracle, broadly termed "marriage" (Matt 19:1–12). It is a crucial part of the play's power to teach such meaning, however, that within it Rosalind remains not a heavenly allegory, nor a male actor, but rather a young women really, passionately in romantic love with a young man. All of the human folly, and wisdom, attendant on this part is thus preserved, though perhaps both can be fully shown not in the political court of Duke Frederick, but rather in God's natural kingdom, the Forest of Arden, the setting to which act 2 of the play now turns.

---

37. Of the many examples of this, see Bi Academic Intervention, *The Bisexual Imaginary*, 115–16.

3

"Sermons in Stones"

"Translating" Eden in the Forest of Arden

The evident corruption of the court establishes the clear need for Celia and Rosalind to depart, but the nature of their destination, the forest of Arden, does not become fully developed until the start of act 2, when Duke Senior and his exiled court singer, Amiens, meditate further on its meaning. For while Charles the Wrestler had compared Arden to the "golden world" celebrated by classical poets, in the forest itself Senior exults that "here feel we not the penalty of Adam" (2.1.5), explicitly comparing Arden to the prelapsarian, pre-fallen garden of Eden. There is an obvious natural referent for Arden, in Shakespeare's time, in the Ardennes, a forest of France which Thomas Lodge made the primary setting of *Rosalynde*. When he adapted Lodge for the stage, though, Shakespeare himself could not have forgotten that his wife's maiden name, Arden, derived from the forest region near her home in England. More universally yet, Shakespeare's audience, living fairly close in time to the "fourteenth-century vowel shift" commonly noted by most historians of the English language,[1] might have consciously or unconsciously compared "Arden" to "Eden," and *As You Like It* certainly encourages this linguistic and theological "translation."

This comparison is developed in many ways by the play, and is extremely important not only to its generally accepted genre, as a "pastoral

---

1. On this commonplace of linguistic history, see Smith and Kim, *This Language a River*.

comedy," but also to its deeper Catholic Humanist theme of the attempt to regain peace in the bonds of marriage. Comparison of the classical "golden world" and of the Christian view of Eden is one of the most common topics of Renaissance poetry and culture,[2] but *As You Like It* offers a particularly compelling example of how Catholic Humanism allows a rhetorical dialogue or argument on the nature and possible value of this topic. From the perspective of Erasmus or More, a "utopian" text is not primarily about the quest for a perfect world, but rather is fundamentally both theological, about our understanding of God, and anthropological, about the human nature that God has created.

There is a strong emphasis on natural goodness in Catholic Humanism, which, as already discussed in chapter 5, can be seen in the position on human nature taken by Erasmus in his famous public debate with Luther on the question of free will.[3] Though certainly rejecting the notion of "total depravity" also developed by Jean Calvin, stressing rather the eternal imprint of the divine image upon human nature (Gen 1:27) and the "original blessing" of creation, Catholic Humanists such as Erasmus or More retain the catholic doctrine of "original sin" by also stressing the flawed or finite nature of any attempt, even *ad fontes*, of regaining any pure, natural paradise. An important part of More's *Utopia* is thus ironic, and in a sense dis-topian, because it stresses most of all the impossibility of utopia in a fallen world. A similar dialectic of hope in God contra the reality of the fallen world exists in *As You Like It*, even, perhaps especially, in the Forest of Arden.

All of these topics are introduced at the start of 2.1. In one of the most important speeches of the play, Duke Senior welcomes everyone to Arden; the speech is worth hearing in full:

> Now, my co-mates and brothers in exile,
> Hath not old custom made this life more sweet
> Than that of painted pomp? Are not these woods
> More free from peril than the envious court?
> Here feel we but the penalty of Adam,
> The seasons' difference, as the icy fang
> And churlish chiding of the winter's wind,
> Which, when it bites and blows upon my body,
> Even till I shrink with cold, I smile and say
> "This is no flattery: these are counsellors
> That feelingly persuade me what I am."
> Sweet are the uses of adversity,

---

2. Rivers, *Classical and Christian Ideas*, 8–19.

3. See Erasmus, *Diatribe on Free Will*, to which Luther responded with *On the Bondage of the Will*. Both works are found in Rupp, *Luther and Erasmus*.

> Which, like the toad, ugly and venomous,
> Wears yet a precious jewel in his head;
> And this our life exempt from public haunt
> Finds tongues in trees, books in the running brooks,
> Sermons in stones and good in every thing.
> I would not change it.

In a technical sense, Senior's opening questions are *erotema*, or rhetorical questions, but their tone and intent is markedly different from both the aggression of Oliver and Orlando or the kindness of Celia and Rosalind. Peacham might call the speech *topothesia*,[4] "a fained description of a place," but Arden is both natural and an ideal world typically found only in poetry and myth. "Old custom," could refer to a lengthy exile, which Asquith and others might liken to the exile of Lodge or other English Catholic emigres, but any melancholy melts away in the music of Senior's words. Surrounded by "co-mates" and "brothers in exile," he asks, "Are not these woods / More free from peril than the envious court?" (2.1.1–4), then answers his own question, *hypophora*,[5] not by reviewing the court's corruption, but rather by praising the climate of Arden, for "here feel we not the penalty of Adam / The season's difference" (2.1.5–6). Yet this "paradise" is not free from cold weather. On the contrary, cold is welcomed, Senior explains, for when "the winter's wind . . . blows upon my body / Even till I shrink with cold, I smile, and say / "This is no flattery. These are counselors / That feelingly persuade me what I am" (2.1.7–11). The diction and thought here is similar to that of a play which Shakespeare probably wrote years later, *King Lear*, where another old man blinded by the malevolence of human nature can yet "see how this world goes," for he sees it "feelingly" (*Lr.*, 4.5.145).

Lear is, of course, a much darker play than *As You Like It*, but the roots of both plays precede either. Nature can remind us of human identity because—as in the famous opening lines of Chaucer's "General Prologue," when "Nature pricketh em"[6] and inspires pilgrimage, or in Herbert's later meditation on "the God of Nature"[7]—nature is created by a Creator who also has a plan and purpose for our lives. For Duke Senior, as is often the case with Catholic Humanists, Nature is an educator promoting self-knowledge, and offering wisdom; as in *The Winter's Tale* reference to the "good goddess Nature" (*WT*, 2.3.104), Nature was as common a positive emblem as Fortune was negative; as John Shaw writes:

4. Peacham, *Garden*, 141.
5. Peacham, *Garden*, 107.
6. Chaucer, "General Prologue," in *The Canterbury Tales*.
7. Herbert, "The Pulley," 114–15.

Nature was often presented by the goddess Sapientia or Virtue, who might sit firmly on a four-square pedestal, eyes open, holding the mirror of Prudence, signifying self-knowledge.[8]

Duke Senior continues his sapiential speech with *paroemia*,[9] or proverb, that foreshadows another crucial moment in *King Lear*; just before he and his fool enter a hovel, Lear tells us that "The art of our necessities is strange, / And can make vile things precious" (3.2.70–71). Duke Senior has a similar way of summing up the far happier place that is the Forest of Arden, while adding the rhetorical flair characteristic of *As You Like It*:

> Sweet are the uses of adversity
> Which, like the toad, ugly and venomous,
> Wears yet a precious jewel in his head. (2.1.12–14)

The toad with "precious jewel in his head" can seem an odd *simile*[10] for sapiential suffering; yet to those educated in a Catholic Humanist curriculum, such as the poet and critic Sir Philip Sidney, the "toad" here probably represents fallen nature transformed into the "golden" world made possible by the power of human virtue and the magic of poetry. As Sidney argues, "Nature never set forth the earth in so rich a tapestry as divers poets have done," for while Nature's "world is brazen," poets "grow in effect another nature," and thus deliver a "golden" landscape.[11] The golden toad, also mentioned in Lyly's *Euphues*, is thus an example of the potentially fearsome or even grotesque reality of nature transformed by the power of the human imagination, which becomes possible by the union of eloquence and sapience that Duke Senior's speech as a whole exemplifies.

The final three lines of Duke Senior's speech employ memorable figurative language that causes us to reevaluate the very meaning of the most common trope, *metaphora*:

> And this our life, exempt from public haunt,
> Finds tongues in trees, books in the running brooks,
> Sermons in stones, and good in everything. (2.1.12–17)

Literary critics today generally distinguish *metaphor* from *simile* according to whether, with *metaphor*, a "being" verb is used, and diverse subjects are said "to be" each other, or, with *simile*, whether "like" or "as" are used to claim rather that the subjects are similar to each other. Yet for Duke Senior,

---

8. Shaw, "Fortune and Nature," 46.
9. Peacham, *Garden*, 29.
10. Peacham, *Garden*, 158.
11. Sidney, *Defence*, 216.

his familiar first objects here are not identified with their alliterative pair, but rather found within that pair in a manner that transforms the whole of the natural object into a source of the initial object.

All of "being," in the philosophical and theological sense of the created world, can thus "be" a metaphor, if one can perceive the "good in everything." Senior's metaphors particularly suggest, therefore, the equation of *sapientia* and *eloquentia* typical of Catholic Humanism. For Duke Senior, despite or rather because of the adversity that banishment has brought him, in Arden he has found that every tree has a tongue, each book becomes a running brook, and every stone offers a potential sermon. One recalls Christ's metaphor after the Pharisee's rebuke of the disciples' praise of him, when He tells them that "if these should hold their peace, the stones would immediately cry out" (Luke 19:40). For Duke Senior, nature in Arden is God's creation, so infused with goodness that each natural object is a source of sapiential creativity.

In performance, the initial issue facing directors of the scene or actors playing Senior is whether to attempt a natural environment that mimics, in any way, the transformative magic of the opening speech's rhetoric. The often naturalistic BBC production of 1978 began with Tony Church, as Senior, washing his face and hands in a cool running brook. Most productions are less naturalistic, suggesting rather a wintry climate implied by Senior's reference to "the penalty of Adam, the seasons' difference" (2.1.5–6). The larger issue, though, is the tone with which to deliver Senior's poetic lines. Church and most older Seniors, such as William Needles at Stratford, Ontario in 1983, adopt a serene, serious tone that clearly enunciates each element of his sapiential eloquence. This tone thus contrasts and soon clashes with a satiric, vitriolic Jaques, who sharply criticize the courtiers' need to live not by wisdom or eloquence alone, but by the organized violence involved in hunting deer. In the 2009 RSC, Philip Bird broke this pattern as a younger, almost carefree Duke Senior; unshaven, with rough, leather clothing, this Senior's words seem almost cynical, and the much older Amiens' subsequent praise of the speech was, with eyebrows raised, clearly ironic. The 2016 Stratford, Ontario, also offered an interesting twist, as both Senior and Jaques were played by female actors. Yet Brigit Wilson, as Senior, delivered her lines with the gracious optimism and hospitable tone typical of most Seniors, while Seanna McKenna was a caustic, typically satiric Jaques. Significantly, especially if one recalls also the nature of Shakespeare's original acting company, in 2016 this gender choice did not fundamentally alter the delivery or primary effect of either major characters' words.

Two modern actresses who in 1983 had played Rosalind and Celia on the British stage, Juliet Stevenson and Fiona Shaw, give another perspective on the relationship of nature and rhetoric in the play. After playing their parts, for them Arden seemed to be

> A strange, weird realm which has the power to transform itself, and in which all things are possible. It is both an image from our nightmares and a place of infinite potential. Above all, we felt, it is a metaphor. But a metaphor for what, exactly?[12]

Setting aside for a moment these actresses' awareness of the darker elements of Arden, their question on metaphor can be approached by recalling Peacham's insight into this central trope. The preface of Peacham's *Garden of Eloquence* argues that tropes originated because

> Wise men calling to remembrance that many things were very like to one another in some aspect of nature, thought it good to bestow a name of one thing to signify another, which did in some part or property of nature resemble it, thus began they to use translated speech: declaring their meaning by similitudes and compared significations.[13]

There is an interesting biblical parallel to Peacham's concept of "translated speech." Genesis 5:24 tells us that Enoch, Methuselah's father, "walked with God" and was not reported to have died, "for God took him," of which St. Paul later writes, in the KJV translation: "by faith Enoch was translated that he should not see death; and was not found, because God had translated him: for before his translation he had this testimony, that he pleased God" (Heb 11:5). The KJV translation of this scripture may or may not have drawn on the rhetorical concept of tropes to describe the radical similarity between the reality of divine life in time and eternity, but Shakespeare found the concept interesting enough to apply it to a sublime moment of comedy from an earlier play, *A Midsummer Night's Dream*. There Bottom, the bombastic actor who wants to play every role on stage, is physically transformed into what his character already is, an ass or donkey, causing the leader of his acting company to say, "Bless thee Bottom, bless thee. Thou art translated" (3.1.113).

This apparently incongruous comment becomes coherent when Bottom awakes from his "dream" and, though not fully remembering the wonders of the Fairy Queen who fell in love with him, has his perceptions altered in a manner that recalls one of St. Paul's most famous promises, that "eye hath not seen, nor ear heard" of the things that "God hath prepared for them that love him" (1 Cor 2:9). Bottom comically but clearly alludes to this

12. Shaw and Stevenson, "Celia and Rosalind," 63.
13. Peacham, *Garden*, 1–2.

passage by describing his own vision: "The eye of man hath not heard, the ear of man hath not seen, man's hand is not able to taste, his tongue to conceive, nor his heart to report what my dream was" (4.1.206–9). One could argue that Bottom has "mistranslated" divine vision, but within the world of his own play Bottom does become an imaginative leader who helps the other players perform a play that Duke Theseus eventually considers good.

The rhetorical and biblical concept of "translation" helps us to understand why Peacham, when he defines *metaphora* as the primary trope, describes it as "artificial translation of one word, from the proper signification, to another not proper, yet nigh and like."[14] Moreover, we can now fully appreciate the comment given upon Senior's speech by his court singer, Amiens, who says:

> Happy is your grace
> That can translate the stubbornness of fortune
> Into so quiet and so sweet a style. (2.1.18–20)

So far from being a comment solely about the linguistic structures of Senior's speech, Amiens sees that Senior has advanced the cheerful debate between nature vs. fortune begun by Celia and Rosalind, yet further "translated" this argument in a manner especially valued by Catholic Humanists; in the simple things of nature, Senior finds words—not incoherent words, but words that allow speech, even books, perhaps even the wisdom of good sermons, for there is good in everything. Duke Senior's speech is thus an apt illustration of what Erasmus calls *copia* of words and things, *de rerum et verborum*, for in nature Senior finds the truth of revelation: after creating the world, God saw that "it was very good" (Gen 1:36). From the perspective, then, of Catholic Humanism, there is very clear scriptural authority for Duke Senior's concluding claim: "there *is* good in everything" (2.1.17).

This is the "original blessing" that those in the Judeo-Christian tradition have usually affirmed as strongly as the concept of "original sin." Yet it is hard to imagine a more complete portrayal of the Catholic Humanist mind than this speech; Duke Senior rests not in nature, nor even in the God of nature, but rather exults in the eloquent wisdom spoken everywhere in nature. The imagery here draws on a medieval and biblical commonplace, that the heavens declare the glory of God because God authors the "book" of nature, and the "book" of scripture and the "book of history," all part of the "book of life."[15] Yet the Catholic Humanists brought their rhetorical emphasis to this

---

14. Peacham, *Garden*, 3.
15. See Jeffrey, *People of the Book*, 139–66.

imagery, reading both physical and human nature to discover the eloquent wisdom freely offered therein by the grace of God.

Another word in Amiens' comment upon Duke Senior's speech also has rich Renaissance connotations which most modern readers are likely to miss: "sweet" (2.1.20). In medieval and Renaissance poetry and spiritual writing, "sweet" refers not to the saccharine taste of candy or other treats, but rather to the exultant experience of communing with God, especially in prayer.[16] Could Duke Senior also be describing a spiritual experience of this kind? In his own "quiet," thoughtful way, the answer is certainly yes, for Catholic Humanists cannot speak eloquent wisdom without listening to God. The "sermons in stones" found by Senior perhaps refers not only to the physical objects of the forest, but quite possibly also alludes to Jesus as the "chief cornerstone" (1 Pet 2:6), or even to the principle that we are all "lively stones" called to worship God (1 Pet 2:5).

Jesus' redemptive presence within our fallen world is fundamental to Catholic Humanism, yet it is also central to Shakespeare's presentation of the "pastoral" genre in *As You Like It* that expectations of an "ideal" rural world are often undercut in the play. Rather, the fallen, not so ideal aspects of our world are never far from view within the play. Arden is not Eden, and immediately in 2.1 we are soon introduced to the figure who will debate Duke Senior, and others within Arden, to remind the audience of the reality of the fall: Jaques. Primarily, Jaques does this by sympathizing with and becoming an advocate for the natural inhabitants of the forest, particularly the deer sure to be hunted to feed the humans now living therein. In a fascinating extension and variant upon the "holy fool" tradition usually developed by Shakespeare, Duke Senior asks what at first seems like another rhetorical question, "Come, shall we go and kill us venison?" (2.1.22), for it is obvious that the courtiers must hunt to eat and survive. Yet Senior himself seems doubtful of his own answer to this question, lamenting that "the poor dappled fools," or deer, should be hunted "in their own confines" (2.1.24).

It is Jaques, though, who develops this "doubt" into a full rhetorical argument that deeply questions whether humans have any right to hunt within Arden. We first hear the outline of this argument from a "First Lord" (the sort of nameless character whom Shakespeare commonly uses to announce a major theme) who reports that Jaques claims that Duke Senior "doth more usurp" in the forest than Duke Frederick does in the court (2.1.27); further, Jaques laments the death of any deer, calling each one a "hairy fool" (2.1.40). The Lord then tells us that Jaques develops Duke

---

16. There are many examples of this use of "sweet" in Medieval and Renaissance authors. To take one from Erasmus's *The Paraclesis*, 105: "there are those who make the Philosophy of Christ sad and morose, although nothing is more sweet than it."

Senior's concerns in a manner that would be familiar to every sixteenth-century student trained by Erasmus' *De Copia*; this "melancholy" man, in a "humor" or state of mind that Shakespeare's age commonly associates with intellectual and linguistic creativity,[17] will "moralize this spectacle" by turning it "into a thousand similes" (2.1.44–45).

The terms here are those of Catholic Humanist rhetoric, not modern liberal ethics. To "moralize" is not to assign the sort of vaguely emotional "moral" that ignores the concrete reality of a situation, but rather to make substantive ethical argument. Nor do the "thousand similes" suggest figurative retreat from concrete reality. On the contrary, Jaques is an orator whose similes begin with concrete reality and then amplify it through comparisons, as Erasmus recommends throughout *De Copia*. We will see and directly hear from Jaques soon in the play, but here the First Lord gives second hand report of Jaques' arguments. "'Poor Deer' quoth he," the First Lord reports, perhaps mocking Jaques' tone, "thou makst a testament / as worldlings do, giving thy sum of more / to that which had too much" (2.1.47–49). The word "testament" here, as now, has religious and legal connotations, so that Jaques' *simile*[18] compares the dead deer both to an appeal to the human soul, and a legal will which bequeaths material goods—in this case, the good of the deer's dead body. The wit of the simile is also enhanced if "worldlings" is also a homonymic pun, or *paronomasia*,[19] for "wordlings," satirically rebuking Senior's utopian words by pointing to everyman's material needs.

This suggestion might seem farfetched, but its unusual rhetoric is typical of Jaques' creative if slightly skewed wit. In the next quotation reported by the "First Lord," Jaques is reported to have said, "'Tis right . . . thus misery doth part / the flux of company'" (2.1.31–32). A literal meaning of "flux" is "bodily discharge," so again the implied *simile*, comparing Senior's courtiers to "flux," satirically suggests that the misery caused to the forest's deer divides Jaques from Senior's party. In a *paranomasia* that would have been obvious to Shakespeare's English audience, however, pronunciation of the French name "Jaques" could be anglicized to "jakes," another name for a "privy" or outhouse. A harsh reading of this pun could suggest that Jaques is "full of shit," but a kinder epithet is the alliterative *metaphora* Jaques terms himself, "a broken bankrupt" (2.1.57). Jaques is isolated, alienated from any source of material advancement, yet this noble orator will employ *sapientia*

---

17. For the later but very thorough summary of this tradition, see Burton, *The Anatomy of Melancholy*.

18. Peacham, *Garden*, 158.

19. Peacham, *Garden*, 56.

and *eloquentia* against any human invasion of the natural world. As the First Lord concludes:

> Thus most invectively he pierceth through
> The body of the country, city, court,
> Yea, and of this our life, swearing that we
> Are mere usurpers, tyrants, and what's worse,
> To fright the animals and to kill them up
> In their assigned and native dwelling place. (2.1.58–63)

Yet rather than regarding Jaques as an enemy to be avoided, Duke Senior asks the First Lord to bring him to the melancholy poet, saying, "I love to cope him in these sullen fits / For then he's full of matter" (2.1.68–69). The key word here, "cope," is an anglicization of Erasmus' key Latin word *copia*, a "translation" that retains the sense of dialectical argument, though modern editors often errantly footnote the term to suggest some physical confrontation.[20] As Robert Burton's *Anatomy of Melancholy* will so richly suggest later in the seventeenth century, Duke Senior recognizes Jaques' intellectual brilliance during "sullen fits," precisely because he is developing copious rhetorical argument or is "full of matter," or intellectual ideas. From the start, then, Duke Senior does not view Jaques as an enemy, but rather an intellectual companion whose unique rhetoric has its own value in developing the humane, peaceful civilization that Senior envisions in Arden. We are reminded of Erasmus' willingness to debate even those who appear to be enemies, such as Luther.

The rhetorical promise offered by Duke Senior's entry into the play is followed by a very short scene in which Duke Frederick presents its political and intellectual opposite, the brief but efficient language of political power through intimidation of others. Beginning with threatening *erotema*, or rhetorical question, "Can it be possible that no man saw them?," Duke Frederick asserts that there must be "some villains of my court" who have helped Celia and Rosalind, "foolish runaways," to escape (2.2.1–2, 21). Positively invoking terms sure to terrify any politically aware audience in the sixteenth century, Duke Frederick concludes by demanding, "let not search and inquisition quail" to bring them back again. Happily, for this is a very happy play, we do not see the standard instruments of state cruelty unfurled, but rather turn to a scene in which old Adam persuades young Orlando that he, too, should pursue a new life in the forest.

The relationship of this scene, 2.3, to those surrounding it in act 2 is unclear, and being unnecessary to the plot it might easily be cut by modern

---

20. Latham, *As You Like It*, 33, footnotes the word to mean not only "encounter," but also "debate with."

directors. From a simple theatrical perspective, there are surely shorter means by which to bring Orlando into the forest of Arden, yet there are thematic and rhetorical reasons, rooted in the Catholic Humanist tradition, as to why Shakespeare would want to portray old Adam persuading Orlando to seek a new life in the forest. The traditional biblical typology of the "old Adam" being sacrificed for the "new man" (1 Cor 15:22) is an important referent for the entire scene, but it remains in the background as the scene begins rather with Adam asking a series of *erotema*, rhetorical questions, which have the opposite effect and impact of those with which Oliver bombarded Orlando in the play's opening scene. Here, the questions imply respect and deep affection, rooted in a strong desire to protect Orlando from harm. Adam "asks" Orlando, "Why are you virtuous? Why do people love you?" (2.3.5), but clearly these questions point not only to the abundant good in Orlando's human nature, but also to the strong love of the old servant for the young man. Adam has become aware that Oliver plans to burn down Orlando's home (2.3.24), so he now wants Orlando to avoid any contact with his older brother, though even to acknowledge this familial relationship has become odious to the old man:

> The enemy of all your graces lives,
> Your brother—no, no brother—yet the son—
> Yet not the son, I will not call him son—
> Of him I was about to call his father. (2.3.19–22)

Puttenham might call the figure here *aposiopesis*, when we "break off" speech because "ashamed, or afraid to speak it out,"[21] but more generally it could also be described as the *euphemism* still common whenever one wishes to avoid political offense. By warning Orlando but avoiding directly naming and thus specifically critiquing his familial lineage, Adam reflects his own commitment to the *ethos* of service, which also now compels the old man to again offer Orlando "the service of a younger man / In all your business and necessities" (2.3.55–56). Orlando recognizes and commends the classical *ethos* of Adam's commitment, "the constant service of the antique world, / When service sweat for duty, not for meed!" (2.3.57–59).

Yet beyond himself, great though that sacrifice is at any age, Adam also offers Orlando, to aid his immediate survival, the "five hundred crowns" (2.3.39) he saved while in service to old Sir Rowland. The young man is understandably concerned with how he can keep body and soul together on his own, but Adam gives his greatest gift by reminding Orlando that he will never be alone. Like Hamlet recalling the "special providence in the fall

---

21. Puttenham, *Art*, 166.

of a sparrow" (5.2.165–66), Adam directly alludes to the famous passage where Jesus reminds his disciples that all people "are of more value than many sparrows," for "two sparrows" are "sold" for little value in human commerce, yet our Father in heaven has "numbered" each hair of our head (Matt 10:29–31). Do not worry, Adam tells Orlando, for though he has lost his earthly father, yet "he that doth the ravens feed / Yea providently caters for the sparrow" (2.3.44–45) will comfort them in any trials they face. Via this direct biblical allusion, old Adam reminds the young man of the possibility of pursuing a new life in which "perfect love casteth out fear" (1 John 4:18). Here, as so often in Renaissance poetry and drama, scriptural reference offers an ethical and theological light in dark times.

Act 2, scene 4 lightens the serious tone of this somber spiritual scene, focusing again on Celia and Rosalind, now in the Forest of Arden and surrounded by rustics. Touchstone remains with them, and puns how he would rather "bear with" the tired young ladies than "bear" them, a probable bawdry that he covers by quickly adding, "I should bear no cross if I did bear you" (2.4.10–12). The puns thus cleverly switch from sexuality to the more socially acceptable realms of religion and money, the disciple's (and fool's) call to take up one's cross and the presence of crosses on most of the "crowns" of coins then printed, any of which Touchstone would happily accept as payment. Rosalind does not respond, blandly remarking, "Well, this is the forest of Arden," and again Touchstone probably replies with a bawdy pun, on "harden," when he agrees, "Ay now am I in Arden; the more fool I" (2.4.14) Bawdy jokes were a staple of most fools' repertoire,[22] and even Lear's Fool will joke about "things [being] cut shorter" (*Lr.*, 1.5.50). It is unclear how fully the young ladies grasp these puns, but that Touchstone offers them at all suggests that, perhaps now due to their disguises, these "young men" are aware of the language once hidden from what Rosalind here (2.4.6) calls "the weaker vessel" (1 Pet 3:7). Paul also teaches, however, that "when I am weak then I am strong" (2 Cor 12:10), and it is this paradox which Shakespeare portrays fully once these young women meet even more foolish men.

A reminder of such men then comes in the form of young Silvius and old Corin, as the old man counsels the younger (obvious pastoral counterparts to Adam and Orlando) regarding his infatuation with Phoebe, a shepherdess. Any counsel is in vain, however, for Silvius doubts that Corin, "being old" (2.4.22), can possibly comprehend the depth and pain of his love for Phoebe. Rosalind is perhaps the only onlooker moved by this rhetoric, for in another sign of her romantic soul she remarks: "Alas, poor shepherd, searching of thy

---

22. See Partridge, *Shakespeare's Bawdy*.

wound, / I have by hard adventure found mine own" (2.4.41–42). The *pathos* generally seen in pastoral love is then strongly undercut by another extended bawdy speech in which Touchstone fondly remembers "Jane Smile," though he concludes with the kind of abstract aphorism for which Shakespeare's fools are also well known: "As all is mortal in nature, so is all nature in love mortal in folly" (2.4.43–52). Erasmus' *Praise of Folly* surely supports this proverb, which Peacham might call *paroemia*,[23] and Touchstone may directly allude to this famous text, but any Catholic Humanist would smile here at Touchstone's pessimism. When Rosalind replies with praise that could apply to any of Shakespeare's "unconscious fools," "thou speak'st wiser that thou art ware of," Touchstone reminds her and the audience of the concrete realism that Shakespearean fools are also typically grounded in: "Nay, I shall ne'er be ware of mine own wit till I break my shins against it" (2.4.53–55).

Celia soon reminds them all of their concrete need for food, causing Touchstone to comically and rudely introduce the courtiers to Corin as his "betters" (2.4.66). The humble old shepherd replies with a simple statement of economic fact, "Else are they very wretched," and soon assents to the aristocrats' offer to buy the "cottage, pasture, and the flock" (2.4.67, 91) of the old shepherd's master. "And we will mend thy wages" (2.4.93), promises Celia, but surely such economic banter, typical of the "court vs. country" rhetoric common in pastoral literature, is but prelude to the summary *paradox* then given to Celia: "I like this place / And willingly could waste me time in it" (2.4.93–94).

Time spent in Arden can seem to be wasted, yet so, most humans at times believe, can any time spent on love. In *As You Like It*'s Arden, as in Eden long ago, young people will learn much about love, and learn especially the difference between passionate love derived from their own will and love given by the will and presence of God. Such learning not only is time not wasted but, according to Catholic Humanism, perhaps the only learning worth spending time upon. Or rather would be, if our world were more Edenic, or Arden-like; however, because men are often un-wise, women especially need the wisdom of fools, if only as an alternative to the "wisdom" of the man to whom act 2 now turns, Jaques.

---

23. Peacham, *Garden*, 29.

4

"Ambitious for a Motley Coat"

The "Matter" of "Melancholy" Jaques

BEFORE INTRODUCING JAQUES, SHAKESPEARE first gives us another song from Amiens which serves to restate Duke Senior's thoughts on the natural goodness of the forest. "Under the Greenwood tree," as brilliantly shown in John Hirsh's 1983 production at Stratford, Ontario, can be an elaborate set-piece in which everyone present, including the audience, is invited to come "hither, hither, hither," into Arden, to let one's natural "merry note" be tuned by the "sweet bird's throat" (2.5.1–4). Through the pleasing rhetoric of music and performance, the entire theatre can thus become a welcoming "green space" full of cheer and happy song, and everyone involved in the play can be transported to what one time Renaissance scholar and later baseball commissioner A. Bartlett Giamatti called the "green fields of the mind."[1] Echoing Duke Senior's initial warning of winter in 2.1, however, Amiens adds a touch of realism in the final line of the song's first stanza: "here shall he see no enemy / But winter and rough weather" (2.5.6–8).

Perhaps human nature might also mar this music, however, for when Jaques requests "more, more," Amiens warns that the song will make him "melancholy" (2.5.9–10). This response might surprise modern audiences, but is familiar to Shakespeareans who can compare the melancholy Orsino's call for music at the start of *Twelfth Night*, or Orsino's payment for Feste's

---

1. Giamatti, "Green Fields of the Mind."

melancholy song later in the same play (2.4). Amiens' fear is that music might awaken the depressed spirit which lurks within this strange figure. Jaques admits, "I can suck melancholy from a song as a weasel sucks eggs" (2.5.11–12). The exceptionally unflattering *simile*[2] here does not so much "moralize the spectacle" of Amiens' song as appear to shatter its harmony. Jaques is clearly different than anyone who has thus far appeared in the play, and there is a real danger that the "matter" of Jaques, both his satirical arguments and personal presence, could suck the very life out of the cheer and goodness that Duke Senior and his court have found in the forest. Jaques' melancholy rhetoric must be responded to, but through means other than the railing and ridicule which he himself practices so skillfully.

Yet it must also be recognized that melancholy can inspire creativity. Though melancholy is understood, by the primitive medicine practiced in the Renaissance, to be one of the four "humors" that, when unbalanced, can indicate illness, melancholy was also thought to foster reflection and wit. Probably the best summary of this tradition, as already noted, is Robert Burton's *The Anatomy of Melancholy*. Burton will follow Jaques in eschewing the "sweet" balanced style that characterizes much sixteenth-century prose, favoring instead unruly sentences and long paragraphs that don't fit any rhetorical mode. This style of writing is in some ways a reaction against the highly patterned, disciplined, "euphuistic" style made so popular by John Lyly's *Euphues*. Jaques, a character not found in *Rosalynde* but rather invented by Shakespeare, prefers "matter" that is often incongruous, unbalanced . . . in a sense, more realistic in representing the "rough patches" that are part of every human life. Jaques is the very embodiment of the melancholy creative thinker whom Burton will later praise. A melancholic thinker faces the dangers of isolation, alienation, and depression, as an almost inevitable result of such thinkers' integrity and lack of concern for social popularity or interaction.

Jaques seems to welcome isolation, yet in his response to Amiens one senses the artistic integrity also valued highly by Catholic Humanism. Amiens at first refuses to sing further, saying "My voice is ragged: I know I cannot please you" (2.5.14). When Jaques first responds: "I do not desire you to please me," we can be sure that we have met an exception to the rhetorical ethic that reigns over most of the play. Yet when Jaques adds, "I do desire you to sing. Come, more; another stanzo: call you 'em stanzos?" (2.5.15–17), he also expresses the common sixteenth-century interest in the forms of art, and in the value of art beyond the hedonistic pleasures it might give. Common human niceties are of no interest to Jaques, who compares

---

2. Peacham, *Garden*, 158.

"compliment" to "the encounter of two dog-apes," and contrasts himself to Duke Senior, whom Jaques deems too "disputable" for company; "I think of as many matters as he," Jaques further claims, "but I give heaven thanks and make no boast of them" (2.5.23–24, 32–34). Evidence for Senior's pride in the play, however, is almost as lacking as examples of Jaques' piety.

Soon Senior and Jaques meet, but first Amiens gives another stanza that, in contrast to the first, has much more pointed political and social critique. This time invited "hither" into Arden are those "who doth ambition shun" (2.5.35), a rather clear exclusion of the usurping Duke Frederick. Jaques himself wants to add a verse to the song, saying he wrote it yesterday "in despite of my invention"; "in despite," perhaps, because in a sense this is "anti-rhetoric" which yet serves to clarify the rhetoric which Jaques typically practices:

> If it do come to pass
> That any man turn ass,
> Leaving his wealth and ease,
> A stubborn will to please,
> Ducdame, ducdame, ducdame:
> Here shall he see
> Gross fools as he,
> An if he will come to me. (2.5.47–54)

As the first speech in which Jaques, as the First Lord had said, "most invectively" critiques not only Senior's courtiers but humanity in general, this is a very important speech by which to understand Jaques' role as satirist in the play. Within the play's rhetoric as a whole, it is certainly notable that the speech both opens and closes with an "if" or conditional clause; the final line repeats "if" through "an," which in sixteenth-century English generally means "if," rather than the article it usually is today. These "if" clauses are certainly different than any so far spoken in the play, however, in opening up a new possibility: all in the forest may become fools. A common synonym of "fool" is "ass," as when Bottom is translated into an "ass" or donkey as the primary fool of *A Midsummer Night's Dream*. More positively, of course, Jaques' invitation could be seen as a willingness to share his wisdom, for the fool as wise man is a proverbial commonplace not only in Shakespeare's plays but, thanks to Erasmus' *Praise of Folly*, in Renaissance culture generally.

On the other hand, Jaques generally does not seem the sort of sociable sort of fool who would welcome sharing with others. Most actors present this key speech as *sarcasmus*,[3] Jaques critiquing class privilege, the "wealth

---

3. Peacham, *Garden*, 37.

and ease," of the aristocratic courtier. Live theatre can make this critique more personal. In John Hirsch's 1983 Stratford, Ontario, production for example, the other actors onstage gathered around Jaques, played by Nicholas Pennel, until he sneered at these fools called "into a circle." In the 2009 production of Thea Sharrock, Tim McMullan plays Jaques as a young, sarcastic, almost nihilistic "bon vivant," and his "invention" is sung as a duet with a much older Amiens, Peter Gale. On the "call fools into a circle" line, though, McMullan points directly at people in the audience, and Gale raises a knowing eyebrow.

While Jaques' "invention" is surely both theatrical and social rhetoric, it is also important to note here the probable allusion to Catholic Humanist rhetoric when Jaques speaks of the "stubborn will." For it is a common error to believe that Catholic Humanist theologians had a simple view of human nature as good, to be contrasted to the Calvinist emphasis on "total depravity." Rather, as Erasmus makes clear in his dispute with Luther, the human will can be so stubborn that it is in fact capable of rejecting the will of God, Who desires to save all men.[4] The logical alternative is the related Calvinist doctrines of "irresistible grace," and "double predestination," since God saves whomever He wishes and "predestines" the rest to die. Shakespeare is clearly familiar with this view; in *Measure for Measure*, for example, the condemned Claudio quotes the central Calvinist scripture supporting such doctrines, Romans 9:14–21, when he speaks of the arbitrary nature of God's judgment: "on whom it will, it will; on whom it will not, so; yet still 'tis just" (1.2.114–15). It is not clear, though, whether Shakespeare would support such notions or the view of Lucio, who earlier in the same scene told us, "Grace is grace, despite of all controversy" (1.2.24–25).

Theological debates aside, the more obvious response to Jaques' speech is Amiens' question, "what's that ducdame" (2.5.55). Modern editors have traced the word to an "ancient British phrase," once common in children's games, "dewch da mi," which roughly translates simply as "come hither" in another language.[5] While Jaques certainly means to replace Amiens' musical invitation with his own satirical challenge, it also would have been possible for the less learned in Shakespeare's audience to form their own interpretation of the phrase. Most obviously, "ducdame" could be a French play upon "dukes" and "dames," or "lords" and "ladies," and thus Jaques might be inviting all powerful aristocrats to give up worldly power for the wisdom of

---

4. See Erasmus, *Diatribe on Free Will*, to which Luther responded with *On the Bondage of the Will*. Both works are found in Rupp, *Luther and Erasmus*.

5. Latham, *As You Like It*, 45.

the forest. The phrase might thus be an example of *cacozelia*,⁶ an affected word invented by Jaques to show himself more learned than the courtiers who have invaded Arden. Elizabethan fools often invent "false authorities" to claim superior wisdom,⁷ and Jaques might be mimicking this practice.

Jaques' response to Amiens' question, "tis a Greek invocation," to "call fools into a circle" (2.5.56), could be interpreted as attempting to place all under his own power. For "invocation" is the term used by a magician who calls enemies into "a circle" to put them under a spell. It is this very use of power that Prospero forswears in the climactic moments of *The Tempest*, which might also be the concluding moments of Shakespeare's dramatic career. Yet it is hard to see Jaques as ever being ruthless enough to retain power. Immediately after defining "ducdame" he reverts to a much more humble "if" clause: "I'll go sleep if I can. If I cannot, I'll rail against all the first-born of Egypt" (2.5.57–58). The allusion here to the death of the first-born Egyptians in Exodus 12:29–30, which led to the expulsion of the Jews from Egypt, or possibly to those "first born" later killed as Herod searched for Christ, threatens further political conflict. Yet Jaques' rhetorical "railing" rarely leads to physical conflict, but rather to debate with those in power, whether those now in Arden or those still in the court of Duke Frederick.

The potentially serious but largely comic nature of this conflict is given added poignancy by a brief scene, 2.6, which reminds us that Orlando and Adam are in the forest, starving, in need of food rather than words. It is a commonplace of Catholic Humanism, and of medieval and Renaissance political thought in general, that without good governance, or legitimate political authority, the people die. As the scene opens, Adam tells Orlando that he "can go no further," that he is so hungry that "lie I down and measure out my grave" (2.6.1–3). To revive Adam's "greater heart" (2.6.4), Orlando's prose response demonstrates how a series of *conditional* clauses can be used not to threaten, as with Oliver, but rather to elicit mercy:

> If this uncouth forest yield any thing savage, I will either be food for it or bring it for food to thee. Thy conceit is nearer death than thy powers. For my sake be comfortable; hold death awhile at the arm's end: I will here be with thee presently; and if I bring thee not something to eat, I will give thee leave to die: but if thou diest before I come, thou art a mocker of my labour. (2.6.6–13)

Perhaps the most important line here is Orlando's admonition that Adam's "conceit," or mental state, "is nearer death" than his "powers," or physical capacity; the implication is that one's spirit can incline one towards

---

6. Puttenham, *Art*, 251–52.
7. See Wiles, *Shakespeare's Clown*.

or away from death, which recalls the Catholic Humanist emphasis on the importance of the imagination in preserving spiritual hope. Yet physical hunger has its own imperatives, and is here driving Adam to the most urgent of indicative statements, which Orlando voices when he first comes upon the courtiers in the forest: "I almost die for food; and let me have it" (2.7.104). If Orlando can share their fellowship, then he and Adam can also experience peace in the forest.

The potential for peace in Arden to be disrupted by a struggle for rhetorical authority, however, has become heated again in 2.7 as Duke Senior and Jaques finally meet. Directors typically contrast the two characters' personalities, usually pairing a serene Senior with a sarcastic Jaques. Sharrock's 2009 RSC, as already noted, was unusual in casting Senior as a carefree middle-aged man and Jaques as a "bon vivant," but only a general tone of merriment can soften the many points of conflict between these two characters. The *metaphora*[8] used to introduce their first encounter is so familiar to a Renaissance audience that it is radically condensed, but its potential relevance to Catholic Humanism is suggested first by Duke Senior's opening lines in the scene, as he tells the "First Lord" that Jaques cannot be found so perhaps "he be transformed into a beast" (2.7.1). Unless his human nature can be found, and reconciled to the other courtiers in Arden, Duke Senior foresees disharmony in the forest: "If he, compact of jars, grow musical / We shall have shortly discord in the spheres" (2.7.5–6).

The *conditional* here introduces imagery based upon one of the central ideas of most Renaissance world views. The "music of the spheres" can be heard, according to pre-Galileo, Ptolemaic cosmology, whenever one realizes that God is ultimately in control of the universe, despite the evidence of temporal suffering and evil which might suggest otherwise. The relationship between heavenly bodies, or "spheres," requires fuller explanation, but the meaning is so popularly known that it can be referenced "short hand" in drama. Thus in *Pericles*, one of Shakespeare's late plays, the title hero is separated from his daughter and undergoes many trials and tests, but finally is reunited with her and hears, "the music of the spheres" (21.215).[9] Duke Senior's phrase "compact of jars" can confuse modern audiences, but no figure of speech seems implied; rather "compact" is a verb based on the infinitive "to compact," meaning "to compose," while "jars" could be a plural noun describing quarrels.[10] The implied trope is in Senior's fear of "discord in the

---

8. Peacham, *Garden*, 3.

9. See Maillet, "To Glad Your Ear and Please Your Eyes," 109–24.

10. Trautvetter, *As You Like It*, based on *Two Gentleman of Verona*, 4.2.67, and *The Taming of the Shrew*, 3.1.39, 73.

spheres," for the forest's harmony—expressed here in familiar cosmological metaphor—is in danger of serious discord.

Yet when Jaques is found, Duke Senior discovers that he appears, "merrily" for, as he explains, he has met Touchstone. Jaques exclaims: "A fool, a fool, I met a fool i'th' forest / A motley fool—a miserable world" (2.7.12–13). The juxtaposition here of "motley fool" and "miserable world" is viewed by some as a typo, so that they suggest reading "word" for "world,"[11] so that Jaques is lamenting that some call such a fine fellow as Touchstone a "fool." However, Jaques' *sarcasmus*[12] could just as easily be based upon how the "world" undervalues the humor and wisdom of a fool. Jaques is very pleased that Touchstone has come to the forest, for he clearly admires the fool, whose traditional purpose in Shakespearean drama and Renaissance courts is to speak truth to worldly power, employing comedy primarily as a means of avoiding the retribution which such speech normally provokes. From Jaques' perspective, he and Touchstone are at least rhetorical allies and perhaps even soulmates.

Jaques specifically expresses admiration for how Touchstone embodies the traditional fool's role. He loves how Touchstone's wisdom is expressed in learned eloquence, behind the disguise of a fool's costume, recalling how he "railed on Lady Fortune in good terms, / In good set terms, and yet a motley fool" (2.7.16–17). As already noted, "railing" is the form of rhetoric that best suits Jaques, who similarly employs traditional schemes and tropes to advance his own arguments. Jaques' initial praise introduces a series of direct quotations, which serve to remind us that most fools, or certainly most Shakespearean fools, express their wisdom through concrete expressions that simply notice reality. "It is ten o'clock," Jaques reports Touchstone observing, then sagely adding, "'Tis but an hour ago since it was nine, / And after one hour more 'twill be eleven" (2.7.22–25). One could describe this observation as a scheme of brevity, a *brachiepa*,[13] but to most listeners the point seems rather literal. Such lines could be related to the play's broader themes on time, but here they are simply common sense.

Literal, common sense jokes of this kind are one of many common features of fools that Shakespeare includes in this part, invented from his own theatrical traditions rather than adapted from Lodge's prose. Whether Touchstone was a part first written for Will Kempe, or for the more intellectual Robert Armin, the role exemplifies the "foolish wisdom" tradition that Puttenham, for example, reminds us of when he writes:

11. See Hulme, *Explorations in Shakespeare's Language*, 208.
12. Peacham, *Garden*, 37.
13. Peacham, *Garden*, 182.

> Most certainly all things that move a man to laughter, as do these scurrilities and other ridiculous behaviours, it is for some undecency that is found in them; which maketh it decent for every man to laugh at them. And therefore when we see or hear a natural fool and idiot do or say anything foolishly, we laugh not at him: but when he doeth or speaketh wisely, because that is unlike himself.[14]

Puttenham's focus upon "decency," here at the end of *The Art of English Poesy*, suggests also the important role of bawdry in Touchstone's appeal. Frequently this bawdry is implied through puns, which are an important part of the fool's appeal to Jaques, as he indicates by quoting from lines that conclude and summarize Touchstone's thinking on time:

> And so from hour to hour we ripe and ripe,
> And then from hour to hour we rot and rot;
> And thereby hangs a tale. (2.7.26–28)

There are two distinct forms of pun here, and both are central to the humor of the play, and especially to the fool Touchstone. One is *paranomasia*,[15] a homonymic pun involving words of similar sound but different spelling, since "hour" is likely a pun on "whore"; "rot," though, is *antanaclasis*,[16] a pun using different meanings of the same word, for the "rot" repeated here might not be simple decay but rather venereal disease that destroys genitalia. Johnson famously called puns the fatal Cleopatra for which [Shakespeare] lost the world,"[17] but in *As You Like It* puns are a crucial part of the world of Arden that is recreated to combat human evil. Puns are so important to the play's rhetoric that my glossary counts them as "figures of thought."

Technically the scheme of repetition here is *diacope*,[18] but the imaginative impact of Jaques' words comes from implied, rather unflattering *metaphora*[19] which suggests that our sexual organs are fruit, mature or ripe for use at one age, but likely to later "rot" through either old age or venereal disease. Most actors use gesture to indicate the bawdy joke here, with Pennell memorably wagging his umbrella (an umbrella also used, comically, to bludgeon other actors onstage). Jaques' rhetoric thus offers the sort of "double entendre" which the Elizabethans always enjoyed: "thereby hangs a tale," a

---

14. Puttenham, *Art*, 297.
15. Peacham, *Garden*, 56.
16. Peacham, *Garden*, 56.
17. Johnson, "Preface to Shakespeare," 222.
18. Peacham, *Garden*, 48.
19. Peacham, *Garden*, 3.

story to be gossiped about, for thus a "tail," or rear end, is publicly destroyed or at least humiliated. This comparison might seem macabre, but is probably Jaques' comment upon the defective human nature that leads men to the prostitutes whom Touchstone had earlier joked about. This humor leads Jaques to a rare literary *simile*,[20] when he adds that Touchstone will make him "crow like chanticleer," the rooster whose lechery is mocked in Chaucer's "Second Nun's Priest Tale," and to laugh "sans intermission" (2.7.30–32).

Such a view of human nature omits any emphasis on its formation by the divine image, but is certainly part of the Catholic Humanist view of the fall. It is probably another bawdry, based on the commonly joked about biblical *metonymia* "know," that Touchstone intends when Jaques reports that the fool also said, "If ladies be but young and fair they have the gift to know it" (2.7.37–38). This *conditional* leads Jaques to one of his most extraordinary similes to describe Touchstone's creative wit:

> in his brain
> Which is as dry as the remainder biscuit
> After a voyage, he hath strange places crammed
> With observation, the which he vents
> In mangled forms. (2.7.38–42)

The *simile*[21] here comparing Touchstone's intellect to a dry biscuit, left over from a sea voyage, is an unusual but admiring praise of the fool's combination of linguistic creativity and dry humor. The "strange places" then mentioned could refer to more "good set terms" of rhetoric, for "places" could be a reference to the well-known "places of invention" which help an orator survey and then plan a speech on any subject;[22] more concretely, "strange places" might mean simply "odd corners" that Touchstone uses to store uncommon nuggets of comical wisdom.[23] To summarize his entire meeting with Touchstone, Jaques concludes with another *conditional*: "O that I were a fool / I am ambitious for a motley coat" (2.7.43–44).

> I must have liberty
> Withall, as large a charter as the winde,
> To blow on whom I please, for so fools have. (2.7.47–49)

There are other Shakespearean passages that describe the wind as "bawdy" (*Oth.*, 4.2.80) and a "strumpet" (*MV*, 2.6.16), and associate "blow" with both the fertilization of eggs and the abuse of rhetoric (*LLL*, 5.2.406–9).

20. Peacham, *Garden*, 158.
21. Peacham, *Garden*, 158.
22. Latham, *As You Like It*, 50, footnotes "places" here as "stock topics in rhetoric."
23. As Trautvetter, *As You Like It*, 77, argues.

Yet it is quite possible that Jaques' *simile* here comparing "liberty," a legal "charter" and the "wind" also carries the bawdy meaning suggested in another line from *Henry V*: "The air, a chartered libertine" (1.1.49). Normally in Shakespeare's texts, well before the vast influence of the American revolution and its constitution, "liberty" is usually associated not with legitimate freedom but with "libertinism," the abuse of sexual liberty. Jaques himself suggests this by adding, "And they that are most gauled with my folly, / They most must laugh" (2.7.50–51). As Touchstone has taught him to laugh at himself, so Jaques wants to show others the folly and humour of their own sexual sins. Thus Jaques finally demands:

> Invest me in my motley; give me leave
> To speak my mind, and I will through and through
> Cleanse the foul body of the infected world,
> If they will patiently receive my medicine. (2.7.58–61)

The *metaphora*[24] here, which presents an orator as a physician whose words are medicine to listeners, is a commonplace but is also self-righteous. The role of sexual satirist arrogantly demanded here by Jaques helps explain why, rather than the amusement that he showed upon first hearing of Jaques' invective rhetoric, Duke Senior now responds with the bitterest words spoken in Arden:

> Most mischievous foul sin, in chiding sin:
> For thou thyself hast been a libertine,
> As sensual as the brutish sting itself;
> And all the embossed sores and headed evils,
> That thou with licence of free foot hast caught,
> Wouldst thou disgorge into the general world. (2.7.64–69)

The *simile*[25] here likens Jaques to the *synecdoche* of a snake, but it is more concrete, material problems that Senior suggests in the key *metonymies* here; "embossed sores," "headed evils" and "license of free foot" probably suggest venereal disease, which Duke Senior clearly worries could be spread throughout Arden as quickly as the wind of Jaques' speech.

Jaques defends himself as satirists typically do, using conditionals and another nature *simile* to suggest that only those already guilty would be bothered by his critique:

> if it do him right,
> Then he hath wrong'd him self: if he be free,

---

24. Peacham, *Garden*, 3.
25. Peacham, *Garden*, 158.

> Why then my taxing like a wild-goose flies
> Unclaim'd of any man. (2.7.84–87)

Yet Senior's accusations largely go unanswered. We cannot be sure if there are factual stories grounding these accusations, but Senior's comments certainly explain Jaques' attraction to Touchstone's bawdy. The point here is not Jaques' personal past, but rather the purpose of his rhetoric in the play and the theatre. Alan Rickman, who played the role, notes that actors often find Jaques' speeches notoriously difficult, but Rickman found that Jaques' words become clear when put "into the mouth of a wounded and trapped animal."[26] There is a desperate disjointedness, an apparent *apostrophe* to courtiers perhaps departing the magic "circle" first drawn by this now humiliated fool, when Jaques cries out: "There then, how then, what then, let me see wherein / My tongue hath wrong'd him" (2.7.83–84). There is an obvious scheme of repetition here, again *diacope*, but clearly the line ought to be delivered in the desperate tone that Jaques' circumstances demand; as Rickman writes: "put rhythm and sense together and you find that yet again Shakespeare has done the work for you."[27]

From a Catholic Humanist viewpoint, the orator who acknowledges his own folly is able to provide wisdom to others, the kind of wisdom that Shakespearean fools typically provide. The importance of charity is also central to Catholic Humanism, however, and the focus on Jaques is temporarily interrupted by the arrival of Orlando, without Adam, and demands, with his sword, some of the food that Duke Senior and his party are feasting on. Jaques replies, "An you will not be answered with reason, I must die" (2.7.100–101), but this *conditional* is answered by a longer series of "ifs" in Orlando's eloquent reply:

> If ever you have look'd on better days,
> If ever been where bells have knoll'd to church,
> If ever sat at any good man's feast,
> If ever from your eyelids wiped a tear
> And know what 'tis to pity and be pitied,
> Let gentleness my strong enforcement be:
> In the which hope I blush, and hide my sword. (2.7.113–19)

The scheme here is *symploce*, beginning and ending a clause in similar fashion; many rhetoricians would call the opening repetition of "if" an *anaphora*. Regardless of terminology, Orlando's point is that "if" Duke Senior and his party are civilized or good enough to feed the starving, then

---

26. Rickman, "Jaques in *As You Like It*," 77.
27. Rickman, "Jaques in *As You Like It*," 77.

he will put away his sword. Here is one of the most obvious moments in the play in which "if" becomes "a peacemaker," because "if" here provides an important means, and alternative to the sword, to allow the suffering to eloquently argue and move the powerful towards necessary charity.

Even in Arden, then, there is the potential for reproducing the kind of personal and political conflict that seems to plague all human societies, and Duke Senior recognizes the wide relevance of the drama he has just witnessed:

> Thou seest we are not all alone unhappy:
> This wide and universal theatre
> Presents more woeful pageants than the scene
> Wherein we play in. (2.7.135–38)

This is also, of course, one of the many "meta-dramatic" remarks in Shakespeare, in which clearly the on-stage action is said to be relevant to the broader society in which the play is being performed. Art can become "universal theatre," Catholic Humanism affirms, because human nature faces similar problems in every "scene" in which humans find themselves. Those who adopt Jaques' perspective, argues Rickman, might dismiss Senior's words as "a universal platitude,"[28] but his *paroemia*, or proverbial wisdom, does provide a valuable prologue to what is probably the play's most quoted speech: Jaques' lengthy discourse on the seven ages of man.

This speech is not particular to this play, but is an oft-cited, well known speech from Shakespeare's time, given here to Jaques because it expresses a view of life, and has the linguistic creativity, that is typical of melancholy eloquence. In the terms of Renaissance rhetoric, the "seven ages of man" speech is *allegoria*[29] in the specific but limited sense of this oft-used term, as a "continued metaphor" of a Renaissance commonplace, the identification of the theatre and the world. Via the emphasis of the first word of his speech, "All," Jaques clearly intends to "one-up" Senior's version of this metaphor, and to provide even more universal thoughts upon its meaning:

> All the world's a stage,
> And all the men and women merely players:
> They have their exits and their entrances;
> And one man in his time plays many parts. (2.7.139–42)

Jaques then describes "seven ages" of human life, from infancy to old age, yet with the melancholy, even cynicism, that we would expect from his character. Perhaps what makes this speech most memorable, especially

---

28. Rickman, "Jaques in *As You Like It*," 77.
29. Peacham, *Garden*, 25.

when delivered by a great actor like Nicholas Pennell,[30] is the opportunity for *mimesis*[31] provided by each part. *Onomatopoeia*[32] is often heard, as Jaques mimics both the pleasure and pains of infants "mewling and puking," or the "whining" and "creeping" school boy, or the "sighing lover" with "woeful" ballad, or how a "big manly voice" turns again to "childish treble [that] pipes and whistles in his sound" (2.7.144–63). Perhaps the greatest challenge for any actor lies in the transitions between these parts, but certainly the concrete details of the speech provide what persuasive rhetoric terms *evidentia*, which serves to convince an audience of its authenticity. There are moments when Jaques shows respect for some human roles, such as his serious description of the Justice's "wise saws, and modern instances," and there are times when he is clearly chuckling at the folly of human life, such as when he sees the soldier "seeking the bubble reputation / even in the Canon's mouth" (2.7.152–56). Yet life as a whole is never entirely happy for Jaques, and his conclusion is particularly chilling:

> Last scene of all,
> That ends this strange eventful history,
> Is second childishness and mere oblivion,
> Sans teeth, sans eyes, sans taste, sans everything. (2.7.163–66)

The concluding "sans" here, like the earlier expression of "sans intermission," could be Shakespeare mocking an abstract French philosopher lost in an otherwise English Forest of Arden. However, the scheme of repetition used for this word here, *symploce*,[33] does work rhetorically with the rhythmic iambic pentameter of this final line, especially a slowly-spoken final three syllables, to allow a competent actor to provide a universal, thoroughly chilling portrayal of death.

Actors portraying any Shakespearean speech as familiar as Jaques' "Seven Ages of Man" face a recurring problem: how to make it sound fresh, and new, even as the audience knows what's coming. The standard contemporary way to do this is exemplified by the 1978 BBC version, where Richard Pasco turns the speech into a campfire story. He and all of Senior's courtiers have been heavily drinking around the fire, until Jaques alters the mood with this stirring but deeply depressing speech. Pasco, like most Jaques, acts out each part, and especially stresses the *onomatopoeia*[34] that Shakespeare

---

30. In Hirsch's 1983 production in Stratford, Ontario.
31. Peacham, *Garden*, 138.
32. Peacham, *Garden*, 14.
33. Peacham, *Garden*, 43.
34. Peacham, *Garden*, 14.

includes, for example, when the voice of the "lean and slippered pantaloon" turns to shrill "treble pipes," slowing down even more for the "last scene of all." Pasco's eyes grow ever wider, and finally his expression conveys a nihilistic disgust at being "sans everything." Some actors convey terror rather than disgust in this last line, while Kevin Kline brought another approach to Branagh's 2006 film. Though Kline delivers the speech while sitting on a log beside the other courtiers, he is clearly in his own mental world while doing so, cut off from them through creative meditation, lost in thought. Though unorthodox, and apparently the opposite of the rhetorical arguments that recur throughout the play, Kline does convey the "anti-rhetoric" that is part of Jaques' role in the play.

Though some Jaques will leave the stage after their speech, and some productions cut out entirely the rest of the scene, it is clear that Shakespeare immediately offers an answer to Jaques' famous speech. As with many oft-quoted, famous speeches in Shakespearean drama, one needs to ask whether Jaques' eloquence, however moving, and disturbing, should also be regarded as the broader wisdom intended by the play? Old Adam soon arrives to give concrete counter-evidence of the vigor and value possible in old age, while the youthful Orlando will soon learn a different view of life from Rosalind. For Catholic Humanism, life does not end in "mere oblivion," and the apparent "nothingness" of death itself is redeemed by the beauty of the glory of God. So far from "childishness" being a state to be lamented, Christ teaches rather that "whoever does not receive the kingdom of God as a little child will never enter it" (Luke 18:17). As orator, however, Jaques offers the counterargument to such a view, and his eloquence must be answered if Arden is to become the peaceful world which Duke Senior envisions.

Rather than Jaques' dark words, Shakespeare closes the scene with more music from Amiens, allowing the "good cheer" of theatrical "green space" to be restored. Though Amiens' lyrics do at times address some of the darker human problems raised by Jaques, such problems are to be endured, perhaps even enjoyed, within the beauty of the forest. Amiens sings:

> Heigh-ho! sing, heigh-ho! unto the green holly:
> Most friendship is feigning, most loving mere folly:
> Then, heigh-ho, the holly!
> This life is most jolly. (2.7.181–84)

The sentiment here is similar to the song in the middle of *Much Ado about Nothing*, "men were deceivers ever" (2.3.62). Yet like the lovers in that play, Amiens does not despair. Rather, just as that play advises one to sing "hey nonny, nonny," (2.3.68) the "nonsense" cheer here is "heigh-ho!" This comical acceptance of human folly is not nihilistic but rather allows the endurance of human folly until a greater wisdom, and true love, can truly make human life "most jolly."

As the political authority which will allow such human civilization within Arden, the last word of welcome to the forest falls to Duke Senior. Beginning with a final *conditional*, "If that you were the good Sir Rowland's son / As you have whispered faithfully you were / And as mine eye doth his effigies witness / Most truly limned and living in your face" (2.7.195–98), Senior tells Orlando and Adam:

> Be truly welcome hither: I am the duke
> That loved your father. The residue of your fortune,
> Go to my cave and tell me. Good old man,
> Thou art right welcome as thy master is.
> Support him by the arm. Give me your hand,
> And let me all your fortunes understand. (2.7.199–205)

In many ways, this is the Catholic Humanist response to Jaques' view of life. Senior remembers his love for old Sir Rowland, and welcomes Orlando to his abundant banquet, such as he can offer in Arden. So far from dismissing Adam as insignificant, Senior takes the old man by the hand and continues to support his walk in life. Such concrete wisdom is the good by which human nature can allow one to understand, and endure, the suffering caused by ill fortune.

5

"Learn of the Wise"

Touchstone and the Foolish Wisdom of Catholic Humanism

JAQUES' VAIN DESIRE TO be a fool is eventually eclipsed, within the play, by the play's proper fool, Touchstone. It is difficult within scholarly prose to capture the right tone of this fool's wisdom, for as already noted its essence is paradoxical: on one hand, the fool is straightforwardly foolish, comically portraying many of the worst traits of human life, inviting everyone's laughter and scorn; yet in the case of "unconscious" clowns like Bottom in *A Midsummer Night's Dream* or Dogberry in *Much Ado about Nothing*, these fools speak wiser than they know, until certainly the play's audience and sometimes those on stage themselves must acknowledge, as the villain Boracchio says late in *Much Ado*, "What your wisdoms could not discover, these shallow fools have brought to light" (5.1.225–27).

Actors playing Touchstone typically stress his foolishness rather than wisdom. So much of Touchstone's humour depends upon being a stylish courtier amongst country bumpkins, and thus, more than most Shakespearean fools, his costume has been extraordinarily eccentric, including a wide range of dreadfully inappropriate urban clothing. Alfred Molina, playing Touchstone in Branagah's 2006 film, is perhaps the epitome of such an approach, wearing a very wide variety of colorful clothing. Budget is obviously no obstacle, though ironically this production cuts more of Touchstone's lines—which would often be unintelligible to a modern movie audience—than most productions of *As You Like It*. Branagh's approach to Touchstone's costuming is certainly suggested by his rhetorical duels with characters such as the old shepherd Corin, representative of traditional pastoralism in the play. Touchstone not only stands out in the forest, but is there able to fulfill his vocation, to make merry and lighten the emotional burden faced by the young aristocratic women he is bound to serve, Celia and Rosalind. As he himself puts it, "Now am I in Arden; the more fool I" (2.4.14). In the forest, Touchstone's role is at once more obvious and more necessary.

In creating wise fools, Shakespeare clearly follows a path of paradoxical wisdom well known within the traditions of Catholic Humanism. St. Paul had a famous chapter on the topic, 1 Corinthians 1, which teaches that the crucifixion of Christ is "foolishness to the Greeks" but that "God useth the foolish things of the world to confound the wise" (1 Cor 1:20–25). Such scripture is the serious subtext and, by book's end, the explicit theme of the rhetorical speech given by the goddess Folly in Erasmus' *Praise of Folly*. It is not hard to argue that, in many ways, Shakespeare's fools are exemplary Catholic Humanists. Touchstone, however, poses a unique critical challenge in being so silly that it is almost natural for those of any moral wisdom to critique or even censor his thoughts, or to simply laugh at him without taking seriously anything he says. Yet there are also moments of wisdom from him in the play, when this "touchstone" of reality gives insightful wisdom essential to the play's thematic development.

In part the wisdom of Touchstone can be appreciated simply by noticing where Shakespeare inserts this invented character within the plot largely inherited from Lodge. Touchstone and Jaques are the major characters in *As You Like It* with no clear parallel in *Rosalynde*. Before returning to the Forest of Arden, however, act 3 opens with a very brief scene reminding us again of the much harsher world of nature, human nature, that yet exists in the court. Duke Frederick is shown, demanding that Oliver bring back Orlando, "dead or living," or himself be banished from the court. Oliver does not object, telling Frederick, "I never loved my brother in my life," but his pledge of loyalty produces no similar response from the Duke. Rather, after Oliver leaves, Frederick orders "an extent," which can be defined as the "seizure of property in execution of a writ,"[1] in order to immediately seize his "house and lands" (3.1.6–17). In performance, and especially in a film such as Branagh's 2006 setting of the play within nineteenth-century Japan, such scenes with Duke Frederick give the play a dark background that make the happy tone of Arden seem even lighter and more pleasant.

---

1. Wells and Taylor, "Glossary," 1260.

Act 3, scene 2 then focuses upon a different yet still very masculine form of rhetoric, as Orlando appears running from tree to tree in Arden, carving poems to Rosalind upon them. The juxtaposition here surely favors poetry over legal writ, yet there are problems with Orlando's "verse." First, the poem read aloud, by Orlando himself (3.2.1–10), has the rhyme scheme typical of Shakespearean sonnets, and its concluding, characteristic rhyming couplet. Yet the "sonnet" here is obviously incomplete, with only two rather than three complete quatrains, and ten rather than fourteen lines. Even more problematic, the closing rhyming couplet, which typically for Shakespearean sonnets summarizes the poem's major themes, praises Rosalind as "the fair, chaste, and unexpressive she" (3.2.10). While one can certainly grant Rosalind's beauty, she has already made clear the procreative intentions typical of a young person in love (1.3.11), and has certainly proven that she is not "unexpressive" (3.2.10). In fact, Rosalind's expressive abilities, or linguistic imagination, will prove to be crucial to any sustainable love between her and Orlando.

Perhaps most problematic of all, Orlando's poetry makes the rhetorical error most dangerous within the volatile world of Reformation England: it makes literal a metaphor, ignoring the distinction between imaginative and literal reality that is so important to the *ethos* of Catholic Humanism. Duke Senior found in the forest "tongues in trees" (2.1.16), but had not authorized the carving of poetry into trees; the theatre is unlikely to show literal carving, and Orlando could pin his verse upon trees, but his opening speech in 3.2 does tell us that in the "barks" of trees "my thoughts I'll character" (3.2.6), and when Celia enters reading one of the poems found it does proclaim: "Tongues I'll hang on every tree" (3.2.124). In considering Shakespeare's intention here, one must remember the Puritanical claim that all fictions are "lies," against which Sidney writes his "Defense of Poetry," and also the simple-minded literalism parodied in *A Midsummer Night's Dream* when Bottom and the other working men plan to perform a play but worry that the roaring of a lion onstage will "so fright the ladies" that it would "hang us" (1.2.73–74).

It is as an antidote to such simple-minded materialism that Touchstone next appears, in conversation, and debate, with the old shepherd, Corin. Their rhetorical conflict comically portrays the court vs. country theme central to the play, and all pastoral literature, as Touchstone clearly disparages part of what Mark Van Doren calls the "proposition" explored in *As You Like It*: that "the country is more natural than the court" and that shepherds "live lives of enviable innocence and simplicity."[2] Yet in having Touchstone

---

2. Van Doren, *Shakespeare*, 128.

make this case, Shakespeare also clearly highlights the inherent comedy of a "fool" displaying the intellectual learning that forms the educational foundation of both grammar school and university in Shakespeare's time: the "trivium" of grammar, logic, and rhetoric. Because of these intellectual qualities, many view Touchstone as a critic within the play. *Pericles* speaks of "gold that's by the touchstone tried," and *As You Like It* does refer to this fool as a "whetstone of the wits" (1.2.224), so it is valid to say that Touchstone "tests all that the world takes for gold, especially the gold of the golden world of pastoralism."[3]

It should not be imagined, however, that Shakespeare intends to propose Touchstone as some pillar of intellectual virtue. Rather, in response to Corin's simple question, "And how like you this shepherd's life," (3.2.11–12), the fool responds with a series of "polite" assertions that show respect for the pastoral life, then quickly follows each assertion with a sharply critical statement from an "urbane" or broadly philosophical point of view. "In respect," for example, that a shepherd's life "is solitary," Touchstone says, "I like it very well," but "in respect that it is private, it is a very vile life" (3.2.15–17). Touchstone's correction of Corin does not have the bitterness of *inter se pugnatia* or *sarcasmus*, but the effect is similar to *leptotes*,[4] or litotes, the negation of an idea through understated restatement, and the opposite of euphuism, the restatement of an idea in more pleasing terms. Here, Touchstone's critical comments negate and ridicule the pastoral ideal, to comical effect. Shakespeare's audience probably recalls that the subtitle of Lodge's *Rosalynde* is *Euphues' Golden Legacy*, and they are certainly aware of the linguistic fad of euphuism in England during the late 1500s. They probably would have laughed at Touchstone's mockery of country life. As "the urbane Court fool entering Arden's country world of rustics," Touchstone may have been played by Robert Armin,[5] the new fool of Shakespeare's company, and intended "as a very self-conscious opposite" to Robert Tarlton or Will Kempe, clowns who in the previous twenty-five years had brought great popularity to "the stereotype of the guileless rustic."[6] Shakespeare's audience probably would have enjoyed Touchstone's mockery of Corin as "a sophisticated game of reversed clowning against the stereotype" which they themselves had laughed at for years.[7]

---

3. Wilson, *Shakespeare's Happy Comedies*, 156.
4. Peacham, *Garden*, 150.
5. Wiles, *Shakespeare's Clown*, 55–65.
6. Gurr, *Playgoing*, 27.
7. Gurr, *Playgoing*, 27.

At the same time, however, Touchstone's treatment of Corin is so condescending that there is surely also an element of self-parody here, showing how foolish "wise" intellectuals can be. Corin gives a reasonable reply, through practical, commonsensical assertions sure to be affirmed by any realistic person—for example, that those lacking "money, means and content" are "without three good friends" (3.2.24–25)—and he shows basic rhetorical skills in constructing *antimetabole* to defend pastoral life: "those that are good manners at the Court are as ridiculous in the country, as the behavior of the country is most mockable at court" (3.2.44–47). Corin receives no respect, however, from Touchstone; when he calls Corin a "natural philosopher," for example, probably Touchstone does not intend simple praise, but more likely is using the word "natural" in the sense noted earlier, to critique the shepherd's mental capacity. As Miriam Joseph has thoroughly illustrated, Touchstone here uses a number of fallacious forms of logic to baffle the simple shepherd and assert his own courtly values.[8] In probably the single best example of this, Touchstone uses another *conditional* or *hypothetical syllogism* to argue not only for the superiority of the courtier's life over the shepherd's, but also that the latter is damned:

> if thou never wast at court, thou never sawest
> good manners; if thou never sawest good manners,
> then thy manners must be wicked; and wickedness is
> sin, and sin is damnation. Thou art in a parlous state, shepherd.
> (3.2.39–43)

Joseph notes that Touchstone here commits the "fallacy of consequent," converting the proposition "those at the court have good manners" to "all those who have good manners are at the court." Corin cannot see, Joseph continues, that "there is a shift in the meaning of good and wicked" in Touchstone's argument, which further invalidates a very weak chain of reasoning.[9] Finally, Corin probably does not recognize the fool's concluding "malapropism," in which the word "parlous" is used when most likely "perilous" is intended. Malapropism was a favorite comic technique of Shakespearean fools like Bottom and Dogberry, probably played by Kemp; Peacham could describe this technique as *meiosis*,[10] an ironic understatement, but it is a vice that often produced the virtue of laughter in Shakespeare's theatre.

Modern actors playing this fool's role cannot expect the linguistic knowledge possessed by an Elizabethan audience. In Czinner's 1936 film

---

8. Joseph, *Arts of Language*, 197–98.
9. Joseph, *Arts of Language*, 197–98.
10. Peacham, *Garden*, 168.

version, perhaps unsurprisingly, many of Touchstone's lines are cut entirely, and the play takes on a fairy-tale atmosphere that loses Shakespeare's undercutting of *Rosalynde*'s romantic pastoral rhetoric. However, *within itself* the play offers models of what one might call "rhetorical incomprehension," and actors playing the fool, or those acting onstage with him, can stress this in order to give a modern audience some idea of what they are missing. For example, in 2.4, Corin is shown hardly able to comprehend the youthful romantic passion of Silvius. In parallel fashion, Touchstone is then shown telling Rosalind about his "night to Jane Smile"; this passage also references his "sword," "peascod," and "cow's dugs" (2.4.45–48), and probably constitutes what Trautvetter call a "series of bawdy quibbles" normally "neglected" in modern editions of the play "because they do not add up to a consistent erotic image."[11] In Basil Coleman's 1978 BBC version, a closeup camera shows Helen Mirren, as Rosalind, and James Bolam, as Touchstone, hiding behind a tree, faces close together, as this strange passage is related. Mirren's face conveys incomprehension, Bolam's a witty reserve, and bawdy is implied without any explicit understanding.

Other actors have found other ways, especially in the theatre, to convey Touchstone's humor. In John Hirsch's 1983 production at Stratford, Ontario, Lewis Gordon, as Touchstone, sat between a naïve Celia, played by Rosemary Dunsmore, who listens smiling while reclining on the fool's chest, while Rosalind, played by Roberta Maxwell, seems more knowing, at times dismayed and other times laughing. In Thea Sharrock's 2009 RSC, Dominic Rowan plays the Jane Smile speech with many hand gestures to suggest their literal meaning, then suggests romantic lunacy by desperately screaming the concluding request that Jane "wear these for my sake" (2.4.50). In general, theatrical production can use gesture and innuendo to suggest the humour to a live audience, who usually "get it," while television or film directors must use the reactions of characters within the play to convey the effect of linguistic humour.

Is Touchstone's use of religious language, such as "sin" or "damnation" significant? Quite possibly, Touchstone employs such terms to prefigure the fuller parody of Puritanism from such fools as Feste in *Twelfth Night*, who plays the interlude of Sir Topas the curate in the darkhouse in order, among other things, to exorcise the "hyperbolical fiend" within Malvolio. Touchstone is not as intellectual a fool as Feste, but with both Shakespeare may have been mocking the literalism of irrational believers, as Catholic Humanist writers often did. The obvious error in Touchstone's argument—the notion that "manners" could be so "wicked" as to constitute mortal

---

11. Trautvetter, *As You Like It*, 58.

sin—not only parodies the concern for appearances typical of the court, but also mocks the pharasiacal (see word in Dante's *Inferno*, canto 24) tendency of some Christians to judge righteousness according to the conventions of outward appearance rather than the honest faith and fruit of one's heart. There is certainly an admirable humility and simplicity in Corin, and these qualities of his nature, as Vickers might predict, allow "natural" use of traditional rhetoric; Corin presents a noble *systrophe*,[12] cast in balanced *compar*,[13] that uses *diazeugma*[14] to limit use of the subject—after the honest, plain speaking, simple use of "I" in the opening three clauses—and instead focuses on broadly defining the shepherd's life:

> Sir, I am a true labourer, I earn that I eat; get that I wear, owe no man hate, envy no man's happiness; glad of other men's good; content with my harm; and the greatest of my pride is to see my ewes graze and my lambs suck. (3.2.74–75)

Corin's noble words, humility, and simplicity of spirit exemplify why the shepherd has always been an especially important vocation within the Catholic faith, a vocation to which Christ likens his own work (John 10:11).

The spirit of gentle mockery explicit in Touchstone's words to Corin, and the implicit critique of one's own folly, is then continued in the play when Rosalind re-enters the stage, reading Orlando's verse. Yet there is also a serious element to the ensuing critique of clichéd romantic verse, for this critique generally follows the lines of Shakespeare's own *Romeo and Juliet*, and his *Sonnets*, particularly the late sonnets to the so-called "dark lady." Romeo's first love, many forget, was not Juliet but, perhaps not coincidentally, named Rosaline, and early in that play he writes verse to her using the clichéd imagery of Petrarchan verse, finding in love "bright smoke, cold fire, sick health, / Still waking sleep" (1.2.177–78). Only upon meeting Juliet, and experiencing true love, does the couple together speak a full sonnet to each other (1.5.93–105), concluding with a kiss after the final rhyming couplet that summarizes the sanctity of their love: "Saints do not move, though grant for prayers sake. / Then move not while my prayer's effect I take" (1.5.104–5). In the *Sonnets*, perhaps the clearest single example is #130, where Shakespeare lists a number of Petrarchan clichés, to stress that his "mistress"—a word that in his time more often refers to "wife," as "master" refers to husband, than to an extramarital affair—is "nothing like" the idealized Elizabethan female—as Anne Hathaway may not have been, given

---

12. Peacham, *Garden*, 153.
13. Peacham, *Garden*, 58.
14. Joseph, *Arts of Language*, 59.

that she was not married until twenty-four years of age. Yet "by heaven," the rhyming couplet concludes, "I think my love as rare / As any she belied with false compare."

In *As You Like It*, Rosalind critiques the lack of rhetorical skill in Orlando's verse, its tendency to simply list rhymes of her own name, but on a deeper level she is critiquing the objectification and simplification of the female that has long been part of the Petrarchan tradition. By 1599, when *As You Like It* was first performed, there had appeared in England many sonnet sequences which followed the same pattern: an infatuated male writes numerous sonnets that idealizes and, from a distance, woos the "perfect" female, until the "unexpressive" she scorns the man, and thus ensures that the poet will remain in love with love rather than with a real person. Rosalind, very likely, sees the same pattern developing in Orlando, and does not want to play the traditional female role. After Touchstone similarly mocks Orlando's poetry and sums up its status as "bad fruit" upon the trees (3.2.114), Rosalind offers a horticultural metaphor for the strategic rhetorical response which she will pursue:

> I'll graft it with you, and then I shall graft it
> with a medlar; then it will be the earliest fruit
> i' th' country, for you'll be rotten ere you be half ripe, and
> that's the right virtue of the medlar. (3.2.115–18)

Rosalind's *metaphora* here, one of the key "figures of thought" in the play, is to "graft" or to breed together different plants in order to genetically produce elements of both. A "medlar," whose fruit was known for "being rotten before having reached ripeness,"[15] is often, due to its shape, or through a pun, associated with erotic imagery (As in *Romeo and Juliet*, 2.1.36[16]). Here Rosalind could intend *antanaclasis*[17] on "medlar," which could mean not only "one who interferes" but also "one who indulges in sexual intercourse."[18] Touchstone's earlier "moral on the time" was, according to Jaques, that we "ripe, and ripe," and then "rot and rot" (2.7.26–29), and the bawdy clown here "meddles" in Orlando's verse by saucing its own romantic flavor with the *paranomasiastic*[19] bawdry he is often known for: "He that sweetest rose will find / Must find love's prick and Rosalind" (3.2.109–10).

---

15. Trautvetter, *As You Like It*, 107.

16. Mercutio tells Romeo, "Now will he sit under a medlar tree, and wish his mistress were that kind of fruit / As maids call medlars when they sit alone."

17. Peacham, *Garden*, 56.

18. Trautvetter, *As You Like It*, 107.

19. Peacham, *Garden*, 56.

Rosalind's horticultural *metaphora* promises to continue the battle of Shakespeare's sonnets, which portray romantic love and art waging war against time and death. Her rhetoric, to borrow a word from Sonnet 15, can "engraft" anew three groups of lovers whose conventional literary roles might consign them to the "mere oblivion" of Jaques' "last scene." Rather, via a series of amorous arguments, the conventionally pastoral love of Phoebe and Silvius, the rustic love of Touchstone and Audrey, and finally the romantic idealism of Orlando are "engrafted" anew by the rhetoric of Rosalind. Our heroine's intention, and probably Shakespeare's, is to "engraft" these deficient forms of love, as one might "engraft" essential genetic forms when breeding plants, with the reality of a real person. Thus will be formed a love "ripe" or "the earliest fruit / i' the country," in that it would be ready for real marriage rather than repeating or recasting the stereotypical tragedy of Petrarchan love. When Touchstone responds to Rosalind's medlar *metaphora* by saying, "You have said, but whether wisely or no, let the Forest judge" (3.2.119–20), the *prosopopoeia* or personification suggests a sentient Forest who will assess, like a judge hearing forensic rhetoric, the various arguments for love that the audience are about to hear.

Rosalind's partner in this project, as in all things in this play, is Celia, who also now re-enters the stage reading one of Orlando's poems. This is an especially long poem, some twenty-seven lines, and includes the traditional Petrarchan *blazon* that lists and idealizes Rosalind's "many parts," though not in base physical terms. Rather, there is a clearly religious tone to Orlando's verse, seeing in his beloved "the quintessence of every sprite / Heaven would in little show" (3.2.136–37). Rosalind, however, does not initially know who wrote the poem, and ridicules it as a "tedious homily" (3.2.152). Only upon learning that Orlando is also in the forest is she inspired to a series of questions (3.2.214–19). After Celia begins to answer by saying, "He was furnished like a hunter," Rosalind replies with the anxiety inevitable for any woman familiar with the Petrarchan tradition: "O ominous—he comes to kill my heart" (3.2.241). The *paranomasia*[20] here, on "heart" and "hart" or female deer, is so familiar that it is almost cliché. Wyatt had famously translated Petrarch to describe Henry VIII's pursuit of Anne Boleyn, "whoso list to hunt I know where there is a hind,"[21] while at the start of *Twelfth Night*, in response to the question of whether he will "go hunt" the "hart" (1.1.16–22), Orsino confesses his very Petrarchan infatuation with the lady Olivia. In *As You Like It*, because Rosalind is truly in love with Orlando, she must find a way to rescue him from cliché while also protecting the life of her own heart.

---

20. Peacham, *Garden*, 56.
21. Wyatt, "Whoso List to Hunt," 350.

A brief reminder that Orlando is worth this effort is then given in the play, as "Rosalind and Celia stand aside" (according to the stage direction at 3.2.247), in order to hear another of the play's many rhetorical debates, between Orlando and Jaques. Unsurprisingly, they are debating whether it is worthwhile to love, as Shakespeare makes comic and philosophical matter of the contrast between the young man in love and the old curmudgeon convinced that love is folly. Somewhat surprisingly, Orlando fares well in this debate, rising to Rosalind's defense when Jaques insults her. When "monsieur melancholy" advises Orlando that "the worst fault you have is to be in love," Orlando is quick to retort: "'Tis a fault I will not change for your best virtue" (3.2.276–77). Most significantly, when Jaques invites him to the self-righteous melancholy that Duke Senior had found especially objectionable in this cynic's habitual persona, Orlando responds with a humility that is truly wise: "I will chide no breather in the world but myself, against whom I know most faults" (3.2.274–75). Perhaps the exercise of his wit against Jaques, as much as his body vs. Charles, has indeed made Orlando an "athlete of virtue," as John Shaw calls him.[22]

What follows is clearly one of the most important moments of the play. Rosalind comes out of hiding and, still disguised as "Ganymede," introduces this moment in an aside: "I will speak to him like a saucy lackey, and under that habit play the knave with him" (3.2.289–90). In Shakespeare's playhouse, which cast together "boys and women" (3.2.398–99) by giving female parts to young boys, Rosalind's aside restates the "external" rhetoric of the play's theatrical conditions. Internally, Rosalind, as "Ganymede," will convince Orlando to play a game in which he will call "him" Rosalind, and woo him as if he were truly his beloved. Throughout this game there is obvious dramatic irony, in that the audience is always aware that the young woman in love is the real source and judge of the "game." This is surely the most important "if" of the play, for within its "conceit" or elaborate fiction lies the central "proposition" of the play: through an exercise of imagination, men can recognize their habitual faults, and learn to offer the true love necessary for a happy marriage. This possibility is the true aim of the "cure" (3.2.410) for love that "Ganymede" offers Orlando, for surely Rosalind does not intend to end Orlando's love for her. Just beneath the rhetoric of her "game" lies a question relevant to anyone contemplating marriage: how can one know if one's prospective spouse is truly in love, and has the real, deep commitment necessary to sustain love throughout marriage?

This is the real question at stake when "Ganymede" begins her discussion with Orlando. Her initial question for him, "what is't o'clock" is the

---

22. Shaw, "Fortune and Nature," 45–50.

kind of very general question that one might ask of any stranger, and there is probably some disappointment implied when Orlando responds, "You should ask me what time o'day? There's no clock in the forest" (3.2.294–95). It is the latter assertion, a pastoral cliché, that Rosalind then attacks through what modern rhetorician Richard Lanham calls an *argumentum ex concessis*. Lanham defines *concessio* as "conceding a point to hurt an adversary or to prepare for more argument,"[23] and it soon becomes clear that Rosalind accepts Orlando's obvious, material point on clocks only to alter his view of time and, hopefully, improve his punctuality. Despite the instruction, Orlando will be late for subsequent meetings in the forest, but this fact simply underscores the importance of "Ganymede's" discourse. Punctuality will remain a major test of Orlando in the play, as it must be for anyone attempting to love in the "real world" outside the forest.

Most likely it is "Rosalind" who replies, to Orlando's initial assertion about clocks, that, "Then there is no true lover in the forest, else sighing every minute and groaning every hour would detect the lazy foot of time as well as a clock" (3.2.296–98). There is implied mockery of male groans and laziness here, but she quickly turns to a broader "figure of thought," as she then uses *prosopopoeia*, or personification, to present Time as a horse rider who "travels in divers places with divers persons . . . who time ambles withal, who time trots withal, who time gallops withal, and who he stands still withal" (3.2.301–4). The repetition and balance of Rosalind's figure, particularly the *epiphora*[24] of "withal," allows her then to both "universalize" her figure, and to provide particular examples of how time alters pace according to individual circumstances. In the situation most relevant to Rosalind, "Ganymede" notes that Time "trots hard with a young maid between the contract of her marriage and the day it is solemnized" (3.2.306–7). "Slow down" is the almost universal advice given by parents but, as with Friar Laurence in *Romeo and Juliet*, there is often a large gap between this advice and the details of a plan needed to allow time to "allay passion." Will haste also mar the potential love in *As You Like It*?

"Ganymede," it can be argued, is teaching a relative though realistic sense of time. Orlando is impressed by "his" eloquence and compliments "Ganymede's" "accent" as "something finer" than most denizens of the forest. "He" attributes this to "an old religious uncle" who "taught me how to speak" (3.2.333–34). There may be external rhetoric here alluding to the fairly common Catholic Humanist practice of home-schooling, pioneered by More with his own children, but the intention of Rosalind to apply this

---

23. Lanham, *Handlist*, 16.
24. Peacham, *Garden*, 42.

rhetoric to feminine issues is shown when Ganymede further tells us that this "old uncle" once "fell in love" and now gives "many lectures" against both love and women. With dramatic *ironia*, Ganymede asserts, "I thank God I am not a woman, to be touched with so many giddy offenses as he hath generally taxed their whole sex withal" (3.2.337–40). If taken literally, "Ganymede's" words could be a repetition of the misogyny common in medieval and Renaissance Europe, but figuratively they become rather a prelude to Rosalind's defense of her own gender.

After Orlando asks for "the principal evils" attributed to women, Rosalind replies with another argumentative technique, a *correctio*,[25] designed to correct the misogyny by paradoxically admitting it. She replies, "There were none principal; they were all like one another as half-pence are, every one fault seeming monstrous till his fellow-fault came to match it" (3.2.343–45). This trope is based on a simple concrete object, "half-pence" coins all appearing alike, but taken as Catholic Humanist *metaphora* Rosalind could be asking us to view all faults as part of the general human fall into sin. Logically, of course, this fall included males as well as females, and while "Ganymede" may not yet be ready to make this point explicitly to Orlando, the masculine pronoun with "his fellow-fault" reminds us of the near universal human curse of sin. Typically, the "illness" that must be "cured" is clichéd Petrarchan love, which rarely ends happily, and thus Rosalind must make sure that by "love" Orlando means much more than the self-centered desire of so many Renaissance male sonneteers. On a broader level, selfishness is one clear sign of the fallen nature that Catholicism sees in all human beings. The "serio-comic" theology of Erasmus, however, is unusual in stressing that "play" is one way to combat the curse of sin. Rosalind's proposed "game" does have a serious side, then, in that she can offer Orlando true wisdom.

It is in response to the "curse" of love that Ganymede offers Orlando a "cure," replacing Jaques as "physician of the forest" with his own medical *metaphora*. But it is probably the young woman testing the young man who says that she will not immediately attempt this "cure"; rather, Rosalind says, "I will not cast away my physic but on those that are sick" (3.2.347–48). Only if she can be sure that Orlando has the "quotidian" or fever of love upon him will she offer her rhetorical medicine. Ganymede then checks for "marks of love" on Orlando, each beginning a balanced rhetorical clause, "a lean cheek . . . a blue eye . . . an unquestionable spirit . . . a beard neglected . . ." but each clause, again using *epiphora*,[26] concludes with the same phrase: "which you

---

25. Peacham, *Garden*, 172.
26. Peacham, *Garden*, 42.

have not" (3.2.361–64). Rather, she uses *epanaphora*[27] and *compar*[28] to make the point more positively: "your hose should be ungarterd, your bonnet unbraided, your sleeve unbuttoned, your shoe untied, and everything about you demonstrating a careless desolation" (3.2.366–69). By contrast, Orlando is "point-device in [his] accoutrements" (3.2.370) causing Ganymede to use *paregmenon*[29] and straightforwardly accuse Orlando of selfishness, of "loving yourself" more "then seeming the lover of any other" (3.2.370–71). Paradoxically, by using rhetoric to deny Orlando's claims of love, Rosalind is demanding that his actions prove true love.

The initial success of her rhetoric is then shown when Orlando tells Ganymede, "Fair youth, I would I could make thee believe I love," particularly as the audience should hear Rosalind reply, "Me believe it? You may as soon make her that you love believe it, which I warrant she is apter to do than to confess she does" (3.2.374–76). Rosalind soon covers up this apparent admission, however, and gives an "example" of another time when she "cured" a lover of his illness:

> He was to imagine me his love, his mistress; and I set him every day to woo me. At which time would I, being but a moonish youth, grieve, be effeminate, changeable, longing and liking, proud, fantastical, apish, shallow, inconstant, full of tears, full of smiles; for every passion something, and for no passion truly anything. (3.2.392–98)

Here Ganymede uses *compar* to list, indeed "pile" up all the misogynist accusations typically made against women.

Rosalind's intention, again, seems to be to test Orlando. Could he remain married to a fickle female? Ganymede then describes such a woman, through more schemes of balance, as one who "would now like him, now loathe him; then entertain him, then forswear him; now weep for him, then spit at him" (3.2.400–401). By playing this part, "Ganymede" caused the suitor "to forswear the full stream of the world and to live in a nook merely monastic" (3.2.404–5). Will Rosalind's rhetoric have the same effect upon Orlando? He does insist, "I would not be cured, youth" (3.2.409), but we are only halfway through the play. Orlando's words do suggest some level of commitment to continue loving Rosalind. But for how long? Truthfully answering this key question is the serious intent of the comic fiction that "Ganymede" closes the scene insisting must be played. In one final *conditional*, she promises him, "I would cure you if you would but call me

27. Peacham, *Garden*, 41.
28. Peacham, *Garden*, 58.
29. Peacham, *Garden*, 55.

Rosalind and come every day to my cot, and woo me" (3.2.410–11). In the language of religious devotion, Orlando promises to do so "by the faith of my love," but his last line of the scene addresses Ganymede as "good youth"; thus "he" reminds Orlando, in "his" final line of the scene, that the drama must be played: "Nay, you must call me Rosalind" (3.2.418).

Actors playing Rosalind and Orlando at this point in the play have an extraordinary challenge: on one hand the disguise of "Ganymede" must be effective enough to allow the rhetoric of the game, but on the other an audience might expect some level of attraction that recalls the couple's initial meeting and foreshadows the reality of their eventual marriage. Czinner's 1936 film provided little of the latter; Elizabeth Bergner tried to turn her accent from thick German to that of an aggressive male, while Olivier, as Orlando, seems only puzzled by the whole exercise. After Bergner gives the final line of the scene, "Nay, you must call me Rosalind," Olivier dutifully responds "Rosalind," but the tepid response surely suggests hesitation to play this "silly" game. In Basil Coleman's 1978 BBC, television cameras bring the couple so close together, with very minimal attempts at disguise, that it is hard for an audience to believe that the lovers don't see through each other; paradoxically, though, the need for both actors and audience to suspend disbelief helps to establish the imaginative reality of the game. In John Hirsch's 1983 production at Stratford, Ontario, Roberta Maxwell, as Rosalind, uses minimal disguise, and a strong but certainly not male accent, yet plays a "saucy lackey" who draws big laughs by pointing at Celia and saying "I thank God I'm not a woman" (3.2.289, 337–38). Near the end of the scene, she softly and hesitantly asks, "But are you so much in love as your rhymes speak" (3.2.382), briefly suggesting that she is in love; for his part, Andrew Gillies plays Orlando as completely obtuse, unable to see through any imaginative game.

A much more assertive Orlando is played by David Oyelowo in Branagh's 2006 film; when he agrees to visit "Rosalind" and "woo" her, this final pledge is made by an arm wrestle that brings the two close. Oyelow chuckles loudly as he leaves the stage, perhaps suggesting that he already sees through the disguise. This possibility might cause Naomi Frederick, in Thea Sharrock's 2009 RSC, and Petrina Bromley in Jillian Keiley's 2016 Stratford, Ontario production, to give Ganymede greater disguise. Neither uses extensive costuming, but rather adapts their original costume through androgynous fashion. Frederick simply lengthens her hair and loosens up a leather jacket, while Bromley adopts the long hair and baggy trousers typical of a late twentieth-century Newfoundland male. Both are effective. Frederick directs "I thank God I'm not a woman" (3.2.337) not to Celia, as in most modern versions, but directly to Orlando, who keeps coming close to her in a way that suggests a desperate attractiveness. Cyrus Lane, as Orlando, seems simply giddy to have found a mate, in Bromley, as dense as he is. In the theatre, if these recent productions are any guide, a dumb Orlando in this scene prepares the audience to see the need for his later re-education, while the witty "game" establishes Rosalind as an imaginative teacher strong enough to deliver this humane education.

Act 3, scene 3 is a far shorter and clearly less serious scene in which Touchstone woos Audrey, comically illustrating how a love inspired by lust differs from the imaginative empathy *ethos* of Rosalind. The tone of the scene is established right away when the fool tells his beloved, "I will fetch up your goats" (3.3.1–2); "goats" as *metonymia*[30] for sexual lust is an Elizabethan commonplace.[31] Perhaps even this symbolism is lost upon Audrey, for Touchstone then asks a much more literal question regarding their romance: "Doth my simple features content you?" Audrey replies with comical *pysma*,[32] "Your features, Lord warrant us—what features?" (3.3.3–4). Pride perhaps stung, Touchstone reverts to *paranomosia* and the "mock learning" characteristic of Shakespeare's intellectual fools, replying, "I am here with thee and thy goats as the most capricious poet honest Ovid was among the Goths" (3.3.5–6).

The comical *simile*[33] here requires some Latin knowledge, in which a "caper" is a male goat, and the Roman poet is well known as the author of the erotic *Ars Amores*, and there is also *paranomasia*[34] in that "goths" could be pronounced as "goats." Touchstone's odd combination of intellectual learning and animal lust coalesce after the simple Audrey asks him, "I do not know what "poetical" is. Is it honest in deed and word? Is it a true thing?" (3.3.14–15). The fool's answer quite probably alludes to Sidney's *Defense of Poetry*, which taught that "a feigned example hath as much force to teach as a true example";[35] similarly, Touchstone answers Audrey, "No, truly; for the truest poetry is the most feigning, and lovers are given to poetry." These noble, paradoxical thoughts, referencing Sidney's complex argument for the value of fiction, are here in the service of lust. Reverting to physical appearances, Touchstone tells Audrey that he would not have her "honest" until she is "hard-favoured," having lost her youthful beauty; then,

---

30. Peacham, *Garden*, 19.

31. See Othello's exclamation of "goats and monkeys" as fears of cuckoldry consume him (4.1.265).

32. Peacham, *Garden*, 106–7.

33. Peacham, *Garden*, 158.

34. Peacham, *Garden*, 56.

35. Sidney, *Defence*, 224.

using *metonymia* to both praise her and further his lust, he offers this comical *paroemia*[36] to "flatter" the young woman: "honesty coupled to beauty is to have honey a sauce to sugar" (3.3.26–27).

This "wisdom" produces analytic commentary from Jaques, in aside: "A material fool" (3.3.28). The pair of lovers have been "followed by Jaques," as the stage direction at scene's opening puts it (3.3.1), probably because of his interest in the Fool, but we must wonder how "Monsieur Melancholy" will react to this courtship. Touchstone's intentions become even more obvious when blasphemously he tells this poor woman, "praised be the gods for thy foulness," then adds, in a line that an actor like Lewis Gordon, at Stratford, Ontario, in 1983, can turn into a comical aside to a theatre audience, "Sluttishness may come hereafter" (3.3.36). The very next sentence Touchstone announces, "I will marry thee," and tells her of his intention to find "Oliver Martext, the vicar of the next village," to perform the ceremony. In aside, Jaques appears excited, "I would fain see this meeting," while Audrey is agreeable in a mock religious way: "Well, the gods give us joy" (3.3.37–42).

Yet even in his lust, Touchstone has lessons for honest lovers considering valid marriage. For surely one of the most common impediments to marriage is the fear of "cuckoldry," or when a spouse commits adultery, leaving one scorned and, in the popular image, "wearing horns" of shame. This commonplace *synecdoche*, in which the "horns" evoke the entire *metaphora* of the "hunted deer" motif of Petrarchan poetry, is directly addressed as Touchstone offers more wisdom:

> Amen. A man may, if he were of a fearful heart, stagger in this attempt; for here we have no temple but the wood, no assembly but horn-beasts. But what though? Courage. As horns are odious, they are necessary. (3.3.42–47)

Touchstone goes on to add several related arguments, as is his rhetorical wont, but the most significant message of the argument is his simple, central word: "Courage." For surely it takes great courage to trust in the loving faithfulness of anyone over the course of a long marriage. Something of Touchstone's wisdom is also advised by Erasmus' Folly:

> A husband is laughed at, cuckolded, called a worm and who knows what else when he kisses away the tears of his unfaithful wife, but how much happier it is for him to be thus deceived than to wear himself out with unremitting jealousy, strike a tragic attitude and ruin everything.[37]

---

36. Peacham, *Garden*, 29.
37. Erasmus, *Praise of Folly*, translated by Betty Radice, 93.

Touchstone is more interested in rapid marriage than theological or literary argument, however, so when "Sir Oliver Martext," suddenly appears in the forest, the fool asks to be married immediately "under this tree" (3.3.59). Martext asks only the question raised by formalities, "Is there none here to give the women?" Touchstone turns this question, through *asteismus*,[38] into another jest on cuckoldry: "I will not take her on gift of any man" (3.3.61–62). Jaques then comes forward, offering to "give her" (3.3.65) as formal marriage requires.

Surely Touchstone is surprised to again meet this strange man in the forest, but perhaps he cannot remember his name, for his greeting becomes *aposiopesis*[39] and, for many actors, *misterismus*[40]: "Good even good Monsieur What-ye-call't"; yet, probably hoping to be paid again for jokes, the fool politely thanks him for their last meeting: "God'ield you for your last company" (3.3.66–68). After Jaques asks whether he would be married, Touchstone arrogantly uses *metonymia* to refer to Audrey as a "toy in hand," then turns to the more sophisticated figure of *taxis* which, distributes to "every subject" its "natural adjunct":[41] "As the ox hath his bow, sir, the horse his curb, and the falcon her bell, so man hath his desires" (3.3.72–73). If the by now familiar "man as animal" *simile*[42] were not clear enough, Touchstone adds, "and as pigeons bill, so wedlock would be nibbling." Clearly this fool is driven towards matrimony more by natural hungers than by romantic or religious forces.

The intellectual Jaques is thereby provoked, and he asks the conventional *pysma* likely to be asked not only by a Catholic, but also by many other stripes of Christians in Shakespeare's audience: "And will you, being a man of your breeding, be married under a bush, like a beggar? Get you to church, and have a good priest that can tell you what marriage is" (3.3.75–78). Otherwise, he adds in a *simile*[43] that recalls his reference to "rot, and rot" (2.7.27), either Touchstone or Audrey "will prove a shrunk panel and, like green timber, warp, warp" (3.3.79–80). There is probably *paranomasia*[44] here, a now lost pun on panel and "parnel," one of many Elizabethan words for a prostitute.[45] Whether or not Touchstone hears this joke is

---

38. Peacham, *Garden*, 34.
39. Puttenham, *Art*, 166.
40. Puttenham, *Art*, 191.
41. Peacham, *Garden*, 60.
42. Peacham, *Garden*, 158.
43. Peacham, *Garden*, 158.
44. Peacham, *Garden*, 56.
45. Trautvetter, *As You Like It*, 137.

unclear; while Jaques' demand for clear theological definition and "a good priest" surely resonates with the "traditional" (both Catholic and Anglican) portion of Shakespeare's audience, Touchstone turns Jaques' warning into a syllogism that is not even hypothetical but clearly justifies a future divorce: "I were better to be married" of Martext, the fool claims, "for he is not like to marry me well, and not being well married, it will be a good excuse hereafter to leave my wife" (3.3.81–84). Logically this statement is a valid *enthymeme*, or condensed syllogism,[46] though Peacham might also call it *syllogismus*,[47] in which the point of the argument is obvious. In a technical sense Touchstone speaks logically, but of course everyone in Shakespeare's theatre recognizes it as the opposite of valid practical wisdom.

There could also be an aesthetic reason behind Touchstone's decision here; whatever denomination he is, "Sir Oliver" is clearly not a good minister, but rather a "martext" in an allegorical sense, for to have a marriage in the middle of the play rather than act 5 would clearly "mar" the conventional pattern of the comic genre. Usually played as a doddering, perhaps mentally incompetent old man, a hilarious alternative was performed in the 2016 production at Stratford, Ontario. Having set the play in nineteen-eighties Newfoundland, on Canada's East Coast, Sir Oliver became a burnt-out hippie. Much of what he had to say, in a cross between East Coast accent and hippie drawl, was unintelligible, but there was an emotional coherence to the rhetorical battle cry with which he leaves the stage: "Ne're a fantastical knave of them all shall flout me out of my calling! (3.3.96–98).

Jaques' objection does raise a more serious point, relevant to the entire play. As Erasmus says, Catholic marriage "is nothing other than an inseparable union for life,"[48] but this union is much happier if lived as a true union of souls or, as Shakespeare puts it in the famous marriage sonnet, Sonnet 116, "a meeting of true minds." Instead of marrying here, Touchstone concludes by rephrasing St. Paul's advice that "it is better to marry than to burn" (1 Cor 7:9); he "beryhmes" Audrey, "we must be married, or we must live in bawdry" (3.3.86–87). While we might cringe at the lustful intent of this rhetorical poetic, the fantastical, fictional fools of the play—principally Touchstone but also Jaques and "Ganymede"—have comically reminded us of what a true vocation to marriage should really mean.

---

46. Joseph, *Arts of Language*, 359.
47. Peacham, *Garden*, 179.
48. Erasmus, *Praise of Folly*, 93.

6

"Not True in Love?"

Comical Confusion of Male and Female Identity

AFTER THE PROGRESS IN the love relationship of Orlando and Rosalind and the near marriage of Touchstone and Audrey, it is necessary to the genre of *As You Like It* that act 3 concludes with two short scenes that delay the expected marriages and develop the play's comic Christian themes. In most comedies, as Lysander tells Hermia early in *A Midsummer Night's Dream*, "the course of true love never did run smooth" (1.1.134); rather, there are complications, or "comic blocks," that delay love and make it at once more complicated and ultimately satisfying for having overcome these barriers. In Shakespearean comedy, due probably to the restrictions on female actors in Shakespeare's time, this confusion is often caused when a female falls in love with the play's heroine disguised as a man. However, the "block" can also be psychological, an interior barrier that prevents a character from loving as they should, if free to do so.

Either kind of folly is often corrected, within Shakespearean comedy, by the wisdom needed to love freely. Catholic Humanism, in Shakespeare's theatre as in much Renaissance art, often plays a key role in helping leading characters overcome their own selfishness. While Catholic Humanist theology must be distinguished from the "total depravity" view of the will also found in Reformation-era Christianity, it should also be noticed that even characters infused with wisdom cannot overcome selfishness solely through their own education. They also need the help of others, particularly friends, and perhaps above all else they need providence, or the intervention of God, to help them overcome barriers to love.

As 3.4 opens, Rosalind is experiencing the typical female frustration with a common male failing, the inability to keep one's promises. Orlando had promised to return to see her this day, and has not shown up. This causes Rosalind to temporarily lose her identity, so that very uncharacteristically she opens the scene by saying, "Never talk to me I will weep" (3.4.1); the lack of conjunctions here could be described as the scheme *asyndeton*,[1] or Rosalind's brevity could be called *brachiepia*,[2] indicating the brevity of overpowering emotion. This line indicates the change of rhetorical role that briefly occurs in this scene, accompanying the "identity" change common in comedy. Rosalind briefly gives up her role as "Ganymede," and returns to being a young woman in love lamenting the lack of commitment of the man she loves. Instead of rhetorically complex lines which often have a "dual" meaning, "Ganymede" educating Orlando *and* Rosalind expresses to the audience a "disguised" passion that dare not speak too openly. This brief scene allows us to peer inside the young woman's heart and hear the anguish now caused by her beloved's absence. Celia—cousin, friend, and companion in the forest—is with her, and provides the strength and quickness of wit needed to remind Rosalind that there are better days ahead. To Rosalind's promise to "weep," Celia responds not with simple sympathy but rather *sarcasmus*[3] that reminds Rosalind of her disguise as "Ganymede": "Do, I prithee, but yet have the grace to consider that tears do not become a man" (3.4.2–3).

Celia's reminder is certainly comedic, but perhaps the connotations of "grace," or simply the habitual relationship that exists in Shakespeare's time between the language of faith and imagery of love, cause the pair's wit in this scene to revolve again around the rhetoric of religion. Rosalind begins with a French cliché to justify why she has "cause to weep," a perhaps irrational or at least unfair *synecdoche*[4] derived from foxes more than men (though Vikings may also be a source); Orlando's "hair is of the dissembling colour" (3.4.6) meaning that it is red. Celia "ups the ante" of the figure by then comparing Orlando to history's most infamous "dissembler," for she immediately "defends" him by saying, "Something browner than Judas" (3.4.7). The apparent "defense," however, soon turns to aggressive *metaphora* when

---

1. Peacham, *Garden*, 52.
2. Peacham, *Garden*, 182.
3. Peacham, *Garden*, 37.
4. Peacham, *Garden*, 17.

Celia adds that Orlando's "kisses are Judas' own children"—an instrument of betrayal against true love (3.4.7–8).

This harsh comparison arouses Rosalind's defense of her beloved and she insists, "his hair is of good colour" (3.4.9), but her own religious *simile* of his "kissing" is more ambiguous. Orlando's "kissing is as full of sanctity as the touch of holy bread" (3.4.12–13), she says, but what modern audiences might take as an unambiguous reference to holy communion could, in Shakespeare's time, indicate something quite different; "holy bread," rather than referring to consecrated communion hosts, could refer to "bread blessed after the Eucharist" and given only to those unsanctified for communion.[5] Rosalind's *simile* could imply, then, that Orlando's absence leaves him unsanctified, but that charitably she wants him to enjoy the fruits of her love.

Celia's rhetorical strategy, by contrast, is to remove any ambiguous sympathy for Orlando by returning to classical imagery whose "baptized" Christian meaning is extremely clear; she continues the witty exchange on Orlando's kissing by adding:

> He hath bought a pair of cast lips of Diana. A nun of winter's sisterhood kisses not more religiously. The very ice of chastity is in them. (3.4.14–16)

Rhetorically, the "cast lips," "winter's sisterhood" and "very ice" here are all condensed *metonymia*,[6] concrete images with symbolic meaning, but the more important point here are the implied *similes*[7] of Orlando's passion to Diana—the classical goddess of chastity often invoked by Medieval or Renaissance artists as a substitute for Mary—or, similarly, to that of a chaste nun. These similes are obviously intended to cast doubt on the "heat" of Orlando's passion, but the almost comical *hyperbole*[8] of Celia's language reminds us that she too is playing a rhetorical role in this scene, acting as the good friend, and spiritual sister, who can support Rosalind in her heartache by rebuking the unfaithfulness of Orlando. Her "role," which she plays with absolute sincerity and faithfulness, is to realistically remind her cousin that Orlando, however romantic he may seem, remains a flawed man in need of education, if ever Rosalind is to marry him. At this point in the play, this "if" remains very uncertain.

---

5. Trautvetter, *As You Like It*, 139.
6. Peacham, *Garden*, 19.
7. Peacham, *Garden*, 158.
8. Peacham, *Garden*, 31.

Given Celia's initial use of images of chastity, the next turn of their conversation is somewhat surprising but perhaps reflective of the bawdy logic and wordplay probably learned from Touchstone. After Rosalind responds to Celia's critical similes by wondering, again with uncharacteristic brevity, "Not true in love?" (3.4.24), Celia employs *asteismus*,[9] when the meaning of a phrase is suddenly turned, to not only shatter the romantic cliché, "in love," but also to offer a potentially bawdy double entendre, stressed through the scheme *epiphora*[10]: "when he is in. But I think he is not in" (3.4.24–25). Prior to this joke, Celia has more philosophically been insisting that "there is no truth" (3.4.19) in Orlando. He is not "a pick-purse" or "horse-stealer," she allows, comically comparing Orlando to common criminals, "but for his verity in love" she has more concrete, damning *similes*[11]: he is "as concave as a covered goblet, or a worm-eaten nut" (3.4.22–25). In other words, spiritually he is hollow, nihilistic, nothing. Orlando's "oath" should be heard, Celia's *similes* continue, as "no stronger than the word of a tapster" or bartender (3.4.27–28). The comparison here evokes a key question; is it Orlando, or Rosalind herself, who is intoxicated with love? Even if this question cannot be immediately answered, Celia continues the comparison by claiming that neither a lover nor a tapster offer a bright future: "they are both the confirmer of false reckonings" (3.4.28–29). In other words, both will charge a higher bill than one initially expects. Celia's witty rhetoric thus casts doubt on whether Rosalind should pursue any further relationship with Orlando, though providing emotional protection and balance for her friend is probably her real purpose.

Nothing Celia says seems to decrease Rosalind's ardor, however, and after some banter about Duke Senior, Rosalind again blurts out a very passionate *erotema*[12]: "what talk we of fathers when there is such a man as Orlando?"(3.4.34–35). Celia answers with another cynical "double entendre," a satirical, extended *antanaclasis*[13] on the dual Elizabethan meaning of "brave"—emphasized with vehemence through the simple repetition of *epizeuxis*[14]—which commonly meant "finely dressed" or "handsome" while also shifting towards the modern sense of "courageous" or "virtuous." Celia critiques Rosalind's passion by disputing, even mocking, Orlando's masculine honor:

9. Peacham, *Garden*, 34.
10. Peacham, *Garden*, 42.
11. Peacham, *Garden*, 158.
12. Peacham, *Garden*, 106.
13. Peacham, *Garden*, 56.
14. Peacham, *Garden*, 47.

> O that's a brave man. He writes brave verses, speaks brave words, swears brave oaths, and breaks them bravely, quite traverse, athwart the heart of his love, as a puny tilter that spurs his horse but on one side breaks his staff, like a noble goose. But all's brave that youth mounts, and folly guides. (3.4.36–41)

One could also describe Celia's use of "brave" here as schemes of repetition such as *diacope*[15] or *paregmenenon*,[16] but as a whole the speech broadly functions as *ironia*,[17] working to persuade Rosalind that Orlando is something other than "brave," at least in any moral sense, despite how attractive she might find him. Celia's concluding *similes* here mock, the "as" likening Orlando to a foolish medieval knight, the "like" to the proverbially proud, silly goose of nature.

Again, though, there is a deeper critique: the more common folly of self-centered egotism that often guides the "brave man." Like many males, Orlando's actions suggest that his own passions, his own impulses, are more important than the heart, or emotional reality, of his supposed beloved. On a yet more universal level, Celia's concluding line critiques "all" youth, both male and female, for the common folly of being guided by physical passion. Celia's directness here is a little surprising, but there can be little doubt that Celia intends to diminish the sexual passion that clearly grips Rosalind after her long conversation with Orlando in 3.2. Do not be guided by a fool like Touchstone! Celia's mockery insists. Fortunately, for Rosalind, Orlando may be of the same gender and species as Touchstone, and thus another male fool, but Orlando does have sufficient spiritual and imaginative qualities to become somewhat educable, and so potentially marriable.

Corin then arrives and invites Celia and "Ganymede" to view, from a distance, Silvius' wooing of Phoebe, "the proud disdainful shepherdess / that was his mistress" (3.4.45–46). The imaginative importance of this is announced in the play by Corin using another pair of "if" clauses or "hypothetical syllogisms" to invite the young women to see this spectacle:

> If you will see a pageant truly played
> Between the pale complexion of true love
> And the red glow of scorn and pure disdain,
> Go hence a little, and I shall conduct you,
> If you will mark it. (3.4.48–52)

---

15. Peacham, *Garden*, 48.
16. Peacham, *Garden*, 55.
17. Peacham, *Garden*, 35.

Corin's invitation to "a pageant truly played" announces a familiar Shakespearean motif, the "play within the play," which typically (as we recall in *A Midsummer Night's Dream* or *Hamlet*) allows an important insight or transitional moment in the play, but can also cause the "confusion of identity" common in comedy. Rosalind uses *paragmenon*[18] to suggest a positive purpose for this "comedy of love," believing that "the sight of lovers feedeth those in love" (3.4.53), but Shakespeare probably intends the "pageant" as another sort of nourishment to her soul. Perhaps the audience is asked to consider the potential ambiguity of Rosalind's key verb here; in other words, what truly "feedeth"? What do lovers really need to sustain their love? In an important sense, the scene will offer Rosalind some objectivity, some distance from which to view another caught in the irrational passion that "love" can become. For what she needs is very different than what her hunger craves to be fed, and Celia's "advice," and cynical commentary, seem to have had little effect upon her.

Rosalind ends 3.4 by telling Corin, "I'll prove a busy actor in their play" (3.4.55), and this meta-dramatic comment reminds the audience that this comedy, both what they are about to see in Sylvius' wooing of Phoebe and in *As You Like It* as a whole, is cast in a clearly artistic key. In that sense, Corin's invitation is another moment in the play in which the audience is invited, in an obvious, self-conscious way, to consider again the value of fiction. The pageant of Silvius and Phoebe is also filled with obvious, traditional rhetorical figures; in the context of their rural, natural love, these figures "naturally" express the honest emotions of both the shepherd and the "scornful woman" already familiar, to Shakespeare's audience, in the sonnet tradition. Rhetorical efficacy joins with poetic *mimesis* to create, despite the laughable clichés, drama worth watching. Rosalind herself must benefit, as dramatic theorists since Aristotle have argued, from the "catharsis" or purgation of emotion that becomes possible when one objectively sees another enacting emotion that also controls oneself. However foolish the *mimesis* of Silvius and Phoebe might seem to others, for Rosalind it will be the nourishment that her soul needs to regain a realistic love for Orlando.

Act 3, scene 5 opens with Silvius pleading, "Sweet Phoebe, do not scorn me," immediately evoking the stereotypical, clichéd form of Petrarchan love that is, by 1599, well known to Shakespeare's audience. Numerous sonnet sequences of the fifteen-eighties and nineties had portrayed an infatuated male wooing a scornful female,[19] and for the most part Silvius and Phoebe are simply pastoral versions of this familiar stereotype. Comedy is created

---

18. Peacham, *Garden*, 55.
19. The most famous of these is Sidney, "Astrophil and Stella," 153–211.

by the *hyperbole* with which each character is fulfilling this stereotype, and the figurative language that each employs to provide "short-hand" reference to the cliché. Petrarchan males often expressed metaphorical fear of "execution" from their "beloved," and here Silvius begs simply that Phoebe have as much feeling as "the common executioner," whose "heart the accustomed sight of death makes hard," yet "falls not the axe upon the humblest neck / but first begs pardon" (3.5.3–6). He concludes with *erotema*[20] expressing his own *pathos* but, in the modern sense, is surely pathetic: "Will you sterner be / Than he that dies and lives by bloody drops?" (3.5.6–7). For her part, Phoebe follows most Petrarchan females by forswearing violence, and simply wants to get as far away as possible from the pursuing male; she tells Silvius, "I would not be thy executioner. I fly thee for I would not injure thee" (3.5.8–9). Yet numerous other Petrarchan clichés fill Phoebe's speech, and at times they suggest violent tendencies; the "deadly darts of eyes," for example, are referenced when she tries to scare Silvius away through another "if" clause: "Now I do frown on thee with all my heart, and if mine eyes can wound, now let them kill thee" (3.5.15–16). The *metaphora* here, of eyes as dangerous weapons, is familiar Petrarchan cliché but, of course, not at all frightening.

Silvius replies with his own "if clause," though one especially marked by clichéd *synecdoche*[21] and *prosopopoeia*[22] derived from the familiar figure of Cupid, the classical archer and son of Venus often mentioned in Shakespeare's comedies of love, but never actually seen. The poor shepherd begs:

> O dear Phoebe,
> If ever—as that ever may be near—
> You meet in some fresh cheek the power of fancy,
> Then shall you know the wounds invisible
> That love's keen arrows make. (3.5.28–32)

Responding to Silvius' *diacope*[23] of "ever," Phoebe replies with her own clichés on time, again using *diacope*, imploring the young man to wait until "that time" which the audience, but apparently not the foolish young man, knows will never come; Phoebe rebukes him:

> But till that time
> Come not thou near me. And when that time comes,
> Afflict me with thy mocks, pity me not,
> As till that time I shall not pity thee. (3.5.33–36)

20. Peacham, *Garden*, 106.
21. Peacham, *Garden*, 17.
22. Peacham, *Garden*, 136.
23. Peacham, *Garden* 48.

Phoebe thus concludes with another "as" or *conditional* clause, but not, as is usually the case in the play, to foster imaginative hope; rather, she strongly suggests that the *catharsis* Silvius hopes for in her—that she will learn to pity him—is not about to take place anytime soon.

In performance, many actors can use the obvious, traditional rhetorical language of both Silvius and Phoebe to lift these characters beyond cliché, making them, if not complex, at least entertaining. Silvius makes the play's dominant figure, the *conditional*, seem rather pathetic, filled with *pathos* rather than *logos*, when he moans a series of these to Corin the older shepherd:

> If thou has not broke from company
> Abruptly, as my passion now makes me,
> Thou hast not loved.
> O, Phoebe, Phoebe, Phoebe! (2.4.37–40)

The final line here could be described as a figure of repetition, *epizeuxis*,[24] but is also a figure of emotional appeal since the lines come across not as a rhetorical scheme, but as the final moans of a dying animal. Most actors play Silvius this way, which is certainly effective, but one must also remember that later in the play Rosalind will give him the privilege of defining "what love is" (5.2.78), and she does not contradict his definition. For her part, Phoebe is slightly more complex, rhetorically tricking Silvius by penning a letter claiming to write "a very taunting letter" (3.5.135) to Ganymede when actually she is expressing her devotion to him. That she is playing a clichéd, literary part, the scornful Petrarchan lady, would have been obvious to everyone in Shakespeare's original audience. Modern actresses can easily convey the same impression through the lines of the play's text, though in the theatre especially the interlude of Silvius and Phoebe often produces laughter. When "Ganymede" meets her, modern actresses generally use wide-eyed stares to convey Phoebe falling into lust with "his" outward appearance.

Rosalind overhears this conversation and eventually becomes enraged by Phoebe's arrogance, coming forward and using *erotema*[25] to rhetorically ask her: "Who might be your mother, / That you insult, exult, and all at once, over the wretches?" (3.5.36–38). Having attacked her lineage, Rosalind further seeks to deflate Phoebe's pride by denying Silvius' praise of her beauty, using *epanaphora*[26] to begin a successive pair of clauses, "I see

---

24. Peacham, *Garden*, 47.
25. Peacham, *Garden*, 106.
26. Peacham, *Garden*, 41.

no more in you than . . ." then varying *metonymy*[27] to deny that Phoebe's beauty is anything special: "without candle may go dark to bed," for she is "the ordinary of nature's sale-work" (3.5.40, 43–44). Rejecting any appeal to commonplace Petrarchan *synecdoches*,[28] Rosalind continues:

> Tis not your inky brows, your black silk hair,
> Your bugle eyeballs, nor your cheek of cream,
> That can entame my spirits to your worship. (3.5.47–48)

There is idolatry, Rosalind's final *metaphora*[29] of herself as worshipper implies, in the idea that Phoebe or any other woman should be treated as a goddess.

Rosalind then addresses Silvius and Phoebe individually, as her rhetorical message to each is very different. With Silvius, Rosalind begins with *erotema* that uses *simile*[30] to paint a comical image of his blustery invocations; yet she also attempts to raise his self-esteem and throw off the self-imposed yoke of Petrarchan masculine devotion:

> You, foolish shepherd, wherefore do you follow her,
> Like foggy south, puffing with wind and rain?
> You are a thousand times a properer man
> Than she a woman. (3.5.49–52)

The key adjective here, "proper," is not figurative, but is rather the sort of clichéd phrase, a kind of *euphemism*, whose symbolic meaning becomes commonly known within a particular culture, such as the urban culture shared by the play's courtiers and, for the most part, Shakespeare's historical theatrical audience in London. Quite possibly, this adjective is meaningless within the pastoral world, and if so would be unintelligible to Silvius, which helps to explain why Rosalind's praise of him has no apparent effect.

As she turns towards Phoebe, the rhetorical aims of Rosalind are largely opposite; she intends to induce humility in the hopes of causing her to treat the poor shepherd better. She begins with reference to the familiar Renaissance image of one's own glass, or mirror, as a source of *sapientia*, having just told Silvius, "'Tis not her glass but you that flatters her" (3.5.55). "Ganymede" then, as Catholic Humanist educators typically sought to do, turns Phoebe towards the starting place of classical wisdom, the oracle of Apollo's famous invocation to "know thyself," and also invokes Christian

---

27. Peacham, *Garden*, 19.
28. Peacham, *Garden*, 17.
29. Peacham, *Garden*, 3.
30. Peacham, *Garden*, 158.

conceptions of heaven and fasting to direct her towards humility. Yet in case traditional philosophical and theological rhetoric cannot move her, Rosalind also invokes *metaphora*[31] of the "market" to remind Phoebe that the goods she sells are not entirely unique or in short supply:

> But, mistress, know thyself; down on your knees
> And thank heaven, fasting, for a good man's love;
> For I must tell you friendly in your ear,
> Sell when you can. You are not for all markets.
> Cry the man mercy, love him, take his offer;
> Foul is most foul, being foul to be a scoffer. (3.5.58–63)

The final *antanaclasis*[32] here, playing on the dual meaning of "foul" as "ugly" and "wicked," sounds like *paromeia*,[33] a proverb, drawing on both moral and "market" wisdom. Yet Rosalind's proverb seems either unheard or, as with Silvius, unintelligible to Phoebe, for she replies, "I had rather hear you chide than this man woo" (3.5.66). As with "Cesario" wooing Olivia in behalf of Orsino in *Twelfth Night*, the "young man's" eloquence here causes the scornful young woman to fall in love with him. Rosalind herself recognizes this reaction, telling Silvius "she's fallen in love with my anger," but nevertheless offering another "if" clause to pledge rhetorical battle: "If it be so, as fast as she answers thee with frowning looks, I'll sauce her with bitter words" (3.5.68–70).

In performance, Rosalind's intervention in the pageant of Silvius and Phoebe reveals her to be both an observant psychologist and a romantic iconoclast. She boldly addresses the root of their problems—Silvius' pathetic lack of self-esteem and Phoebe's pride—then selflessly challenges each to change, for their own good. One can easily critique Silvius' devotion to Phoebe, but when Rosalind directly enters their "interlude" her harshest words are primarily for Phoebe. She particularly uses *erotema* to express disbelief at Phoebe's arrogance, asking her, "who might be your mother that you insult, exult, and all at once over the wretched" (3.5.36–38). As so often in the play, here Shakespeare draws directly on the Catholic Humanist tradition; in Marlowe's *Dr. Faustus*,[34] the seven deadly sins are led onstage by Pride, who proclaims: "I am pride; I disdain to have any parents" (5.282). *As You Like It* probably alludes to Marlowe later, as well, when Touchstone speaks of the possibility that a poet's words can be misinterpreted: "When a man's verses cannot be understood, nor a man's good wit forwarded with

---

31. Peacham, *Garden*, 3.
32. Peacham, *Garden* 56.
33. Peacham, Garden, 29.
34. Marlowe, *Dr. Faustus*, 501–35.

a second child, it strikes a man more dead than a great reckoning in a little room" (3.3.9–12). Marlowe, infamously, had died in 1593 after a violent quarrel in a bar over a "reckoning" or bill.

The possibility of direct allusion in 3.5 is enhanced, further, as "Ganymede" leaves the stage, when Phoebe bids farewell by saying, "Dead shepherd, now I find thy saw of might: who ever loved, that loved not at first sight" (3.5.82–83). The direct quotation from the now dead Marlowe's *Hero and Leander* certainly qualifies as external rhetoric, as well as providing a "wise saw" that comments upon the internal action of the play. James Shapiro has pointed out that the line alludes not only to "Hero and Leander," published in 1598, but also to a poem entitled "The Passionate Shepherd to His love," misattributed to Shakespeare himself in *The Passionate Pilgrim*, a text that pirated some of Shakespeare's poems, without his consent, and was published just prior to *As You Like It*.[35] For Shapiro, the allusions here represent not just name-dropping, but rather rhetorical debt. "One of the lessons Shakespeare learned from Marlowe," Shapiro argues, "is that the most effective way to talk about love without sounding clichéd is to turn what others have written into cliché"; "what Marlowe's characters experience was invented, what Rosalind feels in this most artificial of plays is real."[36]

At least momentarily, however, Rosalind's rhetorical recipe produces no good fruit. Even if Silvius and Phoebe are farcical stereotypes, one can't help but asking the question evoked by numerous other examples of human folly in love: what element of human nature allows such blindness in love? In Christianity, this question is usually posed as part of the extensive evidence of original sin; or, in the terms of St. Paul's famous paradox in Romans 7:15: "what I would, that I do not; but what I hate, that do I." Why? What element of human nature makes us self-destructive? Paul goes on in *Romans* to describe the universal human challenge "to be spiritually minded" rather than "carnally minded" (Rom 8:6), and surely this is a key part of the problem portrayed by the "passion" of Petrarchan love: the tendency to focus solely upon the outward appearance rather than taking the time to become aware of another's spiritual life. Thus Phoebe falls in love with solely the outward appearance of "Ganymede," unaware and unconcerned with the reality of the soul inside this appearance.

This is the essential problem with the "mighty saw," or "powerful proverb," that Phoebe cites. The "saw" is "mighty" because it powerfully describes the reality of many passionate love affairs. Shakespeare's *A Midsummer*

---

35. Shapiro, *A Year*, 228.
36. Shapiro, *A Year*, 218.

Night's Dream makes comic capital out of a "magical" means to create this phenomena—a few drops from a little fairy flower causes the characters in that play to fall in love with the first creature whom they lay eyes upon—but this comedy as a whole plays upon a commonplace of Elizabethan culture. Young women dream, on "A midsummer's eve," of the man they might marry. Is that practice any more rational than love at first sight, or rather simply more evidence, as Duke Theseus summarizes late in that play, that "the lunatic, lover and poet are of imagination all compact" (5.1.7–8). Yet should they be? Rosalind does not appear to agree, and hence her attempt to become "an actor" in the pageant of Silvius and Phoebe, as Puck decides to be "an actor, an auditor too" (3.1.75) in the play of the "rude mechanicals" (3.2.9) in *Dream*.

Initially, however, Rosalind's words seem to have no impact on Silvius and Phoebe, and create rather the confusion of identity characteristic of the middle parts of Shakespearean comedy. Silvius' humiliation will become even more complete, if that is possible, as Phoebe employs him to deliver letters to "Ganymede." These letters will supposedly scorn him, but Phoebe's real intention can easily be grasped by the audience, and seems accepted by Silvius when, in the traditional pastoral *metaphora*[37] identifying a harvester and husbandman, he offers "to glean the broken ears after the man / That the main harvest reaps" (3.5.103–4). While clearly farcical, a continuation of the comic tone that marks the entire scene, Shakespeare also uses Phoebe to raise another key question in the philosophical-rhetorical discourse of love that is central to the entire play. For it is here that Phoebe, early in a long speech that is a typically narcissistic, if not formal aside, offers the "mighty saw" with which I began discussion of rhetoric in this play: "But what care I for words? Yet words do well when he that speaks them pleases those that hear" (3.5.112–13).

In context, this "proverb" is highly ironic, in that her words certainly don't please either Silvius or Ganymede. Phoebe hardly seems to notice, however, for in the long speech that follows she continues to cite a number of Petrarchan *synecdoches*[38] that are commonplace clichés. She dotes especially on "Ganymede's" complexion, which has "just the difference betwixt the constant red and mingled damask" (3.5.123–24). However clichéd, these physical images seem to inspire her rhetorical invention, and she concludes by promising to soon write letters for Silvius to deliver to Ganymede; "the matter's in my head," she promises, and her letters "will be bitter" and

---

37. Peacham, *Garden*, 3.
38. Peacham, *Garden*, 17.

"passing straight" (3.5.140–41). We don't doubt that she is inspired to write, but the parody of a rhetorical-poetic here raises deeper questions.

For while her opening "maxim" on the purpose of words could summarize the rhetorical poetic of much of the best of Renaissance poetry, in Phoebe's mouth these words become a self-centered program of manipulation, "rhetoric" in the worst modern sense of the word. How can the same words mean such different things? Perhaps Shakespeare is here reminding us, as so often in his plays, that the intention of a speaker does affect the meaning of words. Phoebe's intentions are clearly selfish, directed by what Augustine would describe as a "carnal imagination," or at least by the will to lust after outward forms. There is comedy here because Rosalind's outward form, as "Ganymede," makes this lust hopeless, as was Olivia's lust for Cesario, yet Phoebe does express a common human vice. A key purpose of comic drama in Shakespeare's time, perhaps mastered most of all by Ben Jonson, is the portrayal and parody of human vice in order to purge human desire of the vice displayed.

Yet Shakespearean comedy, as many have noted, clearly also does something more, not only critiquing the vice in others but also finding it in ourselves, thus teaching us to laugh at our own folly. Not all cases of "love at first sight" end unhappily in human life, and very rare, nor entirely desirable, is the human who, like Iago (*Oth*., 1.3.319–32) claims to be entirely immune to human passion. Olivia's lust leads to a sudden and apparently happy marriage with Viola's twin, Sebastian, and in this play Phoebe and Silvius do finally marry. In both plays, one can say that it is the imaginative mind and spiritual virtue of the comic heroines, Viola and Rosalind, that allows the happy conclusion, but as we shall see, this cannot be achieved solely through the wisdom of any one human being. Rather, many factors allow resolution of comic confusion, perhaps none more so than the providence of God, which after the Acts of the Abuses in 1605 Shakespeare's late tragic-comedies refer to through the phrase, "the heaven's directing" (*WT*, 5.3.151). *As You Like It* will present this providence through more classical, humanistic means, in keeping with the confidence in art and human nature characteristic of Catholic Humanism.

As so often in life, in Shakespearean drama God is not a direct actor in on-stage events, but rather manipulates circumstances to re-direct our loves to a fruitful purpose, transforming the apparent evil of selfishness into a general good that can be shared by all. For perhaps the central questions raised by Phoebe's "maxim" are: what kind of love can truly "please," and for how long? These are questions far beyond Phoebe's intention, but clearly must be considered by anyone concerned with the long term good of the characters onstage, or of any human being. Phoebe's apparent lack of concern for Silvius is not only mocked but corrected by Rosalind's compassionate intervention, and the simple comedy of the scene thus foreshadows the happy conclusion that this wise comic heroine, herself trapped in the folly of love, will yet create, with the help of Nature's Creator.

# 7

"A Woman's Wit"

Debating Jaques and Educating Orlando

GIVEN THE CHALLENGES FACING her, one might well wonder whether Rosalind, within her unfortunate circumstances in the forest of Arden, has any hope of achieving success. After all, she has no money, strength, or physical power of any kind, and is forced to remain disguised as "Ganymede" in order to remain safe from the commonplace threats of male violence. Yet it is perhaps the conditions of the forest that inspire her to draw upon and magnify the gifts which she does possess in abundance: imaginative wit and eloquent wisdom. These are the talents that Catholic Humanist educators sought to develop in young people, and so Rosalind, in 4.1, continues to develop and model an educational ideal that, while offered in practice primarily to males, could also be aspired to by females.

As already noted, "wit" is a Renaissance word which—while not yet as dominant to describe intellectual activity as in the eighteenth century—certainly connotes being "imaginative" rather than simply "clever." Rosalind has a wit that can't be restrained by convention or repression of any kind; using *metaphora*[1] of imprisonment, she will tell Orlando: "Make the doors upon a woman's wit, and it will out at the casement. Shut that, and 'twill out at the key-hole. Stop that, 'twill fly with the smoke out at the chimney" (4.1.153–56). Like many aristocratic and home-schooled women of

---

1. Peacham, *Garden*, 3.

Shakespeare's time, Rosalind simply needs an opportunity to exercise and develop this wit, and she is happy to seize that opportunity in Arden. However, Rosalind herself must also learn to cope with her own passionate ardor for Orlando.

Before the meeting of these two, Shakespeare first presents a short but crucial conversation between Jaques and Rosalind. For once, the only time shown on-stage during this play, Jaques initiates conversation with another, telling Ganymede, "I prithee, pretty youth, let me be better acquainted with thee" (4.1.1). It is not clear why Jaques approaches Ganymede; perhaps he has overheard and been impressed with the young page's wit, or perhaps he is just bored in the forest. More probably, Shakespeare recognizes that, from a thematic point of view or in order to rhetorically convince an audience of the play, it is essential to the heroine's ability to create a comic conclusion for her to debate, and rhetorically defeat, an obvious antagonist of this love, "Monsieur Melancholy." To do so, Rosalind, as "Ganymede," remains calm and employs the skills of an accomplished Renaissance orator.

Their debate begins with Jaques affirming his love for melancholy, saying, "I do love it better than laughing," but Rosalind replies by advocating balance: "those that are in extremity of either are abominable fellows" (4.1.4–5). Sensing critique, Jaques defends himself: "Why, 'tis good to be sad and say nothing." Probably Jaques means the common Elizabethan meaning of "sad," which normally translates as our modern "serious," but Rosalind might well be aware of the coming linguistic change, and thus shares *antanaclasis*,[2] or pun based on a dual meaning of the word, with the audience. She responds by conceding Jaques' intended point, only to draw an absurd conclusion: "Why then, 'tis good to be a post" (4.1.8–9). A modern rhetorician might term this an *argumentum ex concessis*,[3] though Peacham might instead term the whole argument, *inter se pugnatia*, a "forme of speech by which the Orator reproveth his adversarie. . . . Of manifest unconstancie, open hypocrisy, or insolent arrogance."[4] Jaques is normally arrogant but in playing the role Alan Rickman found a rare moment of humility, as "a curious complicity is established with the audience which allows a lot of warmth in." Unlike modern people who might relax and drop the argument, however, here Jaques is inspired by Rosalind's jibe to develop a *systrophe*,[5] a rhetorical if not logical definition of melancholy:

2. Peacham, *Garden*, 56.
3. Lanham, *Handlist*, 16.
4. Peacham, *Garden*, 163.
5. Peacham, *Garden*, 153.

> I have neither the scholar's melancholy, which is emulation, nor the musician's, which is fantastical, nor the courtier's, which is proud, nor the soldier's, which is ambitious, nor the lawyer's, which is politic, nor the lady's, which is nice, nor the lover's which is all of these; but it is a melancholy of mine own, compounded of many simples, extracted from many objects, and indeed the sundry contemplation of my travels, in which my often rumination wraps me in a most humourous sadness. (4.1.15–19)

Jaques' long definition certainly reflects and perhaps even inspires the developing Renaissance obsession with melancholy, later so eloquently expressed by Robert Burton.[6] While over half of Jaques' definition is negative, saying what he is not, this speech does suggest the unique character of his own melancholy, derived from his unique experiences and meditation, or "rumination."

By "sadness," Jaques probably intends a commonplace Elizabethan synonym for "serious," but Rosalind responds with the modern meaning of "sad," using *asteismus*[7] to now describe Jaques as a "traveler" who has "great reason to be sad," because he has "sold" his "own lands to see other men's" (4.1.20–22). In other words, Rosalind is arguing that Jaques has never really lived anywhere, in that he has remained aloof from others in order to maintain objectivity; more darkly, it seems possible that he has used people also as "objects" from which can be "extracted" melancholy, which unsurprisingly leaves him without social relationships of any kind. Rosalind concludes that Jaques' life reveals that "to have seen much and to have nothing is to have rich eyes and poor hands" (4.1.22–23). There is some respect in this conclusion for the knowledge Jaques has gained, but also a critique of whether Jaques has produced any good fruit from this knowledge. Because "good fruit" is a standard Christian criterion of value, Rosalind's critique reminds the audience of philosophical issues often raised by Catholic Humanists: what is a human being? How should humans gain knowledge of the world, and how does such knowledge become wisdom? More fundamentally yet, what distinguishes a human being from other things in the world? The traditional Catholic response is "the image of God," said to be imprinted upon male and female in the garden of Eden (Gen 1:27), but surely anyone who considers how often this image is defaced is likely to grow as melancholy as Jaques.

Pride causes Jaques to hear only praise from the young page, and he replies, "Yes, I have gained my experience" (4.1.24). Rosalind's reply clearly

---

6. Burton, *The Anatomy of Melancholy*.
7. Peacham, *Garden*, 34.

now employs the modern meaning of "sad" to again question the value of Jaques' knowledge: "And your experience makes you sad. I had rather have a fool to make me merry than experience to make me sad—and to travel for it too!" (4.1.25–27). Touchstone's value seems to be affirmed here, but there could also be a reference to Orlando, who enters wishing Rosalind happiness: "Good day and happiness, dear Rosalind" (4.1.28). Besides the apparent use of an antonym of the modern meaning of "sad," as she responds to Orlando's late arrival, Rosalind perhaps intends, for Jaques, another pun, but one based on *paranomasia*,[8] on the French homonym of "travel," "travaille," which translates as our English word "work." In other words, Rosalind is disputing whether the experience gained by Jaques has been worth the voyages he has gone on, and the work he has put into such trips.

On the page, the meeting of Jaques and Rosalind is a key moment of rhetorical conflict, a meeting of arguably the two major imaginative forces in the play. In performance, however, many actors play this meeting so as to downplay any tension. In the 1978 BBC, for example, Helen Mirren as Rosalind and Richard Pasco as Jaques meet casually, under a tree, Jaques not even interrupting what appears to be a rural adaptation of darts to engage in argument. In Branagh's 2006 film, Jaques and Rosalind speak quietly inside a shepherd's shed. Roberta Maxwell, as Rosalind, in the 1983 Stratford Ontario production, adopts initially an extremely sympathetic tone, then suddenly varies it with the line, "I had rather a fool to make me merry than experience to make me sad" (4.1.25–27). Petrina Bromley, Rosalind in the 2009 RSC, similarly uses this line to almost accuse Jaques of being deliberately bitter.

The tone between Rosalind and Jaques is inevitably varied when Orlando comes on stage; Nicholas Pennell, as Jaques, drew laughs at the 1983 Stratford by almost growling before his "greeting" of the apprentice poet. "God b'wi'you an you talk in blank verse" (4.1.29–30) is Jaques' use, through "an," of the *hypothetical syllogism* to dismiss Orlando, the play's hero. The play's heroine responds with implicit suggestion again of Catholic Humanism. With or without poetry, in another's presence or alone, Orlando is the man, and perhaps the fool, whom Rosalind is willing to travel with, and to work with to create a happy marriage. She sends Jaques off-stage with this summation of their argument:

> Farewell, Monsieur Traveller. Look you lisp, and wear strange suits; disable all the benefits of your own country; be out of love with your nativity, and almost chide God for making you that

---

8. Peacham, *Garden*, 56.

countenance you are, or I will scarce think you have swam in a gondola. (4.1.31–35)

Rhetorically, Rosalind here uses *antonomasia*[9] to rename "Monsieur Melancholy" according to the just mocked vocation of his life, "Monsieur Traveller," and then uses a series of *metonymies*,[10] naturally spoken and included with a range of comments, to summarize and emphasize key elements of his "experience." Some of these terms seem straightforward *misterismus*,[11] as when she mocks Jaques' style of speech as a "lisp," though he has never shown any trouble speaking, and his probable lack of fashion as his "strange suits," though this may simply be generational bias towards clothing. Yet the extended satire here mocks not just external appearance; perhaps more importantly, Rosalind rebukes Jaques' inability to appreciate the gifts of Nature in his own country, and in his own person. As she suggests here, Jaques' central problem is that he does not love his own country; correspondingly, as Catholic Humanists would likely point out, Jaques does not thank God for the nature of his own image, but rather will "chide" even God for the face, or "countenance," that he has been given. The final *metonymia* of "a gondola," however, probably links Jaques to Venice, proverbially known in Elizabethan England as a center of vice, and thus probably alludes again to the "libertine" past earlier critiqued by Duke Senior. These words can seem cruel, even though they echo Senior, but "Lady Love" must clear the stage of lust before leading her beloved man towards the marriage altar.

Yet Rosalind is not immediately happy with Orlando. Rather, as "Ganymede," she rebukes him for failing to show up on the preceding day. She begins with more rhetorical questions, asking, "Why, how now, Orlando? where have you been all this while? You a lover?" (4.1.37–38); the latter question borders on *sarcasmus*,[12] questioning the vocation that this man had earlier professed. She then offers a *conditional* that, if fulfilled, would be the single most destructive consequence for any prospect of peace or happiness in this comedy; she warns Orlando, "An you serve me such another trick, never come in my sight more" (4.1.38–39).

Orlando objects, pointing out, "I come within an hour of my promise" (4.1.40), but Rosalind replies not merely by saying, "that's not good enough," but by teaching him an approach to time that she believes is more

---

9. Peacham, *Garden*, 22.
10. Peacham, *Garden*, 19.
11. Puttenham, *Art*, 191.
12. Peacham, *Garden*, 37.

appropriate to one in love; employing *hypophora*,[13] when an orator answers her own questions, she exclaims:

> Break an hour's promise in love! He that will
> divide a minute into a thousand parts and break but
> a part of the thousandth part of a minute in the
> affairs of love, it may be said of him that Cupid
> hath clapped him o' the shoulder, but I'll warrant
> him heart-whole. (4.1.42–46)

The point here is not simply *hyperbole*,[14] or the invention of another *synecdoche*,[15] "heart-whole," to question whether Orlando is truly in love, but moreover, through her imaginative wit, to teach Orlando an approach to time appropriate to "the affairs of love." Love requires great attention to detail, so that one values each moment of time. One could see Rosalind's words here as "hysterical hyperbole," driven by infatuation, but one could also see her as teaching Orlando the "norm" of an approach to time that is capable of making the commitment, and living the life, that is "natural" within Catholic marriage.

It is another thorny, "realistic" problem that Ganymede / Rosalind then raises by telling Orlando, "an you be so tardy.... I had as lief be wooed of a snail" (4.1.48). This apparent *simile*[16] from nature, however, becomes *dissimilitudo*,[17] to further rebuke Orlando. Preferring a snail over a man, Rosalind explains that a snail "carries his house on his head, and at least "brings his destiny" with him: "horns" (4.1.56). Through this apparently odd comparison, Rosalind raises the problem of adultery, for snails have small protective growths like a deer's antlers, and thus could be said to have "horns"; in Elizabethan literature and probably life as well, any mention of "horns" (as noted earlier when Touchstone argued for their inevitability) acts as *synecdoche*[18] to evoke the image of a "cuckold," the name given to someone publicly disgraced because his or her spouse has been found to have committed adultery. It is this painful marital situation that has caused Ganymede / Rosalind to blithely bring up horns, and to further comment that such a snail "comes armed in his fortune," *asteismus*[19] which clarifies

---

13. Peacham, *Garden*, 107.
14. Peacham, *Garden*, 31.
15. Peacham, *Garden*, 17.
16. Peacham, *Garden*, 158.
17. Peacham, *Garden*, 160.
18. Peacham, *Garden*, 17.
19. Peacham, *Garden*, 34.

the husband's "destiny," but ironically this "fortune" simply "prevents the slander of his wife" (4.1.57–58).

The ironic point here re-establishes Ganymede's "male" voice for, at least in this play, the fear of "cuckoldry" is primarily a male fear. Is Orlando really ready to face such damage to his already limited "fortune"? The female fear hinted at by Rosalind's "hidden" female voice, which the audience remains very much aware of beneath her male disguise, is the fear of slander. Shakespeare dramatizes such fear in several other plays, such as *Much Ado about Nothing*, *Othello*, *Cymbeline*, and *The Winter's Tale*, and it is notable in each case that the woman in question is entirely innocent, the accusation against her pure slander. Nevertheless, the female heroine of each play suffers greatly or even dies as a result of the slander, so Shakespeare is certainly aware that such "slander" is a serious social problem. Within Shakespeare's historical age, of course, Henry VIII's accusations of adultery led to the execution of some English queens, and to various theologians debating the meaning of Jesus' teachings on adultery and divorce (Matt 19:1–12). Orlando's view of this problem is thus important to whether or not he is ready for marriage to Rosalind.

Orlando responds to the thorny issue of "horns" with rhetorical clarity gained through schemes of repetition, *epanalepsis*[20] varied through *paregmenon*[21]: "Virtue is no horn-maker; and my Rosalind is virtuous" (4.1.59). This declaration of trust in Rosalind, and the implicit affirmation of his own virtue, for a moment seems to unmask the real Rosalind disguised within Ganymede, for she exclaims: "And I am your Rosalind" (4.1.60). Celia has to jump in to preserve the disguise, protesting that Orlando "has a Rosalind" of "a better leer," or look, than Ganymede, but the temporary revelation seems to be part of a pattern throughout the scene. Whether because of their passion or simply their familiarity, Orlando seems on the verge of recognizing Rosalind within "Ganymede," and Rosalind seems on the verge of revealing her true identity. Of course it is impossible to know the inner thoughts of these characters, but this impression in the audience is created first because of the grave, serious way that Orlando says "my Rosalind" three times early in the scene (4.1.40, 59, 102) with "Ganymede" apparently assenting to the claim in the line just quoted.

Perhaps this impression is never stronger, however, than when Ganymede continues the "game" in a voice that has to be very close to Rosalind's own desire, if she were present to speak it:

> Come, woo me, woo me, for now I am in a holiday

---

20. Peacham, *Garden*, 46.
21. Peacham, *Garden*, 55.

> humour and like enough to consent. What would you
> say to me now, an I were your very very Rosalind? (4.1.64–66)

Here the *epizeuxis*[22] of "woo me" and of "very" creates the passionate emotion surely felt by the "real" Rosalind, but the key word remains "an," or "if." This word, and the fiction it proposes, is the heart of the game being played, and the word "an" itself has a very interesting role within this scene. It is used as an article, as in modern English, at times in this same scene (4.1.40–41), but there are also three key lines in which the older meaning, as a synonym of "if," is also used (4.1.30, 38, 48). It seems probable that Shakespeare is aware of the meaning of the word changing in his own time; within this very scene, the older meaning must be preserved in order to allow another synonym for the play's emphasis on the *conditional* or *hypothetical syllogism*, the "if" clauses so important to the play's rhetoric.

The "offered fallacy," or, in this case, invited fantasy, is so inviting, and the physical presence of Rosalind so real, that Orlando seems moved to passionate action, for he says: "I would kiss before I spoke" (4.1.67). An actor can plausibly accompany this line with gesture, if Orlando's fantasy or recognition of the presence of "very Rosalind" takes hold, but "Ganymede" both evades this initial advance and seems to invite future kisses; yet if Orlando moves to kiss here, "Ganymede" dodges and explains:

> Nay, you were better speak first, and when you were
> gravelled for lack of matter, you might take occasion to kiss.
> Very good orators, when they are out, they will spit; and for lovers lacking—God warr'nt us!—matter, the cleanliest shift is to kiss. (4.1.69–72)

The relevance of "cleanliness," proverbially of course "next to Godliness," is not brought up again by Rosalind until the play's epilogue, but this is clearly one of those speeches in the play marked by the "playwright's matter." Very explicitly, lovers are compared to orators and, in the rhetorical-poetic yet still comic tone characteristic of this entire play, both depend on the "warrant" of God to remain wise to gain "matter," or rhetorical ideas. As usually argued by Catholic Humanists, *eloquentia* requires *sapientia*.

Due perhaps to the romantic intensity of this exchange, there follows a much less serious discussion which is almost anti-romantic. Rosalind paradoxically seems to assert her own identity to preserve her disguise, and the "game," by telling Orlando, "in her person I say I will not have you." Orlando responds, "then in mine own person I die" (4.1.86–87). This return to romantic cliché prompts a long speech in which "Ganymede" recalls the most

---

22. Peacham, *Garden*, 47.

famous male lovers, such as Troilus and Leander, but concludes that their tragic deaths were for non-romantic reasons. An almost depressed Rosalind concludes with a very literal, almost empirically scientific claim: "Men have died from time to time, and worms have eaten them, but not for love" (4.1.88–101). Her words could be described as "anti-rhetorical," though Peacham might also call them *leptotes*,[23] his word for the modern "litotes," or understatement. Faced with such a bleak future, however, Orlando seems to seize the moment; after brief banter hoping that his "right Rosalind" is not "of this mind" (4.1.102–3), he gives perhaps the most direct, literal address to the woman he must know is standing right before him: "Then love me, Rosalind" (4.1.107).

The romantic passion of this moment, however, is both defused and, in a sense, honored, by another "game" within the play. The rhetorical and imaginative complexity of this "game" makes it among the most fascinating interludes in the play, one whose meaning is sure to be debated. "Ganymede" now proposes a "mock-marriage" in which "he" stands for Rosalind, Orlando acts as himself, and Celia can "be the priest" (4.1.115).

Coming just a scene after Jaques has told Touchstone and Audrey, "get thee to church, and have a good priest tell thee what marriage is" (3.3.76–78), this is a daring and clearly important escalation of the "wooing" game initially proposed by Ganymede. Words and action combine in the scene, though, to make it potentially even more: the moment when Orlando clearly sees through Rosalind's disguise, and the two lovers pledge their love to each other. Shapiro is not unusual in claiming that this is the moment when "Orlando sees through her disguise" and "we know he knows she knows he knows it."[24]

This perhaps hyperbolic claim is based, first, on a fairly well known historical aspect of English marriage. Medieval and Renaissance canon lawyers normally distinguished two forms of wedding vows, *sponsalia per verbo de futuro*, a couple's promise to marry each other, and *sponsalia per verbo de praesenti*, the vows spoken as they formally take each other as man and wife. Both engagement and commitment thus had some legal status, even before public ceremony within a church, and editors and critics of *As You Like It* normally point out that perhaps this is why Celia is hesitant to take part in this game, first saying, "I cannot say the words" (4.1.120). Even after she agrees, when Orlando first says, "I will," the *de futuro* promise, Rosalind immediately replies, "Ay, but when," before requiring the *de praesenti* words: "you must say, 'I take thee, Rosalind, for wife'" (4.1.127). After he does so,

---

23. Peacham, *Garden*, 150.
24. Shapiro, *A Year*, 210–11.

and she responds with the same pledge, the combination of words and actions allow Shapiro, like many other critics, to argue that "playgoers at the Globe" would have seen this as "a 'handfast' or legally binding betrothal," and given that "holy sacraments, including that of matrimony, could not be performed in the theatre," the "Elizabethan audiences would have found the espousal scene in *As You Like It*, where contractual words are spoken, especially powerful."[25]

This claim is surely true, but we must also note Rosalind's words responding to Orlando's vow, spoken just before she makes her own: "I might ask you for your commission" (4.1.130). In other words, "by what authority" can you take me? She thus raises another question which must surely have been on the mind of any Reformation-era audience of the play, "by what authority is marriage sacramental and thus binding?" This must have been especially true in England, where Henry VIII's initial defense of the Roman Catholic doctrine of seven sacraments, *Assertio Septem Sacramentorum* ("The Defence of the Seven Sacraments") of 1521, was infamously followed by his own marital record, the children of which subjected sixteenth-century England to rotating religious regimes. Even in 1599, near the end of Elizabeth's relatively stable reign, Anglican doctrine on marriage was not sufficiently stable to ensure audience response, especially in an audience already divided over many other religious questions. An Anglican "Diocesan Visitation" well prior to the play, in 1578, had said of marriages "without bannes," or public announcement, "it is doubted whether they be married at all."[26]

It is perhaps more accurate, then, to see *As You Like It*'s "mock-marriage" as an extension of the wooing game. Orlando may see through "Ganymede" here, just as he may earlier, but the game is not legally binding or it becomes no longer a game. This is not at all to say it is unimportant. Rather, as with the "wooing" in general, the mock-marriage allows Rosalind to gauge Orlando's commitment, to test whether he would marry when the time actually comes. This could be seen as manipulative, but can also be praised as realistic feminine resourcefulness within a system that might otherwise leave her without a voice. Rosalind herself seems to express this opinion just after she speaks the vow pledging her love to Orlando: "There's a girl goes before the priest; and certainly a woman's thought runs before her actions" (4.1.131–33). In other words, as the play as a whole "argues," prior to any legal reality, love requires "thought," whether one describes such intellectual activity as rhetorical, poetic, or imaginative. Otherwise,

---

25. Shapiro, *A Year*, 211.
26. Quoted in Latham, *As You Like It*, 134.

all marriages could be arranged. Even the often prosaic, proto-typically masculine Orlando here can assent to Rosalind's claim: "So do all thoughts; they are winged" (4.1.134). Both men and women have minds that must be engaged prior to the union of their bodies in marriage.

The Catholic Humanist insight on the priority of personal spiritual and emotional life is thus applied specifically to women, but universalized so as to include men also. In performance, the ambiguous language and rhetoric of the scene allows actors to play the "mock-marriage" scene in at least two very different ways. Orlando can seem entirely obtuse, willingly saying whatever Ganymede tells him to, or the couple can indicate in some way a romantic commitment beyond simple "play." The former method seems clear in Czinner's 1936 film, but in the 1978 version the normally simple Orlando, Brian Stirner, seems lost in thought, clearly stirred within by the mock-marriage. In John Hirsch's 1983 Stratford, Ontario production, Roberta Maxwell and Andrew Gillies speak the vows very seriously, but then fall on the ground laughing, spurred on by Celia's mockery. In Branagh's 2006 film the ceremony is performed with full seriousness, accompanied by solemn music, Bryce Howard as Rosalind especially speaking the vows slowly and solemnly; however, David Oyelowo, as Orlando, pulls away suddenly after the vows, lending emotional depth to the skeptical remarks about men that follow. In Thea Sharrock's 2009 RSC production, the passionate Jack Laskey, as Orlando, practically demands that Celia come out of hiding behind a theatre column to marry them. After the vows, this Rosalind and Orlando kiss, leaving Laskey almost no choice but to come out of the embrace pointing emphatically at "Ganymede." He has probably long before seen through the disguise, like most actors playing Orlando, but a kiss here changes the rhetoric from "probable" to "certain," making physically clear that they are a couple ready to be married.

After Rosalind's long anti-romantic speech, the "mock-marriage" surely lifts Rosalind's spirits as much as Orlando's. It is in this same spirit of commitment that "Ganymede" then asks Orlando to pledge love not "For ever and a day," but rather, using *antimetabole*[27] to reverse the romantic cliché, advises him to "Say a day without the ever" (4.1.137–38). Then, using the scheme *compar*[28] to balance her clauses, and *prosopopoeia* to personify the seasons, Rosalind continues, "men are April when they woo, December when they wed. Maids are May when they are maids, but the sky changes when they are wives" (4.1.139–41). What can allow both men and women to remain happy in a lasting marriage? One might propose various virtues, but

---

27. Peacham, *Garden*, 164.
28. Peacham, *Garden*, 58.

"Ganymede," in this same speech, instead pledges that Rosalind, were Orlando to marry her, would instead torment him in various ways. Speaking in "her" voice, "Ganymede," as Rosalind, offers a very rhetorical pledge, using *compar* of *simile*,[29] hyperbolically heightened by *epanaphora*[30] of "more," to promise to be the opposite of an "ideal" wife:

> I will be more jealous of thee than a Barbary cock-pigeon over his hen,
> more clamorous than a parrot against rain, more
> new-fangled than an ape, more giddy in my desires
> than a monkey: I will weep for nothing, like Diana
> in the fountain, and I will do that when you are
> disposed to be merry; I will laugh like a hyena, and
> that when thou art inclined to sleep. (4.1.141–48)

To which poor Orlando can only ask, "But will my Rosalind do so?," and Ganymede assures him: "By my life, she will do as I do" (4.1.149–50). Why would Rosalind promise such things to her desired husband?

The probable answer is that she is testing whether or not he is prepared to endure the worst moments of marriage, aware that it is these moments that lead to marital alienation. Whereas those engaged in courtship normally reveal only the "best" of themselves, Rosalind's disguise as "Ganymede" lets her also show the worst potential elements of her nature. Perhaps the further purpose of this dialogue is for Orlando to then object, "O, but she is wise," for it allows "Ganymede" to express one of Rosalind's, and Shakespeare's, most memorable affirmations of feminine wisdom. Developing the alliteration or *paroemion*[31] of "wisdom" and "wit," and using the figure *incrementum*[32] to gradually illustrate how feminine wit and wisdom escape imprisoning boundaries, Ganymede tells Orlando that it is precisely because Rosalind is wise, that she acts thus,

> Or else she could not have the wit to do this. The
> wiser, the waywarder. Make the doors upon a woman's
> wit and it will out at the casement. Shut that and
> 'twill out at the key-hole. Stop that, 'twill fly
> With the smoke out at the chimney. (4.1.152–56)

The wit of women is free, and cannot be enslaved, and in this freedom is the potential for wisdom. This speech could be taken as the central theme of *As You Like It*.

29. Peacham, *Garden*, 158.
30. Peacham, *Garden*, 41.
31. Peacham, *Garden*, 49.
32. Peacham, *Garden*, 169.

"Ganymede's" imaginative eloquence even inspires Orlando to enter the game of wit, though his attempts at alliteration, *paroemion*,[33] and verbal puns, or *paranomasia*,[34] cannot help expressing the commonplace male fear of a wife's adultery: "A man that had a wife with such a wit, he might say 'Wit, whither wilt?'" (4.1.157–58). Surely it is Rosalind's voice that responds with a defense of women. For after "Ganymede" warns Orlando of "your wife's wit going to your neighbour's bed," and Orlando demands, "And what wit could wit have to excuse that?" (4.1.159–61), surely it is Rosalind who then turns the tables to remind him that adultery is at least as common a problem among males as females:

> Marry, to say she came to seek you there. You shall never take her without her answer, unless you take her without her tongue. O, that woman that cannot make her fault her husband's occasion, let her never nurse her child herself, for she will breed it like a fool! (4.1.162–67)

References to a woman's "tongue" often function as *synecdoche*[35] in misogynist rhetoric, but here Rosalind alters the symbolic meaning to make the "tongue" an essential source of feminine freedom and identity. Shakespeare, as already noted, often portrays women falsely accused of adultery, but here an eloquent and practical strategy is given to women to employ, even given the abysmal legal and political circumstances of Elizabethan England: each women's wit retains the wisdom to reject false accusations, and to wisely speak so as to encourage male accountability to truth despite the mob of cultural bias that might cause men to irrationally blame women for their troubles.

Rosalind's rhetoric inevitably "lowers the temperature" created by the couple's "mock-marriage," but the gravity of her rebuke is perhaps too much for Orlando to continue the "game" this day, and he then bids farewell: "For these two hours, Rosalind, I will leave thee" (4.1.168). On a positive note, Orlando seems to have learned precision of time, the topic first covered in this day's "education," but Rosalind is clearly unsatisfied with this conclusion. She seems almost angry, in fact, at their farewell, turning the tables on mysognist *synecdoche*[36] by now pointing to a common male vice: his "flattering tongue . . . won me" (4.1.174); "Ganymede" could speak these words, but surely again it is Rosalind's *persona* who challenges Orlando with

---

33. Peacham, *Garden*, 49.
34. Peacham, *Garden* 56.
35. Peacham, *Garden* 17.
36. Peacham, *Garden*, 17.

a parting "if" *conditional*, warning through *metonymy*[37] of the names he shall be called if he fails to keep his commitments:

> By my troth, and in good earnest, and so God mend me, and by all pretty oaths that are not dangerous, if you break one jot of your promise or come one minute behind your hour, I will think you the most pathetical break-promise and the most hollow lover and the most unworthy of her you call Rosalind that may be chosen out of the gross band of the unfaithful: therefore beware my censure and keep your promise. (4.1.178–86)

Orlando responds in the serious terms of Catholic Humanism, with his own conditional for keeping the promise: "With no less religion than if thou wert indeed my Rosalind" (4.1.187). He has accepted and is willing to play by the imaginative rules of the courtship "game." We almost sympathize with Orlando here; we don't know why he has to leave to meet Duke Senior, but there could be good reasons related to his responsibilities to Adam, or other pressures typical of male duties in the world. Rosalind's primary concern, however, is whether Orlando can, in future, keep his romantic commitments.

Yet the tension of their parting also points to how deeply Rosalind is in love with Orlando. There is even a touch of the suicidal passion of Romeo and Juliet when, just after lamenting his "flattering tongue," Rosalind concludes: "'tis but one cast away, and so, come, death!" (4.1.175). Her *metaphora*[38] of love playing dice casts the entire courtship game in an overly dark light. She does not elaborate, thankfully, but alone again with Celia, Rosalind uses *epizeuxis*,[39] *metaphora*, and *simile* to restate her true love for Orlando:

> O coz, coz, coz, my pretty little coz, that thou didst know how many fathom deep I am in love. But it cannot be sounded. My affection hath an unknown bottom, like the Bay of Portugal. (4.1.195–98)

The ocean *metaphora* here is a favorite means for Shakespeare to express the depth of irrational love, and we must sympathize with Rosalind's angst here. Her dear cousin plays upon the often comical term, "bottom," and through *asteismus*[40] cynically questions how real this passion truly is: "Or rather bottomless, that as fast as you pour affection in, it runs out" (4.1.199–200). Rosalind responds with a short speech lamenting the power of Cupid over

---

37. Peacham, *Garden*, 19.
38. Peacham, *Garden*, 3.
39. Peacham, *Garden*, 47.
40. Peacham, *Garden*, 34.

her; using *diazeugma*[41] to ascribe to this one subject, Cupid, diverse actions within her, she tells Celia:

> No, that same wicked bastard of Venus, that was begot of thought, conceived of spleen, and born of madness, that blind rascally boy that abuses everyone's eyes because his own are out, let him judge how deep I am in love. (4.1.201–5)

Rosalind here sounds like someone who has learned the lessons of *A Midsummer Night's Dream*, and sees that the "lunatic, the lover, and the poet / Are of imagination all compact" (*MSND*, 5.1.7–8), but she cannot assert any independence from this passion, concluding by admitting to Celia: "I cannot be out of the sight of Orlando: I'll go find a shadow, and sigh till he come" (4.1.205–6). In addition to simple depression, Shakespeare here could be expressing another meta-dramatic comment through the common *metonymia*[42] of "shadow" meaning "actor."[43] Is a shadow any more or less substantial, a theatre audience must ask, then the lover whom Orlando may be merely "acting" as? What if his devotion is as much a mask as that of "Ganymede"?

In performance, the revelations of Rosalind challenge anyone playing her to reassert her feminine identity, and to reconcile the apparent contradiction posed by such a deeply romantic soul remaining within the rhetorician who has so successfully played a "game" so far. Celia seems tired of the entire exercise, responding only "And I'll sleep" (4.1.207), but Rosalind's passion cannot be dismissed as youthful feminine cliché.

Rather, it is of the essence of Shakespearean comedy, in contrast to Jonsonian satire, that the dramatic protagonists are immersed in the folly being portrayed, not aloof from it. Even heroes or, in this case, the heroine, is human, and flawed; from the standpoint of Catholic Humanism, it is inevitable that such folly should be experienced. Love is a great good, but to understand its goodness one must also be aware of its forms, as Catholic Humanists from Augustine to Dante to Chaucer had all stressed. It is arguable that the passion of this couple, which lets them play at "mock-marriage" long before their words can fully express the good of marriage, is a necessary prelude to them actually marrying, however laughable one might find the scene. There is something deeply honest, and human, in both the lovers' naïvete and personal revelations, however humiliating; following Erasmus, Shakespeare's *As You Like It* invites us not only to laugh at others caught in the folly of love, but to also laugh at ourselves.

41. Joseph, *Arts of Language*, 59.
42. Peacham, *Garden*, 19.
43. Compare, for example, Puck's final epilogue in *A Midsummer Night's Dream*, which begins by asking forgiveness: "if we shadows have offended."

8

"If You Be a True Lover"

Rounding Up Imaginative Realists in the Forest of Arden

FOR *AS YOU LIKE IT* to be a Shakespearean comedy, however, Rosalind must do more than simply educate Orlando. As a comic heroine like Viola, Beatrice, or Imogen, Rosalind also rebukes destructive folly in the play, and harmonizes discordant elements that can be redeemed. Neither she nor anyone else can achieve such things by themselves, but rather must seek viable solutions to conflicts, whether these are presented by time, chance, providence, or God—what *The Winter's Tale* refers to as "the heavens directing" (*WT*, 5.3.151).[1] Because marriage is the foundation of harmony in human society—according to both Catholic Humanism and Shakespearean comedy—Rosalind must especially be prepared to direct solutions to discordant love in order to allow the play's final dance of music and marriage. To do so, she must reveal false conceptions of love that distort romantic love, while enabling what Catholic Humanists might call "imaginative realists," those who can accept the redemptive power of true love in their lives. In pursuing this goal, Rosalind will not act alone; rather, she must speak rhetorically, aware of her audience and its needs, even as she pursues her own romantic desires.

As already noted, one of the greatest threats to romantic love is the cynicism of Jaques, precisely because there is an element of truth in his

---

1. See Maillet, "Fidelity," 219–43.

satiric vision. Act 4, scene 2 is a short scene that reminds us of this threat, and of Jaques' perceptive critique of the *ethos* in Arden. As is inevitable, given the absence of grocery stores in Arden, Duke Senior's courtiers have killed a deer, and are celebrating this successful hunt when Jaques happens upon them. Simultaneously joining in this celebration and mocking it, Jaques asks who "killed the deer?"; he then makes what seems, coming from him, to be a surprising proposal: "Let's present him to the Duke like a Roman conqueror, and it would do well to set the deer's horn upon his head, for a branch of victory" (4.2.3–5). While ostensibly praise, the rhetoric here is clearly caustic *ironia*,[2] cast in a form familiar to Shakespeare's audience, a mock epic *simile*.[3] By comparing a hunter to someone far greater but often also guilty of pride, "a Roman conqueror," Jaques likely intends to deflate the celebration rather than add to it. Ever the cynical satirist, Jaques mocks those around him even while standing in the midst of them.

Jaques then requests a song to "celebrate" the hunt, and the foresters offer one that again gives a professional company an opportunity to turn their theatre into a forest, and the audience into a chorus that can join their own voices to the action onstage.[4] Yet even more so than "Under the Greenwood Tree," there is a darker purpose to this song. For as already noted, the *antanaclasis*[5] and *allegoria*[6] of "hunting the hart," or deer, as an extended *metaphora*[7] for romantic courtship, or "hunting the heart," also included the image of "cuckoldry," of the humiliated spouse wearing the "horn of scorn" after their supposed beloved had committed adultery. This is surely the dark, painful situation that the foresters also sing about in the song's final verse, though here the scorn is accepted with good humor as a potential part of any marriage:

> Take thou no scorn to wear the horn
> It was a creed ere thou wast born.
> Thy father's father wore it,
> And thy father bore it.
> The horn, the horn, the lusty horn
> Is not a thing to laugh to scorn. (4.2.14–19)

---

2. Peacham, *Garden*, 35.
3. Peacham, *Garden*, 158.
4. For an excellent illustration of this possibility, see John Hirsch's 1983 Stratford production.
5. Peacham, *Garden*, 56.
6. Peacham, *Garden*, 25.
7. Peacham, *Garden*, 3.

Clearly, though, the foresters are laughing in something of the same spirit as Erasmus' *Praise of Folly*. As with Touchstone's "courage" before "horns," as noted in chapter 5, so here the fear of adultery is laughed at. As Erasmus' Folly puts it, "Goodness me, what divorces or worse than divorces there would be everywhere if the domestic relations of man and wife were not propped up and sustained by the flattery, joking, complaisance, illusions and deceptions provided by my followers!"[8]

In performance, particularly in exceptionally skilled professional theatre such as John Hirsch's 1983 production at Stratford, Ontario, this song can become a set piece, like "Under the Greenwood Tree," transforming the stage into a wooded world of foresters, song, and friendship. Even in such an environment, though, Jaques can have his say. In the 1978 BBC, for example, Richard Pasco as Jaques looks as though he is about to vomit during the song. At the 1983 Stratford, after the song ended an enraged Nicholas Pennell rushed onstage, shouting "No, no," then clubbing various foresters with his umbrella.

One can almost hear the foresters laugh as they sing. Their rhetorical message, surely, is "don't be afraid" of the scorn that can come while married. The point is not that adultery is acceptable, but rather that one should not be so fearful of adultery that this fear prevents marriage. The message is especially important for males, and the jealousy common amongst males is a vice often focused upon and purged in Shakespearean drama. Although Jaques seems opposed to love, in general, the forester's song reinforces the witty word-play of Rosalind as "Ganymede," who in 4.1 had also sought to make Orlando laugh at the possibility of adultery. Again, the purpose of such laughter is not to regard the entire issue as "a joke," but rather to recognize one's own potential for similar vices, and thus to laugh at oneself rather than condemning others, especially often innocent wives. This is the "serio-comic" psychology of Catholic Humanism, which seeks to transform the human heart from within rather than promoting condemnation of others; it is a very practical, pragmatic method, in other words, to teach us to hate the sin but love the sinner. Or, at least, to laugh with others while laughing at the sinner who is ourselves.

If the song of 4.2 addresses common human and especially male phobias of love, 4.3 depicts more clichéd but still damaging forms of misguided love. Rosalind and Celia begin by lamenting, again, how Orlando has failed to return when he said he would, within two hours, prompting Rosalind to use the word "much" as an *ironic*[9] expression in this moment of disappoint-

---

8. Erasmus, *Praise of Folly*, translated by Betty Radice, 93.
9. Peacham, *Garden*, 35.

ment: "And here much Orlando" (4.3.2). Trautvetter notes other examples in Renaissance drama in which "much" is an ironic expression meaning "little" or "no," but believes this the "only instance of such in Shakespeare."[10] Celia, in response, is more directly critical, pointing out the incongruity of Orlando's "pure love and troubled brain," and expecting that he hath "gone forth to sleep" (4.3.3–5). The attention of both is then turned to Silvius, who offers Rosalind the letter from Phoebe which she takes and reads. Silvius warns, though, that Phoebe wrote with a "stern brow and waspish action," and this outward expression probably means that the letter bears "an angry tenor" for which he can't be blamed, being but "a guiltless messenger" (4.3.10–13).

By this point in the play, Rosalind is familiar enough with the shepherd's and shepherdess's relationship to know what to expect, but after reading the letter even she seems taken aback, adapting a traditional *prosopopoeia*,[11] or personification, of an idea (recall Viola's famous speech on "patience like a monument" (*TN*, 2.4.113) for this rhetorical moment: "Patience herself would startle at this letter" (4.3.14). At first this reaction seems to stem from Phoebe's perfect enactment of the commonplace Petrarchan cliché whereby the pursued female scorns her suitor. As "Ganymede" now tells Silvius, "She calls me proud, and that she could not love me / Were man as rare as Phoenix" (4.3.17–18). The expression that follows, however "Od's my will," meaning simply, "God knows my will," reminds us that inside Ganymede is the will of Rosalind, and the mind of a Renaissance Catholic Humanist. It is this voice that then undercuts the traditional rhetoric of hunting and courtship with a more humbling *antanaclasis*[12] and *metaphora*[13]: "Her love is not the hare that I do hunt" (4.3.19). Rosalind seems to view the clichéd love of Phoebe and Silvius from a distance, yet with dismay at the confusion her disguise has caused.

Rosalind's next tactic might confuse those in the audience, but from a psychological point of view it makes good sense. By accusing Silvius of having written the letter, telling him "This is a letter of your own device" and claiming that the letter "is a man's invention, and his hand" (4.3.21), Rosalind probably hopes to awaken the competitive masculine nature of Silvius and inspire him to challenge "Ganymede" as a rival. She cannot truly believe that Silvius wrote the letter, but by pretending to do so at first she perhaps hopes to inspire in him something other than the passive Petrarchan male we have seen so far in the play. Yet the strategy seems to fail; Silvius replies

10. Trautvetter, *As You Like It*, 167.
11. Peacham, *Garden*, 136.
12. Peacham, *Garden*, 56.
13. Peacham, *Garden*, 3.

only, "Sure it is hers," and then agrees to hear the letter read after Ganymede insists that "Women's gentle brain / Could not drop forth such giant-rude invention" (4.3.34–35). The entire scene seems designed to challenge the view that women are incapable of the cruelty typically shown by powerful men. The purpose of such argument is not to demonstrate the "equality" of the sexes, as one might argue today, but rather a Catholic Humanist commonplace: the common human nature in both men and women, the soul constructed by and in need of communion with God.

In the lines that follow, the first Folio twice includes a rare stage direction, "Read," which could also be Shakespeare's way, as elsewhere in the play, of explicitly foregrounding the process of communication being used, and of focusing audience attention upon the meaning of the letter's written words. The probably illiterate Silvius could not read the letter on his own, but the aristocratic, probably home-schooled Rosalind soon becomes, in reading Phoebe's letter, aware that this is a love letter addressed to Ganymede. As Ganymede begins reading, "he" invents another *prosopopoeia*,[14] turning the young shepherdess' very name into a trope to personify tyranny, much as Hamlet does with a more traditional "tyrant" when he laments, in his advice to the players, poor dramatic delivery, saying that it "out-Herods Herod" (3.2.14). Here, perhaps first scanning the letter, Ganymede from exasperation employs the same figure, saying "She Phoebes me," then exhorts Silvius to "Mark how the tyrant writes (4.3.40). The letter largely consists of standard Petrarchan cliché, humorously (and heretically) presenting how a "god to shepherd turned," "godhead laid apart," can through the "scorn" of "bright eyne" "raise such love" in another (4.3.41, 45–51). It soon becomes apparent, however, that there are other rhetorical intentions in the letter. Phoebe has written:

> Whiles you chid me I did love;
> How then might your prayers move?
> He that brings this love to thee,
> Little knows this love in me. (4.3.55–58)

Even the illiterate shepherd recognizes this reference to himself. Yet poor Silvius has the eloquence only to respond with *erotema*,[15] rhetorical questions reflecting his own inner pain during the reading. "Call you this chiding?" (4.3.65), he sadly wonders, but Shakespeare seems to both be laughing at and lamenting human folly in love. For Phoebe perfectly illustrates how the effect of words can sometimes depend not on the words'

---

14. Peacham, *Garden*, 136.
15. Peacham, *Garden*, 106.

meaning, but rather on how a listener's inner will is disposed to hear the words. Phoebe is herself illustrating this when her letter praises "the scorn" of Ganymede's "bright eyne" (4.3.51) and thus reverses the normal Petrarchan pattern by which the scorn of a female's eye awakens passionate love in a male suitor, as also happens in *Twelfth Night* when Olivia falls in love with "Cesario," the disguise of Viola. Rosalind recognizes that Phoebe's desire is shaped by a cultural cliché, and she must find a means to "re-order" this love if either Phoebe or Silvius are ever to be happy.

Rosalind's strategy to do so is to first rebuke the folly with rhetorical questions of her own, but then also *hypophora*[16] in which she answers her own question. She says to Celia, "Do you pity him? No, he deserves no pity," and to Silvius: "Wilt thou love such a woman? What, to make thee an instrument, and play false strains upon thee?" (4.3.67–68). Figurative rebuke cannot help this simple shepherd, however, despite commonplace, traditional *metaphora*[17]; thus Ganymede describes Silvius as "an instrument" whom Phoebe "plays false strains upon" and "a tame snake" (4.3.68–70), not subtle or dangerous like the snake of Eden, but rather a common garden snake who slithers away without even a tail to put between its legs. Soon Rosalind reverts to the "if" *conditional* clauses central to the rhetoric of the whole play; "say this to her," Ganymede tells Silvius:

> that if she love me, I charge her to love thee. If she will
> not, I will never have her unless thou entreat. If you
> be a true lover, hence, and not a word. (4.3.71–73)

Rosalind will develop similar *conditionals* to help create many "true lovers" at the play's comic conclusion. Yet it is significant that the germ of this rhetorical strategy is here, as the kind will of Rosalind, which "Od's will" knows well, desires not simply her own romantic satisfaction but also to help the at once sad and silly love of Phoebe and Silvius. Rosalind truly feels sorry for both, perhaps because she herself knows the irrational folly of human love. Beyond even her initial intention to "prove a busy actor in their play" (3.4.55), Rosalind becomes a playwright creating conditions for them to become "true lovers," much as Shakespeare does with all of the characters within *As You Like It*.

Signs of an even greater Author, and of the creative power of true love, commence in 4.3 with the sudden arrival of Oliver in Arden. He has a dramatic story to tell, beginning with a potentially ominous *emblem*[18]: "a bloody napkin" (4.3.94). As is common elsewhere in Renaissance drama,

---

16. Peacham, *Garden*, 107.
17. Peacham, *Garden*, 3.
18. Puttenham, *Art*, 102.

including the tragic, infamous example of Shakespeare's *Othello*, a "napkin" is a synonym for "handkerchief," and frequently has romantic connotations. The "bloody napkin" has expressly been sent via Oliver to Rosalind, and it is with apprehension that she here asks: "What must we understand by this?" (4.3.95). Yet rather than relating the *emblem* to the Orlando / Rosalind romance, Oliver answers by saying that the bloody handkerchief signifies "some of my shame," and with further ambiguity proposes another "if" clause to suggest the dramatic story behind this mysterious emblem; listen, he implies,

> If you will know of me
> What man I am, and how, and why, and where
> This handkerchief was stained. (4.3.96–98)

This somewhat labored introduction, employing the still used method of invention known as "the journalist's questions," prefaces a long speech from Oliver of not less than twenty-two lines. Artfully narrating the tale, Oliver's aesthetic method is not simply a technique, but reflects his broader ethical purpose.

Beginning by indicating that he will recount Orlando's travels from the very moment he "parted with" Rosalind, Oliver tells how Orlando happened upon a strange scene in the forest: "a green and gilded snake" is around the neck of a sleeping man, when suddenly the snake slithers off the man and under a bush, wherein is hidden "a lioness" waiting until the man awakens to attack the man. As Oliver explains, summarizing many traditions related to "the king of beasts," it is "the royal disposition of that beast / To prey on nothing that doth seem as dead" (4.3.109, 118–19). Clearly not a "naturalistic" story of a "real" forest, whose snakes are not commonly "green and gilded," Oliver's tale rather "emblematizes," as Allen Brissendon comments,[19] biblical verses such as Psalm 91:13, "Thou shalt walk upon the lion and the asp."[20] Such allusions and emblems effectively preface the ethical issue which Orlando faces once he discovers that the sleeping man is "his brother, his elder brother" (4.3.121).

Will Orlando take revenge by allowing to be killed the elder brother who had denied his inheritance (of even more importance, now that Orlando hopes to marry), and sought to have him killed in the wrestling match? We recall, of course, Orlando's great initial resentment of Oliver, and could see "natural justice" occurring, at the very least, if Orlando were to allow "nature" to "take its course" and slay Oliver through these dangerous beasts. Yet in the snake's fear of the lion there is probably Christian allegory, of

---

19. Brissendon, *As You Like It*, 203.
20. Knowles, "Myth and Type," 12.

Satan slinking in fear away from the "Lion of Judah," and Orlando should also have a healthy "fear" of the true King of beasts. Quite unexpectedly, then, Oliver seems to deliver to Rosalind, and the theatrical audience, a narrative embued with the symbols and spirit of Catholic Humanism.

After this main narrative, a philosophical discussion of "nature" ensues, particularly "human nature." Celia recalls that Orlando regularly described his elder brother as "unnatural," and Oliver here admits that "he was unnatural" (4.3.125). Rosalind, by contrast, can think only of Orlando's safety and asks if Orlando left his brother to the "hungry lionesse?" (4.3.127). Oliver then adds an extraordinary element to the story:

> Twice did he turn his back, and purposed so,
> But kindness, nobler ever than revenge,
> And nature, stronger than his just occasion,
> Made him give battle to the lioness. (4.3.129–31)

In context, particularly, this "battle" seems an especially surprising, "unnatural" act, for Orlando goes against his "natural" inclination to turn his back on Oliver, and instead risks his own life out of love for his enemy. That this enemy is also a brother probably accounts for the word "kindness" here, for the older English meaning of "kind" is cognate with "kin" and in this sense the brothers are of course related by "nature."

Yet perhaps, as Catholic Humanists would surely point out, it is also Nature, as a synonym for God, that here is "stronger than his just occasion" and inspires Orlando to love rather than the human tendency to revenge. In Arden, we might say, Orlando treats Oliver as Abel might have treated Cain, had Adam and Eve still lived within Eden and evil never befell human nature. We might term Oliver's narrative a *fable*,[21] after Aesop's allegorical stories of animals teaching moral lessons, but Erasmus's *De Copia* commends fables of this kind "because the truth is set out vividly."[22]

Orlando's noble love has a radical effect on Oliver. When he concludes the narrative with the words "I awaked" (4.3.133), Celia and Rosalind suddenly realize what the audience has known for some time: the speaker, Oliver, and the man who had been sleeping in the forest are one and the same man. "Are you his brother?" demands Celia, which prompts perhaps the key point of the entire narrative; Oliver replies:

> 'Twas I, but 'tis not I. I do not shame
> To tell you what I was, since my conversion
> So sweetly tastes, being the thing I am. (4.3.136–38)

21. Lanham, *Handlist*, 50.
22. Erasmus, *Copia*, 631.

The repetitive schemes of "I" here, first *epiphora*,[23] then *epizeuxis*,[24] and perhaps most importantly *paregmenon*[25] of the "being" verb, effectively express the crucial topic of conversion, as that concept is understood by Catholic Humanism. Oliver's identity has been changed, and he is no longer the man who, at play's start, treated Orlando so cruelly.

This is an important passage for the authenticity of the comedy as a whole, for it cannot simply be the case that Oliver has arrived in Arden, become "good," and happily provided a male for Celia to wed in the multiple marriages that always conclude comedies. Audience credulity of this kind cannot be assumed without also damaging the credibility of the play's overall thought on love. Rather, Oliver's lines here signify the radical conversion that Christianity teaches is possible through self-sacrificial love of the kind that Orlando has shown. For Catholic Humanists, "atonement" in this sense is commonly a process initiated by disciples of Christ, even as it depends for its power and authority upon the atonement of Christ on the cross. The authenticity of Oliver's conversion is shown here by how he has freely admitted his past sins and evil nature. Also, as noted earlier with Amiens' comments on Duke Senior's first speech in Arden, with Oliver the word "sweetly" reverses Augustine's famous account of how "sweet the sin," and follows medieval and Renaissance spiritual writers who, as previously noted, often describe the experience of God as "sweet." Shakespeare thus signifies, through both internal rhetoric and external rhetoric that appeals to the Catholic tradition, the divine foundation of Oliver's new interior life. In Arden, Catholic Humanists would say, Oliver has put off the "old Adam" in order that the "new Adam" (1 Cor 15:22) might live within him.

Rosalind, however, can still think only of Orlando, and again demands: "But for the bloody napkin?" (4.3.138). Again Oliver puts off this question, replying only "By and by," before commencing another long speech in which he describes Orlando leading him to Duke Senior, whose authority in the forest will allow him to remain there and be governed, as Oliver is now happy to accept, by "my brother's love" (4.3.145). Oliver does offer the romantically interesting information that, as Orlando's wounds were healing in a cave, Orlando "cried in fainting upon" hearing the name of "Rosalind" (4.3.150). Orlando then sent Oliver to the young women, with his story of the bloody "napkin," as penance for "his broken promise" to return earlier. This further revelation of real love causes (as a stage direction prompts) Rosalind to herself faint, and Celia comically can't resist again mocking her

---

23. Peacham, *Garden*, 42.
24. Peacham, *Garden*, 47.
25. Peacham, *Garden*, 55.

cousin's disguise through *diacope*[26] of her assumed name, saying, "Why, how now, Ganymede, sweet Ganymede!" (4.3.158). Oliver himself seems to suggest, through *hypophora*,[27] that he sees through Rosalind's disguise, saying "You a man? You lack a man's heart" (4.3.165–66).

In performance, skilled actors can make this moment of revelation a key turning point in the play. There is an inevitable lull in action as Oliver relates his narrative, which is long and can be delivered in a dull fashion. Some productions shorten his speech considerably, but he and Celia falling in love at first sight, and the swoon of "Ganymede," is always dramatic. When Oliver counsels Rosalind to "counterfeit to be a man" (4.3.174–75), most actors convey, through gesture and tone, that he already knows of her disguise, presumably learned through Orlando. Theatre tends to enhance all of this drama, as John Hirsch's 1983 Stratford showed through something so simple as Oliver telling the tale while standing between Rosalind and Celia, allowing the latter's instant attraction to be conveyed. Oliver's key line—"Twas I, but tis not I"—is then spoken directly to Celia, who turns away, but her hidden smile is visible to the audience.

In Branagh's 2006 film, the "realism" possible in high-budget modern movies allowed a physical dramatization of Orlando fighting the lioness, presented just before lines from 4.3 in the play. Oliver thus has a much shorter narrative to deliver, the audience being able to understand the import of the "bloody napkin" without the full explanation; not having to present the entire speech allows Oliver and Celia a much slower delivery of their lines, and a much more obvious mutual fall into lust. Adrian Lester, as Oliver, physically lifts Romola Garai, as Celia, from a haystack, and almost kisses here there and then. Such action can seem heavy-handed, and it can detract from Shakespeare's emphasis on the narrative art of Oliver. Yet love's ability to suddenly sweep Celia and Oliver away provides an effective contrast or "foil" to the patient love "game" of Rosalind and Orlando, though happily both couples are headed to the same marriage feast.

Awaking, Rosalind tries to cover up the revelation with further fiction, asking Oliver to "tell your brother how well I counterfeited," but his clear-eyed new identity cannot be fooled. "This was not counterfeit," he replies, for he has seen the evidence of the real flesh of Rosalind herself: "There is too great testimony in your complexion that it was a passion of earnest" (4.3.170–72). Forms of the word "counterfeit" are used six times in the scene's final twelve lines, obviously foregrounding the "game" of disguise but also the rhetoric of poetical theatre, which has been accused

---

26. Peacham, *Garden*, 48.
27. Peacham, *Garden*, 107.

since Plato's *Republic* of offering a "counterfeit" of reality. Rosalind closes the scene by again requesting, "I pray you commend my counterfeiting to him" (4.3.182–83) but even she must know that her disguise has worn thin.

Cynical audiences may also be weary of the "game" of "Ganymede," but Rosalind's words here surely recall the Catholic Humanist love of "counterfeit," as noted in both More and Erasmus. Cynically, one could wonder whether Oliver's conversion is "counterfeit," but Celia certainly does not question its reality. Actresses playing Celia here can choose how explicitly to present her falling in love with Oliver, but there can be no question that she does marry him. If Celia did not, there might not be the multiple marriages typical of Shakespearean comedy, but her love is not simply an aesthetic convention. Rather, as Erasmus seems to recognize, without faith in "counterfeit," who could be married at all? To borrow the words of Wilson's 1668 passage in *The Praise of Folly*, "Thus are all things represented by counterfeit, and yet without this there was no living."[28]

Just as essential to the play's imaginative endorsement of "counterfeit" is Oliver's behavior, the actions that follow his eloquent words. Though Oliver clearly sees through Rosalind's disguise, he will "play along" at least up to the time of the couples' wedding ceremonies. Cynical self-interest could be cited, but there is an element of both humility and self-interest in the Catholic Humanist love of "counterfeit." For who does not play a role, or put on some disguise, in the course of human courtship? Do most couples really know each other better than Orlando and "Ganymede" already do? Quite possibly, the "game" they have played has let them know each other's real nature better than through more conventional courtships—just as the shrewish masks worn by Beatrice and Benedick in *Much Ado about Nothing* allow a more realistic preparation for marriage than the conventional courting of Hero by Claudio. Paradoxically, imaginative "counterfeit" has similarly created romantic realism between Orlando and Rosalind.

As is known to Oliver in his conversion, to Catholic Humanist theologians, and to every audience attentive to the conclusion of a Shakespearean comedy, real love ultimately leads towards revelation of identity and the realm of eternal being. By the end of act 4, Rosalind has created the conditions necessary to such a conclusion; one is tempted to add, "in spite of her own infatuation with Orlando," but rather it is precisely because she is so in love, and has been since the wrestling match of act 1, that she is sympathetic enough to care whether or not the good fruit of love will lead to the full harvest of marriage. We can add that Shakespeare certainly helps Rosalind's directing, in no small part by reminding us that neither she nor any other

28. Erasmus, *The Praise of Folly*, translated by John Wilson.

lover acts entirely alone. Whatever the limitations of his imaginative wit or romantic verse, Orlando's moral virtue has saved his brother from both physical harm and spiritual perdition, and in so doing has also convinced Rosalind of his real passion for her. A potential pairing of Oliver and Celia now seems probable also, but before the multiple marriages expected in comic conclusions, Shakespeare returns, at the start of act 5, to the foolish love and common lust of Touchstone and Audrey.

9

"Sweet Lovers Love the Spring"

Finding the Time for Love

As ACT 5 OF *As You Like It* opens, it is clear that many of the main characters are prepared for marriage, yet there remains much uncertainty as to when the appropriate time for this life-changing ceremony should occur. The most influential biblical statement on time is probably Ecclesiastes 3, which begins by reminding us that there is "a time to every purpose, under heaven" (Eccl 3:1). Yet the New Testament, and much of the subsequent Catholic ecclesiastical tradition, also reveals that romantic love is not a fruit always in season, for there can be excellent reasons to practice celibacy in order to live a Christian life, and it is essential to the spiritual life of a Catholic community that celibate love be supported and honored. While it is certainly true that *As You Like It* is not a play that encourages one "to live in a nook merely monastic" (3.2.404–5), we may be surprised to find that the play also insists on an essential distinction being made between love and lust.

The Catholic Humanism of Erasmus and More, however, emerges at a time of ecclesial and political corruption, and this is part of the reason that it celebrates the possibility of personal, romantic love. Yet Catholic Humanist theologians still look to consecrate romantic love through the traditional sacrament of marriage, believing, with historic Christianity, that the presence of God creates the unitive love sought within every marriage. It has to be remembered, however, that much of Reformation Christianity fails to acknowledge this sacrament. Perhaps even more importantly, it is dispute over the nature of marriage that leads to Henry VIII's split with Rome and, subsequently, More's martyrdom. *As You Like It* is very much in the spirit of Catholic Humanism, as advocated by both More and Erasmus, in that the play celebrates the imaginative possibility of romantic love, but acknowledges also the absolute need for the presence of God if marriage is truly to be a time of spiritual harmony.

Complex theological and ecclesial questions are not explicitly raised in the play, of course, but rather suggested through the aesthetic forms of particular characters and themes. In a comedic form, Touchstone gives us the essential theme when he opens act 5 by telling his fiancé, "We shall find a time, Audrey" (5.1.1); then, ironically, and comically, he urges the virtue usually associated in Shakespearean comedy and romance with virtuous females, not virile males like himself: "patience, gentle Audrey" (5.1.1). For her part, she responds by affirming the ecclesiastical validity of whichever church Rev. Martext, whom we recall from act 3, might represent; she tells Touchstone, "Faith, the priest was good enough, for all the old gentleman's saying" (5.1.2–3). It is not clear here whether the latter reference is to Sir Oliver Martext or Jaques, but Touchstone has his own comical sayings, and irrationally rebukes again the hapless parson: "A most wicked Sir Oliver, Audrey, a most vile Martext" (5.1.4–5). The serious point here, if there is one, is as much aesthetic as comic; marriages in the middle of act 3 would have "marred the text" of any comedy, which must wait until act 5 for a full celebration of joy. In performance, especially, 5.1 also helps to reestablish Touchstone's foolish lustfulness, a dramatic foil to the more spiritual marital unions later to occur in act 5.

Before such celebration can occur here, however, Shakespeare adds another character, and short scene, that surely adds humor, and probably also represents a typically medieval and Renaissance form of aesthetic humility. After Touchstone tells Audrey that "there is a youth here in the forest" (5.1.6–7) who also seeks to marry her, there enters onstage a simple shepherd named "William." It is a fairly common practice amongst Medieval and Renaissance authors to either include some humble *persona* of themselves in a text, or to "stamp" or "print" their name as a kind of signature in their work, a practice that Shakespeare himself perhaps follows in texts such as Sonnet 135, whose fourteen lines include twelve uses of the word "Will" in an obvious reference to the poem's author. In perhaps the most incredible yet still fascinating example of this, in the early twentieth century an enterprising seminary student noticed that in the King James Bible of 1611, but not in earlier English translations such as the Bishop's Bible or the Geneva Bible, the forty-sixth word from the beginning of Psalm 46 is "shake"; the forty-sixth word from the end of the Psalm is "spear." Is it possible that

Shakespeare was on the translation team of Biblical poetry in 1610, when he was forty-six years old, and left an "authorial signature" to indicate his presence and influence?[1]

Is it also possible that the simple shepherd "William" allows an extraordinarily humble, exceptionally self-deprecating cameo role for the playwright himself, William Shakespeare? Touchstone does introduce him in a way that suggests authorial revolt against convention and censorship, which was a major problem for Elizabethan playwrights, and ironically recalls the economic importance, to Shakespeare's theatre, of the "fool" characters: "It is meat and drink to me to see a clown. By my troth, we that have good wits have much to answer for. We shall be flouting; we cannot hold" (5.1.10–12). It is also known that Shakespeare did some acting, with his name appearing on the cast list of a play by his friend Ben Jonson, and legend has long held that Shakespeare may also have played the Ghost in *Hamlet*.[2]

Yet when William enters and starts to speak in *As You Like It*, we do not hear a witty playwright. Rather, "William" gives very short, four- to five-word answers as Touchstone "catechizes" the shepherd, or asks a series of probing questions, in the mock-religious practice of similar Shakespearean fools.[3] Some of the questions could poke fun at censorship in the theatre, such as when the fool asks, "Wast born i' the forest here?" "Ay, sir, I thank God," responds William, and all Christians must agree with the fool's approval: "'Thank God'; a good answer" (5.1.22–24). Touchstone then asks another question likely to have been on Shakespeare's mind in 1599, as the Globe was opening: "Art rich?" Unlike the question on faith, William's answer to this has to be ambiguous, "Faith, sir, so so" (5.1.24–25). Touchstone cannot resist comical wordplay, using the familiar schemes *epizeuxis*[4] and *diacope*:[5] "So-so is good, very good, very excellent good; and yet it is not; it is but so-so" (5.1.25–27). The crucial question for any Renaissance artist is then asked, "Art thou wise?," and William seems more confident: "Ay, sir, I have a pretty wit" (5.1.27–28). Touchstone comically critiques this answer

---

1. The legend of Shakespeare as KJV translator is discussed in Black, "Edified by the Margent."

2. This legend originates with the eighteenth-century scholar Nicholas Rowe; for a modern reprint of his work, see Rowe, *The Life of Shakespeare*.

3. See, for example, the "catechism" offered Lady Olivia by her fool Feste in *Twelfth Night*, 1.5.53–68.

4. Peacham, *Garden*, 47.

5. Peacham, *Garden*, 48.

through a "saying" or *paroemia*,[6] that uses *antimetabole*[7] to express the paradox that appears so often in Shakespeare's portrayal of fools:

> Why, thou sayest well. I do now remember a saying,
> "The fool doth think he is wise, but the wise man
> knows himself to be a fool." (5.1.29–31)

As much as this is "internal rhetoric" that continues the play's argument against Jaques, the *paroemia*[8] here could also be "external rhetoric" that comically pokes fun at the central importance of the foolishness / wisdom paradox in 1 Corinthians 1, Erasmus's *Praise of Folly*, and Catholic Humanism generally. More specifically, Touchstone may well be poking fun at Shakespeare himself. As the author of these same lines within *As You Like It*, Shakespeare is laughing at himself, making himself part of the comedy.

Touchstone then turns to much clearer, comically hedonistic "sayings" that reflect both the Fool's characteristically concrete linguistic devotion to bawdry; by contrast to the eucharistic images of a Catholic theologian, he next points out:

> The heathen philosopher, when he had a desire to eat a grape,
> would open his lips when he put it into his mouth;
> meaning thereby that grapes were made to eat and
> lips to open. (5.1.31–35)

There is obviously nothing very "philosophical" about this comment, and certainly does not reflect the typical Catholic Humanist reverence for classical philosophy. Touchstone has other things on his mind, and soon moves to another direct question for "William": "You do love this maid?" (5.1.35). After William simply affirms this devotion, Touchstone takes him by the hand and tries to complicate the matter, asking the simple shepherd, "Art thou learned?" (5.1.37). Very honestly William replies, "No, sir," which then gives Touchstone another opportunity to display his own learning:

> Then learn this of me: to have, is to have; for it
> is a figure in rhetoric that drink, being poured out
> of a cup into a glass, by filling the one doth empty
> the other; for all your writers do consent that *ipse*
> is he: now, you are not *ipse*, for I am he. (5.1.38–43)

There is clearly a comical jab here, as throughout *Love's Labour's Lost*, at the pedantic manner in which rhetoric was often taught in the Renaissance.

6. Peacham, *Garden*, 29.
7. Peacham, *Garden*, 164.
8. Peacham, *Garden*, 29.

We can thus be respectful, but not take too seriously, the lengthy historical and textual analysis of this passage given by T. W. Baldwin.[9] "*Ipse*," for example, is certainly a common term in the grammar school curriculum of Latin rhetoric, and Sr. Joseph also describes Touchstone's speech here as a *disjunctive syllogism*.[10] As drama, however, much more important here is the comedic "mock learning" or "mock authority" commonly used by Shakespeare's fools.[11] One might term Touchstone's diction here a vice of language, *cacozelia*, which Puttenham says orators commit when they "affect new words and phrases . . . to shew themselves among the ignorant the better learned."[12] Or Peacham could suggest terms such as *cacempheton*[13] or *catachresis*,[14] terms for words being misused and out of context, or Touchstone's verbal assault upon William could more generally be termed *cataplexis*.[15] But surely the more dramatic and comical point here is that there is nothing particularly "rhetorical" or "figurative" about either Touchstone's speech or "drink" here, which quite possibly also alludes to onstage action in which the Fool steals poor William's wine by pouring it in his own. The real, and obvious, purpose of the "learned" discourse here is to assert Touchstone's own desire for Audrey.

Finally, simple "William" has a question of his own, "Which he, sir?," and now Touchstone makes his claim: "He, sir, that must marry this woman" (5.1.44–45). Comically, again, for surely this fool is more of a lover than a fighter, Touchstone is prepared to duel for Audrey, telling William:

> Therefore, you clown, abandon,—which is in the vulgar leave,—
> the society,—which in the boorish is company,—of this
> female,—which in the common is woman; which
> together is, abandon the society of this female. (5.1.46–49)

There is "a figure in rhetoric" here, for as Baldwin notes, Touchstone employs a reverse form of the "regular sixteenth-century" procedure known as

---

9. See Baldwin, *Shakespeare's Small Latine & Lesse Greek*, 116–20. Baldwin argues that Touchstone uses "the sixth form" of the disjunctive syllogism in Cicero's *Topica*, wherein one reasons, "this and that are not both true; but this is, therefore that is not." Baldwin also argues that Touchstone quotes "Ipse dixit" from the *Ciceronis Sententiae* of 1558, and that the fool's "cups and drinking" derive from another passage in Quintilian's *Institutio Oratoria*.

10. Joseph, *Arts of Language*, 186.

11. Compare, for example, Feste 4.2.50 in *Twelfth Night*.

12. Puttenham, *Art*, 251–52.

13. Peacham, *Garden*, 30.

14. Peacham, *Garden*, 16.

15. Peacham, *Garden*, 79.

"construeing" in which a schoolmaster translates a classical language into orderly English grammar.[16] As a fool, however, Touchstone gives "a mock construe . . . from the courtly language into the vulgar,"[17] translating each longer, Latinate word into a simple English term that the shepherd can easily understand, sure to give William a very simple message: "get lost!"

Once the *copia* of Touchstone begins, however, his own physical lust carries over into passionate language, and he creates *incrementum*[18] through a diverse rhetorical discourse that first continues to construe, then uses *prozeugma*,[19] *hypozeuxis*,[20] and *epanaphora*[21] to develop hyperbolic threats of violence against William:

> or, clown, thou perishest; or, to thy better understanding, diest;
> or, to wit I kill thee, make thee away, translate thy life into death,
> thy liberty into bondage: I will deal in poison with
> thee, or in bastinado, or in steel; I will bandy
> with thee in faction; I will o'errun thee with
> policy; I will kill thee a hundred and fifty ways:
> therefore tremble and depart. (5.1.50–56)

The *onomatopoeia*[22] of "tremble" and sudden end to the entire discourse invites a comical exit for the simple shepherd. Quite possibly the humor here could derive from the great playwright, and part-owner of the new Globe theatre, being humiliated in this manner. In the "internal rhetoric" of the play, Touchstone's passion finally also provokes Audrey to speak, from charitable concern or concupiscence it is not clear, as she now advises the simple shepherd to depart as the fool wishes: "Do, good William" (5.1.57). For his part, Touchstone ends the scene in a most merry mood, lightheartedly looking forward to lifting the heels of Audrey and almost singing to her, using the now familiar schemes of *epizeuxis*[23] and *epiphora*,[24] "Trip, Audrey! trip, Audrey! I attend, I attend" (5.1.61). Touchstone must yet wait to marry, but onstage many fools playing the part literally dance for joy in anticipation.

16. Baldwin, *Shakespeare's Small Latine & Lesse Greek*, 588.
17. Baldwin, *Shakespeare's Small Latine & Lesse Greek*, 589.
18. Peacham, *Garden*, 169.
19. Peacham, *Garden*, 51.
20. Peacham, *Garden*, 59.
21. Peacham, *Garden*, 41.
22. Peacham, *Garden*, 14.
23. Peacham, *Garden*, 47.
24. Peacham, *Garden*, 42.

Nowhere in the play, however, does the academic analysis of internal rhetoric potentially clash more with onstage performance criticism than in 5.1. Here the play's clown explicitly refers to a "figure in rhetoric," and uses technical Latin terms such as "ipse," yet these lines occur when Touchstone is clearly abusing such learning, using it to intimidate a poor, uneducated peasant in order to take his former girlfriend from him. The scene is inevitably humorous, Touchstone appealing to many of the worst elements of human nature while so energetically turning his learning towards lustful ends, and the potential for an "in" theatrical joke would obviously be enhanced if William represents, in 1599, the fairly accomplished intellect of the play's playwright. Audience members who know nothing of this rhetoric can still enjoy the physical humor that most actors playing Touchstone bring to this part of the play.

In the 1978 BBC production, James Bolam conveys the basic humor of the scene; a wide-eyed William struggles to understand then flee from the increasingly agitated Touchstone. At Stratford, Ontario, in 1983, Lewis Gordon adds physical comedy to the scene, taking off his coat and hat while speaking, and placing them on Audrey, who adopts a pugilistic stance. In Branagh's 2006 film, the exceptionally eccentric Alfred Molina confronts a Japanese peasant whose incomprehension is expected by the film's western audience, though many of Touchstone's lines are cut. The full speech is presented, though, in Thea Sharrock's exceptionally humorous 2009 RCS production, where Touchstone energetically bullies William, who silently mouths and repeats the fool's words, unable to comprehend him. This William does get the last word, though, as his final line in the scene, "God rest ye merry, sir" (5.1.58) is spoken with such *pathos*, and whimpering, that the audience responds "aaagh." As with Corin, Touchstone's learned rhetoric does not always win an audience's approval, and even this comical scene suggests Shakespeare's sympathy for the poor and uneducated, regardless of whether he himself played the role of William.

After the comical "mock rhetoric" of the act's opening scene, 5.2 returns to the central themes of the play, and to the literary rhetoric that presents these themes. Shakespeare begins by portraying a short conversation between Orlando and Oliver, returning to the *erotema* or rhetorical questions that have always characterized their conversation. Yet whereas before these questions were often accusatory, even hostile, Orlando begins the scene asking questions through the schemes *incrementum*[25] and *climax*,[26] expressing growing wonder at the sudden love of Oliver and Celia:

---

25. Peacham, *Garden*, 169.
26. Peacham, *Garden*, 133.

> Is't possible that on so little acquaintance you
> should like her? that but seeing you should love
> her? and loving woo? and, wooing, she should
> grant? and will you persevere to enjoy her? (5.2.1–4)

Oliver responds with a phrase that seems to rebuke these questions, "neither call the giddiness of it in question," but then displays *eloquentia* which suggests that he also has gained some of the *sapientia* of love. Using *prozeugma*[27] and *compar*,[28] Oliver humbly but simply expresses his own surprise at the sudden love between him and the woman whom he knows as "Aliena":

> Neither call the giddiness of it in question, the poverty of her, the small acquaintance, my sudden wooing, nor her sudden consenting; but say with me, I love Aliena; say with her that she loves me; consent with both that we may enjoy each other. (5.2.5–9)

Oliver's conclusion here points to the paradoxical peace, the unity of "we," made possible through love. The trope here could be called *synoeiciosis*,[29] celebrating the unity that love has given both he and Aliena and, in a secondary but important sense, the peace it has brought between him and Orlando.

Onstage, the altered rhetoric allows a radically renewed relationship between the brothers. Orlando's acceptance of Oliver's "love" for "Aliena" is also made easier by an even more surprising promise that follows from Oliver, one that surely gives compelling "proof" of the authenticity of his conversion. Whereas the old Oliver would keep their father's estate entirely to himself, the new man here will give to Orlando "my father's house and all the revenue that was old Sir Rowland's" (5.2.10–11). If one can believe in this promise, it hardly requires any faith to accept Oliver's complete conversion to the pastoral *ethos* of Arden. I, Oliver concludes, will "here live and die a shepherd" (5.2.12).

Orlando is only too happy to consent to an immediate marriage for his brother, but his life becomes complicated again by the arrival of Ganymede, whom he greets as "my Rosalind" (5.2.16). Building on the tension apparent in the couple's last meeting, there is unsurprising acknowledgement of their apparent gender, but this comes initially not towards each other, but indirectly. "Ganymede" greets Oliver by saying, "God save you brother," while he replies, "And you, fair sister" (5.2.17–18). There are at least two interesting points here. First, in calling Oliver "brother," "Ganymede" could simply be

---

27. Peacham, *Garden*, 51.
28. Peacham, *Garden*, 58.
29. Peacham, *Garden*, 170.

recalling their earlier meeting; yet "Rosalind" could be speaking as one who recently "married," in the ceremony directed by Celia, into Oliver's family, or at least plans to marry soon into that family. For his part, in calling Ganymede "fair sister," Oliver—a speaker from outside the wooing "game" created by Rosalind and Orlando—responds not to any male "disguise," but rather to the vivacious young woman present before him. His rhetorical part now played, Oliver exits, leaving the stage to the two young lovers.

Quite probably the romantic tension between the play's comic hero and heroine becomes apparent as conversation between these two commences. When "Ganymede," for example, laments how Orlando has "been wounded with the claws of a lion," he uses *asteismus*,[30] and recalls the *metaphora*[31] of injury following their meeting after the wrestling, in words that seem clearly intended for Rosalind: "Wounded it is, but with the eyes of a lady" (5.2.22–24). "Ganymede" then asks whether Oliver has told Orlando how he "counterfeited to swoon" in the previous scene, but Orlando here suggests that other information was also given: "Ay, and greater wonders than that" (5.2.25–27). Rather than inquiring what these wonders might be, however, Ganymede assumes that Orlando means the wonder of Oliver and Celia falling in love, and turns to developed but long-winded rhetoric to describe their sudden love. As Oliver had employed *climax*[32] earlier to describe the inevitable progression of "love at first sight," so here Ganymede, also uses the same figure to describe the rapid evolution of this love:

> your brother and my sister no sooner met but they looked, no sooner looked but they loved, no sooner loved but they sighed, no sooner sighed but they asked one another the reason, no sooner knew the reason but they sought the remedy. (5.2.31–35)

Reflecting, perhaps, Puttenham's description of *climax* as "the clymbing figure . . . as a ladder,"[33] Ganymede continues with *metaphora* for this scheme, a "meta-rhetoric" which she spices with bawdy *antanaclasis*,[34] playing on how "incontinent" can mean both "speedily" and "without restraint":

> and in these degrees have they made a pair of stairs
> to marriage which they will climb incontinent, or
> else be incontinent before marriage: they are in
> the very wrath of love and they will together; clubs

30. Peacham, *Garden*, 34.
31. Peacham, *Garden*, 3.
32. Peacham, *Garden*, 133.
33. Puttenham, *Art*, 217.
34. Peacham, *Garden*, 56.

cannot part them. (5.2.36–39)

The rhetoric here re-creates an experience like that of "falling in love," an overwhelming, seemingly uncontrollable rush of emotion; yet reversing direction of the metaphorical stream downwards, the progressive steps of the "stairs" signify a movement upwards, towards divine love or at least towards human love directed and ordered by divinity. The "wrath of love" might seem initially to be a much happier experience than the "wrath of God," but the "pair of stairs" leading to marriage, in Catholic Humanism, involves both. The similarity of divine and human love is fundamental to Christ's conception of the two greatest "commandments," and the unity created by both is precisely why, in marriage, whom "God hath joined, let no man put asunder" (Matt 19:6). Not even men with "clubs," for violence cannot end love or part the soul of true lovers.

Onstage, neither audience nor actors are likely to consider such theological questions. Actors playing Rosalind and Orlando in 5.2 must again alter their onstage *persona*, for the "game" of disguise has been replaced by anticipation of physical love. The deeply romantic nature of "Ganymede's" description of love does evoke an almost envious response from Orlando; suddenly jealous again of his older brother, he exclaims:

> O, how bitter a thing it is to look into happiness
> through another man's eyes! By so much the more shall I to-morrow
> be at the height of heart-heaviness, by how much I shall
> think my brother happy in having what he wishes for. (5.2.41–45)

Orlando's despair allows Rosalind to resume her "disguise" as "Ganymede" and rhetorically ask, with mock disappointment, "Why, then, tomorrow I cannot serve your turn for Rosalind?" (5.2.26). Orlando seems finally exasperated by the entire exercise, bluntly stating, "I can live no longer by thinking" (5.2.27).

The "game" has perhaps run its course, having reached its ultimate goal: though Orlando is clearly weary of the disguise of "Ganymede," we can be sure of his deep need for Rosalind. In a rare rhetorical concession, Rosalind then agrees not to "weary" Orlando any longer with "idle talking" (5.2.29). Yet it is a mistake to see their courting game as an "idle" waste of time. From the "safe" distance created by disguise, it has allowed them not only to "get to know each other" on a surface level, but more importantly to reveal the depths of each other's soul. By this point in the play, they are thus in a very different place than those who "fall in love at first sight." As recommended by Renaissance Catholic Humanists, "thinking" through dramatic rhetoric—the "play" of "Ganymede" and Orlando—allows spiritual fruit far beyond its technical or strictly aesthetic value.

The long speech from Rosalind that follows presents this fruit as knowledge, something that can be shared because known. After promising to eschew "idle talking," Rosalind continues by promising instead to teach what Orlando can have "knowledge" of because he is "a gentleman of some good conceit" (5.2.50–53). "Conceit" here does not mean "proud," as in modern English, but rather "elaborate fiction" or "extravagant metaphor," as the word is used of Donne and other seventeenth-century poets whom the twentieth century will praise as "metaphysical." Rosalind is going beyond the physical, into the spiritual, but with the characteristically Catholic Humanist emphasis on art, appealing now to Orlando's faith in what she will propose to him:

> Believe then, if you please, that I can do strange things: I have, since I was three year old, conversed with a magician, most profound in his art and yet not damnable. (5.2.56–59)

The theological terms here, specifically the mention of tragic "damnation" in a play filled with the hope of comic salvation, reflects the traditional Christian distrust of magic when it is the manipulation of others' wills for the sake of power. Distrust of rhetoric for the same reason is also a commonplace, but Rosalind then begins her appeal to the specifically Catholic Humanist art exhibited throughout the play. The "magician" here is certainly a fiction, but the same figurative *persona* as "the old religious uncle" whom Rosalind had told Orlando, back in act 3, "taught me to speak (3.2.328–29). Both are certainly akin also to the "old Religious man" able to convert even Duke Frederick, in the play's final scene, "after some question with him" (5.4.156–57). What all of these figurative characters have in common, along with so many of the aesthetic forms of this play, is an instinctive celebration of the art of communication, of dialogue that finds something sacred, even religious, in the simple fun of good conversation.

Having established this tone, Rosalind then returns to the "if" or "as" clauses that are clearly the central rhetorical figures of the play. "Ganymede" tells Orlando:

> If you do love Rosalind so near the heart
> as your gesture cries it out, when your brother
> marries Aliena, shall you marry her: (5.2.59–62)

In other words, "if" Orlando's outward actions authentically mirror his inward heart, then his soul is ready for Catholic marriage. This is the *conditional* that Rosalind now presents, and it is not a "figurative" proposition in any trivial sense of "a pleasant fiction." Rather, it appeals to the truth of Orlando's self-knowledge, inquiring whether he has now gained the essential "faith" of the play, for the *conditional* posed here applies not just to Rosalind and Orlando, but to anyone who contemplates marriage: is one able to trust in the promises of another's heart, the honesty of another's soul?

Rosalind concludes this crucial moment in the play with a reminder of her own "magical" role in the play, and another call, through an "if" or conditional clause, to believe that "Ganymede" can cause the "real" Rosalind to "magically" appear:

> it is not impossible to me, if it appear not inconvenient
> to you, to set her before your eyes tomorrow, human
> as she is, and without any danger. (5.2.63–65)

There is a probable allusion here to the well-known biblical idea that "with God all things are possible" (Matt 19:26), but one need not make too much of the allegory of Rosalind as "page" to the highest God of Love. Within the internal drama, the essential "fiction" has been the "play" of "Ganymede" and Orlando, but the Catholic Humanist purpose of this rhetoric has been to show both what each truly is, human as they are. This is the "magic" or the imaginative "play" of a playwright who seems not so much "our bending author," as the Chorus to *Henry V* calls Shakespeare (*H5* Epilogue, 2), but rather one laughing with delight.

Similarly pleasing rhetorical imagery continues Rosalind's "project" when Orlando skeptically inquires, "speakest thou in sober meanings?" (5.2.66). No longer mentioning "an uncle," but rather affirming her fictional, or rather "figurative" identity, Rosalind asserts: "I am a magician" (5.2.68). Yet it is the *conditional* magic of the play's "if" clauses that she then employs to continue the "spell" of play with Orlando: "if you will be married to-morrow, you shall, and to Rosalind, if you will" (5.2.69–70). The complexity of this proposition is magnified, however, by the sudden arrival of Silvius and Phoebe. For it is both a literal truth and *antanaclasis*,[35] or *double entendre*, allowed by her disguise when "Ganymede" announces their arrival: "here comes a lover of mine and a lover of hers" (5.2.71). The first clause here surely refers to Phoebe's love of the fictional "page," but the second could refer to Silvius' love of Phoebe, or to Phoebe's love of Rosalind, who knows herself, of course, to be the true identity of "Ganymede." Further imaginative, rhetorical, and linguistic magic is necessary for identity to be clarified, and for love to be possible.

---

35. Peacham, *Garden*, 56.

One important means to achieve clarity, as every student of the logic-rhetoric-grammar *trivium* knows, is definition. Phoebe calls for definition, though perhaps she has concupiscient rather than intellectual motives, and demands that Silvius instruct "Ganymede": "Good shepherd, tell this youth what 'tis to love" (5.2.78). Silvius does so not so much with logic, but again rather with *systrophe*,[36] heaping together romantic *metonymia*[37] bound not with reason but rather with hyperbolical schemes of repetition, *diacope*[38] of "all made" and *epanaphora*[39] of "all." Silvius "defines" love as "to be all made of sighs and tears" and "to be all made of faith and service," before finally expanding the definition to also include other "virtues":

> It is to be all made of fantasy,
> All made of passion and all made of wishes,
> All adoration, duty, and observance,
> All humbleness, all patience and impatience,
> All purity, all trial, all observance. (5.2.89–93)

Commitment alone allows actors to make more of Silvius' rhetoric, in the theatre, than one might expect from reading it on the page. In many productions, though Silvius is obviously a naïve lover, his sincerity creates a tone that passes for idealism.

More *epanaphora* ensues when Silvius concludes, "And so am I for Phoebe," to which she responds, "And so am I for Ganymede"; Orlando chimes in, "And so am I for Rosalind," to which "Ganymede" or rather Rosalind herself affirms, somewhat ambiguously, "And so am I for no woman" (5.2.94–97). The *epanaphora* here recalls Puttenham's comment that this figure is used "when we make one word begin, and as they are wont to say, lead the dance to many verses in turn."[40] However, these orators are not quite ready for a wedding dance, as is shown when their *epanaphora* becomes accusatory *conditionals*, again making *hypothetical syllogisms* instruments of conflict rather than peace:

> Phoebe: If this be so, why blame you me to love you?
> Silvius: If this be so, why blame you me to love you?
> Orlando: If this be so, why blame you me to love you? (5.2.98–100)

The rhetoric here clearly deteriorates from even repetitive art to the kind of mindless response that gives love a bad name. Only Rosalind can

---

36. Peacham, *Garden*, 153.
37. Peacham, *Garden*, 19.
38. Peacham, *Garden*, 48.
39. Peacham, *Garden*, 41.
40. Puttenham, *Art*, 208, though he uses the term *anaphora* rather than *epanaphora*.

break the refrain, and demand, with reason, to whom Orlando addresses his question, since clearly he loves neither Silvius nor Phoebe; very logically, she asks him, "Why do you speak too, 'Why blame you me to love you?'" (5.2.101). He responds with reference to Rosalind, using *paranomasia*[41] or homonymic puns to wittily claim that his words are "To her that is not here nor doth not hear" (5.2.102). Rosalind herself, however, has had enough of the rhetoric of love. She brings the entire set piece to an end by using another simile from nature to liken romantic clichés to animalistic desire: "Pray you, no more of this; 'tis like the howling of Irish wolves against the moon" (5.2.103–4). The critique here is probably not of the Irish, but of all sub-human desires inspired by the romantic allure of the moon, and now facing the cold reality of frustrated desire. The moon, in Elizabethan literature, typically has both symbolic connotations and so, as always, even simple tropes like *similes* become more complex through their range of concrete reference.

Despite her frustration, Rosalind follows the "Irish wolves" *simile* with some of the most personal, and fruitful, rhetoric of the entire play, addressing each person onstage individually, speaking to each words that please their hearer. Such rhetoric in political contexts could always be seen cynically, as advancing the interests of the speaker, but the charitable Catholic Humanist rhetoric of Rosalind is here perfectly enacted: she desires the best interests of each, and uses words to make this "best" possible. Here the by now familiar "if" clauses express humility, in that her aid will require the cooperation of another's will in order to really bear fruit. To Silvius, "Ganymede" promises, "I will help you, if I can"; to Phoebe, the promise is at first more general, but honest, "I would love you, if I could" (5.2.104–5). Rosalind then casts further *conditionals* in the figure of *symploce*,[42] which combines familiar schemes of repetition, *epanaphora*[43] and *epiphora*,[44] but varies each promise by making it specific to the person being addressed onstage. Speaking, in order, to Phoebe, Orlando, and Silvius, "Ganymede" pledges:

> I will marry you, if ever I marry woman,
> and I'll be married to-morrow.
> I will satisfy you, if ever I satisfy man,
> and you shall be married tomorrow.
> I will content you, if what please you contents you,

41. Peacham, *Garden*, 56.
42. Peacham, *Garden*, 43.
43. Peacham, *Garden*, 41.
44. Peacham, *Garden*, 42.

And you shall be married tomorrow.
(5.2.107–12)

The onstage listeners probably hear only the concluding promise to satisfy their romantic desires, but the audience is aware that Rosalind has artfully pledged *conditionals* that she can fulfill.

As she bids the three lovers farewell until their wedding day, Rosalind concludes with further uses of "if" and "as" as synonyms for hope and imaginative possibility, but also words that require responsible action to become truly fruitful. Again using *symploce*,[45] she instructs Orlando, "As you love Rosalind, meet," and reminds simple Silvius again, "as you love Phoebe, meet," before perhaps turning awkwardly away from Phoebe and muttering, "and as I love no woman, I'll meet" (5.2.112–14). In modern grammatical terms, one could see a shift here from the conditional of "if" to the subjunctive of "as" promised by the play's title, from the possibility of fulfillment to a more definite promise or pledge. Figures of *ethos* and *pathos* cited here could include *eustathia*,[46] the promise of constancy, and *epimone*,[47] repetition of speech to convey such constancy. Yet the most apt term might be *euche*,[48] Peacham's term for "a solemn promise or vow," but one that could come both from "condition" and "vehement affection."[49] Reflecting the seriousness and obligations of her marriage proposals, and raising her rhetoric appropriately, Rosalind then qualifies her "as" and clarifies its meaning by calling her final instructions "commands," for this becomes her final "rhetorical term" to them: "So fair you well. I have left you commands" (5.2.114–15). For their part, the three lovers have also learned the value of *conditional* promises, and before departing both Orlando and Phoebe simply but clearly echo the essential condition for all hope expressed by Silvius as he responds to the instructions of "Ganymede": "I'll not fail, if I live"; they return to repetition, promising: "Nor I. Nor I" (5.2.116–18).

Rosalind's performance in this final gathering of the lovers is a tour de force of rhetoric, and onstage gives an actress playing her part multiple opportunities to vary the meaning of her wise words through change of tone. In Czinner's 1936 film, Elizabeth Bergen effectively varies her exaggerated "Ganymede" voice with a love-struck Rosalind on, "so am I for no woman," before genially but forcefully addressing them all. In the 1978 BBC, Helen Mirren is upset by the "howling of Irish wolves," before speaking

45. Peacham, *Garden*, 43.
46. Peacham, *Garden*, 69.
47. Peacham, *Garden*, 70.
48. Peacham, *Garden*, 67.
49. Peacham, *Garden*, 67.

sympathetically to each lover; even to Phoebe, she stresses, "I *would* love you if I could" (5.2.106). In the 1983 Stratford, Ontario production, Roberta Maxwell is disgusted by the "howling of Irish wolves"; in the address to each lover, she seems to fulfill a duty, with the other lovers much happier than she seems to be; she will meet only because she "loves no woman," the tone of resignation drawing laughs from the theatre. In Branagh's 2006 film, by contrast, Bryce Howard seems happy addressing each lover at the scene, clearly anticipating her own marriage; that "she loves no woman" is proclaimed joyfully rather than with Maxwell's regret, and all leave the forest filled with happy expectations. In the 2009 RSC, Naomi Frederick brings a physical energy to the scene, racing about the stage and insisting that she "loves no woman"; laughter from the audience comes when she asks the confused Jack Laskey, "Who do you speak to 'Why blame you me to love her?'" (5.2.101) a comical, rhetorical question often cut by less complex productions. After this almost slapstick comedy, Rosalind issues serious "commands" which indicate her determination to resolve each lover's confusion.

Before dramatizing the lovers' reunion in the play's final scene, Shakespeare gives us 5.3, a short scene in which two boys appear onstage to sing a song. This is a fiction almost as outrageous as Rosalind being "page" to Jove: according to Audrey (that always reliable source of information in the forest), these boys are "two of the banished duke's pages" (5.3.5). *As You Like It* could be drawing on the popularity and availability of child actors, as *Hamlet* also references (2.2.339–52). The child actors' sudden appearance in this play, in Arden, allows these "pages" to create a suitable tone and mood for the multiple marriages about to ensue, when Rosalind will complete the work begun by "Ganymede," page to the high God of Love.

Before the song, however, the scene is introduced by the now almost giddy pair of Touchstone and Audrey. The lustful fool can hardly wait, using *epanaphora*[50] to remind his fiancé of their impending wedding day: "To-morrow is the joyful day, Audrey; to-morrow will we be married" (5.3.1-2). As for Audrey herself, she responds by affirming her "desire" so clearly that she repeats the words three times; in the mouth of a witty speaker, this repetition might indicate *antanaclasis*[51] or some other pun. Yet if there is such here, it is merely the commonplace *double entendre* of "desire" as a word used to indicate both "wish" and "sexual lust," for certainly Audrey seems to stress the latter; of marriage, she assures Touchstone: "I do desire it with all my heart; and I hope it is no dishonest desire to desire to be a woman of the world" (5.3.3–5). Certainly marriage is "of the world," but according to

---

50. Peacham, *Garden*, 41.
51. Peacham, *Garden*, 56.

Catholic doctrine, that is not all it is. What of Christ's invocation that his disciples "be not of the world" (John 17:16)? Such questions raise a potentially more troubling issue: what is the basis for the love of Touchstone and Audrey? While the answer might seem comically obvious, and one can be happy for any engaged couple, these are the kinds of questions that Audrey's implicit, unintended biblical allusion surely raises.

The song of the two "pages" similarly creates a joyful mood while also raising questions about the foundations of any marriage. As their song begins, it soon becomes clear that no surprising themes are being introduced, but rather the pages offer a simple celebration of the rural love that naturally becomes, in "spring time," the "ring time" of marriage:

> It was a lover and his lass,
> With a hey, and a ho, and a hey nonino,
> That o'er the green corn-field did pass
> In the spring time, the only pretty ring time,
> When birds do sing, hey ding a ding, ding:
> Sweet lovers love the spring. (5.3.15–20)

Some rhetoricians would describe the obvious repetition of sound here as *parachesis*,[52] while scholars have often noted the relationship between music and rhetoric in Peacham's *Garden*.[53] No scholarship is necessary to hear comic notes of marriage being struck, though Shakespeareans likely also hear, in the second line of the pages' song, an echo of Balthasar's song midway through *Much Ado about Nothing*, which converts "sounds of woe / Into hey nonny nonny" (2.3.67–68), but in an even less serious tone. Perhaps noticing this similarity, Branagh makes Balthasar's song the concluding song of his 2006 film of *As You Like It*, just as he did for his 1993 film of *Much Ado about Nothing*.

There are many productions where the pages' song at the end of 5.2 is cut, though John Hirsch's 1983 production at Stratford, Ontario, showed how effective it could be in the theatre. As Shakespeare's company probably did, pre-adolescent boys sing the song with great commitment and sincerity, but in Hirsch's production much humor is added by Audrey and Touchstone joining in the song, and singing it even as they go offstage. There is also effective drama at the end of the scene, as Touchstone accuses the boys of not having kept their time. The boys don't laugh, but do turn back for payment when Touchstone says, "God be with you," like good Catholic Humanist students, they assume that even a fool thinks a "labourer worthy of

---

52. Lanham, *Handlist*, 124.
53. See, for example, Butler, "Music and Rhetoric," 53–64.

his reward" (1 Tim 5:18). From Lewis Gordon, as Touchstone, the pages in Hirsch's production receive some well-deserved pay.

The pages' song does have merits; not even a banal bird's song of "hey ding a ding, ding" can dampen lovers' enthusiasm in the spring, "the pretty ring time" when young hearts are hopeful enough for marriage. The final three lines of this first verse also serve as chorus for the entire song, ensuring that the song never progresses to more sobering themes. Even as the pages sing of a "carol" which ominously reminds us that "life was but a flower" (5.3.27, 29)—an image that in texts like Sonnet 18 or *Romeo and Juliet* could certainly be tragic—the rhetoric here celebrates "the present time," when "love is crowned with the prime" (5.3.33, 35) and banishes all worry or fear. In an excellent musical production in the theatre, such as Hirsch's, the pages' song is not out of place, but rather offers a final song—in a different key but with the same theme—as the dominant marital rhetoric and music of the play.

Probably it is only a desire to avoid the customary payment of singers that causes Touchstone to critique the song as having "no great matter," and being "untuneable," but the boys are not afraid to defend their singing skills, telling the fool: "You are deceived, sir: we kept time, we lost not our time" (5.3.42). Perhaps "showing off" to his fiancée how to use *antanaclasis*[54] effectively, the Fool wittily puns on "time" to change its meaning, and implicitly critique the obvious "uselessness" of the boys' song: "By my troth, yes; I count it but time lost to hear such a foolish song" (5.3.44–45).

Touchstone is hardly, of course, a model of adult efficiency, and it has to be with a similarly ironic sense of his own sanctimonious purposes that he bids them farewell with a mock religious blessing: "God b'wi'you; and God mend your voices!" (5.3.45–46). Though we can take seriously neither Touchstone's words nor the words of the boys' song, both remind us that there is a profound connection between the green fields of spring, the natural human desire to procreate, and the divine institution of marriage. Catholic Humanists argue very seriously for the sacred, holy, sacramental reality of marriage, and in both their time and ours, that is wisdom which any fool must be glad to hear.

---

54. Peacham, *Garden*, 56.

10

"To Make All This Matter Even"

Hymen and the Catholic Humanist Marriage Song of *As You Like It*

THE SWEET, INNOCENT SONG of the youthful pages is a prelude to the lavish, orchestrated, marriage song of the god Hymen, who appears onstage in the play's final scene. Modern audiences whose education is limited to anatomy must not imagine primarily biological symbolism in the play's climax. A "theophany" of classical divinity is not unusual in Shakespeare's plays; Hymen is also referred to, for example, in the wedding masque in *The Tempest* (4.1.97). Appreciating the theological importance of this classical figure is an essential element of the play's Catholic Humanist rhetoric, for again the classical is "baptized." In the final scene, the human will must respond to divine Love, as Erasmus argues in his famous debate with Luther on the question of free will, if the dance and music that characterize the conclusion of *As You Like It* is to find a place for the variety of human wills that we have thus far seen in the play. To make this "matter even," one needs not only divine blessing, but also the magic of Rosalind's words. In deed, and in word, Rosalind illustrates, far more successfully than any Renaissance churchman or politician, the beatitude that Erasmus held so dear: "Blessed are the peacemakers, for they shall see God" (Matt 5:9).

It is something close to the language of religious faith by which Duke Senior poses the initial question of the scene, asking: "Dost thou believe,

Orlando, that the boy / Can do all this that he hath promised?" (5.4.1–2). Orlando's response illustrates both his own skepticism at Ganymede's words, and hope for Rosalind's appearance: "I sometimes do believe, and sometimes do not; as those that fear they hope, and know they fear" (5.4.3–4). The *antimetabole*[1] here linking hope, knowledge, and fear probably derives from biblical rhetoric, such as the famous Old Testament maxim: "The fear of the Lord is the beginning of wisdom" (Ps 9:10). Hope, the other key term here, is a central New Testament theme, perhaps never more memorably expressed than when Paul teaches, in another verse that can help us understand the faith of this optimistic play: "And hope maketh not ashamed; because the love of God is shed abroad in our hearts by the Holy Ghost which is given unto us" (Rom 5:5). Orlando probably fears the loss of his romantic love more than he fears God at the beginning of this scene, but the point of the biblical rhetoric here might be that Orlando's imagination, his capacity for hope and for fear, was awakened by his "education" from Ganymede. In this crucial sense, literary as well as theological, Orlando is ready to enter marriage with Rosalind. In Catholic Humanist doctrine, marriage is a state in which one must also encounter the living God, for it is this God who "hath joined together" (Matt 19:6) man and woman in marriage.

Before that encounter is possible, however, in life or in this play, Christian tradition follows the spirit of the Sermon on the Mount, where Jesus teaches, "Blessed are the pure in heart: for they shall see God" (Matt 5:8); sanctification of one's soul is necessary, apparently, before one has the inner clarity needed to see God. Catholic Humanism follows this tradition, with an added emphasis on the importance of the imagination. Convinced of the potential good of creativity, Catholic Humanists insist that imaginative wit helps us to fulfill both of Christ's two great commandments, to love our Creator and those humans near us, our neighbors (Matt 22:36–40). As has often been illustrated in the previous chapters, *As You Like It* expresses this truth through an emphasis on the rhetorical importance of shared dreams, expressed rhetorically as "if" *conditionals*. The play's final scene follows the pattern of Shakespearean comedy in being not just a climax, or conclusion, of the previous action, but also a recapitulation of the play's major themes and dramatic patterns.

We begin the scene, therefore, with "Ganymede" reminding everyone of the importance of a key virtue in any comedy, then restating the agreement within which the preceding "if" clauses have been agreed upon: "Patience once more, whiles our compact is urged" (5.4.5). The first key term here, "patience," is perhaps the central virtue of Shakespeare's late

---

1. Peacham, *Garden*, 164.

"tragi-comedies" but, as previously noted, these plays are classified in the First Folio as "Comedies," so the centrality of this virtue in this mid-career comedy is unsurprising. In most Shakespearean plays, "patience" is a virtue exemplified primarily by females, especially the leading heroines who in large part create the happy conclusions of these optimistic plays. With the other key term here, "compact," there is *metaphora* likening their promised meeting to our modern term "contract," and legal and rhetorical connotations more typical of male roles in Shakespeare's society. "Ganymede" can effectively employ male disguise, one last time, at the beginning of this scene, and audiences of Shakespeare's time might see "him" fulfilling the role of lawyer within Arden. They cannot forget, of course, that the speaker is also Rosalind, the passionate young woman about to be married, and we might expect females in the audience to be heartened by the legal savvy and rhetorical skill with which Rosalind addresses both her father and her future husband.

Would a lack of formal training in rhetoric, since Elizabethan grammar schools were open only to middle-class males, have prevented the women in Shakespeare's audience from appreciating Rosalind's rhetorical skill? There is no way to definitively answer this question, but a positive estimation of their abilities might be argued for based on the extensive use of rhetoric by Lady Mary Wroth, the seventeenth-century sonneteer and niece of Sir Philip Sidney, or by the fact that Puttenham dedicates *The Art of English Poesie* to "the learning of Ladies and young Gentlewomen, or idle courtiers, desirous to become skillful in their own mother tongue."[2] Puttenham further asserts that not even "the Lord Chancelour of England or Archbishop of Canterbury himself" can speak effectively "without the use of figures."[3] To hear *eloquentia* and *sapientia* from a female character thus might have been a source of pride if not political hope.

For any theatrical audience, the final scene makes especially "interesting dramatic use of the *hypothetical syllogism*,"[4] the "if" *conditionals* which we have found to be so important in the play. "Ganymede" first has Duke Senior agree to give his daughter to Orlando, "if I bring in your Rosalind" (5.4.6) slyly negotiating with the potentially marriage-troubling presence of even the most supportive of fathers. "He" then has Orlando reaffirm his commitment to marry, while the more troubling case of Phoebe requires two conditionals. Ganymede asks her, "You say, you'll marry me, if I be willing?," but this question is merely a prelude to securing the promise that

---

2. Puttenham, *Art*, 158.
3. Puttenham, *Art*, 139.
4. Joseph, *Arts of Language*, 185.

matters to Silvius: "But if you do refuse to marry me, / You'll give yourself to this most faithful shepherd?" (5.4.11–14). "Thinking the bargain safe," notes Joseph, "Phoebe readily accepts the major premise" hypothetically offered here; the proud shepherdess will have no choice but to supply "the minor premise" of his *hypothetical syllogism* "by refusing to marry Rosalind," and to accept "the conclusion by agreeing to marry the shepherd whom she had disdained."[5]

Silvius is potentially the most difficult case of all, so he is spoken to first. Pointing to the scornful Phoebe, Ganymede asks, "You say that you'll have Phoebe, if she will" (5.4.16). Silvius' response sounds strange to modern ears, but strongly suggests the Petrarchan sonneteer, in love as much with an "other-worldly" idea of love as much as a person: "Though to have her and death were both one thing" (5.4.16–17). One can appreciate, upon hearing such a line, why so few sonnet sequences actually end in marriage. The supposed "lover" responds to the scorn of the lady not with bold action or even eloquent words, but rather with depressed resignation—a "de facto" acceptance of death.

Nevertheless, Rosalind understands fully her role in creating this "compact," and the promise she must fulfill: "I have promised to make all this matter even" (5.4.18). Her "promise" here can be interpreted as a brilliant pun, an *antanaclasis*,[6] or homonymic pun, on the connection between rhetoric and marriage that Shakespeare has developed throughout the play. For "matter" in Renaissance rhetoric is the "material" of any linguistic discourse, and Rosalind herself might well have in mind her earlier promise to translate the "howling of Irish wolves" into the clear vows of matrimony that make possible a "marriage of true minds," as Shakespeare puts it in his great sonnet on marriage, Sonnet 116. Catholic marriage is also a gift of one's body, however, and the word "even" recalls the physical consummation and openness to children that is also essential. Finally, the word "even" can be taken as a term of peace-making, of making combatants "even" so that they don't have to "even the score" in an endless exercise of one-up-manship (or one-up-womanship) that transforms marriage from a place of mutual love to a platform for power politics.

Secular law can also allow marriage to become a temporary condition created solely for the fulfillment of mutual lust, and the potential for such a state is then comically illustrated by the arrival of Touchstone and Audrey, a couple who may already be "even," or are at least very impatient to consummate their marriage. In part it is commentary on their lust, as at other

---

5. Joseph, *Arts of Language*, 185.
6. Peacham, *Garden*, 56.

moments in the play, that now prompts satirical but also humorous lines from Jaques, here cast in the form of biblical allusion:

> There is sure, another flood toward, and these
> couples are coming to the ark. Here comes a pair of
> very strange beasts, which in all tongues are called fools. (5.4.35–38)

The *metaphora* here of the couple being "very strange beasts" could recall the oft-forgotten order of Noah's ark, when clean beasts were taken by sevens whereas unclean beasts came in pairs (Gen 7:2), but it is unclear whether Jaques is being so precise. He does stress that in any language, even after the confusion of Babel, lustful couples like Touchstone and Audrey can be called "fools," because lust cannot be the basis for a happily married life. Erasmus' *Praise of Folly*, however, argues explicitly that marriage can only be "happy or lasting" due to Folly,[7] and it is also true that Noah's ark is a traditional typological *metonymia*[8] of both the church and marriage. Whatever Jaques' own melancholy thoughts, the point of the biblical allusion here is not the destruction of evil that is the "dark side" of the flood, but rather the renewal of life that becomes possible when "couples" of any kind enter the strange ark known as "marriage."

To do so in any culture has always been a foolish enterprise, especially for women, but better than the alternatives. St. Paul infamously argues that "it is better to marry than to burn" (1 Cor 7:9), and Jaques would probably add that it is better to marry than to drown. Rosalind, moreover, is ready to marry rather than drown in the sorrow of tears that would be shed if she lost Orlando. Surely, at least for the foreseeable future, both Touchstone and Audrey would be very unhappy to be separated, however foolish we find their union. It is the essence of Erasmus' argument in *The Praise of Folly* that God can use human foolishness to teach divine wisdom. Especially after Babel, and the "confusion of tongues," all humans are fools, but *As You Like It* invites us to laugh rather than "cry," as Lear puts it, that "we are come to this great stage of fools" (4.5.178–79).

Further opportunity for Touchstone to display his courtly wit is then given as Jaques welcomes him into the final gathering. Jaques tells Duke Senior that this "motley-minded gentleman . . . hath been a courtier, he swears" (5.4.41–42). Touchstone then seeks to "prove" or validate this introduction by beginning with an "if" clause, but then comically turning to *diazeugma*[9] by making himself the subject of all the most stereotypical verbs

---

7. Erasmus, *Praise of Folly*, translated by Betty Radice, 93.
8. Peacham, *Garden*, 19.
9. Joseph, *Arts of Language*, 59.

associated with courtiers, and using *diacope*[10] of "I have" to stress his own experience. However foolish we might find this "spoofing" of the actions of a courtier in sixteenth-century England, Touchstone does provide a comical *systrophe*,[11] or extended definition of court life, to "prove" the hypothetical proposition that he has been a courtier:

> If any man doubt that, let him put me to my
> purgation. I have trod a measure; I have flattered
> a lady; I have been politic with my friend, smooth
> with mine enemy; I have undone three tailors; I have
> had four quarrels, and like to have fought one. (5.4.43–47)

Jaques then asks how this final quarrel "was ta'en up?" and Touchstone replies that "it was upon the seventh cause" (5.4.48–50). Before explaining himself, Touchstone has another bawdy flourish, telling Duke Senior that he will "press in here" with the other "country copulatives" to marry (5.4.55–56), but this does not sound like a serious commitment to anything other than his own lust. He has come, he says, "to swear and to forswear: according as marriage binds and blood breaks"; the alliteration and parallelism describe this enterprise, for Audrey is "a poor virgin . . . an ill-favoured thing," but, Touchstone affirms, "mine own" (5.4.57–58). It is quite possible that Duke Senior does not understand the fool's words, as generally he describes them as "very swift and sententious" (5.4.62), but it is hard to see how the fool here is wise. Touchstone responds with two puns whose second sense is probably bawdy: "According to the fool's bolt, sir, and such dulcet diseases" (5.4.63–64). A naïve audience member, or even Duke Senior himself, could hear this line as another reference to the fool's fast wit, but the more worldly will probably interpret "bolt" and "dulcet" as *asteismus*,[12] puns that recall the infamous discussion of "sweet sin" in St. Augustine's *Confessions* or, for the less intellectual, Jaques' earlier references to venereal disease.

Touchstone's humor here not only causes laughter but threatens to destroy the idyllic celebration of marriage that ensues. However, his spoof of courtly life does concur with the principle of Catholic Humanist rhetoric that seems to animate the entire play. For after Jaques prompts him to again explain why he quarreled upon "the seventh cause," Touchstone commences a long and apparently pedantic exposition on how he quarrels "in print, by the book" (5.4.88). The quarrel began with a lie, that Touchstone "did dislike the cut of a certain courtier's beard," and progressed through various

---

10. Peacham, *Garden*, 48.
11. Peacham, *Garden*, 153.
12. Peacham, *Garden*, 34.

rhetorical stages, such as "the Retort Courteous," the "Quip Modest," the "Reply Churlish," the "Reproof Valiant," the "Counter-cheque Quarrelsome," the "Lie Circumstantial," and finally to the "Lie Direct" (5.4.90–94).

As with so much Touchstone says, the terms here are not to be taken seriously, but are rather a spoof of books of rhetorical argument. Specifically, Touchstone's speech is often taken as extra-textual reference to two late sixteenth-century books that treat at length "the manner and diversitie of lies,"[13] but the speech could also be taken as *enumeratio*,[14] which Peacham recommends for "the numbering up of the causes . . . of debate," including such information as

> the occasions and efficients whereby it began, proceedeth, and continued . . . who were the motioners of enterprising the same war,
> what hope of each side to get victorie, what boldness on both parts in their meeting.[15]

Touchstone's pedantic, long-winded style thus has sound rhetorical authority, but the rest of his speech, one may notice, does react against Peacham's typical likening of the arts of language to the arts of war. When Jaques then asks whether the fool can "nominate in order now the degrees of the lie?" (5.4.86–87), the request is given because, as a Renaissance satirist, he enjoys parody of formal rhetoric. Touchstone obliges him by pedantically restating each "degree" of the quarrel, in what Peacham might call *eutrepismos*,[16] concluding that dueling may be avoided for each stage, but the dangerous final form of the lie must be qualified by one key word. The wise fool sagely explains:

> All these you may avoid but the Lie Direct; and you may
> avoid that too, with an If. I knew when seven
> justices could not take up a quarrel, but when the
> parties were met themselves, one of them thought but
> of an If, as, "If you said so, then I said so;" and
> they shook hands and swore brothers. (5.4.94–100).

Touchstone concludes with the general principle that seems to animate so much of the play, and provides the title of my study here: "Your If is the

13. Trautvetter, *As You Like It*, 201, identifies the two works as *The Book of Honor and Armes, Wherein Is Discoursed the Causes of Quarrele, and the Nature of Injuries, with Their Repulses*, by Sir William Segar (1590) and *His Practice, in Two Books: The First Intreating of the Use of Rapier and Dagger, the Second of Honour and Honourable Quarrels*, by Vincentio Saviolo (1595).

14. Peacham, *Garden*, 125.

15. Peacham, *Garden*, 126.

16. Peacham, *Garden*, 129.

only peacemaker; much virtue in If" (5.4.100–101). Using *epanalepsis*[17] to begin and end his speech with the play's key word, "if," Touchstone offers wise *paroemia*[18] that is probably evidence of Shakespeare's extra-textual intentions. As Erasmus unceasingly affirmed, making peace, not war, is the ultimate purpose of a rhetorician's learned argument.

Abstract aphorism of this kind is unusual for Touchstone, but not uncommon amongst Shakespeare's fools, particularly after Robert Armin takes over the role from Will Kempe in Shakespeare's acting company. Performing the "7 degrees of the lie" speech surely tests any actor playing Touchstone. Shapiro argues that the speech was "written specifically for Armin" and "now feels dead on the page as well as in performance."[19] Like the "figure of rhetoric" in 5.2, this could be true if Touchstone's lines are taken as dry academic references, without regard for their tone in the scene. However, a number of modern players of Touchstone have suggested approaches to the speech that bring it alive.

In the 1978 BBC, James Bolam slowly and clearly enunciates each of the "7 degrees," but then for some reason, perhaps time, cuts the concluding maxim so important to my study here, "if is the only peacemaker" (5.4.100). Lewis Gordon, in the 1983 Stratford, takes a different tack, rushing through the initial six degrees, then slowing down to give all of the concluding maxim. Branagh's 2006 film unsurprisingly cuts the whole speech, but Dominic Rowan's rendition in Thea Sharrock's 2009 RSC reveals fully how effective the speech can be, even in the modern theatre. As in his earlier speeches, Rowan again uses numerous hand gestures with each "degree" of the "lie," moving like a dancer before miming an archer who has presented his wit like an arrow to the audience. If the British audience misses this reference, Rowan finally appeals also to their national sport, miming a football goalie sending a long ball deep into the crowd. Such actions obviously appeal to a modern audience, but coupled with the words of Shakespeare's text they do convey Touchstone's role as clown and showman.

Given the importance of this play's "if" clauses, the key maxim, "If is the only peacemaker," clearly has further thematic significance. It might remind one of Sidney's argument, in his *Defense of Poetry*, against the Platonic and Puritan claim that poets are liars, that the poet "nothing affirms, and therefore never lieth."[20] Yet there is also an ethical purpose of poetry for

---

17. Peacham, *Garden*, 46.
18. Peacham, *Garden*, 29.
19. Shapiro, *A Year*, 222–23.
20. Sidney, *Defence*, 235.

Sidney, to show what "should or should not be,"[21] and Sidney offers his own *hypothetical syllogism* to support his point:

> If then a man can arrive, at that child's age, to know that the poets' persons and doings are but pictures what should be, and not stories what have been, they will never give the lie to things not affirmatively but allegorically and figuratively written.[22]

In making a similar argument, *As You Like It* thus follows Sidney, an important Protestant Humanist poet of the late fifteenth century, and Cicero, the central classical inspiration of Catholic Humanism, in stressing the relationship between imagination and virtue. Touchstone's concluding *paroemia* can thus be taken as a summary of Erasmus' belief in the importance of imagination to peacemaking. If Erasmus does not quite go so far as to claim that "if" provides the "only" way to peacemaking, he certainly finds much "virtue" in "if." In his late treatise *On Mending the Peace of the Church*, Erasmus begins one paragraph with three successive sentences beginning in "If," each sentence illustrating how human moral life can improve if humans offer moral action as a pleasing sacrifice to God.[23]

Touchstone's aphorism provides an apt "wisdom" introduction to herald the sudden arrival onstage of the god Hymen, honored here and so often in Renaissance culture and literature as "the god of every town" (5.4.44), precisely because marriage is so important in Catholic culture. Nothing in the play's historical or physical setting would prepare us for the sudden arrival of a classical god, and modern critics often share the sentiment of Dover-Wilson, who argues that there "is no necessity for this masque business."[24] Yet the significance of Hymen is thematic, and closely related to the rest of the play's theology. As Isabel Rivers explains in *Classical and Christian Ideas in English Renaissance Poetry*, in numerous Renaissance manuals "almost all the pagan gods and heroes are seen as types of Christ," though "it is not necessary for twentieth-century readers to have recourse to the handbooks to find out why and in what way a Renaissance poet is using myth."[25] Rather, the "context" can tell us, and the broad themes of *As You Like It* as a whole certainly reflect what Rivers notes is the "most widespread" of the "chief uses of myth" in Renaissance poetry, the "allegorical"

---

21. Sidney, *Defence*, 235.
22. Sidney, *Defence*, 235.
23. Erasmus, *On Mending the Peace of the Church*, 359.
24. Dover-Wilson, quoted in Latham, *As You Like It*, xxi.
25. Rivers, *Classical and Christian Ideas*, 24.

method, which Peacham includes via the figure *allegoria*,[26] in which "Pagan myth both adorns and reveals Christian truth."[27]

Although Hymen is a character rooted strongly in Renaissance culture, his sudden appearance can strain audience credulity, and modern directors especially often have trouble presenting Hymen onstage. Basil Coleman's 1978 BBC, for example, opts for the handsome young man of classical tradition, but he speaks Hymen's line with such solemnity and dreary tone that the marriages become boring rather than the joyful ceremonies they are intended to be. A common alternative, then, is to have Hymen played by an actor who has already appeared in the play. John Hirsch's 1983 production, for example, has the same actor play Amiens and Hymen; rhetorically, this sort of works in that Hymen brings a new kind of music to the play. Branagh's 2006 film of the play has Hymen's part played by some sort of Christian clergyman, a plausible re-casting within this film's nineteenth-century Japanese world. Thea Sharrock's 2009 RSC casts Hymen as an older African actor coming directly from the crowd, suggesting the universal relevance of Hymen, "god of every town" (5.4.144). A much more local approach was used in Jillian Keiley's "East Coast Canadian" production at Stratford, Ontario, as Robin Hutton, the actress who led the play's initial "goat dance," again conducted a dance to bring together the play's ultimately married couples. Though sometimes rearranging Shakespeare's lines, Keiley's concluding "goat dance" surely offered the "rustic revelry" (5.4.175) called for by Duke Senior's concluding speech. These alternatives are exciting in the theatre, yet perhaps fail to capture the "baptized" sanctification of marriage that, for Catholic Humanism, the classical god imaginatively represents.

Even before Hymen speaks, Shakespeare indicates the reverence due to Hymen with a stage direction calling for "still music." The same stage direction appears commonly in similarly climactic moments of Shakespeare's late plays,[28] probably representing the well-known element of Ptolemaic cosmology that *Pericles* explicitly calls, "the music of the spheres" (22.215). When one hears this music, one feels the "harmony of the universe" but not due to romantic, intuitive emotion; rather, one fully believes that providence is sovereign, that God is ultimately in charge of what can seem to be a chaotic world, one stained by sin and marred by evil.

Christian allusion often accompanies Classical theophanies in Shakespeare's late plays, and in *As You Like It* the opening words of Hymen's song certainly have theological resonance:

26. Peacham, *Garden*, 25.
27. Rivers, *Classical and Christian*, 24–25.
28. See, for example, 21.210 of *Pericles* or 5.1.52 of *The Tempest*.

> Then is there mirth in heaven,
> When earthly things made even
> Atone together. (5.4.106–8)

There is probably an initial allusion here to Christ's saving atonement, which allows the "joy" in "heaven over one sinner that repenteth" (Luke 15:7), but the focus of Hymen is the joy possible when humans "repent" here on earth by entering the joys, and sacrifices, of marital union. Yet the reference to atonement is certainly relevant, for Catholicism regards the atonement for sin achieved by Christ on the cross as the prerequisite of any potential human joy. The at-one-ment of men and women in marriage can allow them to be "made even" if the physical union of husband and wife does mirror a "marriage of true minds" like that which Rosalind had sought to achieve through her promise to "make all this matter even" (5.4.18).

This classical god's Catholic Humanist rhetoric continues as he presents Rosalind to her father: "Good duke, receive thy daughter / Hymen from heaven brought her" (5.4.109–10). Again, there is clear enough similarity to Christian doctrine—that Christ came from heaven to be human, and to marry His bride the church—for us to see Rosalind here as a type of Christ. Hymen thus, as Rivers would say, "both adorns and reveals Christian truth,"[29] though one hesitates to call this moment in the play *allegoria*[30] because the "other" reference is not essential to enjoying the moment. As is common in many Catholic marriages, the theology and typology implicit throughout the ceremony of matrimony becomes a supporting complement, an almost unseen foundation, for the "natural" human joys about to unfold. Hymen, one could say, is so completely "baptized" that initially He seems almost as irrelevant to the ceremony as many priests or ministers seem to a Christian couple being married.

Significantly, it is Rosalind—rather than Hymen, Duke Senior, or any competent priest or minister (Sir Oliver Martext now being nowhere in sight)—who steps forward to give the bride, herself, away, telling her Father: "To you I give myself, for I am yours" (5.4.114). Yet this conventional gesture of paternal respect is followed, as with other Shakespearean heroines,[31] by Rosalind then immediately turning to the groom; using *symploce*[32] to show she is equally united to both father and husband, Rosalind also says to Orlando, "To you I give myself, for I am yours" (5.4.115).

---

29. Rivers, *Classical and Christian*, 24–25.

30. Peacham, *Garden*, 25.

31. Compare, for example, Desdemona in *Othello*, who says, "I do perceive a divided duty" (1.3.179–88) between her father Brabantio and her new husband, Othello.

32. Peacham, *Garden*, 43.

If both the father and husband take Rosalind's hands here, as in most productions, one can argue for an important dramatic *actio* or gesture at this moment, "a kind of theatrical *synecdoche*"[33] in which "the gesture of the father's renunciation can stand" for the actual performance of the marriage ceremony,[34] and thus eliminate the need for a church wedding as in Lodge.[35] The social conventions here appealed to make the identical words mean something very different to both Orlando and Duke Senior, of course, but both reply with wonder, and another "if" clause. Both wondrously affirm that, "If there be truth in sight" (5.4.116–17), the real Rosalind, faithful daughter and fiancée, has revealed herself. Their *epanaphora*[36] must be altered, however, for Phoebe, because for her this revelation is much less joyful, and produces a rather agonized "if" clause: "If sight and shape be true why then my love adieu!" (5.4.118). Rosalind attempts to quell further "howling" with more *conditionals*, ironically now using *conditionals* to "cancel" *conditionals* and rule out the possibility of any further plot turns; she tells Duke Senior, Orlando, and Phoebe, in order:

> I'll have no Father, if you be not he
> I'll have no Husband, if you be not he
> Nor ne're wed women, if you be not she. (5.4.120–22)

An alert audience may respond with an uproar, since the line reveals, definitively, that Rosalind has been playing Ganymede. As elsewhere in *As You Like It*, however, the play of identity and rhetoric here produces not only an audience's delight, but also onstage confusion. Rosalind's words cannot please everyone, and we can assume from Phoebe's lack of verbal response, and probable gesture of anger onstage, that she remains unhappy.

Hymen must step back in to return all to silence and reassert the authority of the god of Love: "Peace, ho! I bar confusion! 'Tis I must make conclusion of these most strange events" (5.4.123–25). Hymen then creates onstage harmony through the traditional comic conclusions of music and dance. First he draws the eight people onstage into a formal dance, then addresses each couple individually and collectively, suggesting that the lovers find identity in each other:

> You and you no cross shall part
> You and you are heart in heart.
> You to his love must accord

---

33. Peacham, *Garden*, 21.
34. Bevington, *Action Is Eloquence*, 143.
35. Muir, *The Sources of Shakespeare's Plays*, 131.
36. Peacham, *Garden*, 41.

Or have a woman to your lord. (5.4.129–32)

Some critics regard Hymen's four-stress couplets as doggerel unworthy of the Bard, but Agnes Latham reminds us that Shakespeare often uses this style, "the language of prophecy and of gnomic statement," when he portrays the supernatural.[37] Peacham might describe Hymen's sententious blessings more practically, through a term that he notes is "otherwise called *sententia*," *gnome*, "a saying pertaining to the manners and common practises of men, which declareth by an apt brevitie, what in this life ought to be done or left undone."[38]

Universal ethics are also implied by Hymen's repeated term of address, his *epanaphora*[39] and *diacope*[40] of "you," used also by a number of other speakers in this final scene, the impersonal second person pronoun not often used in prose writing because the addressee is unclear. Onstage, however, Hymen does clearly speak to specific couples. Modern editors often add stage directions to assign particular lines from Hymen to particular couples; the lines assigned in most modern editions are fairly standard, beginning with Orlando and Rosalind then moving through the other significant couples. Yet these stage directions are not in the First Folio and, with the exception of lines clearly intended for Phoebe, Hymen could be addressing all four couples at once.

Probably the most important line in this whole speech is another "if" conditional, one upon which depends not only the love of the couples onstage, but all romantic love in general. Couples hoping to marry "must take hands" and "join in Hymen's bands / If truth holds true contents" (5.4.126–28). In other words, if the marriages proposed are to be happy, the individuals within each couple must unite with each other and thus allow what Shakespeare's Sonnet 116 calls "a marriage of true minds." This is the kind of marriage without "impediment" to which no objection can be made, because each person entering the marriage truly knows what he or she is doing and truly intends to remain faithful to marriage vows. This is the universal challenge of Catholic marriage, voiced by the classical god Hymen even as he draws together the couples in a dance to celebrate their marriages. Without truth's "true contents"—the *paroemion*[41] or alliteration

---

37. Latham, *As You Like It*, xxiii. Examples include the fairies in *A Midsummer Night's Dream*, the witches in *Macbeth*, and the Duke in *Measure for Measure*.
38. Peacham, *Garden*, 189.
39. Peacham, *Garden*, 41.
40. Peacham, *Garden*, 48.
41. Peacham, *Garden*, 49.

helping the phrase become almost another *gnome*[42] or *sententia* to guide wisdom—no couple can find contentment in marriage.

One final bit of marital advice is given by Hymen towards the end of his address to the four couples:

> Feed yourselves with questioning;
> That reason wonder may diminish,
> How thus we met, and these things finish. (5.4.136–38)

The imaginative inquiry as food *metaphora*[43] here might sound strange to modern ears, but it is a Catholic Humanist commonplace. Jesus rebukes Satan, in the desert, by reminding us that "Man shall not live by bread alone, but by every word that proceedeth out of the mouth of God" (Matt 4:4). Shakespeare's Hymen does not dispute this teaching, but simply adds to the daily diet of married couples an important means to remain aware of God's presence in their married lives: get to know each other through discussion, through "questioning," as Rosalind and Orlando have modeled in the play. Through revelation of their very identity, the human nature created by and imprinted with the divine, "wonder" can "diminish" the doubt that "reason" must have while undertaking a venture so foolish as life-long monogamy. For this is the true "finish" of marriage, not the ceremonies that begin it, and clearly this race is much harder to run than the simple act of becoming married, however joyful this moment may be.

The song then sung could also be Hymen's, but the approach used by many of the productions studied here, and certainly one in keeping with the Catholic Humanism found throughout the play, is for the couples onstage to sing it in response to Hymen's blessing, affirming and celebrating his words. They begin by honoring another classical goddess, singing "Wedding is great Juno's crown" (5.4.139). This classical reference is also "baptized," for one must remember that the corresponding Catholic "Queen of Heaven" is Mary, and that Mary is traditionally associated with chastity. That might strike moderns as an odd thing with which to remind couples about to be married, but chastity, commonly understood in Shakespeare's time as sexual fidelity within monogamy,[44] is an important virtue of Catholic marriage, part of what allows it to remain a "blessed bond of board and bed" (5.4.140), as the onstage couples use *paroemion*[45] to sing in the song's second line. Yet

---

42. Peacham, *Garden*, 189.
43. Peacham, *Garden*, 3.
44. A good guide to this meaning is Book Three of Spenser's *Faerie Queene*, in which Britomart is a female knight who marries but exemplifies the virtue of chastity.
45. Peacham, *Garden*, 49.

these couples, like most about to be married, are also joyfully aware that "Hymen peoples every town" (5.4.141) and the procreative importance of marriage cannot be overstated.

It is possible that some in the audience, whether Shakespeare's or that of our own time, will see the appearance of Hymen as an example of *deus ex machina*, the classical "god out of the machine" who appears onstage to resolve any lingering plot complications, allowing a play to come to a swift and happy conclusion. Hymen's role has more to do with theme, however, rather than plot, and if the *deus ex machina* role is assigned to anyone it is more likely the heretofore unseen Jaques, the second son of old Rowland. Shapiro notes that "it's hard to avoid the impression that this is something of a private joke on Shakespeare's part," to write "parts for two Olivers and two Jaques";[46] the purpose cannot simply be doubling of actors, since both Jaques are onstage in the final scene. Perhaps the second Jaques is so named to flaunt the rhetorical and literary artifice of this play.

This "second" Jaques suddenly appears in the play's final scene to deliver a sixteen-line speech which serves mainly to resolve a potentially unhappy complication of the plot: the apparent certainty that Duke Frederick will attack those in the forest and cause war to destroy the lovers' apparent bliss. Beginning with a very unnaturalistic but entirely rhetorical line, one appropriate to his "aesthetic" role in the play, this Jaques first asks, "Let me have audience for a word or two" (5.4.149). Jaques then tells us that Duke Frederick entered the forest intending "to take / His brother here and put him to the sword" (5.4.155–56), but then met "with an old religious man," and

> After some question with him was converted
> Both from his enterprise and from the world,
> His crown bequeathing to his banished brother,
> And all their lands restored to them again
> That were with him exiled. (5.4.159–63)

After hearing this, anyone in the play's audience is to be forgiven if they think of another joke, another reason for the second Jaques to be named after the first Jaques; does not the speech of both men remind us that a "jakes" is also a "privy," or outhouse, and thus "full of shit"?

On the other hand, the play has previously appealed to the rhetoric of the hermit, the "old religious man" in the forest who also taught Rosalind the magic of words (3.4.333–34), whom Orlando mentions again at the start of this final scene (5.4.32–34). Branagh's 2006 film does present

---

46. Shapiro, *A Year*, 215.

this figure, hidden in a hovel, when it offers an interesting take on Duke Frederick's conversion. Before 5.3 even begins, Branagh adds a scene with a weeping Duke Frederick hearing how those in Arden have survived "like Robin Hood of old" (Branagh recasting Charles the Wrestler's speech from 1.1.109–13). Branagh then adds scenes of Duke Frederick's own pilgrimage to the forest during Jaques de Boys' speech. These "added scenes" are rhetorically effective within the film because Brian Blessed, as Duke Frederick, has been such a fearsome, frightening figure throughout the production. The once cruel Duke is shown weeping and, during the play's final dance, meditating under a tree. It certainly becomes possible, especially for Catholic Humanists, to imagine the original Jaques soon sitting there with him, hearing the "matter" to be learned from such "convertites" (5.4.182).

One almost expects the "old religious uncle" (3.2.333) to appear at play's end, if only in the form of Shakespeare taking a curtain call. One could see this "hermit" as the playwright himself, Shakespeare, providing the words and plot twists necessary to the play's comic conclusion, but the character could also be seen as a personification, or *prosopopoeia*,[47] of the play's Catholic Humanism. An "old religious uncle" would have been a natural candidate, in Shakespeare's time, for providing the rhetorically-centered home-schooling that might allow a young woman like Rosalind to have such an eloquent, sapient tongue. By the time of the second Jaques' appearance, perhaps, an audience might be "converted" to accepting the connections the play so often draws between language, questions, imagination, peace-making, and the religion of the living God.

Certainly no one on stage scorns or mocks the good news that this new character in the play brings, and Duke Senior welcomes his speech as a wedding gift, saying that Jaques "offer'st fairly to thy brothers' wedding" (5.4.165). Yet before ending the play, Shakespeare turns the spotlight again upon the still melancholy mood of the original Jaques in the play. For after Duke Senior delivers what could be the last lines of the play, "Play, music, and you, brides and bridegrooms all, / With measure heaped in joy, to th' measures fall" (5.4.176–77), the first Jaques intercedes.

Initially, Jaques the "elder" affirms the thematic importance of Jaques de Boy's speech by confirming the news that Duke Frederick "hath put on a religious life"; he then reaffirms his own role as the play's patron of intellectual life by stating that he will seek to continue conversation with him, for "out of these convertites there is much matter to be heard and learn'd" (5.4.182–83). Jaques then uses *compar*[48] to parallel Hymen's earlier address to each couple,

---

47. Peacham, *Garden*, 136.
48. Peacham, *Garden*, 58.

"TO MAKE ALL THIS MATTER EVEN" 263

but significantly he speaks solely to the males on stage. He commends Duke Senior to his "former honor," Orlando "to a love that your true faith doth merit," Oliver "to your land and love and great allies," and Silvius to "a long and well-deserved bed" (5.4.184–88). Cynical words are given only to Touchstone, whom Jaques predicts will in his marriage commence "wrangling," a word that implies fierce disputation rather than loving conversation, and further implies that the marriage of the fool and Audrey cannot sustain a long journey, "for thy loving voyage is but for two months victuall'd" (5.4.189–90).

Jaques clearly sees their marriage as lust-driven and unlikely to last, but this expected cynicism must be balanced against his apparent acceptance of the real love and hopeful marriage of the other couples onstage. In stark contrast to "outsider" figures at the conclusion of other Shakespearean comedies—such as Egeus, Don John, or Malvolio—Jaques' parting words in the play do not imply bitter alienation, but simply the potentially noble choice of an intellectual rather than hedonistic life. After the *compar*[49] of his closing comments to each actor, he concludes with the elegance of a rhyming couplet, which rhetorically one might term *apophonema*, "a *sententia* in antithetical form":[50] "So, to your pleasures: I am for other than for dancing measures" (5.4.190–91). Duke Senior replies, "Stay, Jaques, stay," kind words that Peacham might call *pathopoeia*,[51] his general term for *pathos*; in performance this line is often accompanied by heartfelt gesture. Finally, there is rhetorical peace between the two former antagonists.

Jaques' comments to the male leads onstage cannot end this play, for so much of *As You Like It* reminds us of the importance of also hearing a female perspective. It is thus unsurprising that, after Duke Senior orders all onstage to proceed with their wedding dance, Shakespeare gives a long "epilogue" for the play to Rosalind. This speech perfectly concludes the play not so much because it is spoken by the play's comic heroine, but because she addresses both women and men in such a balanced and complete way. Shakespearean epilogues—which are always part of comedies, never in tragedies, and seldom in histories—normally aim to transfer the onstage experience of the actors to the live, present audience. We can clearly see this in *As You Like It* as Rosalind aims to bring peace to the war between the sexes. So perfectly does this epilogue conclude the play's Catholic Humanist rhetoric that it is worth reading again as a whole:

> It is not the fashion to see the lady the epilogue;
> but it is no more unhandsome than to see the lord

---

49. Peacham, *Garden*, 58.
50. Lanham, *Handlist*, 14.
51. Peacham, *Garden*, 144.

> the prologue. If it be true that good wine needs
> no bush, 'tis true that a good play needs no
> epilogue; yet to good wine they do use good bushes,
> and good plays prove the better by the help of good
> epilogues. What a case am I in then, that am
> neither a good epilogue nor cannot insinuate with
> you in the behalf of a good play! I am not
> furnished like a beggar, therefore to beg will not
> become me: my way is to conjure you; and I'll begin
> with the women. I charge you, O women, for the love
> you bear to men, to like as much of this play as
> please you: and I charge you, O men, for the love
> you bear to women—as I perceive by your simpering,
> none of you hates them—that between you and the
> women the play may please. If I were a woman I
> would kiss as many of you as had beards that pleased
> me, complexions that liked me and breaths that I
> defied not: and, I am sure, as many as have good
> beards or good faces or sweet breaths will, for my
> kind offer, when I make curtsy, bid me farewell.
> (Epilogue, 197–237)

The speech's dominant figure is *antanagoge*,[52] the balancing of positive and negative qualities, which Rosalind skillfully delivers in *compar*;[53] the musical balance is evident, for example, in the epilogue's opening line, as she reminds the audience of the play's initial male rhetoric by telling them: "It is not the fashion to see the lady the epilogue; but it is no more unhandsome than to see the lord the prologue." She then continues with an "if" conditional now familiar to us, here comparing the use of bushes to signify good pubs (a historical reality which many in the audience could recognize) to the value of plays having good epilogues. What really makes Rosalind's epilogue a rhetorical *tour de force*, though, is her unique use of *apostrophe*,[54] the figure of direct address, to speak both to men and women. Her *pathos* and *ethos* become unique in all of Shakespeare's work because, midway through the speech, the male actor playing Rosalind steps out of her aesthetic character, and into his male voice, allowing direct address to both genders of humanity.

Just before this startling transformation, Rosalind sounds almost like St. Paul commanding Timothy (1 Tim 1:18 or 2 Tim 4:1). "I charge you" she tells both men and women, but her commands were preceded by the *metaphora*

---

52. Joseph, *Arts of Language*, 138.
53. Peacham, *Garden*, 58.
54. Peacham, *Garden*, 116.

that the play has earlier presented through the language and conversions effected by the mysterious "religious uncle" (3.2.333). Rosalind's "way" in the epilogue, she has told the audience, "is to conjure you." But she will use no physical magic, instead relying on the enchanting power of dramatic, rhetorical language to convert her audience. In performance, both film and theatre, modern directors and actors have tried to make visual this appeal. The technology of modern film allowed Elizabeth Bergner in 1936 to speak the first half of the epilogue as a woman, the second half as a man, but for the most part modern actresses stay in the female gender for the entire epilogue. In Branagh's 2006 film, Bryce Howard spoke the epilogue after many of the credits have rolled, a working actress returning to her trailer, "out" of her part yet still very much a female. In the 2016 Stratford, Ontario production, Petrina Bromley dropped the "male" lines entirely, substituting playful references to the conclusion of *A Midsummer Night's Dream* and *Romeo and Juliet*, before closing with the actual lines of *As You Like It*. There is an important sense in which the actual lines of the play are connected to the historical conditions affecting gender in the theatre, but Shakespeare's language also makes a more universal appeal: the audience is asked to continue the rhetorical exercise required by so much of the play's action. As in every play, the audience imaginatively accepts a speaker's "mask" in order to hear what he, or she, might reveal both about themselves and humanity in general.

As so often in the play, key to Rosalind's "charge" of both women and men are puns. Women are told to "like as much of this play as please you," and Rosalind concludes by hoping that between men and women "the play may please." The *antanaclasis* on "play" is obvious, applying not just to this play but Shakespeare's entire project as a dramatist, but also to the many plays within *As You Like It* that were so crucial to allowing the romantic play possible now between the married on-stage couples. Rosalind's epilogue is clearly intending the same for the present audience, but the dangers involved in doing do are surely recalled by the other key pun here, on "bear." Touchstone made bawdy use of this word earlier in the play, and it is perhaps this meaning that has the males in the audience "simpering" as Rosalind parenthetically points out that most males are physically attracted to females. "Bear," however, especially used together with "love," has reference also to one of the most famous texts of Catholic Humanism, St. Paul teaching that those in love "bear all things" (1 Cor 13:7). Subtly, without preaching, Rosalind is reminding the audience that real love requires enduring sacrifice.

It is just after this "charge" that the male actor steps forward, paradoxically revealing his real gender through another "if" clause: "if I were a woman." The condition here is necessary to the proceeding words, "I would kiss," but the concluding words play with the literal and figurative senses here. For much of the charge to men—whom we can presume to be the dominant gender present for this play's historical performances—is a quite literal call to hygiene, for cut beards and clean breath. But this literal call to "clean up your act" could also be taken as prerequisite to the "kiss of peace" (2 Cor 13:12) hoped for by Catholic Humanists. The final lines clearly remind us of key words in this play's title, "as" and "like," but the implied term "you" also reminds us again of Christ's second great commandment: "as ye would that men should do to you, do ye also to them likewise" (Luke 6:31). The "golden rule" is surely foundational to Rosalind's concluding message to the genders: if you like clean breaths and faces whilst kissing, clean your own so others like you also.

Rosalind's closing word also include the familiar appeal here for applause to "bid" the players "farewell," and a last bit of fun with gender as the male actor "make[s] curtsy," a familiar feminine gesture. Yet if the epilogue seems too commercial, practical, or literal, we recall how Rosalind's education of Orlando in "the cleanliest shift" (4.1.72) was not just physical but also intellectual, imaginative, and in important respects spiritual. "As you like it" will be how others like it also, and this is nowhere more true, Shakespeare finally argues, then in male and female relations. The male actor hardly needs to tell the males in the theatre that they prefer females who are clean and have breaths sweet to kiss; "as" they like this, the epilogue finally argues, so men should attempt to become "as" this themselves.

Rosalind's conclusion, like her allusions to the play's title, is so obvious that we could call it *epilogus*, a figure that Joseph thinks especially akin to the *hypothetical syllogism*,[55] but by play's end the pleasing power of rhetoric requires no further argument. While the final epilogue of *As You Like It* may lack the high seriousness of Prospero's final appeal to "Mercy itself" and paraphrase of the Lord's prayer at the end of *The Tempest*,[56] it does continue and rhetorically enact the central themes of *As You Like It*. Although presented in a personal and highly concrete way, the epilogue does attempt, like the rest of the play, to promote peace between men and women. The "way" requires imagination, as the "play" of the theatre, with its disguised actors and examples of human folly and wisdom, is proposed finally as a means to promote the "serio-comic" play of peacemaking for which Erasmus had become famous in his own time. Shakespeare's appeal and influence has arguably been even broader, but there is no point in comparison of achievement known only by God. May those who wish to see God continue to play in the blessed art of peacemaking!

55. Joseph, *Arts of Language*, 185.

56. Prospero concludes, "my ending is despair, / Unless I be relieved by prayer, / Which pierces so that it assaults / Mercy itself and frees all faults. / As you from crimes would pardoned be / Let your indulgence set me free" (Epilogue, 15–20).

Conclusion

"If Is for Children"

Rhetoric and the Value of *As You Like It*

IN OUR MODERN WORLD, it is common for many to regard speculation about "if" as appropriate only for children, whose imaginative flights of fancy can be seen as amusing, but not important for building a better world. Such skepticism can be seen not only in the rationalistic worlds of science or economics, but even in the humanities, in the now commonplace reaction to Rudyard Kipling's poem "If—." Once celebrated as a guide to British manhood, to those who can keep their heads "when all about you / Are losing theirs and blaming it on you," today this poem is often denigrated as a symptom of the colonialism that Kipling is now commonly associated with. Such skepticism can also be seen, from the distance of the early twenty-first century, as symptomatic of the cynical malaise of postmodernism, without faith in not only God but in the very existence let alone potential of the human character and imagination.

Such a viewpoint is clearly very far away, in both history and perspective, from the Catholic Humanism that has been shown to inform the rhetorical drama that is *As You Like It*. There is no question that this play amply rewards the rhetorical approach of this study, reminding us that intensive study of the system of communication that educated Shakespeare, and many other great English writers, remains relevant to audiences attempting to hear the art of great theatre, and to actors and directors who hope to authentically produce such plays. One need not go so far as modern critic J.

Hillis Miller, who rhetorically asks "What is the teaching of reading but the teaching of the interpretation of tropes?,"[1] but one can affirm that traditional rhetoric does offer many resources for the interpretation of literature.

This point, of course, becomes especially obvious with a play such as *As You Like It*. As David Young writes,

> As You Like It is, in fact, almost all style, accomplishing its ends through stratagems of language, brilliant verbal juxtapositions. . . . Everyone is drunk with style (not, fortunately, euphuism, although that receives its glances), all sorts of styles and the roles to go with them.[2]

Style is, in this play, the man, and the woman—in the "case" of Rosalind herself, the man and the woman at the same time. *As You Like It*'s wide range of roles and styles make the linguistic detail of Renaissance rhetoric vital to reading the central emotional and intellectual traits of its characters. Renaissance rhetoric proves its value to modern readers by clarifying the linguistic complexity that causes delight in audiences, potentially even helping overcome the aesthetic barriers that prevent such plays from being enjoyed by young students of the play. Moreover, a rhetorical approach to this play can not only draw on the central themes of Catholic Humanism but also respond to some of the most complex questions of contemporary literary theory. In no small part, this is because, as Judith Rice Henderson says, writers in Shakespeare's time

> understood that a work of literature is a communication between a writer (or speaker) and a reader (or audience), neither a well-wrought urn preserving its own meaning for successive ages nor a mirror in which every reader can see only his own face.[3]

The very relevant remaining question of value, however, is whether—box office receipts aside—Shakespeare's cheerful portrayal of making love and peace in the Forest of Arden can or should have any claim upon the imagination or behavior of future generations? Posing this further "question of value" might seem naïve in a world struggling to even preserve the existence of forests, but addressing it fully does seem to be what the play itself invites us to do. Would not all want to be present, if unseen, when Jaques sat down with Duke Frederick and the "old religious uncle" who converted him, precisely because "out of these convertites / there is much matter to be heard, and learned" (5.4.182–83)?

1. Miller, "The Function of Rhetorical Study," 97.
2. Young, *The Heart's Forest*, 71.
3. Henderson, Review of *Shakespeare and the Rhetoricians*, 101.

As You Like It and Peacemaking

This second "question of value" might seem even more naïve then the first, given that our world has so long been bitterly divided by war, by those who would put others "to the sword" rather than arguing in anything like the civil fashion so comically portrayed by Touchstone. Yet it is also arguable that our world is even more divided by the "battle of the sexes," by the ongoing cycle of mutual accusation, divorce, and power struggle that seems an inevitable legacy of the much longer history of inequality and alienation between men and women. Given such a history, it hardly seems realistic to again simply pose the solution so passionately believed in by English Romantic poets, the human imagination. Nor does it seem helpful to hope for the "*deus ex machina*" comically portrayed within *As You Like It*, and within many later works of "fantasy" that hope for a religious solution to the general problem of human conflict: the existence of a religious hermit who can teach divine wisdom to those willing to be converted from the ways of our world.

Yet the question of what *could* convert us is not only a religious question but a rhetorical one. In the traditional terms of classical rhetoric, what *can* appeal to our *logos*, *pathos*, and *ethos*; in English, what *can* appeal to our logical minds, to our capacity to feel, and our ability to make ethical choices? In the terms that have since become more common, our human consciousness has largely been divided by the "Enlightenment" age of Reason, on one hand, and the Romantic emphasis on emotion, on the other; what *can* appeal both to our minds and hearts? Or, in the terms of the much older understanding of the human soul as being made in the divine image, which St. Augustine describes as the trinity of memory, intellect, and will,[4] how *can* we remember who we really are, be intellectually convinced of this identity, and learn to act in accordance with the divine will instead of decrepit human desire? Through such questions, we can at least remember that the discipline of rhetoric need not be primarily technical nor political, but rather more concerned with the existential question of how art or any other form of communication speaks to, persuades, calms, our human souls.

That rhetoric has often been such a discipline can be demonstrated through tracing the many historical connections between rhetoric and poetry, noticing how both help a writer speak to universal human issues through concrete and figurative language. The mutual influence of these disciplines reminds us that both contribute greatly to the nature of dramatic art that emerges in the Renaissance. Like so much of the art that then flourishes,

---

4. Augustine, *On the Trinity*, Book X.

Shakespearean drama vividly portrays the distinct features of humanity, and for this reason is often associated with a revival of Classical Humanism. Yet much of the art of this period, and Shakespeare's is generally no exception, depicts the human being as a creature in relationship with a Creator, and with the Redeemer and Comforter whom together comprise the Christian Triune God. Catholic Humanism can be seen in both the broad features of Shakespearean drama and in many of its specific lines; to take one example, from late in Shakespeare's career, young Perdita tells an old man (the disguised King Polixenes), during the "sheep-shearing festival" of *The Winter's Tale*, "of an art which in [its] piedness shares with great creating nature" (4.4.88–89). Polixenes responds with complex aesthetic philosophy on the relationship of art and nature, concluding that "art itself is nature" (4.4.97), but the young girl has the more essential point. Perdita has seen that the concrete complexity of art imitates the creative diversity and vitality of God's infinite creativity.

Catholic Humanism

This diversity allows the influence of Catholic Humanism upon Renaissance art to be described in many ways, as suggested by part 1 of this study, yet one should not forget nor underemphasize the basic elements of Christian theology which encourage such influence. Genesis 1:27 asserts boldly from the beginning that humans are made in the divine image, while Christians of most denominations affirm that the New Testament reveals that Jesus is, however beyond our comprehension we might find this doctrine, both "fully divine" and "fully human." Whereas modern liberal Christians doubt the former and exaggerate the latter, for much of history the situation was reversed; Catholic Humanism was radical, but orthodox, in finding in Christ a human model. Jesus "knew what was in man" (John 2:25), the gospels affirm and, though reference to the Book of Daniel makes this a messianic more than philosophical term, it is still true that perhaps Jesus' favorite title for himself is "Son of Man" (Matt 24:30; 26:24). Perhaps most importantly, Jesus affirms that the second of His two great commandments, "to love thy neighbour as thyself," is "like unto" the first, the commandment to love God "with all thy heart, and with all thy soul, and with all thy mind" (Matt 22:34–40). Thus there is an essential, divinely authorized connection between loving humanity and loving God, a connection that Jesus completes, with potentially terrifying consequences, by allegorically explaining, through the "sheeps" and the "goats," that God's final judgment of our souls will depend on what we "did" or "did not do" for the "least" of those around us, for such is also done or not to the Son of Man himself (Matt 25:31–46).

The orthodox basis of Catholic Humanism is often forgotten or understated by those who would make its Renaissance era leaders into modern pillars of liberalism. This happens most frequently, of course, to Erasmus, who is selectively quoted to explain why the Council of Trent condemned much of his writing as having "encouraged the Reformation." It is true that elements of Erasmus' thought seem sympathetic to Protestant Reformers, such as his fervent critique of clerical abuses, mockery of Scholastic philosophy, and *ad fontes* return to the source of scriptures. For the entire church's benefit, Erasmus' biblical scholarship not only recovers knowledge of the original Biblical languages but, just as importantly, regains awareness of the scriptures' frequent use of figurative language, particularly puns and paradoxes.

Yet one cannot read Erasmus' debate with Luther over free will without becoming aware of the doctrinal issues that caused him, within his own mind, to remain firmly within the Roman Catholic fold. Other texts by Erasmus are also filled with orthodox Catholic claims based upon not only the New Testament but also Church Fathers such as St. Augustine, and Erasmus' close friendship with Thomas More can remind us of what both held dear. As John Paul II writes in a letter announcing the formal canonization of St. Thomas More in 2000, which also makes positive mention of his friendship with Erasmus, the ideals of such men are "inspiration for a political system which has as its supreme goal the service of the human person."[5] Although the imaginative thought of Erasmus may not have suited the strict logic of the Catholic Counter-Reformation, one could argue that both Erasmus and More were intellectuals who served Christ through the expansion of Catholic intellectual understanding, rather than for the purpose of entrenching church schism.

It is silly, today, to debate denominational division with any attempt to preserve schism, but the valuable vein of theological aesthetics that is Catholic Humanism must be recovered and mined. Gregory Wolfe has led this effort on the Protestant side, founding the journal *Image*, producing an anthology of new religious Humanists, and most recently writing the aptly titled book *Beauty Shall Save the World*. The more conservative Catholic world has also produced outstanding Catholic Humanists, none more influential than John Paul II. The first encyclical of this exceptional pontiff, *Redemptor Hominis*, reminds us that Christ is both the redeemer of man and of human culture, while his later "Letter to Artists" speaks directly of the importance of sacred art in human culture. Many other modern

5. John Paul II, "Apostolic Letter."

Christian artists could be also be cited, leaving no doubt about the contemporary influence of Catholic Humanism upon aesthetic, ecclesiastical, or even political questions, yet there may be no clearer statement of the theological purpose of Catholic Humanist education than that given by the great seventeenth-century Puritan, Milton, in his tract *Of Education*:

> The end then of learning is to repair the ruins of our first parents by regaining to know God aright, and out of that knowledge to love him, to imitate him, to be like him, as we may the nearest by possessing our souls of true virtue, which being united to the heavenly grace of faith makes up the highest perfection.[6]

Students of *As You Like It* might find the virtues of Catholic Humanism particularly relevant to reconsidering one of the most vexed issues of our contemporary culture: gender.

Gender and Catholic Humanism

It is not a stretch, in many respects, to regard the Renaissance Catholic Humanists as the first European feminists, or at least the first male intellectuals to take seriously concerns about the status of women in society. The Spanish Catholic Humanist Juan Luis Vives, in his *The Education of Christian Women*, is one of the first to advocate for the full education of women, and this text's 1529 English translation by Richard Hyrdre, a member of More's household, directly influences the education received by More's daughter, Margaret.[7] In the ideal if yet non-existent state of More's *Utopia*, both men and women benefit, twice per day, from a piece of literature read aloud.[8] Perhaps most influentially, as already noted, Erasmus' *Praise of Folly* praises the particularly Christian wisdom of the weak, lowly, fools present in every society: children and women. In the modern English of John P. Dolan, Erasmus' Folly teaches:

> The whole of the Christian Religion seems to have a certain relationship with some kind of folly but fails to agree at all with wisdom. If you would like proof of this, take a look at children, old people, women, and fools and see how they, more than others, take great pleasure in the things of religion.[9]

---

6. Milton, *Of Education*, 389.
7. Smith, "Humanist Education," 9–29.
8. More, *Utopia*, translated by Paul Turner, 83.
9. Erasmus, *The Praise of Folly*, translated by John P. Dolan, 169.

We recall *As You Like It*'s fun with the concept of "counterfeit" (4.3.168–83), and can by play's end see how Rosalind has exemplified Erasmian seriocomic play. As Feste tells Malvolio during his "interlude" in the madhouse, the actor returns "in a trice" (*TN*, 4.2.126), changing forms so quickly that it can disorient the audience; yet without this capacity for wit, in both men and women, as *The Praise of Folly* argues, there can be "no living,"[10] for life brings its own disconcerting changes of costume and identity.

If Catholic Humanism thus provides both men and women with a capacity for imaginative play rather than direct instruction in doctrinal purity, there is one topic upon which they clearly differ from contemporary assumptions. Whereas most feminists today consider it obvious that "gender" is "culturally constructed" while sexual identity is "biologically constructed," Catholic Humanists follow biblical tradition in generally arguing for a "divinely constructed" view of "gender." The foundational text is Gen 1:27, that God created the male and female genders, "male and female created He them," and subsequent Judeo-Christian tradition generally follows a "complementarian" view of gender which affirms the mutual importance but basic distinction between the two genders. There are "egalitarian" Christians who stress that there is "neither male nor female: for ye are all one in Christ Jesus" (Gal 3:28). Yet historically Christians have generally believed that "oneness" in Christ derives from our common identity being made in the image of God. This image, Christianity normally affirms, is related to how the divine image is reflected in both, but differently, of the two distinct genders. The unity of scripture is also at issue here; one can accept that different texts express contradictory messages, both important to human understanding, but it is hard to believe that fundamental contradiction is the teaching of the one infallible God.

Roman Catholic conceptions of gender—such as those held by More and Erasmus—are complicated yet further by an emphasis upon the role and importance of Mary. She is "blessed . . . among women" the angel Gabriel affirms, due to the extraordinarily important "yes" she speaks to God's plan for incarnation: "be it unto me according to thy word" (Luke 1:28, 37). Later, the grown Jesus will contrast the contemplative way of Mary and the practical methods of Martha; while describing Martha's "careful" but "troubled" ways, Jesus reminds us that Mary's is "that good part" (Luke 10:38–42). At the foot of His cross, Jesus will commend to each other Mary and his beloved disciple, John, who accepts her as his "mother" (John 19:27); subsequently, Mary becomes known as "Mother of the Church." As with all developed Catholic doctrines—most notably the central doctrine

---

10. Erasmus, *The Praise of Folly*, translated by John Wilson.

of the Trinity—the doctrine of the "Immaculate Conception," or "unfallen" nature of Mary (a doctrine which the Roman Catholic Church eventually affirms as infallibly true) must be understood in relation to the whole of biblical revelation.

If one does so, it is arguable that Roman Catholic tradition affirms the female as the superior gender. One can easily denigrate the Catholic Church's leadership as "patriarchal," or its cultures as a frequent perversion of anthropological truth, but it cannot be a cliché within Christianity that "the last shall be first," or that "weakness is strength." Rather these must be "paradoxes"—apparent contradictions that prove true—whose truth provides foundations of theological interpretation, including theological aesthetics. For Roman Catholics, whose greatest saint is Mary, the central question should not be, "why can't women become priests?" but rather, "how can more male monks live as nuns?," for nuns are the true spiritual leaders of the church. Nor should one forget that it is the outcast woman Mary Magdalen, according to the Gospel of John, who first perceives the resurrected Jesus (John 20:11–18).

Terming the Marian paradoxes "Roman Catholic conceptions" might also mislead, given that very similar beliefs are held by Eastern Orthodox believers, making the traditional Marian doctrines by far the majority belief of contemporary Christianity, however disconcerting this fact might be to many Protestants. Such doctrines had usually been deemed irrelevant to the interpretation of literature from pre-dominantly Protestant countries such as Elizabethan England. However, the remarkable growth in Reformation historical scholarship—with its complex view of sixteenth-century England as a Christian country divided in belief between a state Anglican church and the underground but very much alive Recusant (Roman Catholic) and Puritan (which includes a wide range of Protestants) movements—has reopened many questions related to the theological interpretation of literature.

As You Like It and Gender

In the light of Roman Catholic conceptions of gender, the "prima facia" feminism of Shakespearean comedy can be reevaluated. Regardless of Shakespeare's own religious beliefs, of which we will probably never be certain, it remains clear that many of the "happy endings" of Shakespearean comedy would not be possible without the leadership of the play's comic heroine. From Portia to Beatrice to Viola to Paulina, this is a consistent pattern, and certainly Rosalind's leading role in *As You Like It* fits this mould. Rosalind does seem almost a superior creature, her gender never fully disguised, as she consistently mocks but also corrects the naïve "honour" of Orlando, the cynical rationalism of Jaques, or the lecherous lust of Touchstone. Rosalind has her own flaws and is certainly no Marian figure (as Desdemona might well be),[11] but her combination of eloquence and wisdom does express well the "ideal" rhetorical orator whom Catholic Humanists hoped would instruct and lead society.

It is also true that Rosalind does not act as an onstage "priestess." Even Celia's brief turn in this role, while more effective than the ministry of Sir Oliver Martext, requires the appearance of the divine Hymen so that the play's heroine can herself marry. Yet it is Rosalind who has created the spiritual possibility of marriage, has "made all this matter even," by securing the *conditional* pledges of love that make each player on stage imaginatively ready for marriage. In the "co-operative" sense normative to Erasmus' view of the human will, she has worked with divine love to create the "true minds" that Shakespeare's Sonnet 116 tells us are needed to overcome the many "impediments" to marriage. The rhetorical work of Rosalind's eloquent words thus allows each player, and the audience, the honest assent necessary to affirming binding marriage, and the paradoxical affirmation that such marriage can be a place of creative freedom.

Conclusion

The broad value of the *As You Like It*, therefore, is closely connected to the value and importance of marriage, but not simply to the continued existence and practice of this venerable institution within Christian society. Rather this play, particularly Rosalind's rhetoric, prepares couples to experience the romantic love, the marital happiness, capable of producing the common "fruit" of such marriages, the children who will grow up to further develop society. Shakespearean comedy often refers directly to children in the marriages common to its conclusions, as when the fairies bless "the issue" of each couple's bridal beds in *A Midsummer Night's Dream* (5.2.35). *As You Like It* does not include such references to the potential children of its couples, probably because the joy is so full, and the romantic tension so fully developed, that it is impossible to imagine several of the couples—especially Rosalind and Orlando—not being open to the common yet precious fruit of marriage that is children.

The creation of such marriages, within which both love and children can be born and thrive, is "authorized" in the play by the eloquent, wise, words of Rosalind, as informed by the imaginative Catholic Humanist

11. See Maillet, *Reading Othello as Catholic Tragedy*.

rhetoric that pervades this play and Shakespearean comedy in general. According to the Catholic concept of marriage, in which the presence of God unites two human souls, prevents divorce (Matt 19:1–11), and offers the concrete gifts of not only each other's body but also the blessing of children, human wills unite with God's will to "co-create" children. In the Catholic Humanist rhetoric of marriage that *As You Like It* exemplifies, "If" is for children, children of men and women who make homes with the spirit of love and peace, the children of God.

Glossary

Unless otherwise noted, all definitions are from the second, 1593 edition of Henry Peacham's *The Garden of Eloquence*.

FIGURES OF THOUGHT

Antanaclasis: kind of pun "which repeateth a word that hath two significations, and the one of them contrary, or at least, unlike to the other."

Allegoria: a "form of speech which expresseth one thing in words, and another in sense. In a Metaphor there is a translation of one word in an Allegory of many, and for that cause an Allegory is called a continued Metaphor."

Apophonema: "a sententia in antithetical form."[1]

Asteismus: a second kind of pun in which "a saying is captiously taken, and turned to another sense, contrary or much differing from the meaning of the speaker."

Conditional or Hypothetical Syllogism: A hypothetical clause is composed of an "if" clause, called the antecedent, and a "then" clause, called the consequent.[2] Miriam Joseph writes: "The sign of the hypothetical conditional is *if*, *unless* or an adverb of time, such as when . . . [it] is valid if the minor premise either affirms the antecedent or denies the consequent of the major premise, which is a hypothetical proposition."[3]

---

1. Lanham, *Handlist*, 14.
2. Lanham, *Handlist*, 58.
3. Joseph, *Arts of Language*, 361.

Emblem: "a figure or portrait of ocular representation, the words so aptly corresponding to the subtlety of the figure, that as well the eye is therewith recreated as the ear or the mind."[4]

Fable: A "short allegorical story that points a lesson or moral; the characters are frequently animals."[5]

Ironia: "a Trope in which one contrary is understood by another, not so well perceived by the words, as either by the pronunciation, or by the person, or by the nature of the thing."

Metaphora: "artificial translation of one word, from the proper signification, to another not proper, yet nigh and like." Peacham's basic definition of the central trope, for which he uses almost the exact same words as in defining "trope," is followed by a detailed discussion of how to create metaphors using fourteen different means.

Metonymia: when "the Orator putteth one thing for another, which by nature are nigh knit together." The "evocation of an idea through a term for some substitute idea."[6]

Mimesis: "an imitation of speech whereby the Orator counterfeiteth not only what one said, but also his utterance, pronunciation and gesture, imitating every thing as it was."

Onomatopoeia: "whereby the Orator or speaker maketh and faineth a name to some thing, imitating the sound or voice of that it signifieth."

Paradoxon: "the orator affirmeth some thing to be true, by saying he would not have believed it, or that it is so strange, so great, or so wonderful, that it may appear to be incredible."

Paranomasia: a third kind of pun in which "a figure which declineth into a contrarie by a likelihood of letters," is "either added, changed, or taken away." Homonymic puns.

Paroemia: "called of us a proverbe, is a sentence or forme of speech much used, and commonly known, and also excellent for the similitude and significatio."

Prosopopoeia: "the faining of a person, that is, when to a thing senseless and dumbe we faine a fit person." Personification.

---

4. Puttenham, *Art*, 102.
5. Lanham, *Handlist*, 50.
6. Espy, *Garden*, 113.

Simile: "a form of speech by which the Orator compareth one thing with the other by a similitude fit to his purpose."

Synecdoche: "More things or fewer understood and gathered by a word, which the proper signification doth not express: and it is by putting the whole for the part or the part for the whole."

Topothesia: "a fained description of a place, that is, when the Orator describeth a place, and yet no such place [exists]; as is the house of envy, in the book of Metamorphosis . . . this figure is proper to poets, and seldom used of orators."

FIGURES OF *LOGOS*:

Argumentum ex concessis: "reasoning that the conclusion of an argument is sound, on the basis of the truth of the premises of one's opponent."[7]

Dissimilitudo: "a forme of speech which compareth diverse things in a diverse qualitie."

Erotema: a 'rhetorical question' that is "a form of speech by which the Orator doth affirm or deny something strongly."

Enthymeme: An "abridged syllogism, one of the terms being omitted as understood."[8]

Enumeratio: "when the subject is divided into accidents, the matter into the antecedents, the effect into the cause, and into things annexed and following after the effect."

Epilogus: "a figure related to the hypothetical syllogism, whereby after a brief argumentation of those things that have before been spoken or done one infers what will follow."[9]

Eutrepismos: "a form of speech which doth not only number the parts before they be said, but also doth order those parts, and maketh them plain by a kind of definition or declaration."

Hyperbole: Exaggeration, a trope that occurs "when a saying both surmounts and reaches above the truth."

Hypophora: "by which the Orator answereth to his own demand."

---

7. Lanham, *Handlist*, 16.
8. Lanham, *Handlist*, 41.
9. Joseph, *Arts of Language*, 185.

Leptotes: "when the speaker by a negation equipollent doth seem to extenuate that which he expresseth." Litotes, or understatement; "the expression of an affirmative by the negation of its opposite."[10]

Pysma: a type of rhetorical question in which "the Orator doth demand many times together, and use many questions in one place, whereby he maketh his speech very sharp and vehement."

Syllogismus: "by which the Orator amplifieth a matter by conjecture." A "figure even more contracted than an enthymeme."[11]

Synoeiciosis: "a figure which teacheth to conjoine diverse things, and to repugne common opinion with reason."

Systrophe: "when the Orator bringeth in many definitions of one thing, yet not such definitions as do declare the substance of a thing by the general kind, and the difference, which the art of reasoning doth prescribe, but others of another kind all heaped together."

FIGURES OF *ETHOS* AND *PATHOS*

Antanagoge: the "balancing of an unfavorable aspect with a favorable one."[12]

Aposiopesis: "when we begin to speak of a thing, and break off in the middle way, as if either it needed no further to be spoken of or that we were ashamed, or afraid to speak it out."[13]

Brachiepia: "by which the matter is briefly told with no more words than those that be necessary."

Cacempheton: "when good words be ill applied or placed"; Puttenham calls this, "the figure of foul speech."[14]

Catachresis: "whereby the speaker or writer wanting a proper word, borroweth the next or the likest to the thing that he would signifie."

Cataplexis: "the Orator denounceth a threatening against some person, people, city, commonwealth or country."

Correctio: "a figure which taketh away that that is said, and putteth a more meet word in the place."

10. Espy, *Garden*, 107.
11. Joseph, *Arts of Language*, 360.
12. Joseph, *Arts of Language*, 138.
13. Puttenham, *Art*, 166.
14. Puttenham, *Art*, 254.

Epimone: "by which the speaker continueth and persisteth in the same cause, much after one form of speech."

Euche: the "speaker expresseth a solemn promise or vow, either made with condition, or arising from some vehement affection."

Eustathia: the "speaker promiseth and protesteth his constancy concerning something."

Gnome: "otherwise called *sententia*, is a saying pertaining to the manners and common practices of men, which declareth by an apt brevity, what in this life ought to done or left undone."

Hypocore: "the use of pet names and names of endearment."[15]

Inter se pugnatia: a "forme of speech by which the Orator reproveth his adversarie. . . . Of manifest unconstancie, open hypocrisy, or insolent arrogance."

Meiosis: "when a less word is put for a greater, to make the thing appear less than it is."

Misterismus: "when we give a mocke with a scorneful countenance as in some smiling sort looking aside or by drawing the lip awry, or shrinking up the nose."

Paramythia: a "form of speech which the orator useth to take away or diminish a sorrow conceived in the mind of his hearer."

Pathopoeia: "when the Orator by declaring some lamentable cause, moveth his hearers to pity and compassion, to show mercy, and to pardon offences."

Sarcasmus: "a bitter kind of derision most commonly used of an enemy."

SCHEMES OF EMPHASIS, REPETITION, BALANCE AND BREVITY

Asyndeton: "which keepeth the parts of speech together without the help of any conjunction."

Antithesis: "a proper coupling together of contraries, and that either in words be contrary, or in contrary sentences."

Antimetabole: "a forme of speech which inverteth a sentence by the contrary."

---

15. Espy, *Garden*, 100.

Climax: "a figure which so distinguisheth the oration by degrees, that the word which endeth the clause going before, beginneth the next following."

Compar: "a forme of speech which maketh the members of an oration to be almost a just number of syllables."

Diacope: "a figure which repeateth a word putting but one word between, or at least very few."

Diazeugma: "the use of one subject with many verbs."[16]

Epanalepsis: "a form of speech which doth begin and also end a sentence with one and the same word."

Epanaphora: a scheme "which beginneth diverse members, still with one and the same word."

Epiphora: a scheme "which endeth diverse members or clauses still with one and the same word."

Epizeuxis: a figure "whereby a word is repeated, for the greater vehemencie, and nothing put between."

Hypozeuxis: a scheme "which joineth to every thing a due verb, which is the contrary of *zeugma*."

Incrementum: "a form of speech by which degrees ascendeth to the top of some thing or rather above the top, that is, when we make our saying grow & increase by an orderly placing of words making the latter word always exceed the former in the force of signification."

Parachesis: "the repetition of the same sound ('thing') in words in close succession."[17]

Paragmenon: "which of the word going before deriveth the word following."

Paroemion: "a figure of speech which beginneth diverse words with one and the same letter." Alliteration.

Prozeugma: the first kind of *zeugma*, "a figure of speech which putteth some word in the first clause, and omitteth it in the other following,"

Symploce: "a form of speech which maketh many members or clauses following to have the same beginning & the same ending which the first had going before."

---

16. Joseph, *Arts of Language*, 59.
17. Lanham, *Handlist*, 124.

Bibliography

Allen, P. S., ed. *Opus Epistolarum Des. Erasmi Roterodami*. Oxford: Clarendon, 1906–58.
Alter, Robert. *The Art of Biblical Poetry*. New York: HarperCollins, 1987.
Aristotle. *Poetics*. In vol. 9.2 of *Great Books of the Western World*, edited by Robert Maynard Hutchins, 681–99. Chicago: Encylopedia Britannica, 1952.
———. *Rhetoric*. In vol. 9.2 of *Great Books of the Western World*, edited by Robert Maynard Hutchins, 593–680. Chicago: Encylopedia Britannica, 1952.
———. *Rhetoric*. Translated by W. Rhys Roberts. New York: Random, 1954.
Asquith, Claire. *Shadowplay: The Hidden Beliefs and Coded Politics of William Shakespeare*. New York: Public Affairs, 2005.
Augustine, St. *On Christian Doctrine*. In vol. 18 of *Great Books of the Western World*, edited by Robert Maynard Hutchins, 621–98. Chicago: Encyclopedia Britannica, 1952.
———. *On Christian Doctrine*. Trans. D. W. Robertson. New York: Liberal Arts, 1958.
———. *On the Trinity* (*De Deo Trino*). Translated by Arthur Haddan. In *Nicene and Post-Nicene Fathers of the Christian Church*, edited by Philip Schaff, 1–228. Edinburgh: T. & T. Clark, 1993.
Baldwin, T. W. *William Shakespeare's Small Latine & Lesse Greek*. Urbana: University of Illinois Press, 1944.
Barber, C. L. *Shakespeare's Festive Comedy*. Princeton: Princeton University Press, 1959.
Barry, Peter. *Beginning Theory: An Introduction to Literary and Cultural Theory*. Manchester: Manchester University Press, 2009.
Beadle, Richard, ed. *The Cambridge Companion to Medieval Literature*. Cambridge: Cambridge University Press, 1994.
Bede. *Ecclesiastical History of the English People*. In vol. 1 of *The Norton Anthology of English Literature: The Major Authors*, edited by Stephen Greenblatt, 29–32. 9th ed. New York: Norton, 2013.
Benedict XVI, Pope. "General Audience." https://www.vatican.va/content/benedict-xvi/en/audiences/2010/documents/hf_ben-xvi_aud_20101201.html.
Berger, Harry. "Narrative as Rhetoric in *The Fairie Queen*." *English Literary Renaissance* 21 (1991) 3–48.

Bevington, David. *Action Is Eloquence: Shakespeare's Language of Gesture.* Cambridge: Harvard University Press, 1984.
Bi Academic Intervention, ed. *The Bisexual Imaginary: Representation, Identity, and Desire.* London: Cassell, 1997.
Black, James. "Edified by the Margent: Shakespeare and the Bible." Calgary: University of Calgary Press, 1979.
Bloom, Harold. *Shakespeare: The Invention of the Human.* New York: Riverhead, 1998.
Boccaccio, Giovanni. *The Decameron.* Edited by Wayne A. Rebhorn. New York: Norton, 2016.
Boethius. *The Consolation of Philosophy.* Translated by P. G. Walsh. Oxford: Oxford World Classics, 2008.
Branagh, Kenneth, dir. *As You Like It.* HBO Films, 2013. DVD.
Brissendon, Allen, ed. *As You Like It.* Oxford: Oxford University Press, 1994.
Burckhardt, Jacob. The *Civilization of the Renaissance in Italy.* 1860. London: Dover, 2010.
Burton, Robert. *The Anatomy of Melancholy.* Edited by Thomas C. Faulkner et al. 6 vols. Oxford: Clarendon, 1989–2000.
Butler, Gregory G. "Music and Rhetoric in Early Seventeenth-Century English Sources." *The Musical Quarterly* 66 (1980) 53–64.
Cahill, Thomas. *Heretics and Heroes: How Renaissance Artists and Reformation Priests Created Our World.* New York: Anchor, 2013.
———. *How the Irish Saved Civilization.* New York: Bantam, 1997.
Callaghan, Dympna. "Do Characters Have Souls?" *Shakespeare Studies* 34 (2006) 41–46.
———, ed. *A Feminist Companion to Shakespeare.* London: Wiley-Blackwell, 2001.
Caplan, Harry. "Classical Rhetoric and the Medieval Theory of Preaching." *Classical Philology* 28 (1933) 73–96.
"Cedric Messina Discusses the Shakespeare Plays." *Shakespeare Quarterly* 3 (1979) 134–37.
Chaucer, Geoffrey. *The Canterbury Tales.* In *The Riverside Chaucer*, edited by Larry D. Benson, 3–328. 3rd ed. Boston: Houghton Mifflin, 1987.
Chesterton, G. K. "A Turning Point in History." In *The Fame of Blessed Thomas More: Being Addresses Delivered in His Honour in Chelsea, June 1929,* edited by R. W. Chambers, 61–65. London: Sheed and Ward, 1933.
Cicero. *De Oratore.* Edited by H. Rackman, translated by E. W. Sutton. Cambridge: Harvard University Press, 1939.
Coleman, Basil, dir. *As You Like It.* Ambrose, 2004. DVD.
Colet, John. *An Exposition of St. Paul's First Epistle to the Corinthians.* London: George Bell & Sons, 1874.
Cox, John D. *Seeming Knowledge: Shakespeare and Skeptical Faith.* Waco, TX: Baylor University Press, 2007.
Crane, Martin M., and Virginia E. Leland. "Chaucer's Life." In *The Riverside Chaucer*, edited by Larry D. Benson, xi–xxi. Boston: Houghton Mifflin, 1987.
Crane, Mary Thomas. "Early Tudor Humanism." In *A Companion to English Renaissance Literature and Culture,* edited by Michael Hattaway, 13–26. Oxford: Blackwell, 2000.
Crane, William G. Introduction to *The Garden of Eloquence*, by Henry Peacham, xv–xxv. New York: Delmar, 1977.

Crystal, David, and Ben Crystal. *Shakespeare's Words: A Glossary and Language Companion*. London: Penguin, 2002.
Czinner, Paul, dir. *As You Like It*. Mr. FAT-W, 2016. DVD.
Dante. *The Divine Comedy*. Translated by C. H. Sisson. Oxford: Oxford University Press, 1998.
Derrida, Jaques. "Structure, Sign, and Play in the Discourse of the Human Sciences." In *The Critical Tradition: Classic Texts and Contemporary Trends*, edited by David H. Richter, 915–25. Boston: Bedford St. Martins, 2007.
The Dream of the Rood. In *The Norton Anthology of English Literature: The Major Authors*, edited by Stephen Greenblatt, 24–26. 8th ed. New York: Norton, 2006.
Dreher, Rod. *How Dante Can Save Your Life*. New York: Regan, 2015.
Duffy, Eamon. *The Stripping of the Altars: Traditional Religion in England, 1400–1580*. New Haven: Yale University Press, 1992.
Dusinberre, Juliet. *Shakespeare and the Nature of Women*. London: Macmillan, 1975.
Eliot, T. S. "Dante." In *Selected Prose of T. S. Eliot*, edited by Frank Kermode, 205–30. London: Faber and Faber, 1975.
Enterline, Lynn. *Shakespeare's Schoolroom: Rhetoric, Discipline, Emotions*. Philadelphia: University of Pennsylvania Press, 2012.
Erasmus, Desiderius. *The Antibarbarians* (*Antibarbarorum liber*). In *English Humanism: Wyatt to Cowley*, edited and translated by Joanna Martindale, 159–61. London: Croom Hel, 1985.
———. *Collected Works of Erasmus*. Edited by Craig Thompson et al. Toronto: University of Toronto Press, 1974–.
———. *The Colloquies of Erasmus* (*Colloquia familiaria*). Edited and translated by Craig R. Thompson. Chicago: University of Chicago Press, 1965.
———. *A Complaint of Peace* (*Querela Pacis*). In *The Erasmus Reader*, edited by Erika Rummel, 288–314. Toronto: University of Toronto Press, 1990.
———. *Copia: Foundations of the Abundant Style* (*De duplici copia verborum ac rerum commentarii duo*). In *Collected Works of Erasmus: Literary and Educational Writings 2*, edited by Craig R. Thompson, 284–659. Toronto: University of Toronto Press, 1978.
———. *The Handbook of the Militant Christian* (*Enchiridion militis Christiani*). In *The Essential Erasmus*, edited and translated by John P. Dolan, 23–93. New York: Mentor-Omega, 1964.
———. *On Mending the Peace of the Church* (*De Sarcienda Ecclesiae Concordia*). In *The Essential Erasmus*, edited and translated by John P. Dolan, 331–88. New York: Mentor-Omega, 1964.
———. *The Paraclesis*. In *Desiderius Erasmus: Catholic Humanism and the Reformation*, edited and translated by John C. Odin, 92–106. New York: Harper, 1965.
———. "The Poetic Feast." In *The Colloquies of Erasmus* (*Colloquia familiaria*), edited and translated by Craig R. Thompson, 158–76. Chicago: University of Chicago Press, 1965.
———. *Praise of Folly* (*Morae Encomium*). Translated by Betty Radice. Harmondsworth: Penguin, 1985.
———. *The Praise of Folie*. Edited by C. H. Miller. Translated by Thomas Chaloner. London: Oxford University Press, 1965.
———. *The Praise of Folly*. In *The Essential Erasmus*, translated by John P. Dolan, 94–173. New York: Mentor-Omega, 1964.

———. *The Praise of Folly*. Translated by John Wilson. https://www.gutenberg.org/files/9371/9371-h/9371-h.htm.

———. "The Usefulness of the Colloquies." In *The Colloquies of Erasmus*, edited and translated by Craig R. Thompson, 624–26. Chicago: University of Chicago Press, 1965.

Espy, Willard R. *The Garden of Eloquence: A Rhetorical Bestiary*. London: HarperCollins, 1983.

Flecknoe, Richard. *A Short Discourse on the English Stage*. In *The English Dramatic Critics*, edited by James Agate, 1–2. London: Barker, 1932.

Frye, Northrop. *A Natural Perspective*. New York: Columbia University Press, 1965.

Giamatti, A. Bartlett. "Green Fields of the Mind." In *A Great and Glorious Game: The Baseball Writings of A. Bartlett Giamatti*, edited by Kenneth S. Robson, 7–15. Chapel Hill, NC: Algonquin, 1998.

Glasscoe, Marion. *English Medieval Mystics: Games of Faith*. London: Longman, 1993.

Gordon, Walter M. *Humanist Play and Belief: The Seriocomic Art of Desiderius Erasmus*. Toronto: University of Toronto Press, 1990.

Gregory, Brad. *The Unintended Reformation: How a Religious Revolution Secularized a Society*. Cambridge, MA: Belknap, 2012.

Gruenler, Curtis. *Piers Plowman and the Poetics of Enigma: Riddles, Rhetoric, and Theology*. Notre Dame: University of Notre Dame Press, 2017.

Gurr, Andrew. *Playgoing in Shakespeare's London*. Cambridge: Cambridge University Press, 1987.

Hamilton, Donna B. *Anthony Munday and the Catholics, 1560–1633*. Burlington, VT: Ashgate, 2005.

Hart, John A. *Dramatic Structure in Shakespeare's Romantic Comedies*. Pittsburgh: Carnegie-Mellon University Press, 1980.

Hattaway, Michael. Introduction to *A Companion to English Renaissance Literature and Culture*, edited by Michael Hattaway, 3–9. Oxford: Blackwell, 2000.

Henderson, Judith Rice. Review of *Shakespeare and the Rhetoricians*, by Marion Trousdale. *Rhetorica* 2 (1984) 101.

Henry VIII, King. *Defense of the Seven Sacraments* (*Assertio Septem Sacramentorum*). Edited by Rev. Louis O'Donovan. New York: Benzinger Brothers, 1908.

Herbert, George. "The Pulley." In *George Herbert and Henry Vaughn: The Oxford Authors*, edited by Louis L. Martz, 114–15. Oxford: Oxford University Press, 1992.

Hinton, D. A. et al. *The Oxford Handbook of Anglo-Saxon Archaeology*. Oxford: Oxford University Press, 2011.

Hirsch, E. D. *The Aims of Interpretation*. Chicago: University of Chicago Press, 1976.

Hirsch, John, dir. *As You Like It*. Morningstar Entertainment, 2008. DVD.

Hopkins, G. M. "That Nature Is a Heraclitean Fire, and of the Comfort of the Resurrection." In vol. 2 of *The Norton Anthology of English Literature: The Major Authors*, edited by Stephen Greenblatt, 827. 9th ed. New York: Norton, 2013.

Hulme, Hilda. *Explorations in Shakespeare's Language*. London: Longman, 1962.

Hunt, Maurice. *Shakespeare's "As You Like It": Late Elizabethan Culture and Literary Representation*. Basingstoke: Palgrave Macmillan, 2008.

"I Sing of a Maiden." In *Medieval English Literature*, edited by Thomas J. Garbaty, 661. Lexington, MA: D.C. Heath, 1984.

Jardine, Lisa. *Still Harping on Daughters*. New Jersey: Barnes & Noble, 1983.

Jeffrey, David Lyle. "Charity and Cupidity in Biblical Tradition." In *Houses of the Interpreter*, 55–74. Waco, TX: Baylor University Press, 2003.
———, ed. *Dictionary of Biblical Tradition in English Literature*. Grand Rapids: Eerdmans, 1993.
———. *The Early English Lyric and Franciscan Spirituality*. Lincoln: University of Nebraska Press, 1975.
———. *In the Beauty of Holiness: Art and the Bible in Western Culture*. Grand Rapids: Eerdmans, 2017.
———. *The Law of Love: English Spirituality in the Age of Wyclif*. Grand Rapids: Eerdmans, 1988.
———. *People of the Book: Christian Identity and Literary Culture*. Grand Rapids: Eerdmans, 1996.
Jeffrey, David Lyle, and Gregory Maillet. *Christianity and Literature: Philosophical Foundations and Critical Practice*. Downers Grove, IL: IVP Academic, 2011.
John Paul II, Pope. "Apostolic Letter Proclaiming Saint Thomas More Patron of Statesmen and Politicians." Vatican City: Librerian Editrice Vaticana, 2000.
———. "Letter of His Holiness Pope John Paul II to Artists." Vatican City: Librerian Editrice Vaticana, 1999.
———. *On the Dignity and Vocation of Women* (*Mulieris Dignitatem*). Boston: Pauline, 2013.
———. *The Redeemer of Man* (*Redemptor Hominis*). Vatican City: Librerian Editrice Vaticana, 1979.
———. *Roman Triptych*. Translated by Jerzy Peterkiewicz. Washington, DC: United States Conference of Catholic Bishops, 2003.
Johnson, Samuel. "Preface to Shakespeare." In *The Critical Tradition: Classic Texts and Contemporary Trends*, edited David H. Richter, 220–25. 3rd ed. Boston: Bedford St. Martin's, 2007.
Jones, E. Michael. *Logos Rising: A History of Ultimate Reality*. South Bend, IN: Fidelity, 2021.
Jonson, Ben. "To the Memory of My Beloved, the Author, William Shakespeare." In *The Norton Anthology of English Literature: The Major Authors*, edited by Stephen Greenblatt, 648–50. 8th ed. New York: Norton, 2006.
Joseph, Miriam. *Shakespeare's Use of the Arts of Language*. New York: Columbia University Press, 1947.
King, Ross. *Michelangelo & the Pope's Ceiling*. Bournemouth: Pimlico, 2006.
Kipling, Rudyard. "If—." In *Rudyard Kipling, Stories and Poems*, edited by Daniel Karlin, 496. Oxford: Oxford University Press, 2015.
Knowles, Richard. "Myth and Type in *As You Like It*." *English Literary History* 33 (1966) 12
Kuhn, Maura Slattery. "Much Virtue in 'If.'" *Shakespeare Quarterly* 28 (1977) 40–50.
Langland, William. *The Vision of Piers Plowman: A Complete Edition of the B-Text*. Edited by A. V. C. Schmidt. London: Dent, 1987.
Lanham, Richard. *A Handlist of Rhetorical Terms*. Berkeley: University of California Press, 1968.
Latham, Agnes, ed. *As You Like It: The Arden Shakespeare*. London: Methuen, 1975.
Lewis, C. S. *Miracles*. New York: HarperOne, 2015.
Lodge, Thomas. *Rosalynd, or Euphues Golden Legacy*. Edited by Edward Baldwin. Boston: Ginn, 1910.

Lubac, Henri de. *The Drama of Atheist Humanism*. San Francisco: Ignatius, 1998.

———. *Medieval Exegesis*. Vol. 1, *The Four Senses of Scripture*. Translated by Mark Sebanc. Grand Rapids: Eerdmans, 1998.

Lupton, J. H. *A Life of John Colet: With an Appendix of Some of His English Writings*. Eugene, OR: Wipf & Stock, 2016.

Maillet, Greg. "'Fidelity to the Word': Lonerganian Conversion through Shakespeare's *The Winter's Tale* and Dante's *Purgatorio*." *Religion and the Arts* 10.2 (2006) 219–43.

———. *Learning to See the Theological Vision of Shakespeare's King Lear*. Newcastle-upon-Tyne: Cambridge Scholars, 2016.

———. *Reading Othello as Catholic Tragedy*. Newcastle-upon-Tyne: Cambridge Scholars, 2018.

———. "Theoretical Foundations and Educational Applications of Willard R. Espy's *The Garden of Eloquence: A Rhetorical Bestiary*." *Proceedings of the Canadian Society for the Study of Rhetoric* 5 (1993–94) 41–52.

———. "'To Glad Your Ear and Please Your Eyes': Medieval and Renaissance Rhetoric in Shakespeare's *Pericles*." *The Canadian Journal of Rhetorical Studies* 5 (1995) 109–24.

———. *Word Awake: An Introduction to the Novels of Michael D. O'Brien*. Ottawa: Justin, 2019.

Markos, Louis. *From Achilles to Christ: Why Christians Should Read the Pagan Classics*. Downer's Grove, IL: InterVarsity, 2009.

Marlowe, Christopher. *Dr. Faustus*. In vol. 1 of *The Norton Anthology of English Literature: The Major Authors*, edited by Stephen Greenblatt, 501–35. 9th ed. New York: Norton, 2013.

Massing, Michael. *Fatal Discord: Erasmus, Luther, and the Fight for the Western Mind*. New York: Harper, 2018.

McGregor, Brian, trans. *De ratione studii legendi interpretandique auctores* (*On the Method of Study*). In *Collected Works of Erasmus: Literary and Educational Writings 2*, edited by Craig R. Thompson, 661–69. Toronto: University of Toronto Press, 1978.

Meres, Frances. *Palladis Tamia, Wit's Treasury*. New York: AMS, 1994.

Michelangelo Buonarrati. *The Complete Poems of Michelangelo*. Translated by John F. Nims. Chicago: University of Chicago Press, 1998.

Miller, J. Hillis. "The Function of Rhetorical Study at the Present Time." In *Teaching Literature: What Is Needed Now*, edited by James Engell and David Perkins, 95–101. Cambridge: Harvard University Press, 1988.

Milton, John. *Of Education*. In *Seventeenth-Century Prose and Poetry*, edited by Alexander M. Witherspoon and Frank J. Warnke, 388–94. 2nd ed. New York: Harcourt Brace Jovanovich, 1982.

———. *Paradise Lost*. Edited by Alastair Fowler. 2nd ed. London: Longman, 2007.

———. *Paradise Regained*. In *Milton: The Complete Shorter Poems*, edited by John Carey, 417–512. 2nd ed. London: Longman, 2007.

Monti, James. *The King's Good Servant but God's First: The Life and Writings of Saint Thomas More*. San Francisco: Ignatius, 1997.

More, St. Thomas. *The Complete Works of St. Thomas More*. New Haven: Yale University Press 1963–.

---. *The Confutation of Tyndale's Answer*. The Complete Works of St. Thomas More 8. New Haven: Yale University Press 1973.
---. *A Dialogue of Comfort against Tribulation*. The Complete Works of St. Thomas More 14. New Haven: Yale University Press 1976.
---. *English Poems, Life of Pico, The Last Things*. The Complete Works of St. Thomas More 1. New Haven: Yale University Press, 1998.
---. *Life of John Picus*. In *The English Works of Sir Thomas More*, edited by W. E. Campbell, 345–96. London: Eyre and Spottiswoode, 1931.
---. *Response to Luther* (*Responsio ad Lutherum*). The Complete Works of St. Thomas More 5. New Haven: Yale University Press, 1969.
---. *On the Sadness of Christ* (*De Tristitia Christi*). The Complete Works of St. Thomas More 14. New Haven: Yale University Press, 1976.
---. *Utopia*. Translated by Paul Turner. London: Penguin, 1965.
---. *Utopia*. Translated by G. C. Richards. The Complete Works of St. Thomas More 4. New Haven: Yale University Press, 1965.
Muir, Kenneth. *The Sources of Shakespeare's Plays*. London: Methuen, 1977.
Munday, Anthony, and Henry Chettle. *Sir Thomas More*. In *William Shakespeare: The Complete Works*, edited by Stanley Wells and Gary Taylor, 813–42. 2nd ed. Oxford: Clarendon, 2005.
---. *Sir Thomas More*. Edited by John Jowett. London: Bloomsbury, 2011.
---. "Sir Thomas More: Passages Attributed to Shakespeare." In *William Shakespeare: The Complete Works*, edited by Stanley Wells and Gary Taylor, 785–88. Oxford: Clarendon, 1988.
Nauert, Charles G. *Humanism and the Culture of Renaissance Europe*. Cambridge: Cambridge University Press, 1995.
Nietzsche, Friedrich. *On the Genealogy of Morals*. Translated by Walter Kaufmann. New York: Vintage, 1967.
Novikoff, Alex J. *The Twelfth-Century Renaissance: A Reader*. Toronto: University of Toronto Press, 2016.
Olin, J. C., ed. *Christian Humanism and the Reformation: Desiderius Erasmus, Selected Writings*. New York: Fordham University Press, 1987.
Ordway, Holly. *Not God's Type: An Atheist Academic Lays Down Her Arms*. San Francisco: Ignatius, 2010.
O'Siadhail, Michael. *Five Quintets*. Waco, TX: Baylor University Press, 2018.
Owst, G. R. *Literature and Pulpit in Medieval England*. Cambridge: Cambridge University Press, 1933.
Partridge, Eric. *Shakespeare's Bawdy*. London: Routledge and Kegan Paul, 1968.
Peacham, Henry. *The Garden of Eloquence*. New York: Delmar, 1977.
Petrarch, Francesco. *The Secret*. Edited by Carol E. Quillen. Boston: St. Martin's, 2003.
Puttenham, George. *The Art of English Poesie*. Edited by Gladys D. Willcock and Alice Walker. Cambridge: Cambridge University Press, 1970.
Quillen, Carol E. Introduction to *The Secret*, by Francesco Petrarch, iii–xlvi. Boston: St. Martin's, 2003.
Quintilian. *Institutio Oratoria*. Translated by H. E. Butler. Cambridge: Harvard University Press, 1922.
Ray, Steve. *The Papacy: What the Pope Does and Why It Matters*. San Francisco: Ignatius, 2018.

Rebhorn, Wayne A. Introduction to *The Decameron*, by Giovanni Boccaccio. Edited by Wayne A. Rebhorn. New York: Norton, 2016.

Rickman, Alan. "Jaques in *As You Like It*." In *Players of Shakespeare 2*, edited by Russell Jackson and Robert Smallwood, 73–80. Cambridge: Cambridge University Press, 1989.

Rivers, Isabel. *Classical and Christian Ideas in English Renaissance Poetry*. 2nd ed. London: Routledge, 1994.

Roper, William. *The Lyfe of Sir Thomas More, Knight*. Edited by Elsie Vaughn Hitchcock. London: Early English Text Society, 1935.

Rowe, Nicholas. *The Life of Shakespeare*. London: Pallas Athene, 2010.

Rummel, Erika, ed. *The Erasmus Reader*. Toronto: University of Toronto Press, 1990.

Rupp, E. Gordon. *Luther and Erasmus: Free Will and Salvation*. Louisville: Westminster John Knox, 2006.

Rutherfurd, Edward. *London*. New York: Ballantine, 1997.

———. *New York*. New York: Doubleday, 2009.

———. *The Princes of Ireland*. New York: Doubleday, 2004.

———. *The Rebels of Ireland*. New York: Doubleday, 2006.

Saward, John, et al., eds. *Firmly I Believe and Truly: The Spiritual Tradition of Catholic England*. Oxford: Oxford University Press, 2013.

Scaliger, J. C. *Poetics libri septum*. In *A Handbook to Sixteenth-Century Rhetoric*, translated by Lee A. Sonnino, 225–305. New York: Barnes, 1968.

Schmidt, A. V. C. Introduction to *The Vision of Piers Plowman: A Complete Edition of the B-Text*, by William Langland, 145–51. London: Dent, 1987.

Schoenbaum, Samuel. *Shakespeare's Lives*. Oxford: Oxford University Press, 1991.

Shakespeare, William. *William Shakespeare: The Complete Works*. Edited by Stanley Wells and Gary Taylor. Oxford: Clarendon, 2005.

Shapiro, James. *A Year in the Life of Shakespeare, 1599*. New York: HarperCollins, 2005.

Sharrock, Thea, dir. *As You Like It*. 2009. Opus Arte, 2010. DVD.

Shaw, Fiona, and Juliet Stevenson. "Celia and Rosalind." In *Players of Shakespeare 2*, edited by Russell Jackson and Robert Smallwood, 55–72. Cambridge: Cambridge University Press, 1989.

Shaw, John. "Fortune and Nature in *As You Like It*." *Shakespeare Quarterly* 6 (1955) 45–50.

Sidney, Philip. "Astrophel and Stella." In *Sir Philip Sidney: The Oxford Authors*, edited by Katherine Duncan-Jones, 53–211. Oxford: Oxford University Press, 1989.

———. *The Defence of Poetry*. In *Sir Philip Sidney: The Oxford Authors*, edited by Katherine Duncan-Jones, 212–51. Oxford: Oxford University Press, 1989.

Sir Gawain and the Green Knight. In *The Norton Anthology of English Literature: The Major Authors*, edited by Stephen Greenblatt, 112–64. 8th ed. New York: Norton, 2006.

Smith, Hilda M. "Humanist Education and the Renaissance Concept of Woman." In *Woman and Literature in Britain, 1500–1700*, edited by Helen Wilcox, 9–29. Cambridge: Cambridge University Press, 1996.

Smith, K. Aron, and Susan M. Kim. *This Language a River: A History of English*. Peterborough: Broadview, 2017.

Smith, Preserved. *Erasmus: A Study of His Life, Ideals, and Place in History*. New York: Ungar, 1962.

Spenser, Edmund. *The Faerie Queen*. Edited by A. C. Hamilton. London: Longman, 1977.
Sutherland, Janice, dir. *Shakespeare Uncovered: "Twelfth Night" and "As You Like It" with Joely Richardson*. PBS, 2012. DVD.
Taylor, Charles. *A Secular Age*. Cambridge: Harvard University Press, 2007.
Thompson, Craig R. Introduction to *The Colloquies of Erasmus*, translated by Craig R. Thompson, xxi–xxix. Chicago: University of Chicago Press, 1965.
Tolkien, J. R. R. "Letter 142." In *The Letters of J. R. R. Tolkien*, edited by Humphrey Carpenter, 171–73. Boston: Houghton Mifflin, 1981.
———. "Letter 181." In *The Letters of J. R. R. Tolkien*, edited by Humphrey Carpenter, 232–37. Boston: Houghton Mifflin, 1981.
———. *The Lord of the Rings*. London: HarperCollins, 1995.
———. "Mythopoeia." In *Tree and Leaf*, 83–90. London: HarperCollins, 2001.
———. "On Fairy Stories." In *Tree and Leaf*, 1–82. New York: HarperCollins, 2001.
———, ed, and trans. *Sir Gawain and the Green Knight, Pearl, and Sir Orfeo*. London: Allen & Unwin, 1975.
———. *Tree and Leaf*. New York: HarperCollins, 2001.
Trautvetter, Christine, ed. *As You Like It: An Old-Spelling and Old-Meaning Edition*. Heidelberg: Winter, 1972.
Trousdale, Marion. *Shakespeare and the Rhetoricians*. Chapel Hill, NC: University of North Carolina Press, 1982.
Turner, Paul. "More's Attitude to Communism." In *Utopia*, by Thomas More, translated by Paul Turner, xi–xlvii. London: Penguin, 1965.
Tuve, Rosemond. *Elizabethan and Metaphysical Imagery*. Chicago: University of Chicago Press, 1947.
Van Doren, Mark. *Shakespeare*. Garden City, NY: Doubleday, 1953.
Vickers, Brian. *The Artistry of Shakespeare's Prose*. London: Methuen, 1968.
———. *Classical Rhetoric in English Poetry*. Carbondale, IL: Southern University Press, 1989.
———. "Shakespeare's Use of Rhetoric." In *A New Companion to Shakespeare Studies*, edited by Kenneth Muir and Samuel Schoenbaum, 90–102. Cambridge: Cambridge University Press, 1971.
Vives, Juan Luis. *A Very Fruitful and Pleasant Book Called The Instruction of a Christian Woman*. Translated by Richard Hyrde. London, 1529.
The Wakefield Master. *The Second Shepherd's Pageant*. In vol. 1 of *The Norton Anthology of English Literature: The Major Authors*, edited by Stephen Greenblatt, 308–36. 9th ed. New York: Norton, 2013.
Waugh, Evelyn. *Edmund Campion: A Life*. San Francisco: Ignatius, 2012.
Wells, Stanley. "Television Shakespeare." *Shakespeare on Television: An Anthology of Essays and Reviews*. Hanover, NH: University Press of New England, 1988.
Wells, Stanley, and Gary Taylor. "Glossary." In *William Shakespeare: The Complete Works*, edited by Stanley Wells and Gary Taylor, 1327–42. 2nd ed. Oxford: Clarendon, 2005.
Wiles, David. *Shakespeare's Clown: Actor and Text in the Elizabethan Playhouse*. Cambridge: Cambridge University Press, 1987.
Wilson, J. D. *Shakespeare's Happy Comedies*. London: Faber & Faber, 1962.
Wolfe, Gregory. *Beauty Shall Save the World: Recovering the Human in an Ideological Age*. Wilmington, DE: Intercollegiate Studies Institute, 2011.

Wyatt, Sir Thomas. "Whoso List to Hunt." In *The Norton Anthology of English Literature: The Major Authors*, edited by Stephen Greenblatt, 350. 8th ed. New York: Norton, 2006.

Young, David. *The Heart's Forest: A Study of Shakespeare's Pastoral Plays*. New Haven: Yale University Press, 1972.

Zinnemann, Fred, dir. *A Man for All Seasons*. Sony Pictures Home Entertainment, 2006. DVD.

www.ingramcontent.com/pod-product-compliance
Lightning Source LLC
Chambersburg PA
CBHW061431300426
44114CB00014B/1635